ARTISTS' HOUSES IN LONDON
1764–1914

ARTISTS' HOUSES IN LONDON 1764–1914

GILES WALKLEY

with photographs by Niall Doull-Connolly

SCOLAR PRESS

Published by
SCOLAR PRESS
Gower House
Croft Road
Aldershot
Hants GU11 3HR
England

Ashgate Publishing Company
Old Post Road
Brookfield
Vermont 05036
USA

British Library Cataloguing in Publication Data.

Walkley, Giles
     Artists' Houses in London, 1764–1914
     I. Title
     728.09421

Library of Congress Cataloging-in-Publication Data

Walkley, Giles
     Artists' houses in London 1764–1914 / Giles Walkley.

     Includes index.
     ISBN 0-85967-962-4
     1. Artists—Homes and haunts—England—London. 2. Artists' studios—England—London. 3. London (England)—Buildings, structures, etc. I. Title.
NA970.W36 1993
728'.09421—dc20   93–9773
                 CIP

ISBN 0 85957 962 4

Printed in Great Britain by The University Press, Cambridge

33333010391056

To my parents and friends

CONTENTS

PREFACE

IMPRESSIVE, IF not flagrant, size, a whopping option on the world's daylight reserves, a certain diminished stylishness, an ingrained history, an atmosphere ripe for reverie – enter an old studio of even the least grandeur and you are struck all at once by these out of the ordinary qualities. Over the Victorian and Edwardian periods when British painting and sculpture flourished as never before, many hundreds of such studios were built in London, the nation's fine art marketplace. It cannot be denied that these artists' domestic workshops have a bearing on the country's cultural heritage which has for too long been overlooked. On an equally significant level they belong to a singular and remarkably under-publicised building type which nearly all the major architects of the time contrived more than once to telling effect. This review of their development and distribution, their various styles and relative merits, the involvement of their designers and denizens, together with what went on in and around them during the course of 150 years could not have been produced without the collaboration of numerous most helpful people. Especial thanks are due to each of the studio-dwellers who allowed me to visit or measure their homes; to John Miller for his continuing guidance and the provision of several invaluable visas; to Lord Esher for his encouragement; to Niall Doull-Connolly whose expertise more than answered the challenge of a very trying assignment; to Rachel and Johnny Devas for their matchless hospitality; to John Shields, the kindliest of friends at court; to my chief correspondents for their sorely-tested forbearance; and to Carol Shields for her unstinting assistance, particularly on the photographic front.

GW
Soussis and Adelaide
1988–91

LIST OF ILLUSTRATIONS

These illustrations have been obtained from, prepared with the cooperation of, or reproduced by kind permission of the sources, institutions or individuals cited below each title.

Every effort has been made to trace the copyright holders of the works
on this list, but if any have been inadvertently overlooked the publishers will be
pleased to make the necessary arrangements at the first opportunity.

INTRODUCTION:
ELEMENTS OF THE GENRE

. . . Altogether the artists had a famous time of it during the 'fifties and 'sixties.

Thinking that the good times had come to stay, numbers of successful painters who could afford it, and, sad to say, very many other artists who could not, bought houses with gardens attached to them in St John's Wood, Kensington, Hampstead, and other suburban districts, where they built themselves large and luxuriously fitted studios; in these on 'Show Sundays' they were visited by crowds of fashionable people, but on working days such artists at their easels, with their models, always seemed to me to be sadly out of scale with their spacious and magnificent surroundings. I can well remember, for example, John Pettie appearing to me as quite lost in his large studio.

GEORGE LESLIE'S observations in *The Inner Life of the Royal Academy* (1914) bear witness to a remarkable phenomenon. It is a fact that, in London alone, over 1300 domestic artists' studios were erected during the 60 years prior to the First World War. A surprising quantity of these survives. Such an occurrence was not isolated; a similar, if not greater, number will have been raised over the same period in Paris, the centre of the 19th-century world of art. However, it was not commonly seen. Artists in other European cities, Rome, Vienna, Munich, Brussels, for instance, likewise undertook to build their own workplaces, but by no means did they breed a mania for it. Indeed, the great proliferation of a single building type in the English capital was the result of a craze. In some cases it was a craze embraced and pursued to excess; in others, as Leslie relates just as sympathetically, it was a gamble which did not pay off.

What, then, did John Pettie or any other British artist want with a studio in London? Fundamentally, the answer lies in the rise of professionalism among artists. Prompted by improving remuneration for technically superior productions together with their concomitant reproduction fees, painters and sculptors realistically aspired to higher standards of living and better working conditions. Increasing receipts were attributable not only to the effect of longer and more thorough European-style training, but also to a larger, wealthier and more culturally receptive buying public whose patronage had been massaged by critics, dealers and gallery directors. To help matters, the Royal Academy and the various exhibition societies devoted to specific media – institutions established by the artists themselves and endorsed by the Crown – formally enshrined the art market while lending their members respectability and their members' exhibits an enhanced value. Add the natural competitiveness of business to a desire for social advancement and any artist with sufficient wherewithal would follow the latest star towards fame and reward.

The heavenly, all-facilitating studio represented both an inspirational tool and material proof of the professional approach. A properly appointed workplace, whether added to the dwelling, discrete in the back garden, or combined within a purpose-built residence, removed the suspicion of amateurism from the person based erstwhile in makeshift domestic surroundings. According to that person's disposition or specialisation, it could serve supplementary purposes, among them a showroom-gallery, a salon for entertaining, a winter-garden, and even a permanent kind of blind from which to study animals. However, the list of essential attributes required by the typical easel painter, that is, a painter not of altarpieces or frescoes but average-sized oils or watercolours suitable for hanging in the drawing rooms of the middle classes, would be headed by optimum daylighting.

Eighteenth-century painters working in the northern hemisphere were not averse to light from the east, but the more even, entirely sunshine-free light from the north came to be preferred in Victorian times. For the light to reach an adequate working area of the room, a large window with few or minimal glazing bars was usually necessary. Different amounts of the available external brightness might be introduced by the use of extra-large, more than one, or all-glass bay windows. A natural, conventional light source could be recreated by raising the window sill or sills above the normal level. Roller blinds arranged to unfurl from sill to head could cause steeply angled light to be directed to a limited window-side zone. Blinds, or the lower banks of reveal-hung shutters, helped to reduce reflected glare – sunlight bouncing from the ground or lower roofs – while a steep shaft of light meant that the painter's own hands and instruments threw a less obstructive shade over the paintwork. Other angles could be created by manipulating curtains. Overhead daylighting, similarly controllable, might be accessible in rooms beneath the roof. So-called to distinguish it from side light passing through the wall, top light was often enlisted in tandem, in order to render three-dimensional objects more accurately. Many artists and designers believed that all these effects were to be had from a window joined to an inclined skylight – a versatile 'broken-backed' combination – and, duly, numerous such frames were constructed.

Second on the painter's list of attributes essential in a studio would be the generous provision of space. Breadth, to take the best advantage of side lighting, was more desirable than depth, but, like height, had to be kept in proportion. Depth aided the evaluation of works from a distance, whereas height, necessary firstly to contain a tall window, and secondly to accommodate perhaps a hoarding-sized tableau mounted on the appropriate winding easel, could not safely be under-scaled. A practical area of considerable bounding dimensions was obligatory to ensure the manoeuvrability of easels, sizeable works and basic furniture (a cabinet for colours and equipment, library steps, a models' throne – if not a dais as well to raise the subject into the painting light – a lay figure, miscellaneous props, racks or chests of costumes, bookcases, and, usually in addition to a fireplace, a coke stove), without allowing for outsize canvases to be fabricated flat on the floor, or for the elbow-room needed to welcome visitors.

Because, as a rule, sculptors also made initial designs, drawing on paper from the life, they required comparable conditions to those of painters. At the following stage of making a maquette – sketching the subject in miniature in wax or clay at a bench or on an adjustable, revolving stand – when chiaroscuro was requisite to accentuate the sought-after degree of modelling, the benefit of a naturalistic, high-level light stream would be proven. Shaping the clay at full size likewise called for a measure of top light, especially considering that the finished sculpture was commonly to be seen outdoors, in a glass-roofed conservatory or cortile-style hall, or in a public or private blind-walled gallery lit from above. Subsequent mechanical processes – erecting formwork, puddling plaster, casting, breaking moulds, constructing armatures, recasting, and re-assembling a solid plaster version of the original clay model – might be carried out under general manufactory-standard illumination. After filling and filing, possibly by a skilled assistant, 'the plaster' would return to the sculptor's station in order to receive the final refinements of his or her own hand. Should a marble or granite version be commissioned, a pointing device in a separate shop would be deployed (often by hired hands) to transpose points all over the plaster profile to exactly matching points at the extremities of holes drilled into the rough-hewn stone block. Again, the sculptor would put the finishing touches to the work. If a bronze casting were to be ordered, the unassembled plaster would proceed to a foundry – of which London sculptors managed very few capable of reproducing items in any way colossal. Subsidiary, open-roofed buildings to shelter these operations, approaching the heavy-industrial in nature as they do, tended to assume the attractive functional aesthetic associated with railway, canal and dock.

While good lighting meant much, to the practical statuary net usable cubic footage meant more. Certainly, due to the scale of commodity customarily undertaken, be it cameo or colonial monument, the sculptor's ideal establishment could vary widely in overall volume. The typical body-builder who habitually created larger-than-life likenesses of eminent public figures clearly needed a moderately capacious structure – less a booth than a small barn – in which to manhandle plant such as step-ladders, scaffolds and stands; to stow in a dry place such as plaster, sand and sawdust, and in a moist place water, clay or tacky tow; to display a weighty reference collection both of past commissions and hallowed masterpieces; and, of course, comfortably to encompass work in hand. Ancillary areas might conveniently serve to decentralise blacksmithery around anvil, forge or furnace, pointing procedures, and the splitting, carving, grinding, polishing masons' gogglebolstery of forming pedestals and be-spoke architectural ornament. All these activities generated noise, vibration, dust, heat or damp. Knockabout, neighbourhood protest-proof enclosures were required to withstand them; solid floors at ground level, best specified where there was hefty castor-borne ordnance to usher and shunt (although powdered soapstone might sometimes suffice), would be well-planned to open onto street, stone-yard, or both, via doubled coach-house doors.

Whereas the traditional tools of trade – brush and maulstick, chisel and mallet – endured unvaried over the years, the independent artist's workshop in itself evolved in line with the application of new science and revived or modernising architectural styles. The incorporated residential workshop: the 'studio-house', however, while similarly a product of Victorian urban culture, still had its underlying origins in the provincial weavers' terraces with their ribbon-windowed loom lofts and the rural yeoman's hall house with its airy, primary chamber bordered by service rooms or mezzanines. In the following text such analogies will not be exhaustively stretched, but a historical survey of light and space united in the service of London's fine artists is to be found nevertheless. From a significant date in the mid-18th century different unions are seen to develop throughout the 19th and beyond. Over this time-span the city's renowned artists' quarters are visited and, a trawl of the near country interposing, revisited in broadening rotation. Not solely are the privately built permutations of the genre sampled, but so, too, the parallel speculations in rentable property. And not only is the record animated by the contemporary social interaction of all the painters, sculptors, engravers, illustrators, cartoonists, photographers and architects involved, the whole is finally summarised in an orderly, building by building catalogue. It is one exultation of a bountifully conceived architectural agency lodged between lives and livelihoods of the past in the course of rapid erasure – as the rarer imputed values pertaining desert the present.

1

THE GROVES OF ACADEME, 1769

THAT CONTROVERSIAL institution, the English Royal Academy of Arts, was founded in London on 10 December 1768. Thenceforward drawing classes were conducted under its aegis at Old Somerset House, Strand, and an annual exhibition organised at temporary headquarters in Pall Mall, **1**. Thirty-six prominent artists, a group in which a fair cross-section of contemporary fine art callings was represented, were invited by George III to become its first members.[1] A council presided over by Sir Joshua Reynolds was elected to manage its affairs; Professors and Visitors were appointed to supervise the students' education.

When the Royal Academicians mounted their inaugural exhibition, a catalogue accompanied it. For that, and for each of the now over 200 succeeding summer shows, the catalogue has become an invaluable record. Among much else between the lines, it indicates which items were submitted by whom and from what address he or she was working at the time. No less than 33 of the founder members lived in London in 1769, the distinct majority of them collecting in Westminster.[2] More exactly, most resided between Green Park and Lincoln's Inn Fields. Soho and the vicinity of Cavendish Square accounted for two other roughly equal portions, while the City claimed the three-person remainder.

But for their official posts, two of the City-dwellers, George Dance and Richard Yeo, may also have been found in the west. Dance held the office of City Surveyor in succession to his father. With Newgate Gaol on the drawing board, his base at Moorfields would continue to prove handy. Yeo was domiciled at the Mint in his capacity as a seal engraver. The third man lived by choice in Spitalfields. Mason Chamberlin, portrait painter, had secured a pitch in 'Stuart' (Steward) Street, between Spital Square and the market. Yet the only other Academician giving an address east of Temple Bar over the next 100 years was one of Yeo's successors.

What provoked this disenchantment was a decided local want of taste. In Sir John Summerson's words, 'The City contributed nothing to the art of the Stuarts and Georgians; it was content with the robust second-rate'.[3] On the other hand, such unconcern may be interpreted as a worthy sacrifice: 'the mercantile stronghold' devoted itself instead to the supply of finance, commodities and labour. These

1 Edward Burney, *Antique School, Old Somerset House*, Strand, 1779. Harsh sunlight was tempered by muslin or oiled paper screens.

essentials boosted the growth and propped the cultural indulgence of the upstream end of town at the expense of the downstream end – for the citizens whose vocation it was to advance an age of elegance and to identify with its rarer creations sought out suitably congenial surroundings within the uptown Court milieu. Westminster's more formal residential precincts were primed expressly for the upper classes which, more or less obediently, took up social and architectural poses in them.

Happily, the combination of prestigious speculative development and aristocratic affectation produced every opportunity for image-builders. Thus a good third of the first Academicians are seen to be directly engaged in the design and decoration of houses, not only houses in town but new or improved family seats in the country as well. Fully another third painted their owners' portraits, their prize livestock, or flattering views of their landscaped country parks. Yet to gain these commissions in the first place the artists were obliged to woo their potential West End clientèle from close range. Consequently, and insofar as they could afford to, they made themselves conspicuous in and around the likeliest catchment areas. Apart from being in the City, Mason Chamberlin's position can then be recognised as typical. Obviously he judged there were sufficient friends of art among Spital Square society to support at least one portrait specialist.

For an artist to establish himself in the same exclusive neighbourhood as his clients signified both a bid for custom and the tradesman's desire to be treated as a professional. He had to confront a prejudice which ruled that ungloved trade was vulgar and unsightly, that it should be confined to the lowly back streets. But, failing any representation in drawing rooms frequented by people of influence, he was forced to come forward with a sample display of his own.[4] One honourable method

2 Trade card designed by West RA, etched by Bartolozzi RA, 1791. Intimate drawing lessons given by Paul Sandby's son at the premises depicted in **14**.

of attracting ornamental society was to set up a classroom. For many painters, particularly watercolourists, private drawing lessons were their chief source of income. A decent address on an artful trade card did much to seduce the latent patron, **2**.

Patronage was all-important and, indeed, it made survival tenuous for the unconnected or party-shy artist. Virtually all work was done to advance commissions; the designs and decorations for buildings, the portraits, busts and views were clearly spoken for by individual or collective patrons. Among the latter the Crown, the State – which embodied the Church – and the press were the most forthcoming. Speculative work was considerably less common. This state of affairs was due to an almost complete lack of public exhibition facilities. Publishers commissioned and supplied works on paper directly to booksellers whose trade lent its tolerable respectability to printselling. But, aside from print warehouses, commercial galleries were unknown. Auction rooms offered a dubious substitute. Not until the 1760s did membership of either the Free Society of Artists or the Incorporated Society of Artists of Great Britain introduce a regular market for contemporary art under regular control.

However, these two societies had themselves evolved from one, when differences had arisen over the management of the parent body. Renewed squabbling led to the formation of the Royal Academy. Both the 'Incorporated' and the 'Free' continued to stage exhibitions but the RA's superior firepower gradually forced their closure.[5] At last, then, after decades of foreign domination, the British had reasserted a national position in the fine arts.[6] By opening offices along Pall Mall and the Strand, the artists had extended the principle of their personal quests for recognition. They had placed their corporations within the realm of Court and government where they might creditably reflect the grace of ruling class consideration, if not royal endorsement.

A century had passed since the Great Fire, and in this time St James's and Covent Garden had begun to lose their power to magnetise London's artistic element. While the aristocrat-hosts were now more evenly distributed about the capital, the artist-parasites were tending less to tag after them. Just as lawyers and actors had possessed Chancery and Drury Lanes, artists saw their own platforms crystallising between St James Piccadilly and St Mary-le-Strand. It was, undeniably, a prophetic vision and one which gave good reason to keep faith with the area. Sir Joshua Reynolds, leader of the majority of RA founders who shared his preference for it, dwelt at its very centre.

When (Sir) Joshua moved up to 47 Leicester Fields in 1760, William Hogarth was still at No. 30 on the opposite side. No. 30, 'at the sign of the Golden Head', passed into use as the Sablonnière Hotel and a visitor there is known to have remarked, 'I remember the place when it was Hogarth's . . . these d—d fellows have put a billiard table in the very room my old friend built to paint in'.[7] Reynolds's practice had expanded to such a degree that he needed something similar, a purpose-built suite for himself, for his assistants, and for private exhibitions. Although his Charles II terraced house was relatively narrow, its site extended to Whitcomb Street. He had evidently foreseen space enough to add 'a splendid gallery' together with 'a commodious and elegant room for his sitters' leading off the stairhall.[8]

3 Henry Bunbury, *A Family Piece*, 1781. Sir Joshua Reynolds at work: he 'wrought standing and with great celerity'.

The painting room was octagonal, about 20′ long by 16′ broad, and 15′ high. Only one window – no more than 4′ square with a sill just over 9′ from the floor – introduced a painting light. Sitters were brought closer to it by taking a throne raised 1½′ from the floor. At a little distance the master 'wrought standing, and with great celerity', **3**.[9] Not for nothing is he sometimes dubbed 'Sir Sloshua'. That in some part he owed his immense success to these particular arrangements is quite possible, but once 47 Leicester Fields was yielded up by the Reynolds family no other painter was ever tempted to renew the lease.[10] Almost beyond doubt the designs stemmed from William Chambers, the president's right-hand man at the Academy, whose knowledge of the geometry of Oriental pavilions had lately been displayed in Kew Gardens.[11]

If, as he must often have done, the newly-knighted Sir Joshua were to have made his way in an easterly direction towards Old Somerset House in 1769, he could hardly have passed through the Covent Garden district without an excuse to call on any of several colleagues. First, he might have looked up Samuel Wale or John Gwynn, co-tenants of Little Court, St Martin's Lane – beside James Paine's house. The Academy's Professor of Perspective and the pamphleteering architect were typically situated among their own kind; they, too, had come to flirt with the favour of Leicester House.

In Covent Garden proper, John Richards, Jeremiah Meyer and George Dance's brother Nathaniel all inhabited Tavistock Row, a line of Queen Anne tenements on the south side of the Piazza. Richard Wilson, 'the English Claude' (though he was Welsh), could have been found in one of the original arcaded houses on the north side.[12] Meyer, who styled himself 'Enameller and Miniature Painter to the King', and Dance both upheld Covent Garden's name as a centre for portraiture. Landscape painting was not over-highly regarded in this era and only a few of its exponents gained proper recognition. Richards, at least, could count on supplementary scenic work in the local theatres.

These four painters were now rated among the more distinguished residents of the Piazza, a place to which prestige barely still attached. Gone was the cloistral Rinascimento enclave enjoyed by Sir Peter Lely and Sir Godfrey Kneller during the latter half of the previous century. By 1757 the last titled resident had departed,[13] unable to endure a persistent infiltration of Turkish bathers, taverners, thespians, and market traders.

Had Sir Joshua elicited the company of his colleagues and then pressed on through theatreland, he might likewise have prevailed upon the Swiss family Moser. A veteran of the St Martin's Lane Academy, George Moser lived in Drury Lane, no great distance from the main concentration of metal chasers around Newport Square. His daughter Mary won her place in the Academy by virtue of her dainty floral and mythical confections. On the final stretch there arose the possibility of meeting the king's coach-trimmer, Charles Catton. When he was rostered to take up his duties at Old Somerset House, Catton had only to step down from Gate Street on the meaner north-western edge of Lincoln's Inn Fields. Here was a square nearly as old as Covent Garden Piazza, the society of which, however, still appeared to be half a class beyond that of an RA.

Should Sir Joshua ever have planned a similar excursion from Leicester Fields, this time following a roundabout route westwards to the RA's Pall Mall rooms, a historical painter and an architect would again be the first to lie in his path. The painter, Benjamin West, had lately moved to a close called Panton Square which opened off Coventry Street. A painting of a few years before, showing American students under his instruction, is evidence both of the valuable link West maintained with his native colony and the way mounting public regard was reflected in his self-esteem, **4**. A stone's throw away in Vine Street, in the nearest corner of Mayfair, lived the Palladian sculptor-architect William Tyler. Not only was inner Mayfair the acknowledged testing ground of the architectural style popularised by Lord Burlington and his protégés, this particular corner was also strongly favoured by sculptors, not the least of them being Peter Scheemakers who had preceded Tyler to Vine Street and was still resident there in 1769.

In order to flush out the figure and landscape painters Nathaniel Hone and Francesco Zuccarelli, the president would have had to leave Piccadilly and probe the lanes west of St James's Street. By hanging out their signs within sight of the daily parade to and fro the royal parks, these two men passively invited the patronage of the fashionable St James's set. In addition, and more actively, they gave themselves the opportunity to mingle with the same tractable and bountiful beau monde while attending the occasional whim for coffee and conversation at one or other of the local taverns, like the Star and Garter on Pall Mall. Sir Joshua, however, will have been wise to avoid the Star and Garter, conscious that he risked being waylaid there by his fellow Dilettanti – members of the select and learned society which was in the habit of meeting on these premises during this period.[14]

4 Matthew Pratt, *The American School*, 1765. West RA instructing pupils at a house in 'Castle Street, Leicester Fields' (Charing Cross Road) – his address prior to Panton Square.

One further potential gauntlet Sir Joshua stood to run materialised just beyond St James's Palace in the macaroni shape of John Astley. Although a more or less unsung artist, Astley was nevertheless not unknown to the Dilettanti. Yet he must have wished his talent were better appreciated by the Royal Academy, especially since he had been an early campaigner for the creation of such a body. By good fortune Astley had inherited the means to buy the late 17th-century Schomberg House, 80–82 Pall Mall, and to convert it into three dwellings.[15] No. 81, the central section, received most of his attention and it was ready for his own occupation in 1769. From the front the building retained its former appearance save for a third porch placed against the centre. From the back, however, it could be seen that the entire middle portion had been raised. Most of the forward half of the plan was given over to a domed stairwell rising through four storeys; at the top it opened into a rearward painting room. This prettily decorated room was 23′ square and about half as high. It was dominated by a three-centre arched window fully 8′ tall by 7′ broad – leaving little for sill and head-to-ceiling heights. From outside the effect was less overpowering, as the window was contained by proportionate expanses of brickwork gathered into a chaste triangular pediment, 5. Astley was probably resigned to accepting the limited number of actual sitters who could be induced to make the dizzying ascent to his peacock's perch. But the well-calculated view from this perch over Marlborough House to St James's Park was perhaps as fine a reward as any likeness he might produce. Certainly he must have struggled before the outsize window which brought a variable and dazzling light from the south-east.

5 Top floor painting room built by John Astley at the rear of Schomberg House, Pall Mall, before its reconstruction.

Astley was conveniently placed to hawk his unbidden works at James Christie's immediately adjoining saleroom or to study the miniatures at the Academy rooms a few doors farther east. These Pall Mall establishments were hardly less accessible, though, to the next largest geographical group of founder members, those who hailed from Soho. It needs no more than the small sample of Academicians to reveal that Soho's Wardour Street was supplanting Long Acre as the axis around which later 18th-century artists were now inclined to revolve. They singled themselves out against a background of service industries that had become ingrained even as the West End building front tracked so briskly westwards some 90 years before. Craftsmen and manufacturing tradesmen, many of them European immigrants escaping religious persecution, moved in hereabouts to exploit the prevailing taste for modelled ornament. Of the ten Soho-resident RAs in 1769, six of them had foreign origins; it was as though a political asylum still beckoned. In fact, cosmopolitan camaraderie threatened to completely devalue the quarter's remaining high-class preserves, Soho and Golden Squares.

The fading glory of Soho Square eventually became the despair of its Portland Estates landlords. Doubtlessly they regarded Johan Zoffany's arrival at No. 31 as the toehold of Bohemian subversion. But he soon vanished; the estate's prospects even improved temporarily when a Scots sugar planter brought in the Adams to dress up No. 20, and (Sir) Joseph Banks moved in next door at the rebuilt No. 32. Banks had been there before, however; in 1768 he had called to offer Zoffany a place in the exploration party bound for Terra Australis, but the painter proudly refused it. John Baker, whose forte lay in painting flowers, would have been in some ways a more pertinent choice, yet he went unconsulted at his lodgings in Denmark Street, just east of the Square.

Less likely to be considered, despite her similar qualifications, was Mary Moser, who had been living away to the west side before she decamped with her father to Covent Garden. The odds are that the house the Mosers vacated in 'King Square Court' (Carlisle Street) was taken by Mr Moser's compatriot, Agostino Carlini RA.[16] Carlini was then in the process of smoothing off an equestrian model of the king and prosperous enough to employ a number of Italian assistants. There would have been one or two sizeable sheds in a stone-cutting yard close behind the house and separate access for a dray or barrow. These were facilities Carlini more than likely put at the disposal of his precocious Academy student, John Bacon. It can be no accident that the young sculptor was simultaneously renting space across Soho Square in George (now Goslett) Yard. Were he to want more advice, or a square meal, another of his teachers, the venerable history painter and bon vivant Francis Hayman, lived equally near at hand in Dean Street, **6**.

On the other side of Wardour Street, the Academicians were marginally more tightly knit but, with one exception, their contact with Golden Square was looser. Generally their houses were newer, not more than 50 years old.[17] But they were comparable in size and built on the standard two-room plan with a rear closet wing. Not everyone had the means or the freeholder's right to make major alterations, so painters usually took over what would otherwise be the best bedroom – at the front

6 Francis Hayman RA, *Self-Portrait with Patron*, *c.* 1745. Hayman's potato-faced figures are shown in a sparsely furnished, early Georgian painting room.

on the first floor. Besides the extra breadth they gave, front rooms almost always had at least two windows whereas back rooms might have only one. A well-known landscape painter moved into such a house 30 years later; to a friend he wrote decisively, 'My large room has three windows in front. I shall make that my shop, having the light from the upper part of the middle window, and by that means I shall get my easil in a good situation'.[18] Some painters, however, were prepared to forego extra light in favour of an ideal orientation. In this part of Soho, as in the other, the RAs were divided in their choice between north-east and north-west outlooks. Virtually nowhere else in the West End, in fact, could they hope to do better, such is the predominant bias of the street pattern.

Angelica Kauffmann seemed to be content with the north-west for the time she remained in Golden Square. An uncommon sophistication and a well-attuned decorative ability made Angelica a favourite of the salons, a role which allowed her to maintain a house here, in the middle of the south side, until 1781. By contrast, her adoptive countrymen, the painterly designer Gio Cipriani and the celebrated stipple engraver Franco Bartolozzi, though superior artists, could only afford rented rooms, **7.** They both paid the same landlord in 'Broad Street, Carnaby Market', an address also shared by their keen admirer, the school-aged William Blake. Young Blake grew up in famous and influential company, since Bartolozzi could claim to be the leading light in the art of aquafortis while Paul Sandby, who lived around the corner at 58 Poland Street, was the acknowledged pioneer in the science of aquatinta. Thomas Sandby, the Academy's first Professor of Architecture, was employed and housed at

7 John Rigaud, *Agostino Carlini, Francesco Bartolozzi and Giovanni Cipriani*, 1777. Three of the Italian-speaking RA founder members.

Windsor Park in 1769, but he was often needed at Poland Street to help civilise his younger brother's landscapes with picturesque buildings. Seascapes, on the other hand, were the province of Dominic Serres and family in Warwick Street. Like the Sandbys', Serres' house fronted the west side of the street, facing north-east. It bordered on the pucka Burlington Estate which is known to have harboured the Frenchman's most susceptible customers: military, particularly naval, pensioners.

Towards the 1770s, more than a few retired officers had drifted south from the Hanover Square area, one which appears to have first attracted their settlement in Mayfair. Ostensibly it was their party loyalty that prevented much movement in the opposite direction, to the rival Tory lands around Cavendish Square. Although professionally prepared for housebuyers from 1719 onwards, this latter square was still an incomplete hotchpotch 50 years later. Various early subscribers had subsequently withdrawn their pledges to build, the latest renegade being the Society of Dilettanti whose scheme to erect their clubrooms there had been in abeyance for over a decade. Notwithstanding, the Harley family, who owned the surrounding estate, had not relaxed its efforts to sponsor the artistic fraternity.[19] Consequently, the Irishman Francis Cotes RA, encouraged further by the sight of a local building resurgence, decided to chance his arm at No. 24 on the south side between Holles and (John) Princes Streets.

Cotes bought a lease of the six-storey terraced house in 1763, married two years later and, in the unusual medium of pastel as well as oil, settled down to dispense excellent portraits at a profitable rate. But, sadly, the dead hand of Cavendish soon came knocking again. Cotes died suddenly in 1770, aged barely 44, with at least 15 portraits unfinished. He left a surprising accumulation of books and works of art in exquisitely furnished premises which the auctioneers stated 'were in the most perfect repair, a very large sum having been very lately expended in compleating the same', **8**.[20] The expense was principally deployed on 'two large and well-proportioned rooms with skylight and dome ceilings, added to the first floor, forming an elegant suite' together with 'a pupils' room' – 'a lofty room with a Portland chimney-piece, etc.'[21] at the end of the garden. On the first floor, the accommodation was extended to the rear by a double-cube 'shew room' half the width of the house. This picture gallery led in turn to a painting room the full width and almost square. Upon his mahogany machine chair, or sitters' throne, Cotes thus obtained a northern side light from the resultant half-width area. Supplementary light came from the overhead lantern. Peter Toms, 'the drapery man', and John Russell, the most gifted pupil, had to make do with male and female lay figures in the sunless garden room. But they

8 Three pages from the sale catalogue listing the effects of Francis Cotes RA auctioned at 24(32) Cavendish Square in 1771.

(9)

7 Two pair of canvas window blinds in mahogany frames, and an open work fender, shovel, tongs and poker
8 A *Turkey* carpet 11 feet by 10 feet, and a small *India* mat
9 Two brown enamell'd basons
10 Two enamell'd scarlet jars, and 2 bottles
11 Two enamel'd paned jars and covers
12 Two beautiful enamell'd image jars and covers, and 2 beakers ditto

Numb. VIII. *The Painting Room, and Room adjoining.*

1 Six mahogany stool back chairs, covered with crimson mixt damask, brass nailed, on casters, and crimson serge covers
2 Two elbow ditto
3 A large mahogany commode, with a desk top, variety of drawers, and mask and fluted corners
4 A mahogany writing table on a pillar and claw, and 2 mahogany stools
5 A *Wilton* carpet 19 feet 6 inches by 18 feet
6 A stage covered with carpetting, with a mahogany machine chair cover'd with mixt damask, and crimson serge case
7 A mahogany box for colours, mounted with brass, on a stand, with a drawer
8 A wainscot tool chest with tools
9 An high pair of steps, and a serge window curtain, with a brass rod
10 A mahogany nest of drawers with folding doors

The Shew Room.

11 A *Turkey* carpet 9 feet by 7 feet 7 inch. a shovel, tongs, poker, bellows and brush
12 A brazier, and an high pair of steps
13 Nine canvas spring window blinds
14 An *India* floor mat, 22 feet 6 inches, by 14 feet 6 inches

B   Numb.

(10)

Numb. IX. *The Pupil's Room.*

MODELS in CASTS and PLAISTER.

1 Sundry parts of figures, boys, gladiators, &c.
2 Ten arms moulded from nature
3 Eight feet ditto, from *Bernini*
4 Eight ditto
5 Fifteen boys from *Fiamingo*, &c.
6 A colossal foot, and 2 others, from the antique
7 A boy from *Fiamingo*, and 2 trunks from *Bernini*, and the antique
8 Four masks from the antique
9 Five ditto from nature, a fine boys head by *Fiamingo*, and a trunk of *Daphne*, &c.
10 Two trunks from *Bernini*, and a satyr's mask
11 A crouching *Venus*, an original cast from the antique
12 The *Gladiator* and the *Antinous*
13 Three heads of *Niobe's* mother, &c.
14 Three ditto, *Bernini's Proserpine*, the *Apollo* of the *Belvidere*, and 1 of *Niobe*
15 Three antique heads of *Jupiter*, *Seneca*, and another
16 Three ditto from the antique
17 Two heads of *Homer* and *Minerva*, and two of *Niobe's* family
18 Three figures, *Germanicus*, a fine cast, *Roubilliac's* anatomy, and another from *Bernini*
19 Three, a fine head of *Augustus Cæsar*, 1 of *Attalanta*, a mask from *Fiamingo*, and a ditto from the antique
20 Ten pieces, boys from *Fiamingo*, arms and heads from ditto, &c.
21 Nine ditto
22 Nine ditto, and a greyhound
23 Eight heads from *Fiamingo* and the antique
24 Three busts, *Plautilla*, *Niobe's* daughter, and *Milo*

N. B. *The remaining Lots of this Number will be sold To-morrow; see Page* 13.

Third

[13]

61 A man and a woman by *Metzu*
62 Two landscapes in water colours by *Marco Rice*
64 Two ditto
65 A large view by Mr. *P. Sandby*
66 A ditto
67 *Cupids* in crayons by *Cotes*
68 A *Venus* and *Cupid* by ditto

Numb. IX. *The Pupil's Room*; *continued from Page* 10.

25 Three figures *Antinous*, 2 from *John de Bologna*, and a bust of *Venus*
26 A very fine terra cota model by *John de Bologna*
27 A bust of the *Venus de Medicis*
28 A terra cota model of history by *Rysbrack*
29 A fine cast of the infant *Hercules*
30 A bust of *Carracalla*
31 A ditto of *Lucius Papyrius's* mother
32 The trunk of Mr. *Lock's Venus*, 2 legs from *Fiamingo*, a head and 2 feet
33 The group of wrestlers, a fine cast
34 King *William* on horseback by *Rysbrack* (bronzed)
35 Three fine casts from *Rysbrack* of *Fiamingo*, *Inigo Jones*, and *Palladio*
36 A fine cast of *Venus* from Mr. *Pigalle's* model
37 A ditto of *Mercury* from ditto.
      N. B. These are rare original casts from the model
38 A marble statue of *Diana*, from the antique
39 A skeleton of a lay man
40 A large lay woman
41 Three eazells
42 A mahogany, and a painted ditto
43 A prophyry stone to grind colours, and a muller
44 A box of very fine lake
45 Thirteen glass jars with variety of colours, 5 empty glass jars, and 12 boxes with variety of colours
46 A marble stone for mixing of colours, several boxes with crayons, and a shagreen case with instruments
47 A colour box, a crayon ditto, a ditto for drawings, 3 pallets, and a parcel of pencil brushes
48 A German stove and pipe
49 A wainscot table with drawers, a chair, and a stool

Fourth

also had a staggering array of antique plaster trunks, limbs and digits to guide them in the warmth of the open fire and a German stove.

His firm friend's death is said to have reduced Peter Toms to a state of terminal melancholy. Although a technically capable painter in his own right, Toms had chosen his Wimpole Street address primarily to speed his comings and goings as Cotes's assistant. John Russell had likewise sought lodgings nearby and was happy enough not to move from the locality for the rest of his life. Wimpole Street in 1769 had not yet been pushed all the way through to Marylebone Road, the 'New Road' opened in the late 1750s. Nor had Great Portland or Great Titchfield Streets, which were aimed at the same target. These two thoroughfares originated either side of the Oxford Market, a site in no way central to the estate and surely placed there to localise any low-class infection transmitted by Soho yahoos. Nevertheless, when Joseph Wilton, Edward Penny and Francis Newton moved to this animated quarter the greater nuisance of construction noise had passed to a frontier slightly farther north. Wilton used his position as 'Sculptor to the King' to set up his workshops on relatively fresh ground, where he was necessarily less constrained than Carlini by an existing urban infrastructure. Newton, the Academy's secretary, and Penny, its Professor of Painting, both opted for Mortimer Street. Together with Cotes they set a very worthy figure-painting service before the up-and-coming society about to buy into the Adam brothers' resplendent architecture up and down Portland Place.

At this time the Scots architects could barely keep abreast of their own enterprise, although the opportunity to coordinate the design of an entire London square, for example, eluded them till the 1790s. Nonetheless, they made late contributions to five or six well-established West End squares, including the showpiece of the Portman Estate, Portman Square. Their sound-alikes, the Adams brothers, had built terraces in this square soon after it had been surveyed in 1761;[22] residents began to occupy its southern range seven years later, by which time Portman-style subdivisions criss-crossed much of the rest of the Harleys' inner Marylebone holdings. Portman Square itself was cradled by major axes projecting from both the Portland (Cavendish-Harley) Estate and the similarly orthogonal Grosvenor territories. Orchard Street, which formed one of these axes at the onset of speculative 'Portmania', was also the address given by the prodigal George Barret RA. His line in country-house views presented a further temptation to the increasing numbers of wealthy squires already tempted to invest in immodest pieds-à-terre towards this side of town. The bloodstock portrait, however, Barret ceded to his near neighbour, George Stubbs, whose house and stable lay tellingly close to open fields and the traffic of the Oxford Turnpike.

The westernmost parts of Marylebone and Mayfair never proved especially popular with painters. Stubbs was one of the first men to quarrel with the RA to his disadvantage and he remained out on a limb in Somerset Street until his death. Joseph Wright (of Derby) was another early dissenter, but his Margaret Street rooms of 1769 put him, on the contrary, on the threshold of the London artists' Promised Land.

This turned out to be the cleaver-shaped Berners Estate – Cleveland Street representing its handle and Wells Street its cutting edge – which occupied land beyond the Portland Estate to the east. Attention turned to the Berners Estate when James Paine began building Middlesex Hospital in 1755. William Chambers had had his eye on it during his stay in Poland Street, and after the Seven Years' War he made his move. Having entered into partnership with his friend Thomas Collins, a speculator and master plasterer, Chambers undertook to build 20 terraced houses in Berners Street.[23] Chambers himself moved into No. 13 in 1765; the other 19 houses built to his designs were completed over the following six or seven years. No. 13, like its neighbours, appears to have been a house of sober refinement on a conventional plan. However, it is possible that the garden front was decorated with papier-mâché chinoiserie of the sort occasionally prepared for the architect by Wilton. More certainly, there were stables at the end of the plot and, adjoining these, a drawing office with an east-facing Venetian window. Domestic privacy was effectively

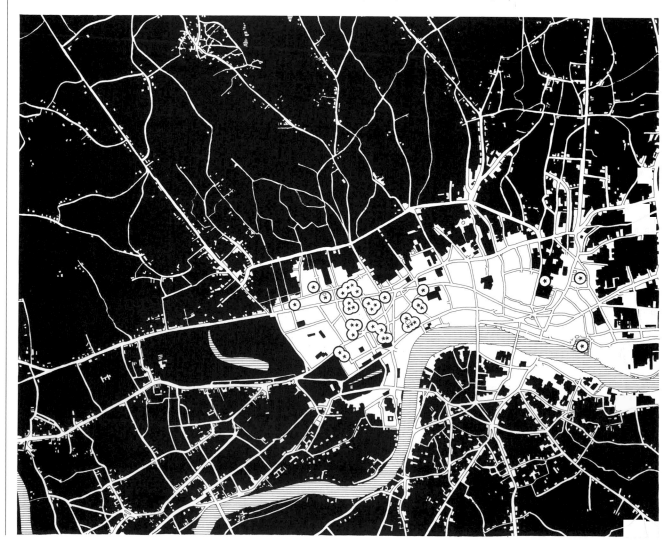

defended, as the office also opened into Berners Mews, four doors from Castle Street.

Chambers really needed a drawing office. In 1769, besides a handful of draughtsmen, he was employing John Yenn and Thomas Hardwick to assist him deal with no less than 20 concurrent jobs. His professional standing was doubly underlined when George III ratified his investiture in the Swedish nobility, creating him a 'Knight of the Polar Star'. Our honourable Sir William, then, had disdained to build a mansion in a square but he did hold sway over half a street of dignified houses. And even if they were in sub-urban 'North Soho', he could confidently expect clients to search him out there. Thus, however much his title helped him, he had brought about a token inversion of the formal approach to patronage.

To the artists who forthwith sailed in to colonise North Soho, Sir William's action looked more like a declaration of independence. Astonishing numbers came up Wardour Street and settled the Berners Estate; yet development here actually lagged behind that immediately to the east, where a tangle of non-patrician estates absorbed just as many again. It could truly be said that a new republic had been proclaimed between Marylebone High Street and Tottenham Court Road, in every state of which an RA was already governor – such was the respect that a chosen few could now invoke by virtue of that regal suffix, **9**.

9   London in 1769, showing the locations of the first RAs. For the distribution of current RAs at later stages, see **20** and **40**. White denotes built-up areas.

2

FROM GEORGIAN CONTIGUITY
TO VICTORIAN SEMI-DETACHMENT

BETWEEN 1769 and the turn of the century, 33 new members were elected to maintain the Academy's full complement of 40. Over this period, 22 of the 33 took houses in that inner portion of St Marylebone and St Pancras parishes; another half-dozen founder members also transferred there. And that is to say nothing of the considerable camp-following composed of artists just as good – some better, many worse, some from the other societies, most unaffiliated – which closed in behind them.

At first the estimation of the painter rose only in the eyes of his fellow painter. Liberation from class servitude remained some way off yet. But if the artists appeared over-ambitious to stand up in one place and be counted they had, in fact, acted with a good deal of foresight. For a start, London's population had begun to accelerate quite noticeably. From 1750 to 1801 it would increase about 25 per cent to reach 900 000. The resultant demand for new housing hastened the speculative builders' advances on the ducal estates. It was becoming clear that the area enclosed by the royal parks, Edgware Road, the New Road, Gray's Inn Lane, Temple and the Thames would be entirely built over by the time numbers passed one million. Sensitive souls looked away from the congested, fire- and plague-prone centre to the only pastoral and picturesque verges which were left. These were at once the bright horizons of a Georgian Golden Age.

Wherever the artists pitched down on the West End perimeter, they could easily maintain contact with their societies and the art markets, with their patrons and the salons. So it mattered little that Mayfair tended to give them the cold shoulder; it was even fortuitous that the Duke of Bedford had postponed development on his half of Lamb's Conduit Fields. Channelled into North Soho instead, they then got the benefit of cheaper accommodation from less exacting landlords and a reassuring contiguity with their familiar 'old' Soho stamping-grounds. Further, developers did not lose sight of the value of building residential squares in the West End. Their faith was repaid by the constancy of the cultural élite, so that dowagers and dignitaries ended up more and more evenly distributed. Obviously there could be no point in the artists' sidling courtship of the square-dweller if squares were to become common-place.

10 Plan of Benjamin West's premises at 14 Newman Street, Marylebone. The 'Great Room' (**21**) was not added until 1820.

11 Plan of John Bacon's house and workshops at 17 Newman Street, Marylebone, adapted from 1774 onwards.

11

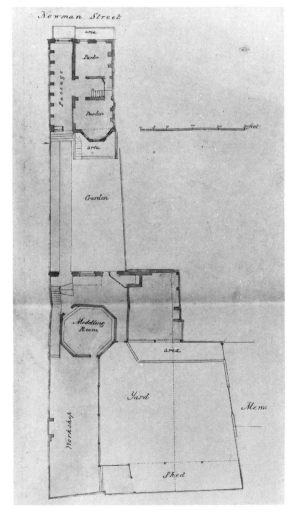

Houses, too, suffered a loss of individuality due mainly to the marriage of mass-production and master planning on gridiron lines. Stylistic consistency was admirable, but it could easily end in rigid facelessness. The contemporary thrust of 'Metropolitan Improvement' thus brought mixed blessings. However, most people welcomed its major architectural instrument, the Building Act of 1774. Thenceforward every dwelling in central London was guaranteed a (provident) minimum spatial content and a (safe) minimum standard of carcase construction. As far as rank and file artists were concerned, the Act put them in line for a lodging with greater dimensional coherence, lighting in proportion, and better ancillary servicing. They began to catch up with these modern conveniences in their improved municipal setting northwards of Wigmore, Mortimer and Goodge Streets, and in various vacant pockets southwards.

The advent of the modern 'rated' house must have immediately cheapened unlet properties built prior to 1774 and, no doubt, there were bargains to be had. Benjamin West had been on the look-out for more spacious premises once he had the King's blessing to realise his dream of painting the world's grandest history pieces. In 1775 he decided to buy 14 Newman Street with its imperial vista down Castle Street and its extra ground at the rear, **10**. In due course the backward view would be equally impressive, **21**.

Initially, however, it seems that West improvised with a detached painting room that gave onto a mews behind Rathbone Place. Adjacent outbuildings were converted into 'Two small Colour Rooms' and a 'Light Gallery'.[1] Extensive undercrofts and other connecting rooms furnished him with plenty of storage space. At 29' × 22' the painting room was not over large, considering the prodigious tableaux which he could easily spring upon unwary clients. But the subsidiary rooms indicated he was employing a back-up team both to prepare his palettes and to garnish his works under a variety of lighting conditions. Nevertheless, it was a remote and irrationally-assembled complex that barely improved on Reynolds's arrangements and only in terms of total space on those of Cotes.

Farther along Newman Street the house plots were more abruptly curtailed by a cul-de-sac opening out of Newman Passage. One of these, No. 17, duly came to the attention of the up-and-coming sculptor, John Bacon. His bread-and-butter employment at Mrs Coade's artificial stone factory, a swelling order book, and a litter of five children all under the age of eight, meant that he could well afford to better his latest cramped position in Wardour Street. Accordingly, from mid-1774, he obtained a lease of the Newman Street house,[2] little knowing he had probably supplanted the future president of the Academy. Bacon gradually gained control over the loop of buildings at the end of the cul-de-sac, barring the roadway to enclose an open-air yard. Within the walls of the existing coach-house he constructed an octolateral 'modelling room'. Separate stairs led to a storage loft or 'bust room'. Flanking the yard on the east side was an open-fronted shed, while on the west stood the former coach-house of 18 Newman Street, **11**. Bacon annexed this to house his own foundry.

RA honours were not conferred on him until 1777 but John Bacon was already a byword in sculpture by then. Patrons and privileged visitors would attend the master in his front parlour before being conducted through a broad hallway lined with niches displaying specialities of the house. Only after they had passed beyond the far garden wall would the function of that squat pagoda glimpsed from the back steps find an explanation. The casts on view in odd compartments of the top level showrooms might have been seen approaching their final state down below in the hands of up to 20 assistants. From this standpoint – beside a heavenly temple and ringed by flinty immortality, with a prospect beneath of humanity in harness heaving hammer and tongs around the fearsome crucible – Romantic spirits unacquainted as yet with industry in revolution must have felt halfway between Valhalla and Gehenna.

Such a scale of operations was sure to have been resented by the crabby and tight-fisted Joseph Nollekens RA. In 1770 he had followed Penny and Newton to a sensible end-of-terrace situation astride the block separating Little Titchfield and Mortimer Streets. His double-fronted house backed directly onto a workshop of somewhat lesser size than Bacon's but otherwise convenient for the two disengaged elevations it presented to the north and east. Nollekens remained here for over 50 years, minimising his overheads and, as a result, amassing a fortune even greater than that of his rival. Not counting Wilton, the other major contemporary sculptor in these parts was Thomas Banks. By the late 1770s he, too, had secured property in Newman Street. Although the house at No. 5 was itself very small, the tail of another service yard provided him with ready-made workspace and the rear access Bacon was finding indispensable to easy delivery and despatch.

Before the turn of the century, two more RAs had joined their colleagues in Newman Street. One was the crayon portraitist John Russell; the other was Thomas Stothard. On buying the freehold of the quite ordinary No. 28 'for the very modest sum of £1000' in 1794, the prolific illustrator was said to be 'fairly established in *Artists' Street*; for in a few years so was Newman Street designated by the neighbourhood in familiar discourse; and well it might be so'.[3] Those few years witnessed the deaths of Bacon, Banks and Russell and their replacement in the street by a fresh crop of Academicians under West's new presidency.

Much the same was to occur in Charlotte Street, St Pancras. Grafted onto Rathbone Place in the early 1760s, Charlotte Street seemed to be heading nowhere until Fitzroy Square had been planted at the north end 30 years later. However, it and its offshoots had quickly found a place in art history: Penny had already passed through and, when the careers of Wilson, Toms and Hone had dwindled to an end there, those of Joseph Farington and Robert Smirke Snr had just begun to bloom.

Nathaniel Hone made his last move to North Soho in 1780. Although his reputation was not helped by *The Conjuror* affair of 1775,[4] he blithely stayed on at his former Pall Mall address until he felt he had out-stared the Academy and seen it re-installed at New Somerset House. He had first settled Pall Mall in 1774, the year that Thomas and Margaret Gainsborough took their lease of the western third of Astley's Schomberg House.[5] Gainsborough had arrived to do battle in the lucrative London portraiture field. For a man accustomed to the elbow-room of his house in Bath, 80 Pall Mall will have been chosen more on the merits of its prime location and the serviceable garden ground behind. Since he was withholding his work from public exhibition at this period, one can safely assume that the two-storey annexe subsequently built upon the garden contained both a painting room and a private gallery. It comprised, in fact, just two rectangular rooms, each about 33′ × 21′ × 15′, placed one above the other and separated from the house by a timber-framed corridor, **12**. Gainsborough had evidently taken note of the extension at Cavendish Square but, in order to preserve an outlook for his back rooms, it meant that the similar intermediate link ended up no wider than a picture-hat.

The architectural precision and skylighting of the link at first floor level suggests that the upper room (with roof-lighting likewise possible) completed a squiggly sequence of gallery spaces starting at the front hall and continuing up the lantern-lit main staircase. It probably did double duty as the painting room once said to be 'of a most admired disorder'. One envisages Sarah Siddons and J C Bach posing beside an end window at least as large as Astley's and similarly mal-oriented. But Gainsborough's room was also much deeper: twice the area of either Reynolds' or Cotes' and bigger again than West's. Below, the corresponding window stretched almost from side to side of a salon given over, more than likely, to entertaining. Outside, the park presented a reminder to Gainsborough of an ideal country landskip.

No doubt these garden rooms were a welcome refuge from the rumpus issuing next door from a sort of massage parlour for fainting hearts, managed between 1781 and 1784 by the notorious quack, Dr James Graham.[6] Astley had given up any attempt to compete with his tenants and retired, via Barnes, to Cheshire. He had allowed his own apartments to be turned into a 'Temple of Health and Hymen' where 'medico-electrical apparatus' was administered to very gullible or altogether befuddled devotees. Hounded by charges of trumpery, Graham soon moved away, ultimately to meet total discredit. No. 81 was then rededicated to the art of portrait miniatures as Richard and Maria Cosway came to occupy it for somewhat longer.

Cosway was the natural, unnatural heir to this Pall-Mall sideshow. Like Astley, he

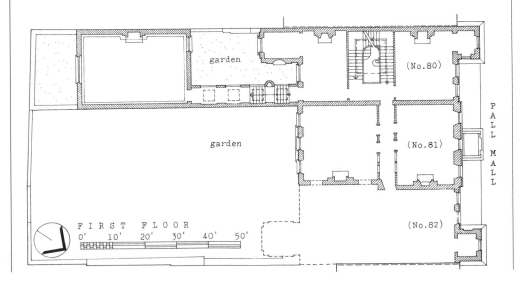

12 First floor plan of Schomberg House, 80–82 Pall Mall, including Thomas Gainsborough's annexe of *c.* 1789 at the rear.

was a social-climbing fop; like Hone, he had a monstrous self-regard, affecting coats of mulberry silk embroidered with scarlet strawberry sprigs and, like Graham, he held a belief in animal magnetism as well as a personal franchise for raising the dead. Patrons who sat in the topmost room during the week mounted the stairs again on Sundays for Maria's intimate musical soirées or Richard's mystical séances, **13**.

Widowed in 1788, Mrs Gainborough survived only another four years, but long enough to observe the Cosways pack up their articles of virtu and voodoo and take them to Stratford Place. Now more or less appropriately adapted, Schomberg House soon took in other painters. For, although the Royal Academy had deserted Pall Mall, the street itself maintained an alluring cachet for artists and fine art businesses, especially once the Prince of Wales had taken up residence at Carlton House.

Indeed, starting in 1787–8 with Macklin's Poets' Gallery,[7] British artists gained access to at least five new Pall Mall outlets in quick succession. These significantly assisted selected painters in the sale of engravings, and wound down a trend towards one-man shows. But, when the enemy occupation of Europe seriously bottled up the print trade, the cry went up again for more venues. Far from subduing the national product, the Napoleonic Wars stimulated heroic, violent works in one quarter and picturesque, contemplative studies in another. Remote campaigns generated interest in foreign parts yet Albion's isolation also bred an academic introversion. With native topographical painting thus coming to the fore, the reopening in 1806 of Boydell's Shakespeare Gallery as the British Institution (BI) both compelled the RA to be more receptive and brought the artists a timely reinforcement to their marketplace. The space provided at the BI for non-Academicians, or 'Outsiders', was supplemented almost simultaneously by what developed into the Old Watercolour Society (OWS) exhibition. But restrictions crept in and dissatisfactions arose again such that by 1832, the year of the Reform Bill, a rebel group of Outsiders had formed the Society of British Artists (SBA) and a New Society of Painters in Miniature and Watercolours (NWS) had developed from 'the Old'. Each of these later societies similarly established their showrooms on the Pall Mall–Strand axis where the National Gallery was soon to take its place as well.

Many years later, the NWS moved its headquarters to Piccadilly and adorned a grand new building with the busts of eight celebrated watercolourists, among them Paul Sandby and George Barret. Quite apart from their artistic distinctions, these two London-based Academicians were the first to break clear of the West End perimeter altogether. Not that they went very far. In 1772 Barret retired to healthful Westbourne Green;[8] in the same year Sandby took his growing family from Poland Street to a smart terrace looking south over Hyde Park, just a few yards along the present Bayswater Road.

To the east of the Sandby house lay the formal graveyard belonging to St George's, Hanover Square; to the west and behind only mature poplars intercepted the view towards Harrow – a fine spot to build a belvedere. This the painter did, making it as useful as it was decorative. Contained within an essentially cubical block sitting athwart the narrow plot, its taller upper level was reserved for a painting room. Twin façades in the form of double-decker triumphal arches were perhaps the contribu-

13 Richard Cosway RA, William Hodges RA, *A View from Mr Cosway's Breakfast Room, Pall Mall*, 1789. Maria Cosway looks from the window shown in **5**.

14 Paul Sandby RA, *The Artist's Painting Room, St George's Row, Oxford Turnpike* (RA 1809). A rural retreat of *c.* 1775 on the edge of the West End.

tion of Paul's brother Thomas, the old-school architect well versed in garden building lore.[9] Some of the details such as the low-relief panels and lacy fanlights are clearly borrowings from the neo-classical Adam houses of about 1774 near Portland Place.

Paul Sandby's oil painting of this subject contrasts a foreground of ordered, concrete enclosures and domestic bondage with a background of untamed parkland and leisure activity, **14**. More so than Gainsborough in his contemporary Pall Mall annexe, the artist here, like the cat on the fence, could face either scene at will from answering windows. Gradually other notable men joined the Sandbys in St George's Row: the mezzotint engraver and publisher John Raphael Smith; the marine painter Dominic Serres (author, with his son, of the *Liber Nauticus*); and, for a period around 1801, the watercolourist Thomas Girtin – coincidentally another of the NWS figureheads.[10]

Paul Sandby probably stayed with his brother at Windsor Great Park but he could not, it seems, afford even a small country house of his own. Although very few painters who were likewise tied to London by official, contractual or teaching commitments could take such a material step, a movement to cultivate the Picturesque on the outskirts had certainly got underway. Sir James Thornhill and William Hogarth, for instance, were appreciating its salutary subtleties at Chiswick well before Horace Walpole had introduced its sickly excesses at Strawberry Hill, Twick-enham. Sir William Chambers had already passed this way, too. In 1765 he had acquired 'Whitton', a modest villa on the Isleworth River. In due course the shady sweeps of the upper Thames also worked on the sensibility of Sir Joshua Reynolds. Familiarity with the 'small decorated mansion' built near Strawberry Hill some time before by his teacher, Thomas Hudson,[11] is sure to have helped. Charmed, anyway, by the prospect from Richmond Hill, he bought a patch of the slope and had Sir William run up a bachelor's retreat for him there in 1770–2.[12] Guests brought down for the day persuaded Sir Joshua, much to Sir William's annoyance, to enlarge it by adding a floor and two sets of bow windows. Notwithstanding, the alterations were a success and the idea of a 'sketching lodge' took root, **15**.

Several other friends and Academicians – retirees like Zoffany and cadets like DeLoutherbourg (at Hammersmith from 1785 onwards) – began to court the riverside. But it was another twenty-odd years before the general invigoration of British watercolour painting led John Varley and the young J M W Turner to reawaken the old interest in Twickenham. Varley hired a cottage as a rural base for his drawing classes; Turner, apart from abjuring an architect, took after Reynolds. In about 1813, close to the site of Marble Hill, he cobbled a toy villa of his own. In mock dudgeon he called it Solus Lodge. Its unlikely Alpine–Palladian exterior belied interiors of an attenuated grace worthy of Soane. French doors were arranged to open from a central room in which the owner liked to paint the sun rising over the watermea-dows, **16**. Turner kept on the little house, renamed Sandycombe Lodge, until late in life.[13] Even then he returned to the Thames, becoming a lodger on Cheyne Walk

15 Joseph Stadler after Joseph Farington RA, *From Richmond Hill down the river*, 1793. Sir Joshua's Wick House of 1771 is on the right.

where the view across Chelsea Reach was again south-easterly.

Not all painters yearned for river scenery. George Romney seemed to prefer marshes and mountains. In common with most overworked portraitists, he would grab any chance to head for the countryside. 'He cheers up', wrote his host William Hayley, '. . .when he goes to Eartham; he works at his big *Tempest* picture in the wooden painting room that he built for himself, and finishes it in 1790 . . .'.[14] In London he started spending the nights in Hampstead and only the days in London; on other occasions, deluded, he would tramp the Edgware Road on his way to a phantom rendezvous with his model and soulmate, Emma, Lady Hamilton. Late in 1792 he was actually about to buy and build in Pineapple Place, Maida Vale, but his son recommended the cheaper course of additions and alterations to an existing house on Holly Bush Hill, Hampstead.[15]

Romney's dream was to devote his savings to a kind of spa-village study centre within walking distance of London. This was to embrace a reference museum of antique casts (already selected and despatched by Flaxman from Rome), a painting room cum picture gallery for his personal use, and nothing less than a pantechnicon in which to store the unsold and unclaimed canvases that threatened to engulf his premises in town. To complete the plan, Romney anticipated that 'youths of respectability' would visit, draw, and receive his instruction.

He took his son's advice, bought the Hampstead house together with some bordering property and, to an academic architect named Bunce,[16] rashly gave a glimpse of the full depth of his pocket. The site of some quite adequate stables having been chosen for the major extensions, building got underway with their

16   William Cooke after William Havell, *Sandycombe Lodge, Twickenham*, 1814. Turner's sketching lodge which he designed himself *c.* 1813.

extravagant replacement in the autumn of 1796. It appears to have been decided that the existing two-storey dwelling would be retained largely untouched and that just two well-lit, polyvalent spaces would be attached to it to answer for every other need. Mr Bunce superimposed these two vast rooms, connecting them to the house along their western side by a common two-level hallway. A heavy porch at one end balanced a compact staircase at the other, **17**. The lower of the 'Westmorland House Fine Rooms' was only sparingly decorated, suggesting its use for teaching, painting and storage. Upstairs, reserved for Romney himself, his pictures and the sculpture, the ceiling height was increased and a little extra floorspace derived from a slimmer, weatherboarded superstructure. Giant 24-pane Dutch windows, bigger again than those below, poured in a skyful of daylight past reeded architraves and a dignified march of fluted gilt pilasters.

The key to the utter magnificence of this room, this essay in the Beautiful, lay in the fact that all the dimensions had been adjusted to conform to the Golden Section. An acute judgment of scale was then applied to perfect proportions. Even the upper hall, or ante-room, possessed a subtle, skewed symmetry. Visitors could ascend

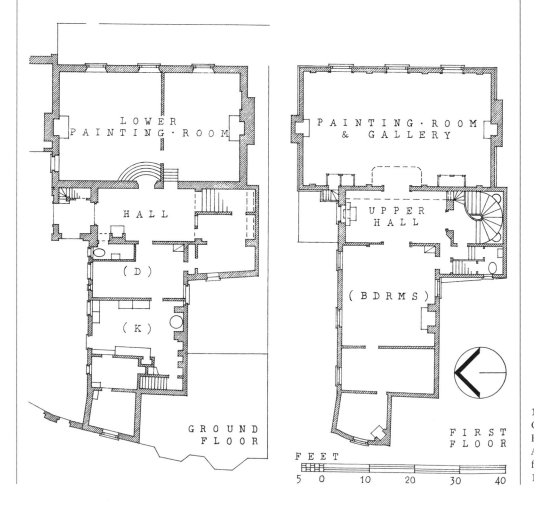

17 Lower floor plans of George Romney's house, Holly Bush Hill, Hampstead. Additions by S Bunce date from 1796. Modified in 1929–30 and subsequently.

further to the catwalk here and penetrate to a balconette where a new angle might be obtained on the entire spectacle. But few visitors ever came. By the time the building was complete in the autumn of 1798, Mr Bunce had long since slipped away. Romney had been in and out supervising the remaining works, although he continued to paint by day in the West End. Faced with a bill upwards of £2750, he not only disposed of his town house but also appears to have let the living accommodation at Hampstead. Thereafter he is reported to have camped in the 'singular fabric' adjoining, from a point in which 'without moving from his pillow he could contemplate . . . a very magnificent view of the metropolis'.[17]

On the same pillow, Romney's original dream turned into a Fuselian nightmare. At one point there was room to begin his long-postponed religious tableaux; at the next, canvases were being consigned to an open riding-house outside where they were either spoiled or stolen. One winter was enough to break his spirit and convince him of his folly. Addled and miserable, he was forced to return to Kendal where his neglected but faithful wife took him in. An auction of the land and buildings in 1801 brought in only a pitiful fraction of his overall outlay.[18]

Romney could never have sunk so low had he not risen so high beforehand. After buying the lease of 24 Cavendish Square which had lain unused for five years since Cotes' death, he had kept himself and his assistants extremely busy in both painting rooms for the rest of the century.[19] His competition in the immediate vicinity remained slight until the big guns – James Barry, Henry Fuseli, John Opie – erected their blinds along to the east on the Berners Estate, and even then these men tended to hunt mythical beasts rather than heads and half-lengths. A more positive challenge in the portrait painters' electorate, however, was being mounted from the south. The presence in Mayfair of influential connoisseurs and collectors like Sir William Hamilton and Charles Towneley alone provided sufficient incentive for ambitious young men to put up their plates there. The rapid rise of James Northcote's and (Sir) Thomas Lawrence's stars in Clifford and Old Bond Streets, the renewed favour shown to Singleton Copley at 25 (St) George Street, and the ready absorption of superior topographical painters, miniaturists, gem engravers and illustrators indicated the breadth of patronage which lay at hand, particularly in the 'Burlingtonia' estate extending north from Piccadilly to Hanover Square. Between 1797 and 1804, Copley and Henry Tresham would gaze across George Street in wonder at No. 8 where (Sir) William Beechey, who had already warmed up the other two Mayfair Squares, was ushering in sitters by the phaeton-load. Possibly Beechey's greatest catch was Admiral Nelson; calling at the Hamiltons in 1800, the man of the moment might have legitimately excused himself for being on the Mayfair tack. The passage into the big room at No. 8 was indeed well trodden by the high and mighty when Thomas Phillips took over. Elected RA, like Beechey, soon after his tenure began, Phillips maintained a steady, if less slick, portrait service here for 18 years and his son Henry carried it forward another 20 years until 1864.

A residency of 20 years would be exceptional among Mayfair portraitists earlier in the piece. Northcote stayed 10 years before withdrawing to the Carnaby market area while Lawrence, who served a similar term, leapfrogged to a 'comparative retiredness

... both pleasant and advantageous'[20] on the edge of Soho Square. Beechey would soon decamp too, but in a different direction. With so many senior Academicians inclining to the region countenanced by West, room was left for fresh gambits on the wider Marylebone chequerboard. Like (Sir) Martin Archer Shee, who jumped into the breach left by Romney in Cavendish Square, the energetic Beechey made a knight's move across two squares to 13 Harley Street. From 1804 onwards, he enticed more and more sitters to a bay window overlooking the Mycenaean palace of the latest arbiter elegantiarum, Thomas Hope, in Duchess Street. Contemporary moves brought J M W Turner first to 64 Harley Street and then to the adjacent 47 (now 23) Queen Anne Street. England's champion watercolourist appeared infrequently at these houses but constructed makeshift picture galleries in both which he entrusted to his father's management. George Jones painted an impression of the second, dating from *c.* 1820, which showed it to be a crooked enfilade of poky attic space accidentally illuminated by virtue of two or three graceless skylights and several poorly patched holes in the roof.

For a one-time trainee architect and Professor of Perspective, Turner's effort was not very flattering. What was more likely to divert the casual gallery-goer lay a few blocks away on the eastern corner of Henrietta Street (Place) and Welbeck Street. In 1806 Peter Stroehling, a German miniaturist trained at the expense of the Russian court, arrived here after a stay on Pall Mall. During 1810 he interposed between the house and the mews behind it a miniature Egyptian-style propylaeum facing Welbeck Street. Its centre portal led to his painting room (about 30′ × 25′); the secondary doors were probably as bogus as the cyclopean masonry and the archaeology of the hieroglyphs. Surmounting the facade was a Zeus-like bust; lower down was a Greek neologism describing lifelong tribulations, **18**. Each alluded to the importance and experience of the denizen. Stroehling inveigled himself into English royal circles also, but his methods were dishonest and his career mercurial.[21] Patrons intrigued by his

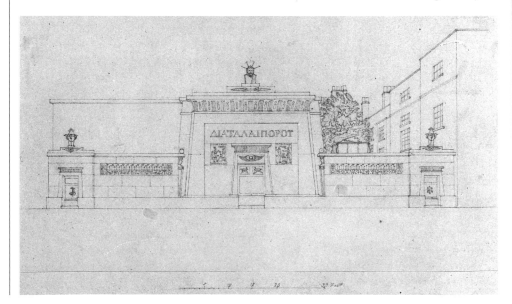

18 Peter Stroehling's Egyptian-style studio of 1810 on the corner of Henrietta Place and Welbeck Street, Marylebone, from the west.

exotic premises might enter wholeheartedly to obtain a passing pocket likeness, yet emerge financially disembowelled.

This three-dimensional conceit was a distinct novelty in Regency London. Its building marginally predates even the Egyptian Gallery in Piccadilly by P F Robinson. Scholars like Thomas Hope had been promoting primitive styles among the English intelligentsia at the time and several designers, including Robinson, could thus be suggested here. Nevertheless, Stroehling himself seems to have been an entirely capable pasticheur.[22] No one else had brought this potentially arresting class of building out into the open before; an artist's self-advertisement was suddenly given a new exterior sphere. A recherché label, exclusive until now to dilettanti, became public property too, and that foreign but easily-pronounced word 'studio' thenceforth took its place in the English language.

It would take another generation before London artists in general made so bold as to shrug off the Georgian architectural uniform and put on fancy dress like the upstart Stroehling. Doubtlessly landlords had a hand in suppressing proposals of this kind where they could, since public exposure of workshops would seem to have been constantly imminent, especially where sculptors were concerned. The relative ease for sculptors to find sizeable serviced space outside the regulated metropolitan area, plus a certain assertion of independence by painters not beholden to the convenience of West End sitters, strengthened the tentative local emigration movement. In 1806, for instance, one of the successful Sartoriuses, the sporting painter John F, struck off down the King's Road towards Chelsea. His brother C J, who painted marines, joined him a few years later next to the Queen's Elm, Chelsea. Among RAs there was (Sir) David Wilkie, the popular Scots genre painter who tried both Hampstead and Chelsea before taking up a handsome terraced house in Kensington High Street in 1811. And prime among sculptors was the example of (Sir) Francis Chantrey.

After marrying rather advantageously in about 1810, Chantrey chose to buy a largish house and grounds opposite Eccleston Bridge in lower 'Belgravia'. Greater Belgravia had barely been conceived at this date; there was thus little likelihood of the sculptor anticipating a new fund of patronage or finding his light industry subject to zoning laws. He was more interested in the fact that cumbersome lumps of marble could now be delivered to his very doorstep by the barges that docked in the creek alongside (later the Grosvenor Canal).

Chantrey's career took off smartly. For the rest of his life his annual profits seldom fell below £15 000. For busts he had no rivals except, perhaps, William Behnes, and for monuments only Sir Richard Westmacott could touch him. His tremendous productivity was made possible by improved pointing machines and an apprentice workforce comprising nearly every young British modeller of promise to emerge between 1815 and 1840. Very soon the Chantrey workshops covered some 12 000 square feet on two or more levels. They were grouped around a narrow courtyard which was entered from Eccleston Place. By the 1830s this doughnut plan incorporated galleries and a heavy-duty bronze foundry. Sir John Soane is known to have streamlined the approach to the main gallery; Soane's pupil, C J Richardson, claimed to have constructed a small showroom shortly before Sir Francis's death in 1841.[23] Many sculptors advanced by Chantrey settled near him, often with workshops of their own. His chief assistant, Henry Weekes RA, united his next door shops to those of his master after 1844 and maintained the house style with distinction for another 30 years.

In addition to heading west and south-west, pioneer emigrants started for the north and north-west. A parallel proliferation of sculptors and masons could be identified near the stone depots along the Regent's Canal in North London. What occurred in lower St John's Wood was significant, even though the Belgravia situation, strictly speaking, presented itself in reverse: John Charles Rossi RA was already a force in the region by the time the canal came to serve it in 1815. Carew and Sievier, to name but two, were among the Late Romantic sculptors who approached it shortly afterwards.

Rossi had suffered mixed fortunes in the terracotta business, but in about 1800 he took one or two of his sons into a new partnership and thereafter ran a moderately profitable live-in factory on the New Road, opposite Marylebone parish church. (For a man with 16 children from two marriages it was difficult to get ahead.) Then, in 1810, he secured a farmhouse on the corner of Lisson Grove and Rossmore Road which at last brought everyone relief from a harrowing torment of heat and dust. But their trials were not over. Having fallen on lean times again seven years later, Rossi was forced to take in the nearest deserving lodger – Benjamin Haydon, the world's most misunderstood history painter.[24] With the aid of £60 (borrowed) advanced by Haydon, Rossi offered him 'his gallery for a painting room, and to fit the rooms near it into a house large enough for a bachelor'.[25] Once the alterations were made Haydon rejoiced:

> The pure air of this part of the town, the escape from the continual rush of fashion, which never left me any rest in Marlborough Street [Soho], the quiet and peace of having a painting room and a parlour to live in with my books around me, was heavenly.[26]

Over the coming years these quarters were the scene of the 'immortal dinners' and drawn-out beery breakfasts attended by the greatest poets, painters and patrons of the day, **19**. This cannot have pleased Rossi père in the first place. In the second it became apparent that Haydon's henchmen were using these rowdy occasions to pour scorn on the Academy. Indeed, his address had become a centre of operations leading to the formation of the opposition Society of British Artists in 1823. Haydon was duly evicted and replaced by C R Leslie, another painter in the same orbit but, pointedly, also the Academy's latest darling.[27]

Despite the colonisation of these outposts by figures as prominent as Wilkie, Chantrey and Rossi, the academic mainstream still ran deep through those groves first blazed in the 1760s. Cases in point were the positions of Chantrey's chief artistic rivals, Westmacott and Behnes, and that of the Academy president. As indicated by the varied collection of graphic artists already noticed there, Mayfair remained a

19 Benjamin Haydon's studio and lodgings on the Rossmore Road corner of Lisson Grove, Marylebone, adapted for the painter by John Charles Rossi in 1817.

prime repository of elevated taste and sponsorship up to and well beyond 1800. In 1797 Westmacott (the future Sir Richard, RA) began to capitalise on contacts his father (Richard Snr) had made over the 15 years he had been operating a small statuary practice behind the family house at 25 Mount Street. With Henry Westmacott in partnership, by 1818 the practice flourished to the extent that it outgrew both 24 and 25 Mount Street and was transferred to 14 South Audley Street. These larger premises had similar back access, and space enough for a bronze-casting pit. It was probably the colossal Hyde Park *Achilles* modelled here that hindered any earlier construction at the rear of the house of 'a broad top-lit corridor leading to a single storey room . . . which perhaps functioned as studio and gallery'[28] from *c.* 1823 until the 1850s. The Dukes of Westminster must have made special allowances for Sir Richard to pursue his antisocial art at such a scale on their premier estate. But they called a halt to any further expansion there in 1829, with the result that Sir Richard's

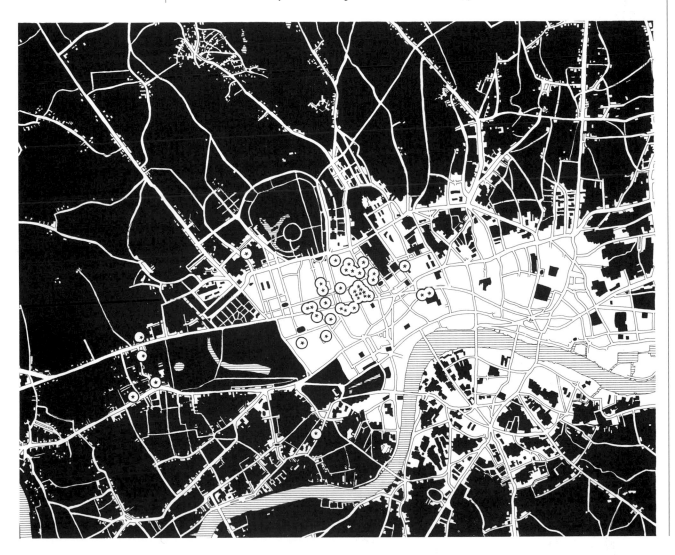

20 London in 1819, showing the distribution of current RAs. Although they are concentrated in North Soho, six have detached themselves from the inner West End. See **9** and **40**.

rising son, Richard III, was banished to 21 Wilton Place on the far border of second-ranking Belgravia.

When William Behnes turned 28 in 1823, in no way could he boast £16 000 worth of commissions as Sir Richard did at the same age. Yet, having made a promising start in his profession, he fully expected to be able to do so by 1824. As it turned out, he seriously compromised the remainder of his career by erecting 'a modelling room high enough to admit statues of heroic proportions' in and around inherently inflexible existing buildings at the top end of Dean Street, Soho.[29] Artists who suffered from megalomania usually paid for it in the end. Some, however, could afford it as well. Just before his death in 1820, Benjamin West invited John Nash to build him a memorial gallery of unstinted amplitude, **21**. This resulted in 'a Great Room . . . at an expense of nearly £4000, with Skylights constructed on a highly approved principle for diffusing light'.[30] West intended to enshrine dozens of unsold paintings here and let his children benefit from the admission fees. Although no one could say the gallery made a compelling afternoon out, they had to agree Nash had successfully rationalised the 14 Newman Street backyard.

Since the next three Academy presidents, Lawrence, Shee and Eastlake, lived in Russell, Cavendish and Fitzroy Squares respectively, the north-central section of the West End continued to be regarded as London's Latin quarter. But while an increasing number of shows were being put on behind the scenes that justified this view, the only new outward sign of an artist's presence was the heightened window. James Ward RA gave one demonstration of this. In 1828 Ward took over a house[31] a few doors south of Behnes at 83 Dean Street. His success with comfortably easel-borne landscapes and animal studies having led him to reckless emulation of West's exaggerated approach, he found himself raising the first floor ceiling to accommodate bigger canvases in the front room. Naturally the first floor windows rose in proportion. Whereas a normal ceiling height suited most other artists well enough, they did see the need for extra light, and a higher shaft of it, in similar lower storey rooms. From the 1820s onwards they began to achieve this effect cheaply by heightening a window but raking up only the portion of ceiling local to it.

When, for example, James Sant first determined to settle in Soho Square in 1844, he had to rest content with No. 19 where a direct northern outlook was denied him by the extended neighbouring house occupied by Henry Pickersgill RA. He was therefore obliged to 'cut up' an east-facing window at the rear, **22**. The tax on window glass, not finally repealed until 1845, formed no real deterrent to such a small increment and alterations ensued throughout the district under review. Quite possibly it was the sculptor E H Baily RA who introduced the expedient to Percy Street, North Soho, when he moved to No. 8 from Dean Street about 20 years earlier. To this day, No.s 1, 2 and 7 also possess central first floor windows of the same kind, **23**.[32]

While greatly outnumbered by Outsiders, RAs had been prominent in Fitzrovia since the very beginning. As time went on, the long stretch between Rathbone Place and Fitzroy Square would rank equally with Newman Street as their favourite province. Within 100 years of 1770 a total of 25 current and future members were to give

21 John LeKeux after George Cattermole, *Benjamin West's Picture Gallery*, 1821. The 'Great Room' (see **10**) designed by John Nash in 1820 to adjoin West's Newman Street house and rearward painting rooms.

22 James Sant, *Self-portrait, c.* 1845. Sant has had the window of his cramped back room in Soho Square 'cut up' in order to introduce a higher shaft of north-east light.

their addresses there, with the number mounting to a peak of 12 between 1830 and 1840. John Constable, for instance, replaced Farington at No. 35 (now 76) Charlotte Street in 1822, painting in the formal studio[33] or a backyard glasshouse that otherwise provided an all-weather playground for his children. To No. 54 (105), Edward

23 South side of Percy Street, St Pancras, from the west. Central first floor windows have been cut up at No.s 1, 2, 7 and 8.

Armitage followed Ramsay Reinagle who had himself taken over from Richard Westall. At best the painters' houses had built-on rooms or converted coach-houses; most men satisfied themselves with cut-up windows in former parlours.

Seen in one light the artists' preference for Fitzrovia invited a measure of ridicule; it had become a tribal reservation. Yet most tenderfoots would acknowledge that a spell in Charlotte or one of the adjoining streets was an unavoidable thorn on the path to prosperity. Everything, after all, was readily available there: cheap rooms easily altered, comradeship, expert advice, models, drawing schools, colourmen and frame-makers. No upper floor in those parts could be proof against requisition – except in Fitzroy Square. Somehow the south and east sides of the square kept the hordes at bay until all four terraces finally enclosed it in 1835. Over the next 50 years, however, more than a dozen newly-elected or potential RAs, together with worthy Outsiders like Ford Madox Brown, also made their marks there, especially in the older Adam ranges. Extra-tall windows lighting the converted coach-house of No. 2 can be ascribed to the successive residencies of William Dyce, James Sant and (Sir) Frank Dicksee.[34]

Wherever there were painters, engravers were never far distant. Fitzrovia had its share, starting with Woollett (who is said to have brought the cannon which he fired to salute the triumphant completion of larger plates). William Sharp and Charles Turner, to name but two, cashed in on the illustrators' Regency heyday, and William Strang prolonged the association well into Victorian times. Not too many monumental sculptors, on the other hand, could find suitable yards around Charlotte Street; instead they resorted to Somers Town or to the Southampton Estate near Marylebone (Regent's) Park. These positions promised close contact with the New (Euston) Road for ease of access; later the Cumberland Basin of the Grand Union Canal made them more sought-after still. Frederick Breamer and Charles Peart were among the first, in about 1790, to set up shop between Hampstead Road and Albany Street. Very soon afterwards, due to the rash of cheapskate masons in artificial stone which broke out alongside, their New Road frontage became known as 'Quickset Row'.

The progress of one of the more scrupulous 'New Road statuaries', J C Rossi, has already been charted. In 1826 the young Edwin Landseer bounced away from the Fitzrovia launching-pad and landed just beyond him in St John's Wood Road. This road was not entirely unheard of at that date. Thomas Heaphy, the first president of the SBA, had moved to No. 7 five years earlier, and J F Lewis, who had studied animal anatomy with Landseer, was on the point of renting No. 21. But whereas the Heaphy and Lewis houses were new stucco villas on suburban plots, Landseer's vintage farmhouse came with a paddock of several acres reaching down to the canal. Having the original farm barn in which to study his more refractory bullocks and bulldogs and, after 1830, the zoo in Regent's Park for everything else except portrait sitters, he saw no need to modernise for nearly 20 years. Both his older brothers stayed in town with their father until, in due course, they also found nearby houses in St John's Wood.

Were it not for the closeness of the family and a dependence on Edwin's sure-fire engraving subjects, the eldest brother, Tom, may have headed up the Hampstead Road instead. The curious general tendency for engravers to leave the West End for Camden and Kentish Towns did not gain momentum till the mid-century. Before that time there were noticeably few 'outworkers'. One of the most important, however, was S W Reynolds, best remembered for his mezzotint translations of Sir Joshua's works. In 1822 he left Poland Street for Ivy Cottage, Queensway, to which he attached an 'engraving room' for his various assistants, presses and associated trappings.[35] Not only did the extra work generated by the introduction of steel engraving plates persuade Reynolds to obtain a bigger, brighter workroom and employ more staff, but he was also able to give himself a pleasanter walk to the parkside palaces in his other capacity as a royal drawing master.

To painters and sculptors alike, both the semi-rural separation and the courtly overtones of an address near Kensington Palace, especially after the accession of the willing patroness Princess Victoria, presented a tempting combination as never before. Of course the semi-rural condition disappeared rapidly, with individual villas on one-acre grounds giving way to terraced houses with barely a flagstone each. In between lay the ultimate picturesque compromise of the semi-detached villa with, perhaps, a quarter of an acre. Early in 1828 these alternatives were being considered by two former John Varley pupils, William Mulready RA and John Linnell. Mulready, Wilkie's Irish counterpart, bought a brand new south-facing half-house in romantic-ally named Linden Grove (Gardens), off Notting Hill Gate. While he built a modest loggia onto the rear and laid out his own garden, there were indications he would have liked a studio annexe similar to the one joined by the landscapist Thomas Creswick to another of the Linden Grove houses soon after 1838.[36]

The portrait painter John Linnell crossed to Bayswater looking as much for clean air as the royal approval that Mulready eventually secured. Taking complete charge, he installed his young family in a semi-detached house near the park. But immediately he wanted a larger, more substantial detached one, and only he was capable of designing it. Under personal surveillance embarrassingly 'vitiated by amateurism', he therefore erected the lower storeys of both 38 and 36 Porchester Terrace between 1829 and 1837.[37] In 1837 the two distinct fronts illustrated the succession from an indiscriminately disciplined, Georgian architectural tradition to a more functionally responsible, Victorian one, **24**.

Mindful of the locality and his role as an upright paterfamilias, Linnell had initially created a four-square villa in tightly-laced Regency clothing on the one plot. By 1835, however, this was again pronounced too small; there were nine children, mostly teenagers, and some were wanting to set up easels beside their father's. Although Linnell had provided tall windows (quite as if they were 'cut up') at No. 38, they were neither wide nor plentiful, thanks to his miserly reaction to the prevailing glass and window taxes.[38] Another move or an extension appropriate to the circumstances was called for. He chose to extend. Seeing, with a speculative prescience, that the neighbouring site was still vacant, Linnell bought it to put up, as a first priority, a painters' 'workshop' – he disdained the term 'studio'. At 50′ × 20′ with an 8′ square eastern side light, three skylights and a generous hallway, it expressed a hitherto stifled desire for a businesslike organisation and a choice of lighting at all costs. As a

24   36–38 Porchester Terrace, Bayswater. John Linnell built No. 38 in 1829, its studio annexe in 1837. See also **144**.

result of this advanced sideways step – externalising internal exigencies at the expense of polite, conventional form – standards rose and commissions multiplied. Of course Linnell continued to meddle left and right. But by 1851 his interest in landscapes had completely overtaken his interest in portraiture, and he moved away to a property in Surrey.

The painter Richard Redgrave did not go so far as to renounce London in mid-career like Linnell, but he did begin to rusticate at weekends at much the same date. It was a small luxury he could afford after working his passage from Fitzrovia to Kensington Square on the strength of costume pieces and an emergent specialisation in soft-core social realism. Once Redgrave had thus penetrated the west London courtier class, he and his brother Samuel wished to go further, to buy land nearby and build their own houses. In this venture they were joined by Richard's new friend and competitor for Academy associateship, Charles West Cope. Cope was earning a good living from historical and religious works, while acclaim for his Westminster Hall panels would follow shortly. Redgrave measured up due to part-time activity as a teacher, industrial designer, writer and administrator. There was now an opportunity to prove himself as an architect as well.

It seems that Redgrave fully designed his half of the semi-detached pair that was built at 27–28 Hyde Park Gate, South Kensington, in 1841, whereas he obtained just 'outline planning permission' for Cope's half. (Samuel Redgrave leased two adjoining plots and developed them separately.)[39] The amateur architect invented raw brick double fronts bracketed by outlandish chalet gables and emboldened by severe, boxed porches; but the hierarchy of Georgian windows betrayed an essentially standard internal arrangement. If the intention here was to hazard a jokey 'New Brutalism', then Linnell's guarded brand of Classic geometry – his chic pilasters and his decorative tickles – deserved its more adhesive appeal. On the inside, further-more, Redgrave's grasp of elementary planning loosened somewhat towards the rear; Cope started with the same ideas and likewise foundered at the stairs and back elevation, **25**.

Notwithstanding, the two men were making the first attempt to integrate a painter's studio into a modest family house. In order to gain unimpeded side and top light they projected 1½-storey rooms beyond the main body of the building into the garden. Cope gave himself a larger space[40] in anticipation of orders for mural cartoons and altar-pieces, while it followed that the high ceilings and 'galleries' would also allow for winding easels and elevated vantage points.

Why did they go to this trouble when Linnell and many others before him had shown that a normal house with an annexe was a tolerably workable arrangement? In addition, having already done so, Linnell had decided on behalf of all artists that it was thenceforth acceptable to place one's big stock-in-trade window directly onto the street in a respectable residential neighbourhood – and the Redgrave–Cope site also faced the east. The two Academicians-to-be were more cold-blooded and sophisticated, however. They wanted a true north light; it was not a matter of shyness. Moreover, being less well-off, neither was able to buy two plots like Linnell, and certainly the pairing of their houses was effected for its theoretical economy.

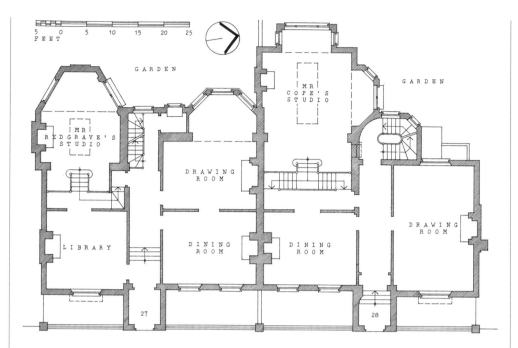

25 Ground floor plan of 27–28 Hyde Park Gate, South Kensington. Semi-detached houses incorporating studios designed by Richard Redgrave for himself and Charles Cope in 1841.

With regard to the integration, perhaps there was a Utopian streak in Redgrave which caused him, consciously or not, to promote the notion of a model house for the professional suburban artist. Thus planted or otherwise self-sown, it was a seed that did eventually germinate in the propitious Kensington mulch. For the moment the geography was right, the season and climate not quite.

Taking an overview at the start of Queen Victoria's reign, it could be said that London's typical, recognised artist, carried along by a faith in decentralisation, had progressed to a middle ground and blended into a middle society. First he had excused himself from kowtowing in Mayfair and Marylebone; then he had delivered himself from Soho, Fitzrovia and the central West End altogether; next, in preference to the teeming town terrace he had discovered the farm cottage, the modern middle values of the semi-detached villa, and even the exclusive independent villa. Now there appeared an experimental semi-detachment of workplace and domicile within the house itself. Although this was all no more than cottage industry brought up to date, it would soon be taken to extraordinary extremes.

3
BOURGEOIS EMPIRE-BUILDING

IF THE model houses put forward by Redgrave and Cope did not exactly galvanise the early Victorian art world, they did draw attention to the pleasantness of the sheltered cul-de-sac in which they were sited. A little closer to Old Kensington is another of these leafy backwaters: Victoria Road. With The Gore at its head and Christ Church at its bottom, Victoria Road forms the residential spine of Kensington New Town, a development which gathered pace during the early 1840s. By 1850 the orderly collection of short terraces, semi-detached houses and single villas was almost fully tenanted. Similar mixtures of two-, three-, and four-storey houses of brick and stucco were going up in the side streets.

The original lessee in 1843 of the southern corner house on Douro Place and Victoria Road was the sculptor John Bell, a contemporary of Cope at Sass's art school. Workshops that Bell set up against the back fence and gradually extended were ultimately coupled to an edifice known as Villa Vigna. Although Bell was capable of dynamic and noble works such as *The Eagle Slayer* (1837) and the Albert Memorial *America* (1864), he also designed decorative items in the most execrable period taste and, indeed, Villa Vigna attracted criticism for its intrusive originality. Within a short time two more sculptors arrived in the same neighbourhood. James Legrew, a learned and quite sought-after Chantrey-ite, took up at 1 St Alban's Grove – directly south of Bell's sheds – in 1845, and in 1851 Alfred Stevens moved into 7 Canning Place. The latter, the man with the 'unnatural and unnational skill in the arts', initially used the tiny terraced house as a pied-à-terre while teaching in Sheffield; after 1856 his superlative *Wellington Monument* began its difficult life here as a small competition model in the back room, or 'study'.[1]

After Legrew committed suicide and Stevens departed, Bell was the only active sculptor of any reputation to stand fast thereabouts.[2] But in subsequent years the New Town became thoroughly infested with painters and engravers who left it the richer by a good dozen studios. The list of these artists is an impressive one. Early comers included the RAs Herbert, Uwins, E M Ward, Ansdell, Cooke, Elmore and Barlow, while Samuel Palmer, A H Corbould and Frederick Stacpoole stood out among the Outsiders. Thomas Uwins, for example, lived from 1845 till 1856 at

Auburn Lodge on the south-west corner of St Alban's Grove and Victoria Road. His successor there was the distinguished engraver T O Barlow, and it is to him that the mullioned picture window and much later rear additions may be attributed. Of the pioneer builders, however, the 'Liverpool Landseer', Richard Ansdell, was surely the doyen.

From the moment he had shadowed Uwins to the semi-detached house opposite Auburn Lodge at 7 (now 39) Victoria Road, Ansdell's route to fame and financial security seemed to be shrewdly mapped. To the exposed north side of No. 7, he forthwith added a wing which was later extended rearwards and fitted with skylights. He next bought the adjoining No. 8 and a vacant plot alongside Legrew's house in St Alban's Grove. On the latter – which was really a small agistment paddock for the painter's models – a sizeable studio went up. The final stage of the master plan was approached in 1861, Ansdell's ARA election year, with the building of a mini-mansion (Lytham House) to join the studio, and the leasing of No.s 7 and 8 Victoria Road to the painters Henry O'Neil and Frederick Bridell.[3]

In the meantime another passable sporting and portrait painter, Alfred Hitchens Corbould, had commissioned the Tudoresque Eldon Lodge on the north corner of Eldon Road and, four doors up, the marine painter Edward Cooke had settled into 'The Ferns' (No. 33, now 44). Whereas The Ferns is of the typical stucco-coated semi-detached variety, Eldon Lodge, as first built in 1850–3, stood alone in an heterodox red-brick nakedness. Compromised here hardly at all by compo trim, the red brickwork of Corbould's tall cottage would, within another 15 years, become a distinguished feature of the modern bespoke artist's house. Corbould's other origi-nal touch was to stretch a 30′ × 15′ annexe across the rear of the house. This was probably a flimsy more-glass-than-wall affair, but at its north end it made contact with the hall and at its south with a sizeable stable building. It was therefore possible for the artist either to open a door onto animal subjects in their stalls, or to tether them just outside the window, or even to lead them into the informal end of the room. Notwithstanding these advantages, Alfred Corbould was unable to convince the public that his flair for architectural design extended much to painting, and by 1867 he had surrendered his interest in Eldon Lodge altogether.

Edward Cooke, or Edward 'van Kook' (Dutch-style sea pieces which he signed in this way would appear doubly authentic), on the other hand, possessed the talent to rise to Academy associateship during his time at the far less propitious No. 33 up the road. In 1855, however, within six years of taking that house, he had predictably bought another half as big again in Hyde Park Gate while dreaming of something grander still in the depths of Kent. Over the same period the pastoral jeweller, the painter-etcher Samuel Palmer, dreamt of his return to a beatific microcosm not far distant. Following three years in one half of a jerry-built Victoria Road crib, Palmer moved to 6 Douro Place, 'a hideous little semi-detached house with a prim little garden at the back and front',[4] in 1851. Yet, like his father-in-law John Linnell in Bayswater, he would not complain of the sunny light at his co-opted parlour window or the view, mercifully oblique, of the Bell establishment opposite.

It only needed an Irishman to complete the picture in the 1850s. Alfred Elmore, newly elected an RA, duly secured Legrew's vacated house in 1857. The historical genre painter quickly improved the fabric but, somewhat cowed by his neighbour's tactics, did not counter with a conjoined studio of his own until Ansdell had quite finished. In actual fact, there was a good deal of professional cooperation between the New Town artists: Elmore obtained a chimneypiece from Alfred Stevens; Barlow and Stacpoole (in Eldon Road) engraved Ansdell's paintings; Ansdell often painted the animals in his friends' landscapes; and so on. One origin of this spirit of reciprocity was The Etching Club, founded c. 1837 by fellow students of Cope and Redgrave and reunited in Kensington. Not just a weekly excuse to swill whisky and seltzer, it was also a commercial enterprise. Meeting at each other's house in turn, members etched or engraved illustrations to classic texts which they combined for sale in portfolios. Verse by Goldsmith and Shakespeare had already appeared when Gray's *Elegy* was issued in 1847. Cope, Redgrave and Bell were the only local members to contribute in that year, although Ansdell and Palmer were to figure later.[5] Half the other contributions came from more senior members – Creswick, Webster, Tayler and Horsley – who had been based since the early 1830s in the Old Kensington lorded over by Wilkie and Callcott. Their patch was clearly close enough to the New Town to provoke more frequent informal meetings and increase the number of professional exchanges.

Any qualified artist wishing to join this exclusive club stood a better chance if he lived nearby. James Clarke Hook, for one, was elected soon after he came to Campden Hill. Though just behind the parish church, for some decades Campden Hill was only sparingly studded with biggish lodges occupied by the likes of Lord Macaulay and the Duke of Rutland. But subdivision of the steeper land suddenly quickened at the mid-century; terraces and semi-detached houses were rushed up and not a few artists were among the takers. Hook moved into what he named Tor Villa before the paint had dried in 1851.[6]

Benefiting from both his father's will and his elevation to ARA, Hook transformed some recently made sketches of Tuscan architecture into two semi-detached houses with the aspect of one villa. His own corner house (he let the other) measured about 25' wide by 35' deep, including a porch and stairhall that rose into 'a sort of campanile'.[7] Not counting the stairhall, the entire rectangle on the first floor could be thrown into a single space by unfolding central doors. A generous window admitted north light from the rear; a shallow bow at the front and a canted bay at the side provided other options. While Hook lived at Tor Villa, his forte still lay in historical subjects for which the cold constancy of north light was an asset. But he was also trying out vigorously brushed country and coastal scenes, strengthening his colours under full-blown afternoon and evening skies; hence the southern bow and the western bay. Hook forfeited the direct contact with the garden which Redgrave and Cope enjoyed – and Corbould was about to – but gained an inviolable workspace wholly, neatly and economically within the one set of walls. Tor Villa could almost be called a 'studio-house', so nearly did the one take priority over the other.

As he had already done in Brompton, Hook was soon complaining of importunate society callers and bad city air. So, shortly after his second son's birth in 1856, the family left for the country. No. 1 Tor Villa was promptly let, unfurnished, to another Etching Club member, William Holman Hunt, along with his acolytes Michael Halliday and Robert Martineau. Hunt and Ford Madox Brown each designed furniture to add to some donated pieces, but the painting room remained bare, **26**. At least for a while there was a clear position before each window – all the usual clutter and stuffing went into the paintings instead. Hunt's *Finding the Saviour in the Temple* and Martineau's *Last Day in the Old Home* were both completed here.

The threesome at Tor Villa would have been regarded a little suspiciously by a miscellany of old-stagers and reformed rebels which had also decanted itself on Campden Hill in the wake of Hook. It had only taken a matter of months for this second wave to break. The venerable Academicians J J and A E Chalon came to end their days at 'El Buen Retiro' on Campden House Road where they would overlook Little Campden House, part of which Augustus Egg ARA had found available. Egg had lately fallen in behind the Scots genre painter John Phillip and the sculptor William Theed, each of whom acquired one of the four semi-detached South Villas just below Tor Villa on Campden Hill Road. Another of the second wave arrivals was John Horsley, who briefly rented 2 Tor Villa after 1855.[8] But, however ill-assorted these fellows first appeared, they were all connected one way or another. Until 1851 the Chalon brothers were the mainstays of The Sketching Society, a winter drawing circle undoubtedly the inspiration of The Etching Club. Horsley, though still an etcher, was

26 John Ballantyne, *William Holman Hunt, c.* 1862. Dressed for the part, Hunt is painting *Finding the Saviour* at 1 Tor Villa, Campden Hill, built by James Hook in 1851.

shifting his allegiance to a summer camp based in Kent known as The Cranbrook Colony, of which Webster was the leading light. And Egg and Phillip were once members of The Clique, an anti-RA ginger group not unrelated to Holman Hunt's Pre-Raphaelite Brotherhood. Those early suspicions soon dissolved and Hook was proud to remember 'a small coterie of artists, all living in much the same quiet comfortable way, and enjoying the mutual hospitality that was so free from constraint'.[9]

While on the subject of The Clique, it is worth noticing that, of the three other members, W P Frith had simultaneously landed close by in Notting Hill and Henry

27 William Frith, *Self-portrait with model*, 1867. Frith shows himself at work in the generously proportioned parlour of 10 Pembridge Villas, Notting Hill.

O'Neil was heading for Victoria Road. A reunion on common ground looked to be quite premeditated; someone of Frith's stature might otherwise have gone anywhere. As it was he contented himself with a ready-made front parlour studio at 10 Pembridge Villas, **27**. But the parlour was bigger all round and better lit than most, suiting an expanded vision – first expressed in *Ramsgate Sands* of 1853 – which called for larger canvases. The great success of this seaside fiesta accelerated Frith's promotion to RA and urged him to plan similar panoramas of modern life. Yet, were he set up in a room the size of Hook's, the painting which followed, *Derby Day*, might well have exceeded the comparatively modest 7'6" × 3'6".

Frith coped wonderfully just the same; he was a fine judge of the market[10] and deserved his rewards. Equally organised and deserving but far less commercial, an artist washed up by a freak Post-Raphaelite tide, was George Frederick Watts. Albeit by accident, Watts had reached Kensington, like his coeval castaway Alfred Stevens, in 1851. Having gently leant on his patron Lord Holland to install his friends, the Thoby Prinseps, in the family dower house (Little Holland House), Watts succumbed to a periodic frailty and, at the new tenants' insistence, joined them there to convalesce. In Mrs Prinsep's famous phrase, 'He came for three days; he stayed thirty years'.

To all intents and purposes, Watts's High Art, like poor Haydon's, never sold.[11] But he could always raise cash by painting society portraits, and until 1852 retained a room in Mayfair for exactly that purpose. Thereafter he was lodged upstairs in the rambling dower house; 'a gap between two walls was filled up' to make a working studio, 'though in the heat of summer he found it too sunny and for this reason he built another later on the north-west side'.[12] 'Signor' or 'The Divine Watts' became the resident prodigy of Little Holland House, the prime though reluctant showpiece of Mrs Prinsep's regular talent-spotting salon.

The talk of the earliest of those gatherings cannot have been other than what Mr Prinsep, a retired East India Company man, passed in his escape from Kensington to the Oriental Club – the Great Exhibition in the Crystal Palace. Everyone could take some pride in this celebration of Britain's entry into the railway age, its pre-eminence as a trading and colonial power. Notwithstanding the numerous extraordinary feats of mid-century engineering and craftsmanship displayed within, the crowning wonder of the piece was really the Palace itself. Its unstoppable progression from blotting pad doodle to full-scale triumph revealed the supremacy in technology and methodology of one nation before all others. Its swift and sure assembly in 1851 was one demonstration, its reassembly at Sydenham a few years later was a telling proof.

Manufacturers of prefabricated buildings, especially iron and glass systems, could have received no better advertisement for their wares. Indeed, major foundries subsequently did such a roaring trade supplying portable churches, theatres, shopping arcades and the like to the colonies that in 1854 'an artist of distinction' suggested they ought to make pavilions for intersuburban painters and sculptors. Accordingly, Bellhouse & Co. of Manchester presented a range of 'Iron Removable Studios for Artists', resembling pseudo-Classical Nissen huts, **28**. Erected in London, a small one 14' square, 'inclusive of stove, papering, painting etc.', would cost £60.10.0.[13] Perhaps thankfully, the idea sold very slowly. Watts, for instance, ordered

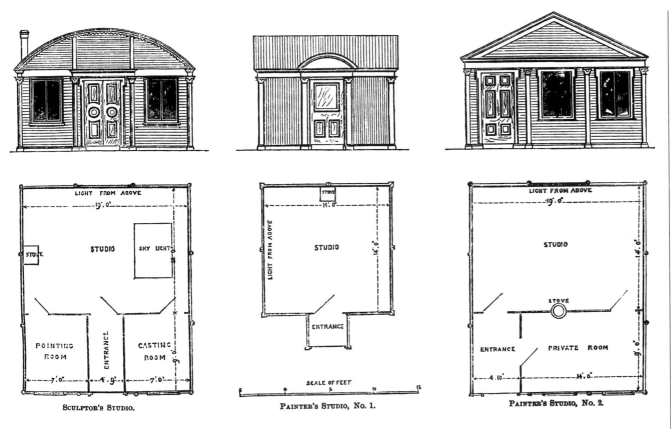

SCULPTOR'S STUDIO.   PAINTER'S STUDIO, No. 1.   PAINTER'S STUDIO, No. 2.

28 A range of off-the-peg 'Iron Removable Studios for Artists' manufactured by Bellhouse & Co. of Manchester from 1855 onwards.

one to his own specifications in 1874. His so-called 'Tin Pot' was a semi-detached model about 40′ long, its other half charitably intended for the use of Edward Burne-Jones.[14]

Watts's alteration of the standard article to suit himself was the typical reaction of a sensitive artistic individual. White-collar city-dwellers, on the other hand, generally embraced the machine aesthetic and welcomed mass production unquestioningly. This middle layer of mid-century society had begun to enrich itself quite noticeably in the supply of consumer goods and commercial services generated by the revolutionary inventions of the recent past. Company and corporation investment was transforming the face of British towns. Everywhere were new banks and chambers, town halls and churches, markets, institutions, hotels, shops – and houses. In London, a handful of super-rich land barons, mining magnates and railway chiefs raised massive piles like those in Kensington Palace Gardens or at the corners of Belgrave Square. But the bourgeois majority satisfied its self-esteem with superior variants of the mass-produced dwelling, terraced or semi-detached. In the 25 years either side of 1850, these were the sterile and stolid stuccoed blocks of Cubittopolis and the sugar-frosted stock designs that enveloped the inner West End. Partly due to the uniformity of entire neighbourhoods, domestic expressions of status and comfort tended to be heaped up on the inside. Rearguard action to turn the outside to effect only became evident at the onset of the 1860s. By this time Pugin and Ruskin had encouraged the revival of some more lively architectural formulae to aid the interpretation of an individual personality.

It was here, pandering to a Victorian obsession with materialistic display, that so much money was to be made by architects, builders and decorators in particular. The call for architectural, monumental and ideal sculpture almost matched that for portraits, landscapes and narrative paintings. Producing an abundant variety of relatively small-scale pictures to cater for mid-depth pockets and medium-sized dwellings, easel painters captivated an impressionable age. Large-scale decorative jobs were harder to come by, but the Westminster Hall competitions of 1843–7, which gave Cope, Armitage and Maclise years' worth of work, were the forerunners of a constant trickle of civic and ecclesiastic patronage. At the opposite end of the range lay the field of book and magazine illustration. Cheap hearthside weeklies like *Punch* (founded 1841) and the *Illustrated London News* (1842) rapidly achieved mass circulations at the expense of occasional highbrow folios sold by subscription. Opportunities for illustrators, cartoonists, artist-reporters and engravers increased in line with the splurge in every department of the publishing business. One could earn a living, if not a knighthood (*viz.*, Sir John Gilbert RA, Sir John Tenniel), from black and white work but really substantial wealth was more likely to come from selling reproductions of oil paintings.

After its setback at the turn of the century, the print trade was again in full swing. In 1854 the first dealer since John Boydell was elected Lord Mayor of London. Francis Moon, along with Ernst Gambart, Victor Flatow and Thomas Agnew, was one of the more flamboyant trader-publishers who both bought and commissioned potential reproduction bonanzas and charged a sum to view them in private galleries. As early as 1846 Moon was paying Landseer £1500 for a single canvas and an equivalent amount for the copyright. Handsome royalties, however, were still forthcoming after the same painter's *A Stag at Bay* (also 1846) had been re-engraved for a third copyright-holder 20 years later.[15] Too often, though, it was the artist who underestimated the value of a sensational subject. Gambart paid Holman Hunt 5500gns for *Finding the Saviour* in 1860, is said to have collected £4000 at the exhibition turnstiles, made £5000 profit from print sales, and then resold the painting for £1500.[16] Prices and returns at double these figures were recorded later in the century. Not every artist could turn out blockbusters, but the incentive was obviously enormous. Sadly the lust for gain caused painters as highly skilled as Millais to set about *Twa Bairns* (1884), *Bubbles* (1886) and similar nursery dribble. On the other hand the engraver, long since unfairly treated, could justifiably hoist his fee. George Doo received £185 for translating Mulready's *The Convalescent* in 1842; in 1873 Samuel Cousins RA was able to charge Agnew £600 to engrave Millais' *Yes or No?*.[17]

Representation by dealers was not the sole means by which artists started to get ahead in the world. Tighter copyright regulations and more specific guarantees under the provisions of the Printsellers' Association were two further contributing factors. Another was the effect of the art unions – the immensely popular lotteries which offered a wide range of prizes in the form of works of art. The value of the

29 1–5 (formerly 1–6) Cromwell Place, South Kensington, built by Charles Freake in 1858–9. The unit second from left was originally a gentleman's studio-house similar to the present No. 5.

works – between £10 and £400 – and the frequent open competitions for their preselection gave the small-time Outsider a better chance of making a sale and a name. A fourth factor, and not the least, was the huge advantage brought about by technical advances and labour-saving devices. Without copying machines, electroplating, electrotyping, photography, chromolithography and much else, far smaller profits and production volumes – and far slighter achievements – would have been realised right across the board. Yet more circumstances operating in Victorian artists' favour were the pro-arts standpoints of Disraeli and Gladstone, in their capacities as chancellor and then prime minister for the Tories and the Liberals respectively. Of course the political climate had been primed from the outset by the exemplary art-lovers, Queen Victoria and Prince Albert. The royal family's genuine friendliness towards very many artists, both great and small, made it specklessly clear that, more than ever, to adopt a career in the fine arts had become thoroughly acceptable, even among the well-born.

Prince Albert's unprecedented example extended to the National Art Education Project, a programme launched after 1851 in a bid to breed better designers for industry. In London the Project's headquarters lay within a tract of South Kensington bought with the profits of the Great Exhibition and dedicated to the creation of a new cultural centre for capital and country. By the date of the Prince's death, 1861, only the 'Brompton Boilers' (an Iron Removable Museum) existed and the nuclei of the permanent museums and art school barely begun. But his initiative was pursued throughout the century and beyond until 'Albertopolis' was a majestic reality.

One of the kinder-hearted benefactors to support Albertopolis was the speculative builder (Sir) Charles Freake. It will have struck this astute Cubitt disciple that he could help to make South Kensington, with its nascent counterparts to the British Museum and University College, into another Bloomsbury. As a result he had lately been building Italianate terraces for one- and two-carriage households along Prince's Gate, Exhibition Road, and between Fulham and Old Brompton Roads, notably Onslow Square. Now, further acknowledging the prosperity and professional ascendancy of an artist class, the patronage of which he was proud to share with Prince Albert,[18] Freake included two houses expressly for painters in his development of Cromwell Place. No.s 5 and 6 of the six-unit east side terrace were built during 1858–9, **29**.[19] Each house rose on a square plan with a typical sub-basement, an upper ground floor of three rooms plus stairhall, and an undivided first floor under a mansard roof. Much larger overall than its neighbour, the first floor studio of No. 6 measures about 34′ square with a deeply-coved ceiling springing from an elaborate cornice 17′ above the parquet floor. A formidable guillotine-style, or double-hung, window 14′ high occupies the centre of the east wall. The opulent hall prepares the visitor for the splendour above, but it is disconcerting to see the promising first flight of stairs shrink into a steep curve and halt just before the studio door; a sudden outward swing and paraplegia beckons.

With the entire top floor given over to the studio – even the stairs had been pushed clear of the main envelope – Hook's arrangement at Tor Villa had been properly rationalised. But Freake is unlikely to have referred to it. Instead he adapted a cross-section that had already become a standard feature of Parisian painters' houses. Freake may have been inspired at first hand, or perhaps he saw the sophisticated example illustrated in the 1858 issue of *La Revue Générale*, **30**, **31**.[20] This marvellously-disciplined building of 1856–8, designed to face a canyon-like city street, lifted the painter's north light to the skyline and established a traffic-free space well away from sources of noise. Many British designers caught up with these and the other ideas revealed chez Jollivet in the years to come.

Freake's investment paid dividends. No. 6 was snapped up by Sir Coutts Lindsay of Balcarres, landowner, man-about-town and dilettante artist. With Charles Hallé, Comyns Carr and Blanche Fitzroy, his Rothschild bride of 1864, he is best remembered for founding the Grosvenor Gallery in New Bond Street. No. 5 went, very briefly, to the third Earl Somers, Lord Eastnor of Belvoir, another landed proprietor and fine weather watercolourist. Lord Eastnor reputedly fell in love with Watts's portrait of his future wife, a sister of Julia Margaret Cameron. He had already taken up photography himself. As with the other houses in the terrace there were rapid changes of tenancy. Lord Eastnor abandoned No. 5 and Lord Thynne, who had taken No. 4, backed off into the wings. Coutts and Lady Lindsay then amalgamated No.s 4, 5 and 6, in the process eliminating the studio at No. 5.[21] In the meantime Freake had built up the west side of Cromwell Place, the first lease of the (then) northernmost end-of-terrace house going to J E Millais ARA in mid-1861. A lean period that drove the former young Turk to illustrate books ended abruptly when Gambart stepped in with 1000gns for *The Black Brunswicker* (1860). It was time to reharness the adulation, to bring his divorcee wife squarely, bodily into their aristocratic dining circle, to get a house at least the equal of Hunt's .... Perhaps tipped off by Sir Coutts, Millais therefore reserved No. 7 and engaged Freake[22] to build a modest studio over his mews behind. Several more big sales paved the way to full RA honours; *My First* and *My Second Sermon* (1863–4) turned out to represent the initial irreligious downpayments on a baronetcy.

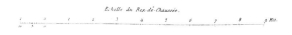

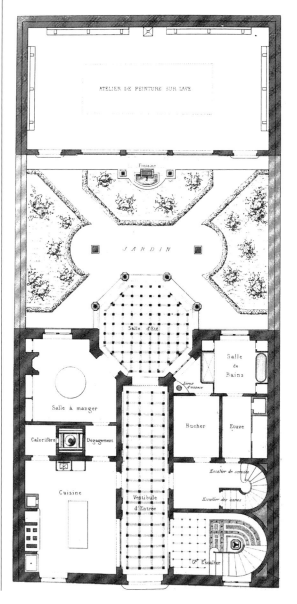

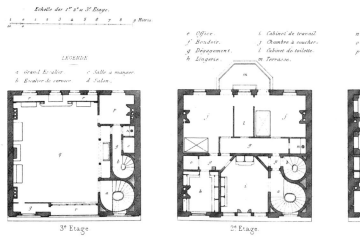

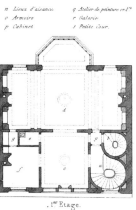

30 Plans of Pierre-Jules Jollivet's premises at 11 Cité Malesherbes, Paris 9, designed by Anatole Jal in 1856. Parisians had already developed an efficient form of studio-house.

31 Cross-section of **30**. M. Jollivet possessed a garden pavilion for enamel painting on lava as well as a galleried house studio for 'la peinture ordinaire'.

To counter a more testing lack of popularity, Millais' Pre-Raphaelite Brother, Thomas Woolner, had likewise reckoned that a transfer to the heartland of the art consumer was called for. In his opinion, this still lay in the central West End. After six years' searching, his agents found a lease of 29 Welbeck Street on the market for £1200. No. 29 is a solid Georgian house on a deep plot running through to Marylebone Mews. Following Georgian precedent, Woolner planned to exploit the rear access and replace the stables with studios. 'I think it will be a most beautiful place,' he wrote to Emily Tennyson in October 1861, 'with five rooms for workshops besides a large kitchen below . . . [for storage], and this advantage is equal to another shop.'[23]

COUPE LONGITUDINALE SUR L'AXE DU VESTIBULE D'ENTRÉE

32 Thomas Woolner's sculpture workshops behind 29 Welbeck Street, Marylebone, designed by (Col. Sir) Robert Edis in 1861.

By New Year's Eve, Woolner was installed and the waggish James O'Shea was treating him to floral corbels under the roof trusses.[24] O'Shea and his brother had recently executed decorative carving at the University Museum, Oxford, designed by Woolner's friend Benjamin Woodward. Had the architect not suddenly died, Woolner would surely have brought this team together again here. Instead he entrusted the brief to a 22-year-old novice named Robert Edis. The fractured prisms that he constructed of plum brickwork dressed in red, grey slates and scads of bluish glass admirably reflect the Ruskinian Gothic of both Woodward's crystalline Museum and

Butterfield's tightly packed All Saints', Margaret Street, **32**. Edis shoehorned the five rooms into a rectangle less than 45′ deep and 30′ wide. At ground level a delivery and despatch bay, (1), occupies half the mews frontage; the other half, profusely lit through cascades of glazing, served as Woolner's own modelling studio, (2). This engages a larger skylit space for carving and casting, (3), that crosses the plot behind. Below (3) is an equal-sized pointing shop, (4), receiving high side light from the sunken kitchen courtyard. Storerooms under (2) contained a cistern and small furnace while above (1), on the first floor, sits the drawing office, (5), also skylit.

Thus visibly organised behind and respectably housed in front, Woolner soon overcame the slur he had suffered in cheerless Somers Town. Helped further by the scandalous favouritism of a critic who was his own lodger and a 13-figure order for the Manchester Assize Courts, within twelve busy years he was employing eight assistants in London and farming an 80-acre estate in Sussex. By settling in Welbeck Street Woolner had evaded the stigma of the New Road. He had similarly stopped short of Lower Belgravia where sculptors were also exceedingly common. Weekes RA and Calder Marshall RA held sway down there in the 1850s and '60s, although Woolner's only real stylistic rival was his contemporary, Alec Munro. Munro had inherited the seasoned workshop at 6 Upper Belgrave Place[25] when Marshall chose to begin afresh around the corner in 1851. However, as Pimlico was steadily absorbing many a rich and titled house-buyer turned away from Belgravia, any local artist was still on a fairly good wicket at the mid-century. Another Scot, James Rannie Swinton, rightly reasoned there was a niche for the portrait painter as well as the portrait sculptor.

Swinton's thorough training had ended in Rome where his sittings became a fashionable station on the Grand Tour. This entrance to British high society would assure him a network of important patronage as long as he kept within reach of it in London. In 1849 he bought the lease of an impressive end-of-terrace house just across Elizabeth Bridge in St George's Drive, Pimlico. All went well; the 1850s were his most profitable years. Viscounts, politicians and bankers flocked to him for excellent heads in chalk (cheap at 35gns[26]), but it was their wives and daughters who made a veritable cult of his powers, returning for replicas and full-length oils (150gns). Famous men such as Louis Napoleon sat to him, yet the ladies made for prettier pictures, with the glamorous *Sheridan Sisters* group of 1852 perhaps his most successful. A dozen or more portraits easily repaid their engraving fees. Although academic recognition eluded Swinton, he nevertheless managed to invest £1500 a year and keep up appearances in Rome every other season. In due course his healthy bank balance, his Continental tastes and, more pressingly, the expansion of railway services at Victoria put him in mind to build a town house of his own that fulfilled all the needs of a 'steamer-set' professional.

Pimlico had been kind to him, so in 1858 he proposed moving into it a little deeper. A certain George Morgan was appointed to design the house and mews on a double plot alongside St Gabriel's, Warwick Square. Jackson & Shaw won the contract with a tender of £6610 early in 1860.[27] Evidently the effect aimed for was of a stately Rinascimento villa which would not look amiss beside the Italianate stucco of

33 George Morgan's perspective drawing of 33 Warwick Square, Pimlico, built for James Swinton in 1858–60. Much of the conciliatory stucco trim was abandoned in the end.

Cubittopolis. But the already extravagant budget must have proven too tight, since the formal trim originally proposed was finally discarded. The Classical pretensions of the exterior are largely gainsaid by a pile-up of contrary Picturesque elements anyway, **33**. Stripped of compo ornament, an eclectic selection of windows stares out from a spartan tartan of red, yellow and grey brick walls girdled in Portland stone. In fact the house appears to be cocking a snook at its sober-suited surroundings.

Not just a piece of architectural roguery, 33 Warwick Square showed itself to be another new-fangled studio-house – the first in London to be built privately. Even more so than in Freake's version, Morgan made the studio take precedence over every domestic conventionality and govern the planning of the whole, **34**. Due north lies towards Victoria; the architect therefore wrapped the principal room around the forward corner of the site in order to align the painting light precisely. Probably for working up his occasional landscapes, Swinton asked for a second, more intimate studio with a 'warmer' light, so this was attached to the first and given another outsize window onto the north-west. A top-lit picture gallery was connected to the opposite side along St George's Drive;[28] sitters and callers could then step in directly from the road. Beyond the additional noise buffer of the inner hall open the dining room and library, both heavily decorated in an English Palladian style devoid of the twinkling touches of Neo-Classicism. While the library is a chaste Doric exercise, it is humoured by a tricksy chimneypiece wherein the mantel mirror rolls away to give a surprise view of St Gabriel's.

Swinton clearly anticipated the social obligations incurred by his marriage in 1865 to an Irish baron's daughter, Blanche de Ros, as a sumptuous ballroom at the head of the broad, easy-paced staircase goes to confirm. Adjoining the ballroom is a hand-

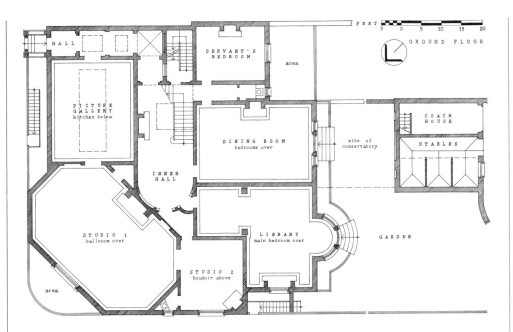

34 Ground floor plan of 33 Warwick Square. Sir Joshua Reynolds's painting room was also octagonal but one third the area of this one.

some, though rather starchy, boudoir cum retiring room. Elsewhere, however, the grand manner dwindles into High Victorian mediocrity. Unfortunately, Swinton's portraiture went the same way. In 1875 he sat back amid his 'ornamental china, glass, bronzes, and other objets de virtu',[29] hardly ever to receive another sitter. Two years after his death in 1888 (when an estate worth £23 750 was declared), the house was sold for considerably less than it cost to build. Pimlico never caught on as an arty district; the younger generation was definitely going west in the 1860s.

Such was the case with the church decorator, Nathaniel Westlake. He was lodging near Eccleston Square when he first teamed up with John Bentley, later the architect of Westminster Cathedral. Their association quickly led to Bentley's first domestic commission: during 1863 he designed a new house for Westlake on a corner site in the potteries area of Notting Dale. Though 235 Lancaster Road could not be called a studio-house, the three exposed sides of the building are full of capricious detail and the topmost storey seems to be the result of some sort of anomaly in the brief. One way or another the artist gave up the house and it has now succumbed to municipal blight. Hindsight shows it to have been a mild aberration; the true path lay in the fields under the eye of Watts and his friends.

Now that South Kensington, Kensington New Town and Campden Hill had all been conquered by artists, attention centred on the nearest frontier westward, Holland Park – or what became so when Lady Holland sold a portion of her property for building land. Not the last to hear of this sale were the Prinseps, secure for the time being in Little Holland House. Four of their sons had stayed behind in the East; the fifth, schooled at Haileybury, edified at Mrs Prinsep's salon of savants and dazzled by Watts, was resolved to become a painter. Young Valentine (b. 14.2.1838) was duly given every encouragement.

Aged 19 in 1857 Val, 'the roughs' and the prize-fighters' pal', was allowed to join Gabriel Rossetti's fresco frolic in Oxford. At 21 he toured Italy with Edward Burne-Jones prior to attending the Atelier Gleyre in Paris. On his return he wintered at Frederic Leighton's former rooms in Rome. Val's first Academy offerings – historical mayhem and colourful femmes fatales – were sent from the centre of Fitzrovia. Once he had sold two or three, it was agreed he should make a high-handed bid for greater recognition by showing that, materially at least, he had already arrived. When the Holland land became available he was advanced a sufficient amount to buy about an acre and to put a substantial house on it. Spoiled to the last, Prinsep would have the house architect-designed and fitted up as well as any of the *hôtels de peintre* he had seen in Europe. His choice of architect in 1864, Philip Webb, was a natural one. Already the designer of William Morris's Red House and 'Fairmile' for Watts's pupil Roddy Spencer-Stanhope, this slightly testy man was now constrained to draw up a master plan for a nabob's son heading for the top.

Luckily Webb warmed to the task, inventing extra geometric challenges of his own. His execution of the three-stage plan – the builders of stage 1 were, significantly, the same as Swinton's – was indeed masterful, shaping what looked like a Middle Pointed village rectory into a cathedral town bishop's palace in Mannerist Tudor. But the first two stages, which together cost 'rather less than £3000',[30] were the more intriguing. Webb proceeded with deceptive ease to fit all the required accommodation into a neat 40′ square, his starting point the 40′ × 25′ Parisian-style studio asked for by Prinsep. Apart from this and the small parlour by the entrance especially for business interviews, the house might well have been for a celibate vicar with a good living. The major private rooms were placed on the north, garden side, partly because the southern approach was a charmless mews behind St Mary Abbot's Terrace. In effect, 1 Holland Park Road turned its back on the outside world. Artist at work; please do not disturb.

Aloft in the studio almost every kind of lighting was built in: sky light, top light, three northern side lights – both the Gothic marvels being double-glazed – and a western oriel for sunbathing after hours. Across the south wall stretched a gallery, a feature previously encountered only at Romney's house. Beyond that and behind the back stairs lay what at the first building stage was the maid-of-all-work's bedroom. Both before and after conversion this room served as a retreat for the men, women and children (the latter two often chaperoned) whom Prinsep invited to pose for his figurative works. The Victorian moral code specified that these socially untouchable people should come up the back stairs, fully concealed from the resident family. More often than not, Val the pal let them come up the main stairs, even after his marriage.

A serious love-affair (he finally married Florence, daughter of F L Leyland, the Liverpool shipowner and art patron, in 1884) induced Prinsep to mend his Bohemian ways and make the house more hospitable. While the dining room actually became a drawing room, the second stage alterations resulted in the layout shown by the illustrated drawings, **35**. Further servants' quarters and storage space also formed part of the clean-up, but they were really incidental to an enlargement of the studio

35 Garden front and drawings of Valentine Prinsep's house in Holland Park Road, Holland Park, by Philip Webb, 1864–76. These drawings take in the alterations and additions of stage 2.

made necessary by a fabulous commission received in 1876 from the Indian government. Poor Webb absolutely scourged himself in an effort to coax all the new work into his original square plan. 1876 was the year Queen Victoria became Empress of India, and Prinsep was asked to paint the massed military proclamation ceremony, *The Delhi Imperial Durbar*. His representation of the event was assembled on a canvas 30′ × 12′. His ultimate need to paint with a north light side-on to the full-width tableau meant that, if he were to work in the existing studio, it would have to be widened considerably. Webb ingeniously achieved an optional extension by bridging the two southward wings of the house – bringing about the 'Part of Studio' indicated on the first floor plan. Since the gallery was still an impedance, its critical length of floor was made into a drawbridge and its balustrade into a pair of gates, **36**. Getting *Durbar Day* out of the studio into the RA four years later was simply a matter of removing one of the purposely adapted north windows. Acceptance was automatic since Prinsep had been elected ARA in 1878.

Oriental accents never left the house, however. Rubber plants and pieces of old china cropped up everywhere. Small squares of Japanese leather paper lined the dados, the doors, and the panelled main staircase. Gold-framed cane-bottomed chairs glittered in the drawing room, the only one where the woodwork was spared Bournville brown paint in favour of Webb's patent juniper green. Here the walls were entirely hung around with old Italian tapestries. Elsewhere, except in the studio which was distempered salmon pink, they were covered with Morris papers just as the windows were draped in 'Morris-like patterned stuffs'.

In the 1860s much of this decor was thought to be excitingly novel. Novelty of another kind distinguished the exterior. Webb's composition still betrayed his training under the ecclesiastic architect G E Street. But muted Gothic forms nonetheless tallied with medieval culture, a branch of approved Pre-Raphaelite doctrine to which his client then subscribed. Native and naturalistic traditions were also endorsed. Webb referred to these in a personal way by reviving aspects of the Dutch-influenced late 17th-, early 18th-century vernacular architecture of south-east England. He banished the artificialities of Latin stucco, casing the house instead in bare red bricks and plain red tiles.[31] A stinging hot–cold contrast was introduced by small-paned sash windows painted in white. Functionally appropriate in size and shape, their vertical alignments cleverly regulated an apparent rustic randomness.

An overall outline symmetry was used to unify the street facade when Val acceded to triple the accommodation in 1892. Comparatively fancy brick and stone ornament had already been incorporated in 1877 to mitigate the selfish public image of stage 1. Thus the final stage was garnished in a similar vein. In the interim Val's subjects had gone from literary heroines to lusty Campagna scenes, from domestic genre to vaguely erotic Egyptian history – all in a bid to win the popular vote for Royal Academicianship with its superadded social credibility. Eventually, after completing the house and launching his second novel, he rallied once more and made the grade.

Right next door to the Prinsep house, at 2 Holland Park Road, another house was being built at almost exactly the same time. No. 2 was also a brazen red brick upstart; it even had red mortar. There was something indefinably odd about its creamy stone

36 Val Prinsep, aged about 45, poses in his studio. Above *The Bookworm,* the gallery floor can be seen retracted.

furbelows and its jutting hindquarters, **37**. It was said to be the doing of another eccentric bachelor artist who had returned with some strange ideas from the Continent. He could be seen daily, inspecting every last brass screw for optimum tightness. His name was Frederic Leighton.

Few artists ever underwent a course of study as thorough as this Scarborough doctor's son. His drawing and design skills were learned at the academies of Florence and Frankfurt. In Paris, as in Brussels and Rome, he had his own studio.[32] Throughout the 1850s Leighton extended his acquaintance among the leading figures of the day at home and abroad while getting to know Lord and Lady Holland, the architect George Aitchison, George Watts and Val Prinsep. Permanently settled in London by 1860, his comprehensive grounding and faultless tact led him to undertake every commission from woodblocks to portraits and to acquit each one with professional promptitude. Works he showed at the RA usually sold at the private view; in 1864 Gambart strode forward with a 1000gn cheque for *Dante in Exile*. It soon became plain that Leighton would get mildly rich and enjoy a fêted career. Election to ARA also came in 1864 but, setting his sights higher, the compleat painter felt the next step would be hastened by use of the compleat painter's house.

Taking advantage of his contacts, Leighton bought a slice of the newly released Holland land adjoining Prinsep's. He and his affable young friend had obviously compared notes; in terms of content their houses would be to a large degree similar. But Leighton wished to enlist both the trust of the conservative plutocracy and the admiration of the culturally radical from the very outset. His belief in the ultimate superiority of Classical art was firm yet still flexible. Therefore he would express definitive taste by exposing a timeless, modular villa façade to the street yet spice it with fresh materials and hints of a synthetic stuffing. Hence the red bricks and Neo-Pompeian Caen stonework.

Knowing him to be sympathetic to his ideals, Leighton asked George Aitchison to prepare the drawings. Although it was an exacting brief, Aitchison was a competent constructor and decorator with a passion for reinventing antique details. At least two stages of building were envisaged, the final product to revolve around a central circulation space. The general layout was thereby not dictated solely by a north-facing studio. Over a basement of domestic offices Aitchison placed a top-lit stairhall between two three-storey blocks, the forward one being the decoy villa front. This initial stage is shown in essence by the parts of the plan in black, **38**. Plus a sequin or two for landscape gardening, the contract sum amounted to £4500.[33] Why this should be so much more than his neighbour spent becomes clear on closer scrutiny.

On its completion late in 1866 Aitchison's design came justly under fire[34] for its 'barrenness of outline' compared to Webb's 'pleasing arrangement of gabled mass' next door. But the spaces are well conceived and the decoration quite remarkable. Bespoke mouldings in both timber and plaster possess a breadth and crispness every bit as unusual as the black lacquered doors, architraves and skirtings. Incised with organic motifs picked out in gold, these lend the effect of ebony and ivory while intensifying adjacent colours. Crossing the lofty, glass-vaulted stairhall, one enters the drawing room with its floorboards painted ash blue and its walls covered in cigar

37 Garden front of Sir Frederic Leighton's house as it looked in 1880. The upper floor studio has already been lengthened once and the Arab Hall added to one side.

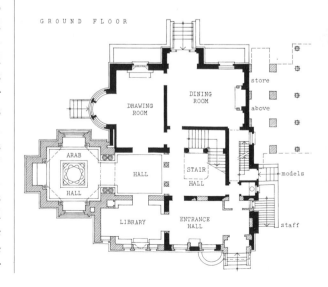

38 Plans of Lord Leighton's house in Holland Park Road, Holland Park, designed by himself and George Aitchison, 1865–95.

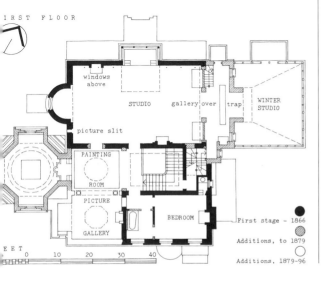

brown cloth. Although this room was specially contrived to take four panels by Corot and a ceiling roundel by Delacroix, the tight bow and the gimmicky see-through chimneypiece are all too reminiscent of Swinton's library to be wholly original.[35] Alternatively, one may enter the dining room where, as Mrs Haweis puts it in *Beautiful Houses*, 'Above the door, the infcription "Profit" greets us like a good omen'.[36] (To find this over the studio door might have been more understandable.) Here the walls were once a 'deep red', the ceiling a 'dull red'. Weighty furniture in plain oak and a baronial fireplace surround competed with a modern ebonised sideboard, although the differences between these were soon obscured by massed travel souvenirs. Upon leaving the dining room to mount the stairs, 'which wind like a treble passage out of bass chords' (Mrs Haweis), a balustrade of blackthorn shillelaghs demands respect on the right while masterful works in titanic baroque frames bear down from cliff-like walls on the left. Thus by the time one steps from the top landing to cross the studio threshold Leighton has shown his hand from every angle. It is all the more stunning, then, to be engulfed in another echoing space not dissimilar to a Romanesque chapel drenched in pink light.

At the time, the western apse, the eastern gallery and the clerestory windows supported such an impression only for the great north bay in the centre to squarely spoil it. This giant, combined side and sky light rises from a sill 5' above the sitters' dais to a ridge 18' higher up.[37] Every side is double-glazed and, formerly, each could be independently shaded with canvas blinds matching the Indian red of the walls. The modest eastern window was formerly flanked by black-and-gold cabinets for storing colours and sundries. Above the window ran a gallery, its pierced stone front propped on polychrome shafts seemingly taken from some sequestered suspension bridge in the Border Country, **39**. Leighton needed the gallery 'to get studies of objects at a moderate elevation'; he could reach it via the service staircase. Models also used the back stairs, approaching a side entrance and ascending unseen to the servants' door – a somewhat stricter defence of propriety than Prinsep cared to provide. Changing facilities, however, were less specific. Prinsep and his models may have fared better with regard to heating, too, but Leighton's tall, narrow door, or 'picture slit', by the apse much improved on his neighbour's method of despatching oversized canvases.

Making the most of his superior working conditions, Leighton attained full Academy membership in 1868. Nevertheless he still felt his technique, already an ultra-scrupulous one, was handicapped by the studio. Aitchison responded by extending it 10', enlarging the east window, and organising a nifty sub-floor lumber room.[38] By partly enclosing the extension and drawing the gallery back over it, the painter obtained both a spot to garage his easels and a little more privacy for his models. Thenceforth it became possible to transform a workshop into a 'show studio' with minimal effort. Similarly the broader gallery, then said to be 'for statuary and hangings', became a more comfortable perch for a violinist or soprano when Leighton threw a ball or chamber concert.

In sharp contrast to Prinsep's pre-emption of an apparent position of eminence, both the first stage of 2 Holland Park Road and the amendments to it rewarded

Leighton's legitimate advances through the ranks. Although the second stage was begun in 1876 – before our hero accepted presidency of the RA and a knighthood – these promotions were decidedly inevitable. Attendant increases in responsibility and social exposure gave Sir Frederic ample excuse to show off his virtuosity in the cause of public relations. Chief of the stage 2 additions, of course, was the Arab Hall, the freakish culmination of a chinamania that had long since affected the whole house. Yet the lustrous pleasure dome only found its place in the hopscotch figure of the new plan after the sage green library-study and an intermediate hall, the Hall of Narcissus – so-named after a centrally sited statuette – had been inserted. And while the latter was connected to the Arab Hall by a portal of visceral marble columns, the corresponding tawny brown, top-lit painting room above looked in with a shadowy black mashrabiyya. In 1880, with the studio become as much showplace as sanctum, the house contained no less than six public areas.

Once into his fifties, despite submitting to a hectic round of official duties, Leighton settled down to produce his best work (*Captive Andromache*, *The Bath of Psyche*). He kept crashing down his own frontiers, surpassing himself now in fresco (*The Arts of War*, *The Arts of Peace*), now in sculpture more Greek than the Greek (his earlier, revolutionary *Athlete Wrestling* was worthily followed by *The Sluggard*). It was about this time that an RA quizzed Whistler about King Jupiter. 'Leighton? That man's doing a fine job as your president. Stands well with royalty. Distinguished appearance. Makes a first class speech. Good linguist. No mean musician – (pause for reflection) – paints a little, sculpts a little.'[39] Universal admiration for universal qualities resulted in the baronetcy of 1886, a sure sign that further additions to the house were imminent. Indeed, not satisfied with the overhead lighting of his intimate new cupolar painting room, he would also have a 25′ × 20′ glasshouse. This allowed him to paint '*en plein air*' while undercover, or on winter days when the light was too dim anywhere else. To knit it into the fabric of Studio No 1, in 1889, Aitchison had to unravel the existing gusset at the east end.

Life resumed its course, but Leighton was not yet done. His final fling entailed filling the space over the library. Down came the outer painting-room wall; up went one more neatly balanced top-lit chamber establishing the umpteenth inviting enfilade. Decorated in olive green and the standard black trim, it had different names: Silk Room, Music Room, Picture Gallery. Sir Frederic barely lived to appreciate it in any guise. Burnt out at 65 he died in 1896, but not before being raised to the peerage. That could only mean he was projecting still another refinement.[40]

If they were not known as artists in their own right, Swinton, Prinsep and Leighton would have passed for typical socially and academically accomplished new Londoners, married severally to property rents, merchant shipping, and the fine arts personified. In other words, they were virtual nouveaux-riches members of the upper middle classes; their standard of living was easily equivalent. But they distinguished themselves by the individuality of their houses, and by their houses they hoped to distinguish the paintings they produced in them. Exclusive gifts were more likely to be found in distinctive wrappings. Visitors saw a new type of house differentiated not only by its integrated studio and its relevance to the client's past

39 Sir Frederic Leighton's studio in 1880. The gilt-lined gallery 'for statuary and hangings' crosses behind custom-made cabinets; a clay sketch for *An Idyll* lies under the big north window.

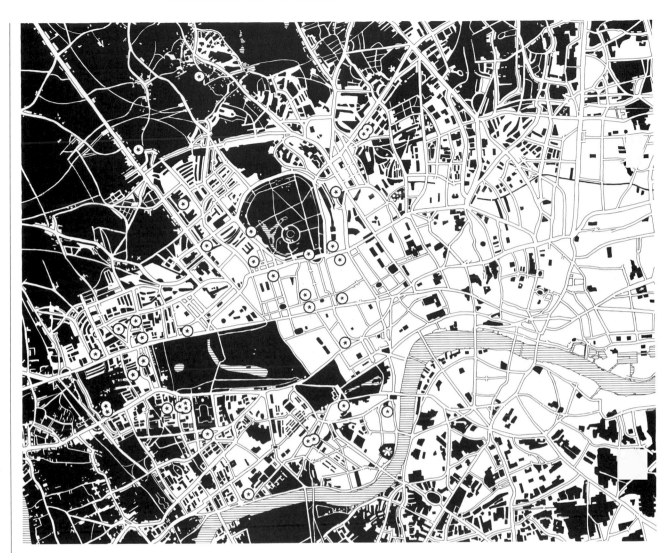

40   London in 1869, showing the distribution of current RAs. While six men had moved away from the inner West End by 1819, now only six remain within it, while another half dozen have left London altogether to live in the country. See **20** and **9**.

experience and future plans, but also by the collaboration of artist and architect in the design. Once they, too, had seen what was possible on a budget of £6000, £4000 or as little as £1500, painters and sculptors began falling over themselves to display their own talents. By 1870 no more signs were needed to prove that a London-wide craze for studio-houses had become a definite prospect, **40**.

4

ESTABLISHMENT KENSINGTON: MELBURY ROAD

GEORGE HOWARD, heir to Castle Howard and the earldom of Carlisle, was not too bothered about the cost when he asked Philip Webb and William Morris to design and decorate a 50-room town house for him opposite Kensington Palace at 1 Palace Green in 1867. He was more anxious to make sure he ended up with a three-dimensional Pre-Raphaelite masterpiece. Though Howard had plenty of artistic ideas of his own, spending much of the year on sketching tours, he preferred to hand his specifications to a team of friends whose avant-garde style he was most in sympathy with. Of the £3500 minimum that the Crown lease obliged him to outlay on the house, most must have drained away merely on provision for horses and servants. However, there was a good deal left over for a painting room under the roof. While this room was hardly the raison d'être of the six-storey mansion, its presence was unmistakably conveyed by a vast pointed window in the east front gable. On plan the studio took up five-fourths of a 20′ square, the fifth fourth serving as an anteroom below and a gallery above. French doors within the frame of the great window opened onto a balcony over the tier of canted bays beneath.

Let loose with a big budget, Webb designed the sort of house he considered most appropriate to London and to that park-side section of Old Kensington in particular. His original scheme was to have been built almost entirely in full-blooded red bricks. Compared to Prinsep's stage 1 façades, Howard's were to be full of incident, with changes of plane, texture and local pattern but unrelieved, as the Crown Commissioners complained, by sufficient stonework or any important horizontal mouldings. Neither were they happy about the unusually steep pitch of the roofs. Webb strongly defended his proposal, congratulating himself that the Commissioners' consultants could not decide to which style or period the building belonged. But as he became more irresistible they became more immovable. Apparently Howard's embarrassment was such that he sneaked away to beg William Butterfield to submit an alternative design; but there, unfortunately, he met an even sterner man of principle. Butterfield scoffed at the worldly frivolity of the whole exercise and sent him back to Webb, who finally consented to revise the drawings. Construction began in 1869.

A token amount of stonework was admitted, most notably in the form of a

41 Dining room detail, 1 Palace Green, Kensington, by Philip Webb for the Hon. George Howard, 1867–70. Burne-Jones, Crane and Morris & Co. contributed the decoration.

moulded band at first floor level and a spearhead of giant Portland blocks[1] surrounding the studio window. As a parting shot at the authorities, Webb devised a jumbo, storey-height cornice of corbelled and pilastered brickwork that encircles the house and disguises the extent of the roof. Suggestions for the decoration of the interiors went unchallenged so that the work of Morris's firm nicely complemented Webb's crossbred fittings. Burne-Jones contributed the beginnings of a *Cupid and Psyche* frieze for the dining room, **41**. A few years later this was brought to completion by Walter Crane, he and his wife having been asked to stay at Palace Green when a house move and the birth of Lionel Crane coincided.[2]

Were Howard's address not in such a sensitive neighbourhood, Webb would probably have had his own way completely. As it was, his favourable compromise made it easier for contemporary architects to design with impunity in a similar fashion. Though this and Webb's other London houses revealed several elements basic to that fashion, the so-called Queen Anne Revival, they are really in a class of their own. W M Thackeray may have unwittingly kindled the 'Queen Anne' movement in 1860–2 by remodelling the old house at 2 Palace Green to resemble a late 17th-century villa. Within another decade, so much more Queen Anne flavour had been filtered out of the air that The Red House, the architect J J Stevenson's own house on Bayswater Road, was a wholly conscious attempt to exhibit a range of typical features. Very soon the easy option of remixing a fleeting, therefore fluid, and relatively recent historical style loosened the cramping grip of academic Classic and Gothic shackles. And once these dropped from the hands of clever young designers, a passage was tunnelled to an architecture – especially appealing to artists – of sweetness and light.

Early evidence of an architect struggling free of a Classical mould is to be seen in F P Cockerell's town house for Reginald Cholmondeley of Condover Hall, Shropshire. Cholmondeley dabbled creditably in portraiture and sculpture. In the one he worked alongside Charles Couzens and Sir Coutts Lindsay; in the other he acted as both patron and assistant to George Watts. In 1869 Cockerell was presented with a wedge-shaped site at 33–37 Palace Gate that offered a view to the north towards Kensington Gardens. Asked for a family house incorporating a painting room, he responded with a five-storey stylistic mish-mash. He built on all but the apex of the wedge in red bricks bound together with yellow stone bands. One facet sported a Venetian arch, another a Dutch gable and French dormers; most of the windows had Jacobethan mullions and transoms. More slenderly-framed windows at first floor level on the north side singled out the painting room. A blend of side and sky light was given by positioning a glazed bay over the front porch, bending the glass over the window-head and raking it up to the ceiling line. This means of lighting a studio sandwiched between floors was quite satisfactory and much imitated, but Cholmondeley's interest in painting suddenly waned. Although he was able to let the house after 1878, it failed to attract another artist until Frank Baden-Powell, elder brother of the peer, came along in 1904.

Apart from the natty glazed bay there was little in Cockerell's design to catch the eye of the artistic client, yet he completed three more houses for painters and sculptors during the 1870s. His early death prevented him from keeping pace with another architect slightly his senior, the Scotsman Norman Shaw. Formerly G E Street's chief assistant in succession to Philip Webb, Shaw already had four painters' commissions under his belt by the end of 1871. In 1874 he undertook his fifth, a house at the top end of Queen's Gate, South Kensington, for J P Heseltine. Though principally a stockbroker, Heseltine became an early supporter of the Society for the Protection of Ancient Buildings and a Trustee of the National Gallery. Membership of the select Etching Club where he rubbed shoulders with Redgrave and Millais established him as an artist of some ability.[3] In most of these respects he took after George Howard and, like Howard, he required a decent workroom in his new house. Shaw provided one of similar size on the fourth floor at the back, also with a balcony, but fairly unremarkable in the context of the building as a whole. For a 14-bedroom house on a narrow plot the planning is most adroitly resolved and the street front a complementary tour de force of red brick specials. The architect seemed to be playing off old values against new ones as the windows rose beyond view, delicate Old English leadlights metamorphosing into coarser 'Queen Anne' square-paned sashes.

In fact, this was a sign that Shaw's workload had become too heavy to sustain a high degree of intricate detailing. When his favourite contractor, W H Lascelles, started building the Heseltine house, plans for three more large town houses – a pair

42 View and drawings of Marcus Stone's house, Melbury Road, Holland Park, by Norman Shaw, 1876. There are three gates – one each for servants, family and models.

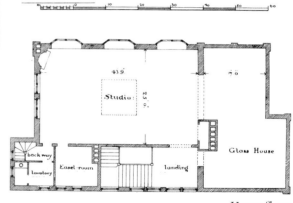

Upper floor

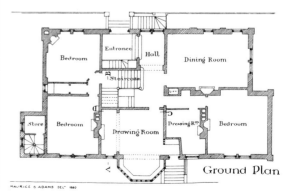

Ground Plan

on the Chelsea riverfront and one for himself in Hampstead – threatened to swamp the drawing board. Then two further projects for painters arrived, and the office was truly awash. Shaw never skimped but he temporarily simplified his exteriors, finding smoother, straighter solutions for the businessmen and barristers (17–19 Chelsea Embankment) while reserving a studied off-beat suavity for himself (6 Ellerdale Road) and the artists.

Notwithstanding, the first of the two studio-house designs, dating from mid-1875, falls somewhat between the two styles. It is at No. 8 in the then newly-formed Melbury Road, Holland Park, just over Leighton's back fence. The client was the young bounder, Marcus Stone, or Marcus 'Apollo Belvedere' Stone as he preferred to be known. So ingratiating was he that he sold his scenes of flirtatious dalliance faster than Landseer used to sell his of performing monkeys, and he did very well from engraved reproductions. Stone saw how Norman Shaw's frothy historicism could effectively trumpet his latest bid to dominate the developing market in Regency romps and *Vanity Fair* friskiness. Shaw had built only one fully-fledged studio-house prior to this commission (in 1870) and that was on a country site. There he was able to semi-detach the studio, placing it over the kitchen wing. On the tighter town plot in Melbury Road, the house had to be compactly planned and brought close to the street to allow for the largest possible garden. In addition to a 45′ × 25′ studio, Stone wanted a glasshouse about half that size to open out of it. When Shaw united these two spaces under their own roofs, the overall extent of the house was roughly settled, **42**. At that date Stone was the first painter to specify a winter studio 'en suite';

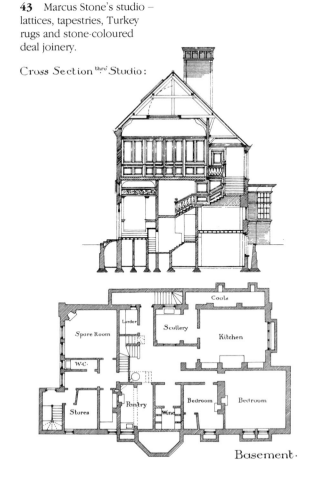

43 Marcus Stone's studio – lattices, tapestries, Turkey rugs and stone-coloured deal joinery.

43

Front · Elevation ·

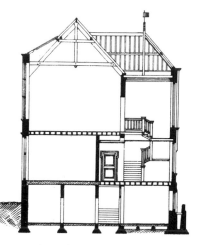

+·Section·of·Studio

Back · Elevation ·

this convenience, which guaranteed a perennial springtime atmosphere, allowed the painter to pose his ever-popular canoodling scene between dizzy young Dorothy and the dashing Captain of Guards whenever he wished, even if it was actually snowing outside.

In the studio proper, all the woodwork was painted a neutral off-white as requested but, after blocking up the original west windows, Stone proceeded to cover the panelling with garish tapestries. His gabled leadlight oriels were almost more ornamental than practical yet their light could be supplemented by bringing the novel ceiling deflector into play, **43**.[4] Other firsts at No. 8 include the room specifically for storing easels and props, and the models' staircase – quite separate from the servants' back stairs. Extra storage and the models' changing room were accessible from it. In order to free the north wall above the front door, the main staircase was taken through the house to the back. It was made to ascend at its full width right up to the studio mainly to satisfy Stone's vanity, since there are no upper floor bedrooms. Although the stairs thereby trample over the drawing room, the architect has shamelessly used copious falsework to create a wagon ceiling and an ingle-nook. Shaw did come unstuck, however. For instance, the corner fireplaces are appropriate on all floors but the chimney stack is only a questionable success. And, in the same way, the sensible internal placement of the lower front windows does not automatically produce a chiming 'picturesque assortment' on the outside.[5]

With the second studio-house in Melbury Road that he began designing in 1876, Shaw redeemed himself considerably. No. 11 (now 31) was designed for a newly-wed couple with whom the Stones had recently spent a winter in Paris – Luke and

44 Drawings of Sir Luke Fildes's house, Melbury Road, Holland Park, by Norman Shaw, 1876–7. A terrace and a day nursery surmounted by a glasshouse were added to the rear at later stages.

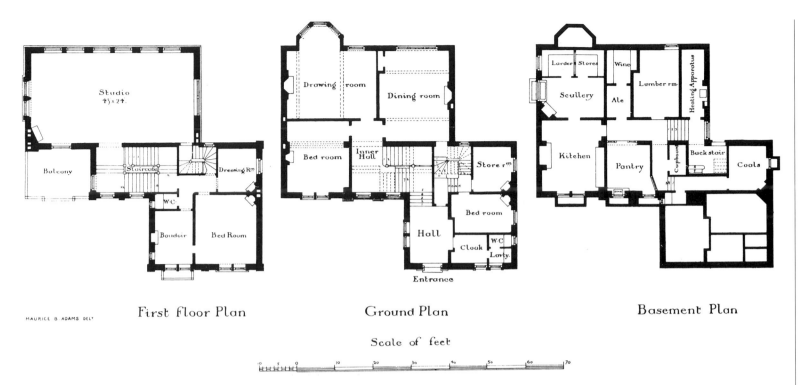

First floor Plan

Ground Plan

Basement Plan

MAURICE B ADAMS DEL?

Scale of feet

45 Reginald Cleaver, *Luke Fildes painting 'The Doctor'* (1891). Fildes's studio was easily large enough to mock up a full-size cottage interior within it.

Fanny Fildes. The Liverpudlian Fildes had barely graduated from pen drawing to oil painting before *Applicants for Admission to a Casual Ward* (1874) rocketed him to prominence. Like Stone, he calculated that a house from Shaw would give him a further boost, hopefully straight into the RA orbit. As the Fildeses went so far as to sink all their money into the venture – tenders came in around the £7000 mark – they were gratified to see a palace rise that 'knocked Stone's to fits'.[6]

A palace it certainly is. No. 11 is half as big again as No. 8, although the studio is no larger and at first there was no glasshouse. This time Shaw avoided trying to fit all the accommodation into a volume generated by the boundary of the studio floor. Instead, he deliberately defined an entrance–bedroom block and a service–living room–studio block. The half-level difference between these two was resolved where they overlapped by the staircase system. Having distributed the bulk of the building, it was left to Shaw to articulate its extra surfaces and corners. This he did with great flair, varying the roof shapes, sprinkling on balconies and a lantern, and lining up a modular range of paired windows set between pilasters or mounted in panels, **44**.

On the north side, a large, square window and a polygonal bay similar to Stone's announce the dining and drawing rooms respectively; the terrace connecting them to the garden is a later addition. Above are the tell-tale signs of the studio: a barrage of coupled leadlights topped by a continuous array of skylights. Inside, the north light could be minutely modulated by moleskin blinds stretching up to the ceiling a full 23′ from the floor, **45**. But for Fildes there could never be enough of it. Shortly after improving his earning power by virtue of his self-assured rise to ARA (1879), he had the middle pair of leadlights joined into one and carried up to the parapet. Six years later he was cursing London's grey, fog-bound winters while his wife's brother, Harry Woods ARA, was crowing about the azure January skies over his 'Palazzo Cristallo' in Venice. Fildes decided to have a glasshouse too, so it was built along the lines of Stone's, sheltered from western sun by the eastern studio gable. The Fildes children were delighted to use the glasshouse as a stage for home theatricals, the former eastern studio window making an ideal proscenium.[7] Other aspects of the Stone house already present were the Gran Turismo staircase, the discreet access and changing facilities for models, and the corner fireplace in the studio – the luxury of supplementary underfloor heating allowed this to be quite a distance from the painting light.

Norman Shaw's two clients were far from the last artists to buy land and build in and around Melbury Road. One of the more ascetic characters to make a home there in 1877 was Albert Moore. As an easel and mural painter, Moore out-Leightoned Leighton in his exhaustive search for perfect forms and colour harmonies, a dedication resulting in serene, supernally lit figure groups such as *Dreamers* (1875) and *Midsummer* (1887). His house, which he designed himself,[8] never failed to bemuse its visitors. His pupil Graham Robertson recalled a 'curious building at the corner of Holland Lane . . . consisting of two huge studios, a sitting room with nothing to sit upon in it and, I suppose, a kitchen'.[9] Edward Godwin noticed that the walls and ceilings were 'cut about in a most remarkable manner'. From this he understood that, by minimising the number of right-angles, Moore hoped to reflect as much daylight as possible without extraneous windows. On that account Godwin deemed the house 'very dodgy and well worthy of consideration by every artist'.[10] When Whistler called he found the place overrun by stray cats and strewn with large funnels in pots

46 Plans and view of the George Watts house, Melbury Road, Holland Park, by F P Cockerell and George Aitchison, 1874–80.

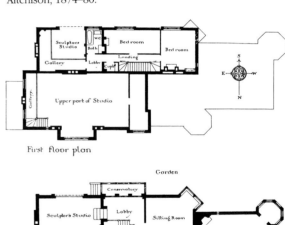

First floor plan

Ground plan

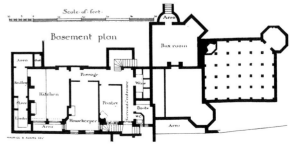

Basement plan

47 Thomas Rooke, *George Watts's Studio, Melbury Road*, 1904. Complete with picture slit and gallery but as much a living room as Stone's next door.

– to catch the drips from numerous leaky roof junctions.[11] In fact Moore's nonpareil was so dodgy it had to be condemned within 20 years of its erection.

Before going any further, it should be remembered that the spate of studio building in Holland Park, beginning with Val Prinsep's house, was ultimately due to George Watts. Studious 'Signor' had not been idle in the meantime at Little Holland House. In the 1860s he developed his interest in sculpture, the figure of *Sir Thomas Cholmondeley* (1864–7) being the first of some dozen monuments and ideal pieces executed over the next 40 years. In 1864, aged 46, he was pushed into marrying Ellen Terry, aged 16. Fifteen months later he was single again, without ever parting from his first love. To model the larger sculptural commissions he had accumulated, he built a fully equipped wooden barrack adjoining the main house. However, at that point the landlady, Lord Holland's widow, informed Watts and his hosts, the Thoby Prinseps, of the £40 000 she stood to gain by demolishing Little Holland House and laying out Melbury Road with the rubble. Conscious of his debt to the Prinseps, Watts set about building them a retirement home on the Isle of Wight combined with a couple of studios for himself as a replacement. The Prinseps transferred to the island early in 1874, leaving Watts behind to thrash out portraits to pay for it all. Because these fine portraits were essentially Signor's lifeline, he realised he could never afford to move away from London permanently. Reluctantly he faced up to finding still more sitters to finance another base in the capital close to where he was already well established.

Val Prinsep willingly sublet a portion of his garden that would front the proposed line of Melbury Road, and this was the site Watts handed to F P Cockerell (his friend Reginald Cholmondeley's architect) in the spring of 1874. Together with a major painting room and a minor modelling room, Watts wanted a knockabout sculptor's workshop; there would be no dining room as such and just one bedroom beside his own. While Cockerell contended with the 'drunkenness, idleness and dishonesty'[12] of the builders, Watts suffered the brutishness of the breakers at Little Holland House until the very last. A further six-month wait before the completion of 6 Melbury Road in February 1876 forced him to order the aforementioned sizeable iron studio for temporary storage.

With amazing carelessness, Cockerell brought about what looked like a collision between a London Board school and a commercial laundry, the mechanics of which Signor only worsened with his second thoughts, **46**. Soon after Cockerell died in 1878, Leighton's architect George Aitchison was called in to make alterations. He succeeded in ramming a public swimming bath onto the west end. In reality this addition incorporated a top-lit picture gallery and a lean-to store; the gallery was designed to clear the decks and keep unwanted visitors out of the studios. The erstwhile modelling room became an extension to it. To the left of the pinched front door, the major studio originally measured 50′ from end to end with a viewing gallery along the south wall. Under orders, Aitchison pushed this gallery to one side (where the steps snarled a picture slit) and blocked the second north light with yet another lumber room, **47**. Watts could then look down through the conservatory or spy on his assistant in the sculptor's workshop. Two colossal equestrian statues, *Hugh*

Lupus for the Marquis of Westminster, and *Physical Energy*, an abstract version of the same for himself, occupied Watts for the next 15 years and more. The full-sized models for these were built up on a pivot-table trolley that ran on rails from the hangar-like workshop to a paved apron. Signor worked on them in the open air, sunstroke and rheumatism permitting. While the workshop gallery put upper parts of the models within reach, Watts was also able to appraise the final effect of the statues on their pedestals by looking out from the basement box room.

In common with Swinton's interesting but inefficient house, there were really too few basement functions at No. 6 to match the extent of the ground floor. The alternative strategy of placing the major studio on the first floor pointed to a smaller overall plan area, an imposing mass of building, and the opportunity for a triumphal staircase. But Watts was not so materially minded. If one were fully aware of Signor's self-denial it might be said that the big kitchen, pantry and wine cellar were rather over-provident, too. Every evening, without variation, he ate nothing but the cold leftovers of a dull mess of lentils that had been hot for his lunch, washed down with a glass of milk and barley water. This same spirit of 'plain living, high thinking' pervaded the house as a whole. Rare, exotic furnishings usually turned out to be tea chests covered with flea market brocade. Signor's second wife, however, put him on

48 View and drawings of Sir Hamo Thornycroft's house and its neighbour, Melbury Road, Holland Park, by John Belcher, 1876–7. On the right: a house, gallery, and comprehensive complex of sculptors' workshops.

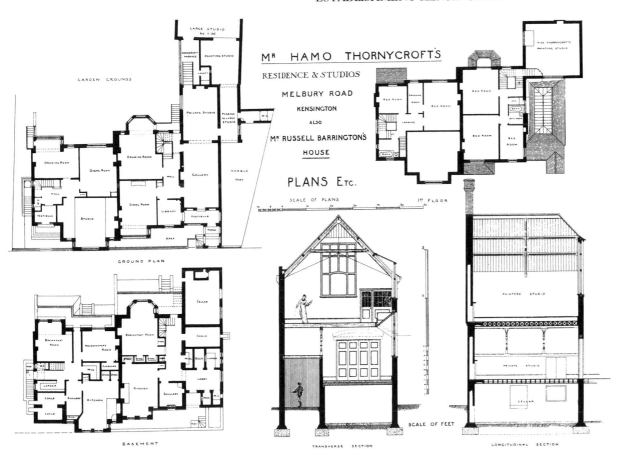

MR HAMO THORNYCROFT'S
RESIDENCE & STUDIOS
MELBURY ROAD
KENSINGTON
ALSO
MR RUSSELL BARRINGTON'S
HOUSE

PLANS ETC.

raw beef and wheeled in a real piano.

A bare month after Watts moved into 6 Melbury Road, proposals to build houses on the next two plots westward became known. Both houses, a dissimilar semi-detached pair, were commissioned from the architect John Belcher by the engineer-sculptor Thomas Thornycroft. Then on the point of retirement, Thomas had rounded off a profitable career with *Boadicea* and *Commerce* (Westminster Bridge[13] and Albert Memorial, London). Thomas's wife Mary was also a distinguished sculptor and still active. No. 4 Melbury Road was to be a painter's studio-house expressly for letting; No. 2, Moreton House, was for themselves and their grown-up children, four of them exhibiting painters or sculptors. Indeed, the most talented sculptor, (Sir) William Hamo, who turned 26 in 1876, was largely responsible for designing the attached complex of studios which were built simultaneously.

Belcher's two house plans show a healthy modernity. They are well lit, handily connected to the outside, hygienic and hospitable. There is even a smack of socialism about the basement breakfast rooms and the absence of back stairs. The punchy, asymmetric fronts, all in red, paraphrase native domestic styles with a resolute avoidance of superficial 'Queen Annery', **48**. Hamo Thornycroft's rearward sequence of workshops had its merits, too, not least in the separation of living rooms from drilling, hammering and grinding rooms. The inclusion and placement of the gallery, or Thornycroft Hall of Fame, was instrumental in this respect and others. As at Watts's house, it kept private and working life free of the incurious gatecrasher, allowing the artists to run working studios regardless of appearances. Moreover, since the gallery was used after hours as an extension of the drawing room, its homely furnishings lent the works on display an appropriate non-commercial setting. Adjoining the gallery – giving the option of doubling its area – lay Mrs Thornycroft's personal studio. Her single cut-up window, the cellar housing an apparatus for ducting warm air throughout the annexe, and the square, first floor painting room used by Alyce, Helen and Theresa Thornycroft can be seen in the cross-section. Beyond the conservatory corridor and a semi-enclosed shop for rough-hewing marble and carving pedestals opened the 'Large Studio' – 35′ × 30′ and soaring well over 30′ to the skylights. In here the sculpting Thornycrofts, including Alyce, supervised the scaling-up of their clay sketches, the forging of armatures, and the pouring and breaking of plaster moulds. A wide doorway on the garden side enabled work to be taken out into the open. Beyond again, stretching to the far garden fence, Hamo arranged a modelling room for himself, **49**. And, divided from the main body of this by a partition under the tall north-east side light, he positioned his study. Secreted in there, or at large on the little roof deck above it, he explored his ideas for *Teucer* (1882), the naturalistic *Mower* (1884), and memorials, e.g., *General Gordon* (1888).

Success came quickly to Hamo. He was elected ARA in 1881 and RA seven years later. Added to his sisters' increasing productivity, his marriage in 1885 and the multi-figure job of embellishing Belcher's Institute of Chartered Accountants building in the City (1889–93) gradually told on the capacity of No. 2. A convenient solution lay in the building of 2a, a new Neo-Baroque-style studio-house right next door, of which Belcher was again the designer in 1891.[14] Great and deserved popularity as a portrait sculptor, especially in the field of colonial monuments, kept Thornycroft 'full of work' into his seventies. By that stage he was no longer obliged to be polite to the Russell Barringtons, the tenants at No. 4. Mrs Barrington, the self-appointed biographer of Watts and Leighton, had been told about the possibility of renting the property even before it was built. Though she aspired to be an artist as well, she did not take advantage of the painting room in the house. Until a secluded studio was built for her at the bottom of the garden, she preferred to potter in Signor's Tin Pot next door.

Mrs Barrington was not the only person to have inside information on Melbury Road developments. William Burges secured the plot at No. 9, on which he spent the six years before his death building a polymesmeric replica of King René's honeymoon hotel, while almost opposite at No. 14 the marine painter Colin Hunter brought in his fellow Glaswegian, J J Stevenson, to design Queen Anne's resurrection pledge – Lugar Lodge.

Since Lugar Lodge represented an eleventh hour revision of Stevenson's original concept, not surprisingly the new scheme of 1876 still needed some ironing out. In practice, the constricted, sector-shaped site worked against a sprawling plan with a

49 Sir Hamo Thornycroft's personal studio with his den beyond the curtained north-east side light. A sketch of the *Turner Memorial* (1882) is on the modelling stand.

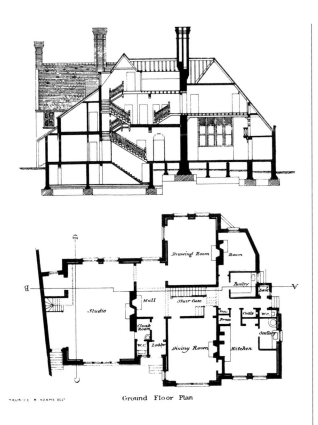

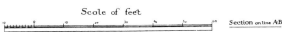

Scale of feet

Section on line A·B·

50 Drawings of Lugar Lodge, Colin Hunter's Melbury Road house, designed by J J Stevenson in 1876. An uneasy composition by a leader of the Queen Anne Revival.

ground floor studio and ground floor kitchen[15] (an arrangement theoretically more progressive still than Belcher's at No. 2), such that the outer rooms had to be squashed and staggered; uneasy roofs and ad hoc windows also appeared, and a low cellar became necessary anyway. But, behind Stevenson's façade with its terracotta appliqué contrived to disguise basically ungainly proportions, the Hunter family found a comfortable, if costly, house, **50**. From the day nursery across the road, the little Fildeses semaphored wildly to the little Hunters at the angle bay of theirs; on the quieter side of the house Colin Hunter waved gently at his canvases. Choosing to curtain off two south windows and having no skylights, he relied on a single gaping north light to brighten his relatively modest, sombre-toned studio. However, those two south windows were later made to look into a glasshouse. Seascape props could be redrawn here under a reproduction summer sky. Promontory views could be obtained from a gallery along the east side of the studio proper and, underneath, space remained for a cabin-like office, a models' room, and a vestibule to the models' side entrance.

Despite *Their Only Harvest* winning Chantrey Bequest selection in 1879, Hunter struggled to ARA in 1884 and rose no higher. Perhaps gawky Lugar Lodge possessed a lesser power to invite adulation than the Stone, Fildes or Thornycroft houses. (Watts's academic recognition was overdue when it came in 1867; he refused a baronetcy for the first time in 1885.) Yet what did it matter, when the fellow could set sail in a Mediterranean-bound yacht weeks before the Academy's sending-in day, his year's exhibits already sold and paid for at £300–£500 apiece?

In a sense, Melbury Road seemed to lead to Burlington House. But not every artist allowed himself to be affected by the craze for a red brick house in Holland Park.

After all, it was also said that Queen Anne Street led to Harley Street. While some wealthier types continued to submit to fashionable and autocratic architects, others chose instead to create striking individual interiors in mass-produced houses. Frank Dillon, for instance, pillaged the Near East on his painting expeditions, returning to construct a genuine Egyptian divan within the walls of 13 Upper Phillimore Gardens.[16] Linley Sambourne, the tirelessly inventive *Punch* cartoonist, took a typical Kensington house at 18 Stafford Terrace and furnished it to the hilt against a tastefully coordinated blur of pictures, papers and painted decoration. Of all the formal altars loaded with ornamental cruets and graven images on the first floor, his penman's laboratory at the rear offered the one true sanctuary.

Dillon settled in 1860, Sambourne in 1874. In the interim the slopes of Campden Hill summoned and dismissed more and more painters. Around 1867 (Sir) William Quiller Orchardson toyed with a garden studio at 1a Phillimore Gardens. R B Martineau died before he could benefit from a pavilion built for him on Gloucester Walk in 1869.[17] A little higher up, a similar fate was to befall Edward Sterling. Son of the Irish poet John Sterling and husband of Marcus Stone's sister, Edward bought a double plot at 18 (38) Sheffield Terrace. In 1876 he put his brief in the capable hands of Alfred Waterhouse, warning him that they were required by the lease to build at the scale and in the character of the adjacent houses. Totally ignoring the proviso, Waterhouse brought in W H Lascelles (also Stone's contractor) to set a blue-black wolf of a building amid the neighbouring grey-stuccoed sheep, **51**. Though it bares some Gothic fangs and a taut upper dewlap, the stone-muzzled bay gives a more accurate indication of the decorative character to be found within. A square plan at basement level slims to a broad rectangle under the roof. There the stack of expertly positioned compartments reduces itself to three: the stairwell in the back corner, a models' room behind the dog-ear gablet at the front, and a roomy north-lit studio about 30′ × 30′. Having forfeited a career in the army (during which he helped form the Artists' Rifles volunteer corps), Sterling was now showing his firm commitment to art by spending over £5500 on a thoroughly solid and well-equipped painter's house.[18] Very sadly, however, he died of a gastric ulcer in June 1877, just before the house was ready for occupation.

Another of the unfortunates living on Campden Hill was the portrait painter Henry Wells RA. Soon after his first move to this region Wells suffered the death of his wife, having already had his livelihood as a miniaturist handicapped by strained eyesight and 'photographic artists'. He battled back to prosperity nevertheless, taking a lease of Thorpe Lodge at the head of Airlie Gardens in 1874. By the end of the '70s he had joined on a studio worth £1500 to the designs of the church architect J L Pearson.[19] As much as for his portraits Wells is remembered for his saintly charm and his adenoidal advice to RA students concerning the importance of delicate brushwork, such as, 'Fload id od, by dear boy! Fload id od. A gossaber! A filb, a bere filb!'

Henry Wells actually ended up nicely placed between two renowned arty party-givers, Arthur Lewis at Moray Lodge, and George Boughton at West House, 118 Campden Hill Road. Boughton and his neighbour around the corner at 80 Peel Street, the landscape painter Matthew Ridley Corbet, both bought their plots in 1876.

51 Edward Sterling's 38 Sheffield Terrace, Kensington, by Alfred Waterhouse, 1876–7. 'A blue-black wolf of a building'.

House at Campden Hill Kensington.

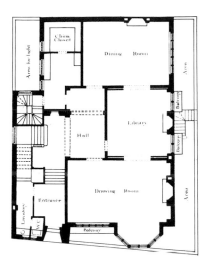

Plan of Ground Floor

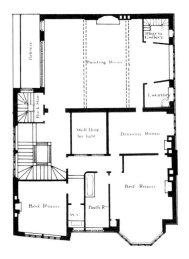

Plan of First Floor

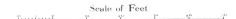

Scale of Feet

52 View and plans of George Boughton's West House, Campden Hill Road, Kensington, by Norman Shaw, 1877–8. Ridley Corbet's skew-sited 80 Peel Street is in the background.

Corbet built on his first, a simple pitched-roof shoebox with a studio along the short axis. It is not entirely ordinary, however, since the whole plan has been turned to face true north instead of meekly following the established street line. From the beginning friends – including Edwin Abbey and Matthew White Ridley – borrowed the house while Corbet was away sketching, and soon it was let permanently. (Sir) Frank Dicksee occupied it for 13 years from 1884.

West House, on the corner site next door, is a more pretentious affair. Like Stone and Fildes before him, Boughton was a rising painter appetitive of high society and Academy endorsement. To draw up his dowry he therefore applied to Norman Shaw who duly produced clever designs in 1877. Boughton's mean site and full brief forced Shaw to build against every boundary. Balconies had to compensate for a garden; only half the overall plan area could be given over to a studio, **52**. Perhaps at Boughton's request Shaw reverted from the swaggering urbanity of Fildes's house to the Wealden manor style he usually prescribed for his country clients. In consequence, a hauberk of red weather-tiles was pulled halfway on quite successfully, but the left sleeve came adrift at the shoulder. The exposed yellow skin of the midriff is pierced by traditional stone-framed leadlights, that of the arm by timber-framed ones in modish red brick surrounds. While further 'Queen Anne' motifs can be traced in the doorcase and balcony railings, a rarefied Sambourne touch characterised the original interiors.

53 Interior of the studio at West House. Boughton has forfeited the western side light in favour of a gold-lined alcove.

54 Sir John Millais' 2 Palace Gate, Kensington, by Philip C Hardwick, 1873–8. A massive scarlet and grey palazzo 'into which the Aestheticism of the day does not enter'.

George and Kate Boughton had rehearsed their decorating skills at Grove Lodge, Kensington Mall;[20] thus a certain reputation preceded the inevitable visit of the *Queen* reporter, Mrs Haweis. Turning into the drawing room at West House, Mrs Haweis attempted to explain its 'soft indescribable bloom' as the result of blending pinks and blues in the carpet, walls and frieze.[21] The mantelpiece, however, was painted 'in two yellows, like the primrose' – a scheme which drew the rider, 'That this does not clash with the blue and pink is strange, but true'. 'The *ensemble* of the room is decidedly mother-o'-pearl-like', she concluded. The Boughtons' reputation as generous hosts also advanced them and this accounted for the suite of reception rooms separated by sliding doors. Passing the first set into the nacreous greenness of the library, the tall wainscot was seen to be 'of such a green, or blue, as an infant pea forming in the pod'. Morris & Co. chintzes covered the furniture here, while in the dining room peacock blue upholstery complemented a general amber tone. Midway up the stairs Mrs Haweis paused at the mezzanine room over the entrance and continued towards the studio. There she found Shaw had recommended a gallery and wagon ceiling, **53**. Models, as usual, had been cunningly catered for. Upper parts of the room were finished in 'greyish drab' whereas the walls and recesses took on darker greys and gold linings. This combination properly set off Boughton's gilt-framed paintings, his colourful Eastern rugs and ceramics.

Compared to the leather-paper dados, the richly-figured burgundy wallpapers and the embroidered fabric friezes in Colin Hunter's house, Boughton's decor positively carolled with aesthetic refinement. Contrary to Mrs Haweis's final analysis, where

55 Plans of 2 Palace Gate. Servants and models are restricted to the back passages.

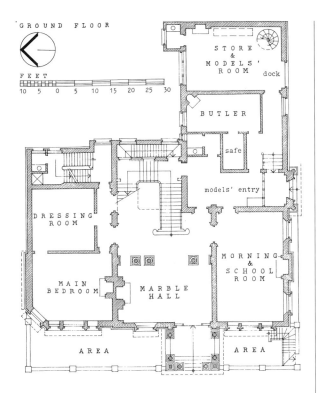

GROUND FLOOR

FEET
10 5 0 5 10 15 20 25 30

STORE
&
MODELS'
ROOM   dock

BUTLER

safe

models' entry

DRESSING
ROOM

MORNING
&
SCHOOL
ROOM

MAIN
BEDROOM   MARBLE
HALL

AREA   AREA

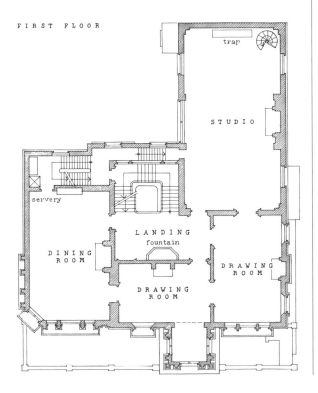

FIRST FLOOR

trap

STUDIO

servery

LANDING
fountain

DINING
ROOM

DRAWING
ROOM

DRAWING
ROOM

praise was accorded equally, it was far more worthy of him than his historical costume-pieces, like *Evangeline*, or his glossy, shampooed vamps, like *Black-eyed Susan*.

Further studio building ensued on and around Campden Hill, a good deal of it speculative,[22] especially where it amounted to studio-flats. Everyone was at it, from the hoi-polloi to the royal family. Keeping up with the Howards of Palace Green, the Dukes and Duchesses of Rutland converted an outbuilding at Bute House, opposite Tor Gardens. Probably the best use of this was made by the 8th Duchess, Violet – ethereal beauty, artistic Egeria of The Souls (the aristocratic fin de siècle literary circle), and a gifted painter-sculptress. Nearer to the Howards' home base, Princess Louise, another hobby sculptress, obtained an undemonstrative workshop from E W Godwin in the grounds of Kensington Palace. Sir Alfred Gilbert made use of Her Highness's facilities here following his return from Europe in 1926.

Whereas Princess Louise paid about £670 for her workshop, John Millais RA handed over ten times that amount for his new building site alone. The new house at 2 Palace Gate cost him maybe twice as much again. Millais' friend, the railway hotel architect P C Hardwick, had finished the drawings by July 1873 but it was not until 1878 that the well-qualified palace builders, Cubitt & Co., were finally discharged. When Thomas Carlyle came to sit for his portrait he was amazed to ascertain that 'mere paint' had financed it all. He went away muttering how many fools there were in the world. This double-edged remark was lost on Millais who believed he had very properly bought himself into the aristocracy – as, indeed, he nearly had.

2 Palace Gate differs from the Melbury Road houses in that it is really a reactionary's mansion by an old-fashioned architect, **54**. Racy red brickwork is outgunned by the Renaissance regalia in Portland stone, snazzy cherrywood joinery cancelled out by the quarryful of veined and rouge royale marble columns and revetments. Though the studio forms an essential part of the plan, it is more like a peninsula rescued from continental drift, and in no way does the house relate to a garden, **55**. Similarly, there is no subtlety about the approach from the splendiferous marble hall to the spacious piano nobile. Wrought iron scrollwork lines the broad stone steps ascending to a gaze-in-wonder landing watched over by a swart hydraulic seal. While Sunday sight-seers were shown from this to the studio, family and guests had the freedom of a suite of living rooms along the lines of Boughton's. The enormous dining room, or banqueting hall, and the middle drawing room give views straight up the Broad Walk of Kensington Gardens. All these saloons were richly fitted out and decorated with everything from horse brasses to a Giambologna relief. Millais himself designed the ironwork, panelling and carvings.[23] Parlour furniture overflowed into the studio where the un-English chalky white wall treatment changed to plain oak wainscots and maroon-bordered Beauvais tapestries. In like manner the 'cold Scotch accent . . . the drawling stoniness' of Effie Millais gave way to the chirpy throne-side banter of the nation's most cherished painter.

North light poured into the 50'-long studio through a whopping 16' × 11' plate glass window; steel roller shutters were used instead of blinds. Three small sun-burners, preferred to a single large one, allowed Millais to continue working after hours. Proof of overtime activity lay in a relentless press of groaning easels beyond the fireplace. If you had visited in the winter of 1881 you would have found portraits rubbed in on four of them and *Cinderella* on another. Behind the easels the architect had positioned a wide floor trap, like Leighton's, and a spiral staircase, both communicating with a fair-sized north-lit storeroom below. Combined here were provisions for the despatch of mammoth canvases and the reception of models. By the mid-1880s the Millais studio had become very big business. At this point his income was reckoned at £30 000 p.a. – or £100 a day, since nine weeks of the year were spent felling pheasants or hauling salmon from the Tay tributaries. In 1885 Millais became the first English artist to accept a baronetcy; in 1896 he took over the RA presidency from Lord Leighton but died in office the same year.[24]

Towards the end of the century it was difficult for prospective builders to find a vacant plot at any price in this eastern part of Kensington. Just the same, a sculptor named Edward Geflowski found one in Eldon Road. It was an unpromising slot

56 James Beadle's 17b Eldon Road, Kensington, by W H Collbran, 1882, and Edward Corbould's Eldon Lodge, Victoria Road, extended by Thomas Watson in 1863.

between No. 17a and the rear of Eldon Lodge, the corner house on Victoria Road built for Alfred Corbould. Edward Corbould, the watercolourist and royal drawing master who had succeeded Alfred there, had made it unpromising in 1868 by planting a very bulky, 'very modern Gothic' enlargement of his relative's studio against the eastern boundary.[25] When his building application was refused, Geflowski probably half-suspected the intolerance of the neighbours but was astounded to learn that the judgment came from a district surveyor all of 86 years old. Since he did not reapply, the site was sold to an officer in the Indian service, Major-General James Beadle, whose son of the same name was a student of painting still in his teens. No objections were received to the studio-house proposed on the Beadles' behalf by an entrepreneurial local architect, W H Collbran, and construction proceeded in 1882.[26]

Collbran politely took his cue from the adjoining Eldon Lodge which was not so much 'very modern Gothic' as blunt Neo-Tudor. A raw and bony but well-knit house of four storeys, No. 17b was lifted out of the ordinary by a last minute dab of chinoiserie in the form of a porch-top conservatory, **56**. Bespoke fittings in oak and mahogany likewise beefed up a basic Victorian interior framework. Dining and drawing rooms occupy the upper ground floor; above these lie the main bedroom and painting room, the latter dominated by a pair of plain, 15'-high windows. Young Beadle would seem to have been not quite up to 15'-high windows. Indeed, he did not immediately take full possession of No. 17b, finding himself either still committed to the Atelier Cabanel in Paris or to sketching assignments in the latest foreign war zone. Rather than let a fine studio lie idle, however, the experienced house-sitter Edwin Abbey was invited to keep it warm for Beadle's return. And while the highly-rated historical painter was there, the military specialist Richard Caton Woodville, another artist of American parentage, entered into a four-year tenancy of Eldon Lodge. With friends and Victoria Road neighbours like these, an expensive education begun under Boehm and finished by Watts, not to mention a £3000 house that begged to be filled by the frenzy of renown, James Prinsep Barnes Beadle might well have been remembered for several more major works than his pointed Boer War testament, *The Empty Saddle*.

Although Abbey soon found a permanent base of his own, he was also no stranger to the home of Gustav Natorp.[27] Art studies begun by this wealthy German bachelor at the Slade School when he was already over 40 were completed under Rodin in Paris. After a while he 'managed to have his works exhibited at the RA by means of influence and ghosting',[28] but he was always better known as a connoisseur, a gastronome, and the genial host of lavish Sunday beanos. For most of the 1880s the Natorp home was Grove Lodge, previously George Boughton's address, but by 1888 it was situated at 70 Ennismore Gardens, South Kensington.

No. 70 was a finely modelled wedding cake in the Jacobean, or 'Anglo-Jackson', style designed by T G Jackson's follower Basil Champneys. Champneys' earlier job for the Holidays in Hampstead bore no resemblance to it except in its organisation. Strict outward symmetry belied a looser pattern of internal spaces in two banks, the rearward bank subordinate to a full-width first floor studio, **57**. An outline balance was nevertheless restored to the major rooms through the use of ingle-nooks,

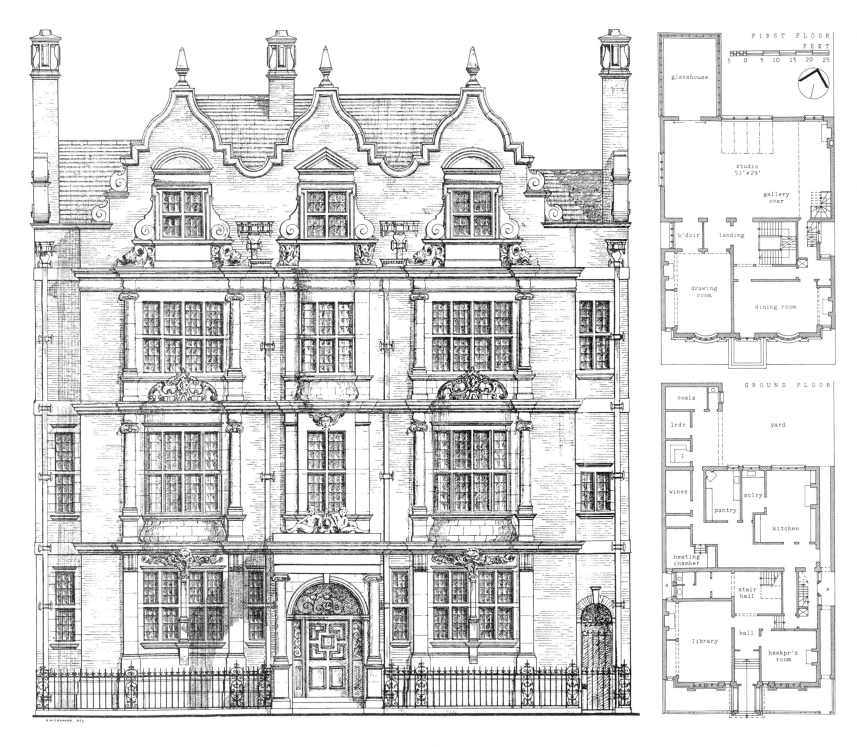

FIRST FLOOR

FEET
5 0 5 10 15 20 25

glasshouse

studio
51'x29'

gallery
over

b'doir   landing

drawing
room

dining room

GROUND FLOOR

coals

lrdr

yard

wines

sclry

pantry

kitchen

heating
chamber

a   a

stair
hall

library   hall

hsekpr's
room

R.W. GODDARD. DEL

alcoves and shaped ceilings. And though the front rooms gave only the slimmest view of the garden square, several openings were aligned to take advantage of the northern outlook towards Hyde Park. The 30-yard enfilade from drawing room through boudoir (a rarity in a bachelor's house) and studio to the glasshouse was also calculated to unravel knots of buffet guests.

Why Natorp needed a galleried studio bigger than Millais', plus a glasshouse, when his work ranged in size from medallions to statuettes, was open to question. However, fashionable people all over Kensington would do much less and still want a House Beautiful of the same kind – an artistic hypersalon in which to entertain and show off. These were the dilettante dupes and precious poseurs egged on by Oscar Wilde and Mrs Haweis only to be ridiculed by George du Maurier and W S Gilbert. Passionate Brompton, Voluptuous Belgravia and Delirious Chelsea had their fair share of Cimabue Browns and Russell Barringtons, too. In Chelsea, certainly, there was no need to go to such great expense:

> Though the Philistines might jostle, you would rank as an apostle
> in the high aesthetic band,
> If you swanned down Cheyne Walk with just a sunflower on a stalk
> in your medieval hand.

57 Front elevation and plans of Gustav Natorp's 70 Ennismore Gardens, South Kensington, designed by Basil Champneys in 1886. Neo-Jacobean splendour for a wealthy Hamburg-born bachelor.

5

AESTHETIC CHELSEA:
TITE STREET

ON THE whole, Chelsea society did not take itself as seriously as that of Kensington. New riches, however, could turn anyone's head, instilling an envy for the latest accessories of a fashionable social presence. By the time Lily Langtry, for instance, had sat to several painters and photographers, she saw that she might enhance her glamour by posing permanently in a studio atmosphere of her own. Accordingly she went to Oscar Wilde's friend Edward Godwin and in March 1882 obtained sketch designs of a very individual private house.[1] No sooner was this done than she backed down, but an anonymous design (financed, allegedly, by the Prince of Wales) was later built for her on the same site, a shallow gap in the north-east range of Cadogan Place. Godwin had proposed a five-storey house with Mrs Langtry's double-height studio-salon in the body of it. An equally tall bay was to have been hollowed out of this to provide an airy palm court overlooking the public gardens opposite. With brickwork striped like Jersey rock, a jaunty Arthurian oriel and a skittish Dutch dormer, the building would have made a cheerful splash in a dowdy neighbourhood.

It was not always so, nor would it be in the future. In the 1850s and '60s Sloane Street harboured a good number of vital characters: stone-carvers and sculptors operated in the backyards giving onto Pavilion Road; painters raised windows to face the east, and photographers erected glasshouses on the roofs. Painters already resident in Sloane Street when young Burne-Jones made his first London bridgehead at Sloane Terrace in 1856 included T M Joy and J B Burgess. Five years later the portraitist Felix Moscheles, son of Mendelssohn's fellow composer Ignaz, found a cottage that was actually situated on the Cadogan Place gardens – 'opposite 94 Sloane Street', as he used to say. His 'immense studio' there was frequently the venue for impromptu concerts by visiting European virtuosos.[2] Sculptors were represented by G Gamon Adams, whose uneven work issued from 126 Sloane Street from 1853 to 1885, by Charles Bacon and John Birnie Philip. Whereas the *Art Journal* was able to call Adams's *General Napier* (1856) 'perhaps the worst piece of sculpture in England', it completely gagged at the mention of Bacon's *Prince Albert* (1874). Bacon had set up shop at 121 Sloane Street in 1863. In this same year Birnie Philip applied to occupy the kitchen wing of 'The Pavilion', the architect Henry Holland's run-down mansion at the south end of Hans Place. Though heavily committed to reredorses and effigies, Philip had just agreed to sculpt 99 figures for the *Albert Memorial* in nearby Hyde Park. His residence was short-lived, however. Together with George Prince's exclusive sports club alongside, The Pavilion was demolished to make way for Pont Street West and Cadogan Square. Prince's Cricket Ground, Chelsea's rank-pulling answer to Lord's, likewise came to be buried beneath Lennox Gardens in the late 1870s.

Three or four other pioneers of the buff stuccoed terraces just beyond Prince's, notably the sculptor Thomas Earle (Vincent Street) and the painter Edwin Long (Ovington Square), had either died or passed on before the scarlet fever betokening the 'Queen Anne' vogue swept up to discomfort them. But Brompton figured more prominently in Chelsea's art history towards the end of the century. In the meantime artists occasioned a resurgence of interest in the riverside streets between the Royal Hospital and World's End. Although painters had established a very early association with Chelsea Reach, the first Academician in several decades to revisit it, in 1846, was William Dyce. He lived briefly at the upper end of Cheyne Walk, at No. 4. In due course Dyce was followed to the same house by his contemporary, Daniel Maclise, while in 1850 J M W Turner, alias Captain Booth, retired from life at the lower end, at No. 119. Outsiders came in plenty, however, not the least of them being John 'Mad' Martin who was still working on his *Last Judgment* series at Lindsey House, 95–100 Cheyne Walk, when he died in 1854. But somewhat better remembered characters were the occupants of No.s 101 and 16 – James McNeill Whistler and Dante Gabriel Rossetti.

Renewing a previous acquaintance with the river, the American-born Whistler settled into Lindsey Row in 1863 with two friends, his Irish model – *The Little White Girl* – Jo Heffernan and the French painter, Alphonse Legros. Within three years Legros had left his hosts in Lindsey House next door and the various masteries of Manet, Albert Moore and the Japanese printmakers had coalesced in Whistler's mature painting style. Even Gambart had called to make a £100 purchase. Further cultivation of aesthetic niceties would lead to the controversial portraits and night-scapes, the symphonic 'arrangements' and 'nocturnes', of the 1870s. Drawing on his new slant-eyed view of space and his supreme, natural colour-sense, Whistler set about decorating the Lindsey House flat. His favourite approach was to pitch vivid accents onto expanses of unpatterned pastel tints, delimiting the latter with substantial contrasting margins. In the drawing room, walls painted pinkish yellow were hemmed with white woodwork; in the dining room, pale blue was teamed with dark blue.[3] While a set of 15 kakemono-style posters was hung in formal array around this blue room, the sunless studio, gull grey edged in black, was selectively dotted about with warm-coloured Japanese prints and the odd cold etching, **58**. Furniture was deliberately kept to a minimum, elegant Oriental screens and cabinets forming the bulk of it. In the china department, however, Whistler's taste verged on that of Rossetti, since both men became maniacal and insatiable collectors of old Blue and White.

58 Walter Greaves, *Whistler in his Lindsey House studio, c.* 1871. Whistler reproduces the colour scheme of his painting room at Chelsea Reach in *The Artist's Mother.*

Widowed and desolate, Rossetti had meandered upstream from his Blackfriars Bridge tenement late in 1862. Proposing to console himself in company and great style, he bought a lease of Tudor House, a genuine Queen Anne house with a dozen bedrooms, an acre of garden, and remarkably cheap at £100 a year. Gabriel asked five members of his family to join the household, but everyone except brother William made their excuses when the rascally poet Swinburne was also invited. To help make up the numbers, the novelist George Meredith was prevailed upon to take two rooms while Gabriel's assistant, Walter Knewstub, was allotted another.

Against the odds, this literary brotherhood held together for the best part of a year and then Meredith bowed out.[4] As the others slipped away their quarters were turned over to Gabriel's numberless unusual pets; the woodchuck and the wombat (though it had a weakness for cigars and cut flowers) were seldom let out of doors. Gabriel himself shared the back room with a barn owl and a hatful of white mice. It was found too dim to paint in even in midsummer so that, as William solemnly recorded, 'after a while [my brother] got a considerable improvement introduced into the lighting'.[5] In July 1864, however, the intention was different. With commissions for large works in the offing, the painter was urgently quizzing Philip Webb about building a 'thoroughly good, but not showy studio' between the kangaroos and armadillos, in the garden. 'Would an iron thing be feasible. . .?' he asks.[6] But Webb proved to be elusive, the large works seemed never to materialise, and in the end nothing was put up except a tent for lunching and lounging in. Triggered by Morris, cajoled by Howell, or tickled by Fanny Cornforth, Rossetti could be the most engaging and inspiring of companions. 'No artist, you know, but charming and a gentleman', offered Whistler. He made many friends – in the hopeful '60s some had keenly followed him to Chelsea, among them the painters Boyce, Smetham and Bell Scott – though few stood by him in the reclusive whisky-and-chloral funk of his latter days.

George Price Boyce, the son of a prosperous pawnbroker, had already trailed Rossetti to his former lodgings only to find them due for demolition. After 1864, then, he was hovering around Cheyne Walk in search of new accommodation. His flimsy topographical watercolours were selling well enough for him to consider building a small house of his own. Having himself been an architectural improver, he chose his consultant as carefully as he did his site. Philip Webb was preferred to Burges and Godwin, probably on account of his recent fine showing in Holland Park for Val Prinsep. The site consisted of the bluebell-bordered asparagus beds in the garden of Chelsea Old Church rectory. One corner of it touched Glebe Place, presenting a vista down Cheyne Row to the river. Boyce received Webb's estimate of £1843 on 20 March 1869; on 3 March 1870 he slept in West House for the first time.[7]

Although he was neither constrained to play up to a blue-blood nor forced to build in stone against his will, Boyce's commission allowed Webb another masochistic spree. West House showed a return to the economical use of red bricks and plain tiles but, just to compensate for loss of aggravation, Webb reverted to the strictly square overall layout he had adopted for Prinsep; it was an even smaller square demanding even tighter planning. To the great good of the design, however, the front door was brought forward to the pavement in a three-storeyed porch. Within the square, the house was divided into four main parts, each of them distinguished externally by axial window groups. Two parts faced a walled garden on the west; the studio was principally lit from the north through sashes approaching the size of Romney's, **59**. Unlike Prinsep, Boyce did not need a studio that stretched right across the plan. Space was left at the blind end for a models' refuge reached from the back stairs. (Since Boyce was an incurably weak figure-drawer, he did not really need this either.) Alternative access lay beneath another redundant, but quaint feature: the gallery. Sparsely balustered and propped on contrary oak shafts, it occasionally elevated musicians invited to play the ancient instruments of which Boyce was a keen collector.

Though not without its bright spots, the house was darkly finished and furnished. Densely patterned Morris papers and low-toned – including the inimitable juniper green[8] – paintwork were consistent with the black-pointed brickwork of the entrance and stair halls. In nearly every room, however, Webb, renowned for designing stone mouldings with the stoniest of profiles, provided a flinty, ash grey fireplace. Larger ones might be lined with Delft tiles; corner ones, like that in the dressing room, possessed all the craftiness of a mason's handshake. This dressing room and the dining room bay were added in 1876, in the year following Boyce's marriage to Augustine Soubeyran. The former, with its midget gablets and foolscap attic lights, unfortunately spoiled a three-way view from the purposefully placed stair landing. But even from the back of the studio the Boyces could still look down at William de Morgan's lustreware kiln in Cheyne Row or, beyond, to the gleety Thames. Sadly, typhoid got the better of the painter in the end; he died in 1897. Two of the Glasgow Boys, (Sir) James Guthrie and E A Walton, obtained a tenancy of West House later the same year.[9]

While 'Webb's Wonder' remained Chelsea's sole studio-house for nearly ten years, local garden studios had, as usual, preceded it. Giovanni Fontana, a not inconsiderable sculptor who eventually made his mark, more than anywhere else, in New South Wales, had built behind the eastern Glebe Place – King's Road corner in 1865. In the following year, the Scots historical painter and spiritualist Robert Hannah had made sizeable additions at 153 Old Church Street. And in 1870 Birnie Philip had again begun moving his works to another seedy villa, this time in Manresa Road. Boyce's neighbourhood would eventually become choked by artists, but for the time being more far-reaching events were unfolding down by the Chelsea Physic Garden. The Metropolitan Board of Works was releasing building plots hereabouts after embanking the Thames to the far end of Cheyne Walk. Well-heeled parties snapped up the riverfront property first, engaging architects prepared to work in the favoured

59 Drawings of George Boyce's West House, Glebe Place, Chelsea, by Philip Webb, 1868–76. Cussedness and crossbred styling contribute to extreme particularlity within a remarkable unity.

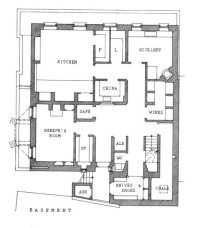

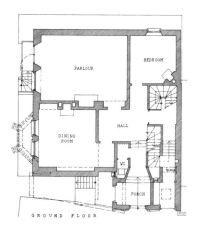

'Queen Anne' style. Edward Godwin designed 4, 5 and 6 Chelsea Embankment; Bodley & Garner, I'Anson and Shaw designed some others. No. 7, built in 1878–9 for the judge Sir Robert Collier, later 1st Baron Monkswell, was a rare essay by Phené Spiers, architectural master at the RA.

Described in the building press as a 'mansion',[10] No. 7 is indeed practically a Victorian country house brought to town. Its chief interest, in fact, lies in the combined male preserve and honeymoon suite facing Dilke Street at the rear. On the ground floor, Spiers provided a billiard room with a small north-lit annexe where Sir Robert could tune up his holiday sketches. Upstairs he planned an almost self-contained flat for Sir Robert's younger son, John Collier, who was about to marry Marian Huxley. Both fiancés being professional portrait and figure painters, the flat was mostly taken up by a proper painting room complete with models' facilities and separate access. But living in a mews, and subject to his parents, soon inclined John to save up for a house of his own. He formed a fair idea of what to build by looking across Dilke Street to Tite Street.

SECTION B–B

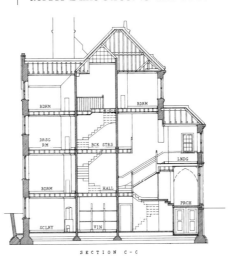

SECTION C–C

STREET ELEVATION

FEET

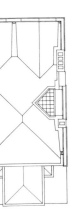

FIRST FLOOR

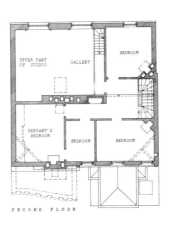

SECOND FLOOR

Tite Street was, and perhaps always will be, synonymous with Whistler and The White House. From his 'unfurnished symphony' in Lindsey House, Whistler had lately made a considerable name for himself. The portraits of his mother and Thomas Carlyle – mere excuses, he argued, to compose pleasing settings in grey and black – had made nearly as much impact as the colour-coordinated Japanese happening he had organised for his first one-man show on Pall Mall. Orders for portraits and decorative schemes were trickling in, etchings and engravings were selling, money was accumulating. Another sideline involved him in the painting of furniture designed by Godwin, the one architect with whom he ever saw eye-to-eye. These minor successes swelled Whistler's head enormously, but it took a fellow American to describe his colossal conceit as 'so colossal that it is really delightful, and – cheek!'[11] Once convinced of his importance to the future of British art, the Master resolved to construct an exemplary arrangement in bricks and mortar: Godwin would translate his aesthetic theories into a house and teaching atelier. And neither his break with F R Leyland in the sequel to *The Peacock Room* decorations, nor Ruskin's libellous damnation of *The Falling Rocket* picture, nor the resultant abatement of sales in general, nor the cretinous behaviour of the Board of Works were going to put him off his stride. But from the spring of 1877 to the autumn of 1879 he would have to inveigh against the Philistines all the way.

Whistler's leasehold site in Tite Street backed onto the Royal Hospital gardens, allowing a sidelong view of the river. Godwin, who was to attempt to solve the studio-house problem for the first time, received his brief and a cost limit (about £1700) in the summer of 1877. Most of the architect's preliminary designs left the teaching studio adrift of a main block containing a smaller personal studio, but by September he had compressed all the accommodation into one three-storey volume with the larger studio, measuring 47′ × 29′, under a tip-tilted roof. There was nothing especially unusual about the planning except the clumsiness of the stairs, a recurrent Godwin foible, **60**. It was the street front which was so extraordinary. Inspectors from the Board of Works compared it to 'a deadhouse'; they complained that it was 'all roof'[12] and demanded the addition of modelled ornament. Conceit playing its part, their absurd demand was treated lightly until, in February 1878 when the structure was nearly complete, they threatened to withold the lease.[13]

At this point, the façade still had the smooth texture and graphic balance of line, form and colour both Godwin and Whistler intended. With only a storeyed porch rising above it and the Portland stone doorcase, a rectilinear field of white brickwork and assorted white plaster panels underscored a fine expanse of grey-green slating. Openings were as precisely positioned in the field as the prints on the wall at Lindsey House – no more in answer to functional requirements than the combined effect of their size, shape and number. 'Art for Art's Sake', in other words. Framed in white or grey against blinds of white or primrose and lipped with red stone sills, the windows blinked blearily beside the gleaming peacock blue doors: a chromatic scherzo played over the pallid undertones of a revolutionary fantasia, **61**.

But, like Webb and Howard at Palace Green, Godwin and Whistler were compelled to compromise. New elevation drawings were submitted and approved. Reconstruc-

60 Cross-section and plans of The White House, Tite Street, Chelsea, for James Whistler by Edward Godwin, 1877–8. Godwin regarded a studio as 'at once a workshop, a reception room and an exhibition building, and designed it accordingly'.

61 Front elevation of The White House as proposed in September 1877 – with 'the smooth texture and graphic balance of line, form and colour that both Godwin and Whistler intended'.

tion proceeded whereby the parapets were raised to reduce the apparent extent of the roof, moulded brick surrounds were added to selected windows, and areas were set aside for sculptural embellishments. While the rejection of the plaster panels and the admission of modelled ornament were regrettable, the new asymmetrical arrangement of the parapets improved the design considerably, **68**.[14] Yet Whistler could not bring himself to appoint, let alone afford, a sculptor. Consequently the lease was still unforthcoming. After a heated exchange, it was finally granted upon the condition the work would be done within a year.[15] But it never was; nor were a number of interior jobs, and no wonder. Whistler was obliged to pay £1910 according to the first estimate, £920 for the reconstruction, and then the contractor, B E Nightingale, asked another £635 for 'overages'.[16] 'The Nightingale hath soured his song', moaned the obdurate painter who was already existing on credit and facing a torturous mortgage.

Financial embarrassment did not stop Whistler, assisted by a butler and his first lady Maud Franklin, extending a typically eccentric hospitality at The White House. His 11.45 a.m. Sunday breakfasts became as famous for their conviviality as their

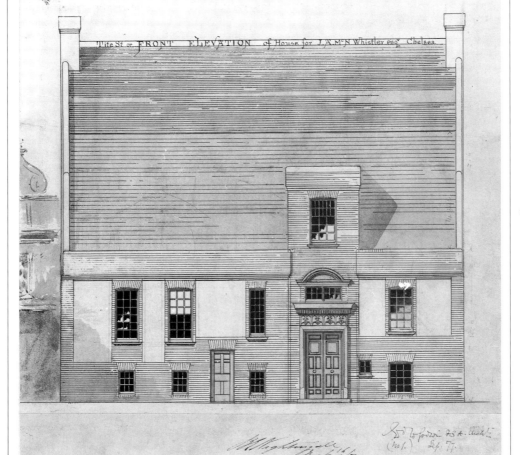

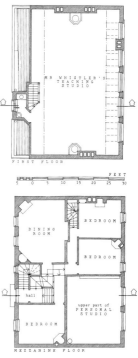

menus. The latter might consist of buckwheat cakes toasted by Whistler himself, mint juleps ditto, or merely the contemplation of goldfish in a bowl. Certainly it was quite easy to conjure the sanctity of a tea ceremony in rooms so sparingly decorated with the shippô from Lindsey House. Casual callers, other than creditors of course, were also encouraged to inspect the Master's latest creation. Charles Dowdeswell, the art dealer, remarked on the terracotta tone of the lower studio walls and the matching serge covers on gilt and ebonised Godwin furniture. Edwin Abbey climbed the breakneck stairs with their Japanese balustrades to the teaching studio, finding 'an immense room with white walls and one side all windows like a bare country church'.[17]

Apart from painting and etching equipment the studios remained bare. Sitters stayed away and Whistler's only students were the bailiffs who came to mind him once his bankruptcy had been fully proven. This was already imminent in late November when he brought his legal action against Ruskin, won token damages, but was denied costs. Yet another six months of reckless living would follow before his effects were carried off at auction. In September 1879 he cleared his name by selling the house to the Philistine enemy for an unrealistic £2700. Rossetti gibed:

> Alas for Jimmy Whistler! What harbour of refuge now, unless to turn Fire King at Cremorne? . . . A Nocturne Andante in the direction of the Sandwich Islands, or some country where tattooing pure and simple is the national school of Art . . .?[18]

Not quite; advanced a small sum by the Fine Art Society, the Master and Maud stumped off to Venice, not to return for over a year.

Early in 1878, while The White House was being built, Godwin began designs for a Tite Street site directly opposite. The Hon. Archibald Stuart-Wortley commissioned a double house, Chelsea Lodge, with two studios, one for himself, the other for his friend Carlo Pellegrini – better known as 'Ape', the captious caricaturist of *Vanity Fair*. Due mainly to a common interest in blood sports, Stuart-Wortley, a grandson of Lords Wharncliffe and Wenlock, had studied painting under Millais. Besides hunting subjects he also painted portraits, becoming both an authority on the grouse and a specialist in sporting personalities. His links with the Beefsteak Club and the Grosvenor Gallery put him in touch with Pellegrini and Whistler. As for Ape, his admiration for all things Whistlerian was as strong as his attachment to Archie. This meant he had to take up Whistler-style portraiture and they had to set up house together. And nowhere but in a Tite Street studio by Godwin could he be close enough to his inspiration.

Godwin struggled to find a satisfactory solution for the difficult Dilke Street corner until another small plot was added to the north.[19] From then on the scheme went unhampered, Nightingale simply moving his plant across the road to start building in June 1878. Allowing for the oddity of the site and the brief, Godwin's architecture was straightforward, if somewhat severe and chunky, **62**, **63**. Evidently the smooth red and rough yellow brickwork together with the fashionably curly Dutch gables

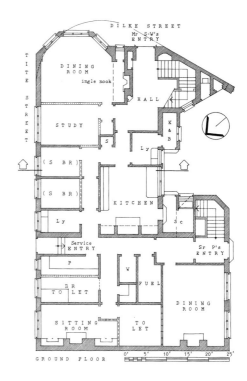

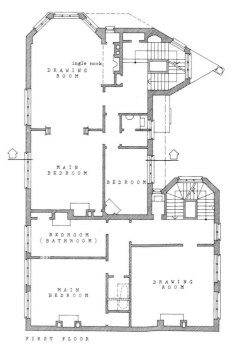

62 Plans and section of the Stuart-Wortley–Pellegrini house (Chelsea Lodge), Tite Street, by Edward Godwin, 1878. Alterations for the Hon. Slingsby Bethell soon obscured the workings of this double household.

63 Chelsea Lodge, as altered for the use of Slingsby Bethell, Edwin Abbey RA, and subsequently.

satisfied the Board of Works with regard to ornament. Nonetheless, the roofs were just as dominant as Whistler's and the windows, though orderly and standardised, seem to have been caught shuffling off to a suspect Oriental rhythm. The plans show the extent to which the two households were communal, particularly on the ground floor. Both studios were originally similar in size and shape to Whistler's atelier and neither had galleries. Pellegrini had told Godwin, 'I wish to have nothing but light – walls and roof and everything',[20] and up to a point he got it. His companion settled for two 16'-high side lights and a sunny bay. Few Japanese features could be detected but Godwin took every opportunity to frame alcoves and doorways with his distinctly un-English architrave-mantel-shelves.

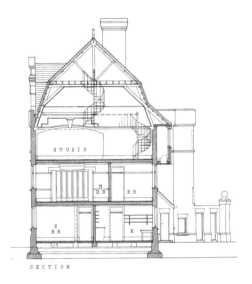

SECTION

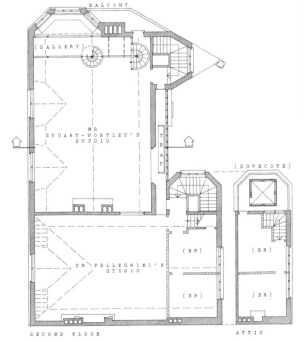

SECOND FLOOR   ATTIC

63

One way or another the Archie-Ape cooperative was too unlikely to succeed; after about six months it broke down. Chelsea Lodge was sold in August 1879 and in October work started on a completely new house across the street for Archie alone. Perhaps he had heard society whispering of scandal and decided to withdraw defensively behind his title in a castle of his own. Ape had trouble changing into a Butterfly, especially after Whistler himself had been all but disgraced. Unable to retain and convert his share of the house he took up part-time cartooning again and slipped back into Mayfair. He remained loyal, however, to Archie – the sole benefactor of a meagre will announced at his death ten years later.[21]

Chelsea Lodge was bought by the Hon. Slingsby Bethell, younger son of Lord Westbury. Bethell looked on himself less as a barrister and clerk in the Lords as a member of the aesthetic peerage. Keen to have a riverside studio at least the equal of Lord Monkswell's, he almost agreed to engage Godwin to build him a whole block of them next to The White House. In the end he preferred to have the architect enlarge and gentrify this one. Bethell and his son Lionel were occasional painters, so he retained part of the northern studio; the southern one, recast as a grand saloon, was spanned by a minstrels' gallery. Other whimsical additions included a charmed-snake stairway to an attic with a fo'c'sle window, and a dovecote over a one-man smoking room. Sir Alfred Wills succeeded Bethell in 1891 and Edwin Abbey RA took over from

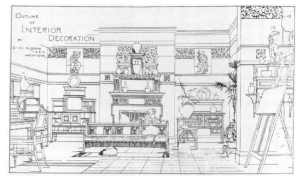

64

65

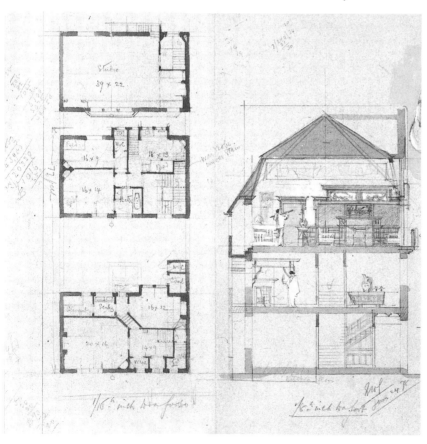

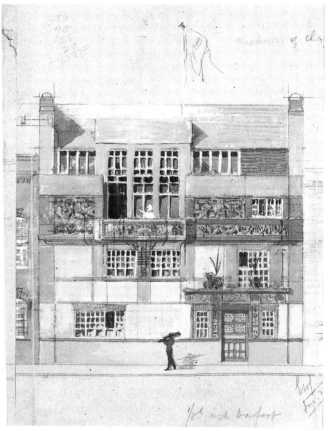

64   Decoration and furniture designed by Edward Godwin prior to 1881 in an arrangement typical of Aesthetic School publicity.

65   Edward Godwin's preliminary designs for the Frank Miles house, 26(44) Tite Street, Chelsea, March 1878 – architecture some 30 years ahead of its time.

66   Front elevation of Frank Miles's Keats House, Tite Street. Forced to alter his radical initial proposals, Godwin came up with a design no one could possibly dislike.

66

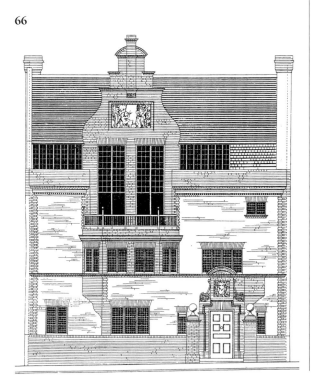

him in 1899. No doubt it was Abbey who reunited the studios and broke in the extra window between the twin gables.

Notwithstanding official restraint and the possibly ruinous consequences of its adoption, the Whistler–Godwin style in art and architecture was undeniably catching, **64**. Commentators such as Mrs Haweis, who only the day before was gushing over the sugary prettiness of George Boughton's Campden Hill interiors, was now urging people tired of ornament, whether mismanaged or simply excessive, to revert to plain surfaces. She wrote in 1880:

> A fashion for plainness and simplicity in decoration is convenient in more ways than one. It is convenient to the new-made *virtuoso* who likes it because it may imply that he could have done the contrary if he had chosen; convenient to those born without taste for it saves them fiascos; convenient to the impecunious, for it saves them money; convenient to decorators who have crept into notice by good luck, not merit . . . for it saves them trouble.[22]

Summing up, she extolled '. . . the whole *farouche* protest against "shaped" and blazoned vulgarity; we know it is aesthetic, and let us be aesthetic or we are nothing'.

To Frank Miles and Oscar Wilde, the two young bucks who next struck out for Tite Street, this rallying cry was already a creed. Miles was a vicar's son of wealthy and artistic West Country family. He was winning acclaim for his seascapes and chalk portraits when Wilde, a friend of some years' standing, came down from Oxford to share his lodgings off the Strand. Together they transferred to Miles's Keats House in August 1880. Proposals, again by Godwin, for the new studio-house had been tabled more than two years earlier but the Board of Works had refused to pass them. 'Why,' the Board members spluttered, 'this is worse than Whistler's!'[23] Godwin, however, thought it the best design he had ever produced. He had good reason: even today it could be mistaken for a sketch of around 1905 by Frank Lloyd Wright, **65**.

While owing much to the original White House scheme in terms of outline and surface variegation, Godwin's initial proposal here was markedly more daring in its asymmetrical distribution of windows. The balconies, though they derived from Chelsea Lodge, were also requested by Miles, an avid gardener who wanted places to exercise delicate imported plants. On his drawings, Godwin showed them copiously enriched in the hope of forestalling the censure of the Board. Obviously it could not have been a lack of relief to which the authorities objected so much as a lack of 'shaped and blazoned vulgarity'. The modernistic stratification and capricious play of solid and void clearly confounded the 'retired farriers and cheesemongers who never drew a line nor saw a drawing until yesterday' as Godwin styled them. Obliged to get the design approved, however, he 'introduced a number of reminiscences of a visit to Holland and', naturally, 'the thing was pronounced charming'.[24]

Along with the sinuous treatment of the north light gable, the majority of the initial angularity was softened by a lighter touch in the detailing, **66**. The windows were rationalised, too, although the winsome effect of a new canted bay was achieved at

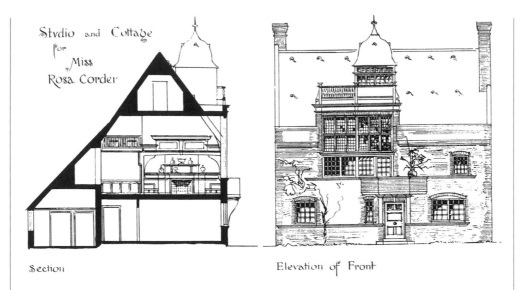

Studio and Cottage for Miss Rosa Corder

Section

Elevation of Front

67 The sou'-wester section and pretty front elevation of the projected studio-cottage for Rosa Corder, by Edward Godwin, 1879.

the expense of the middle floor planning. Godwin atoned for this by specifying variations on the Anglo-Japanese fittings devised for Whistler.[25] Miles, in turn, took the fashion to extremes, dressing his maid like a geisha on the occasion of his 'studio teas'. If guests strode up unannounced and Frank and Oscar were caught unprepared, Oscar could always resort to a secret staircase which dog-legged down to his bedroom.

One of the worthier works of art to emerge from Keats House was Wilde's *Poems*, first published in 1881. Soon afterwards the author left to expound his genius in America but he returned to 16 (34) Tite Street, five doors up, three years later. Wilde had bought a lease of this ready-made terraced house on his marriage in 1884, asking Godwin to decorate and furnish it. A rather off-beat scheme was evolved[26] which transformed a second-hand Castle Bunthorne into the original House Beautiful. The Wildes lived here until Oscar's imprisonment, outstaying Frank Miles who was removed to a lunatic asylum four years before his early death in 1891. Miles's house was let to the Misses Dixon, a trio of lady artists. In 1892 it was bought for G P Jacomb-Hood, illustrator and painter, who raised the roof and had top lights put in.[27]

Back in mid-1879 not all the Tite Street plots had yet been spoken for. It was then, angling for another client, that the self-same Godwin secured an option on a small one south of Miles's. Perhaps a less devious approach than this would not have seen the shameless swindler, Charles 'It's-all-profit-to-me' Howell, rising to the bait. As Ruskin's secretary, or Whistler's salesman, or Burne-Jones's guard dog, or exhumer of Rossetti's poems, Howell cropped up everywhere.[28] Only he could have raised and then dropped the idea of building a studio-cottage for his mistress and protégée, Rosa Corder. Howell had already installed her in Newmarket where she painted racehorses, and in the West End where she faked Fuselis and Rossettis. Miss Corder, whose 'wonderful pale hair . . . lay upon the ground several inches when she was standing',[29] had recently been the subject of a Whistler portrait – somehow paid for by Howell with the Master's own money. Thus she was familiar with the ups and downs of Tite Street. By the time Howell had wriggled off the hook, Godwin's project had advanced some way beyond the published drawings. It was to have been a two-storey version of the Miles house with a cosmetic femininity created by throwing in a few more conciliatory reminiscences of the trip to Holland. The sou'-wester section revealed the Japanese influence still present, but a new departure was the models' open gallery on the way up to the belvedere and balcony, **67**.

While the Corder project came to nothing, Godwin was soon able to get the unqualified go-ahead for the second Stuart-Wortley house. Construction of Canwell House began late in 1879 at 9(29) Tite Street, three doors up from The White House, (see **121** map). Godwin's powers of invention were not deserting him, but Canwell House seemed to concede tiredly to conventional taste, not to say the Norman Shaw manner, **68**. Red and yellow brickwork resurfaced together with the well-tried

68 East side of Tite Street, Chelsea, in May 1880. From left, Canwell House for Archibald Stuart-Wortley, 1879–80; house for Frank Dicey, 1880 (rusticated pilasters); projected studio-flats offered to Slingsby Bethell, 1879 (archway and tower); The White House as built, 1877–8.

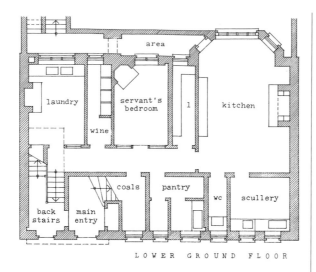

LOWER GROUND FLOOR

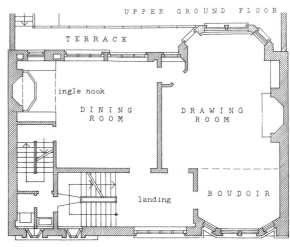

69 Plans of Archibald Stuart-Wortley's second Tite Street venture, Canwell House, by Edward Godwin, 1879–80. 'Godwin's powers of invention were not deserting him'.

parapet, syncopated like the sill and drip courses. But mullions and transoms had become endemic while fancy bay windows and tile-hanging were also taking hold. Nonetheless, the small-scale incident usefully fragmented the bulk of the five-storey building. In a similar way, the larger internal spaces were made more intimate by introducing nooks and recesses. A range of rooms fuller than that at Chelsea Lodge suggests Stuart-Wortley was either intending to fill the house with children or carefully considering resale prospects, **69**. To the first end he married the comic actress Nelly Bromley in 1883, a date transparently soon after his father's death. But there was no holding him; being the elder son may have obliged him to attend to the family's Yorkshire estates. In 1885 Canwell House passed to Miss Mary Grant, a gifted and dogged old sculptress. Miss Grant was replaced after 1901 or so by the Quaker portraitist Percy Bigland who, meeting diminishing success, later sold out to the Victoria Hospital adjacent and went to farm chickens in Buckinghamshire.

Meanwhile the two plots between Canwell House and The White House, No.s 31–33, had found firm buyers. In 1880 a studio-house went up at No. 31 and a block of studio-flats at No. 33, both designed by Col. Robert Edis. The house builder, Frank Dicey, a minor figure on the French side of Whistler's acquaintance, netted Edis at the end of the protracted leasehold negotiations. Although the house was smallish – hardly more than a bedroom and rear dining room under a studio-salon – the architect used plenty of 'Queen Anne' trimmings to make it look imposing. On the garden side, dozens of 2′ square panes tumbled down from a gambrel roof, little changed from the sort he had given Woolner 20 years earlier. Somewhat Frenchified decor foreshadowing the recommendations of Edis's handbook, *Decoration and Furniture of Town Houses* (1881), endowed the interior.

Frank Dicey left No. 31 shortly before his death in 1888. In 1901 it was bought by John Singer Sargent, who, remarkably enough, had coped for the previous 15 years in minimal quarters alongside on the ground floor of No. 33.[30] These quarters were taken from Whistler who was the first to occupy them upon his return from Venice. It

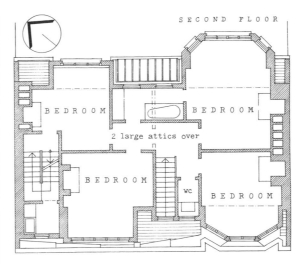

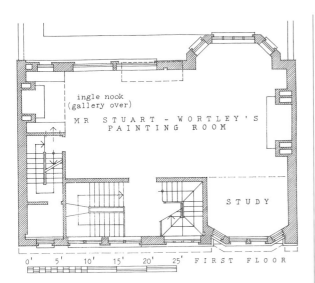

70 Tite Street studio-houses for the Hon. John Collier (left) and Anna Lea Merritt, both designed by F S Waller & Sons, 1881–2. Genteel Jacobean versus the callow and brash.

was in that city that Whistler realised his countryman might pose a threat to the impact of his British comeback, although Sargent had no intention of settling in England then. 'Don't fret, Jimmy,' joked Harry Woods,[31] 'one sergeant doesn't make a battalion any more than one whistler makes an orchestra.' Sargent kept on the suite at No. 33, knocking through the party wall with No. 31 to provide intercommunication. In 1897 he was elected RA, a dubious honour in disestablishment Tite Street. Ten years later, exasperated by la-di-da sitters queuing on both sides of the Atlantic, he could honestly admit, 'I HATE DOING PAUGHTRAITS!'[32] What did it matter; he was already a dollar millionaire by then.

When 31–33 Tite Street were being built, vacant plots were still on offer opposite at No.s 50 and 52. These were simultaneously bought by Mrs Anna Lea Merritt and the John Colliers. Anna Lea, widow of the critic and highly regarded picture restorer Henry Merritt, was another American figure painter. Having been Whistler's neighbour at Lindsey House, she knew about Tite Street. She then fell in with the newly wed Colliers who were living over their Dilke Street mews. The upshot was that in 1881 both parties asked Mrs Collier's brother-in-law, Frederick W Waller,[33] to design studio-houses side by side, **70**. No. 50, which Mrs Merritt pretentiously named The Cottage, took on an appearance not unlike the Dicey house, though decidedly more callow and brash. So barefaced is it that the Board of Works must have lost its nerve to insist on sculptural decoration. Halls lead from the front and side entrances to meet in the centre of the deep, square living–dining–main bedroom floor. Stairs rise a further three flights to a gallery commanding the barn-like studio. Would-be Oriental balustrades here only emphasise how roughly the provincial architect had grasped the finer points of the Aesthetic approach. By contrast Mrs Merritt was a well-schooled artist, but her allegorical pieces, like *War* (1883) and *Love Locked Out* (1889), had a soppiness that belied their earnest titles. After a stay of ten years she moved to Andover; the same Percy Bigland who later bought Canwell House took this one in the meantime.

Ten years in Tite Street often proved quite long enough. John and Marian Collier remained just five years before Marian tragically went mad and died. John's mother, Lady Monkswell, then disowned him for the very idea of proposing to marry Marian's sister, Ethel. Undeterred, John and Ethel eloped to America, married in 1889 and returned to build a new house near Swiss Cottage where, as John said, 'nobody cared what you did'. Earlier in the decade he was reasonably concerned what you did so that, inside and out, No. 52 – More House – strikes a typically Victorian eclectic compromise. Social dissipation represented by the loose 'Queen Anne' styling confronts moral responsibility represented by genteel Jacobean. Accordingly, a few showpieces of pinkish carved stonework were volunteered to tone up the usual mixture of red and yellow brickwork. Answering the prominence of the porch on the left, the chief of these is a bracketed skylit bay on the right. The trade-offs continue inside. Because individual comforts came first, the common staircase was narrowed to such a degree that bigger paintings had to be despatched through a trap in the studio floor above a passage leading to the service entrance. Generous models' facilities and grandstand galleries like Mrs Merritt's find no place, but an ingle-nook and conservatory amply compensate. In the same vein, though plain oak joinery prevails, Waller has licensed the odd star turn in the major rooms.

More House enabled John Collier to make a name for himself before misfortune visited. Thinly disguised excuses to pose nude girls, such as *Pharaoh's Handmaidens* (1883), interspersed publication of two painting manuals and the usual round of portraits. After Collier's departure a naval man, Captain Jephson, lived in the house. He made some alterations of a nautical flavour before selling to Laura and Adrian Hope in 1892. Laura was the artist, painting fairies and pastel portraits of children in Frank Miles's manner. A command to paint 22 of Queen Victoria's grandchildren made her reputation in one swoop; beauty and poise made her the doyenne of Hyde Park's society cyclists. In view of the name Tite Street had gained, it was ironic that Mr Hope should be appointed joint guardian with Mrs Wilde of Oscar's children after the débâcle of 1895.[34]

At least one other unexpected relationship was established in this ethical toboggan of a street. At No. 54 nestled shy little Dhu House, a dwelling taken early in the piece by Mrs Frances Birnie Philip. Having become Godwin's mother-in-law in 1876 she will have watched with wry amusement as his egregious buildings rose around her. Ten years later she renewed her role when Godwin's widow remarried Whistler, leading show pony in the same circus.

Whistler nearly passed over Beatrix Godwin in favour of Louise Jopling, another of his portrait subjects and herself a tolerable painter. Before she married the water-colourist Joe Jopling, Louise also drew the admiration of William Burges. In 1879 Burges was consoled by the task of designing a pair of garden studios for Louise and Joe behind 28 Beaufort Street. By the spring of 1880 Louise was pleased to say hers was 'a delightful room to work in, and big enough to make my piano, a large grand, look lost in it'.[35] Burges's muscular Gothic style must have been in evidence because, when Joe died suddenly in 1884 and Louise could no longer afford to keep the property, the studios were readily converted into a Catholic chapel. Before they changed hands, Louise let one to the languorous Circe whom Burne-Jones had tangled with, the budding sculptress Maria Zambaco.

Returning to the Belgravia side of Chelsea in the early 1880s, one would have appreciated great changes. Though substantially built up, Cadogan Square had not quite taken its final shape. When it did, F W Lawson, an industrious illustrator and social-realist painter, ended up at No. 61a more or less by accident. Having built against the pavement at 40 Cadogan Terrace in 1881, he awoke one morning soon afterwards to find a service road in the south-east corner of the square laid across his back garden. Since the site was never an auspicious one, the north side of the house, which reveals a 1½-storey studio between floors, is the result of a rather self-conscious scramble for aesthetic resolution. Several notable designers, including Stevenson and Shaw, contributed to the square, but one of their contractors probably takes the credit here.

A Norman Shaw design having become a passport to a position of artistic credibility, the architect was besieged by applicants. In 1882 he launched into drawings for

71 Preliminary Walton Street elevation of Walton House, designed for Edward Kennedy by Norman Shaw, 1882–4. Kennedy and his wife Florence required separate studios.

his seventh studio-house, this time on the square leg boundary of the old Prince's ground, now the corner of Walton Street and Lennox Gardens Mews. Like Lawson's, it was an awkward site but as close as Edward and Florence Sherard Kennedy – Sunday painters with private incomes – could get to newly fashionable Lily Langtry-land. Although he had to let the elevations look after themselves, **71**, Shaw worked miracles with the plan and section. Not only was he asked to duplicate the studio but also to fortify the proper Victorian zoning system, in order that models approached separate changing rooms unseen and from opposite ends of the house. Sadly, all this acrobatic moral observance was contrived for a man who would see no irony in his treatment of *Darby and Joan,* and a woman who was perhaps telling the very same story with *Love Me, Love My Dog.* Minor variations to the contract prevented the Kennedys from setting up their easels in exclusive privacy until 1884.

A much more equitable family atmosphere existed at a contemporary house deeper in Chelsea, however. Paul and Isabel Naftel, their daughter Maude, Mrs Naftel's sister and mother all lived together at 76 Elm Park Road. The first four were landscape or still-life painters of some stature. Paul, the most successful exhibitor, had also advanced himself by teaching at St Peter Port in his native Guernsey. Borrowing heavily, he bought a respectable villa in the town and added a tiny 'Early Geometric Gothic' studio to it with the help of the Ruskinian architect John Pollard Seddon.[36] Within six years of 1865 his investment had paid off, so he brought his family to Bayswater, resuming part-time teaching. At last, in 1883 when he was

72   Right to left, 74–78 Elm Park Road, Chelsea. J P Seddon devised the playfully anachronistic No. 76 for Paul Naftel and family in 1883 – a design almost worthy of Alfred Waterhouse.

nearing 70, Paul Naftel was able to build his own studio-house on a newly released Chelsea estate. J P Seddon was resummoned to furnish the designs.

Seddon's designs are fairly typical of an office which had a large stake in ecclesiastical work. Hence the unabashed pointed arches on a façade that would be worthy of Alfred Waterhouse were it not for the over-strong competition between the right-hand tower and studio gable, **72**. Just the same, Seddon's usual package tour for the short-sighted of medieval highlights – all prickles and polychromy – has been exchanged for the immediacy of the Red Cross tent after a formation skiing accident – all blood and bandages, flayed bones, and gristly dislocated joints. Moreover, if the St Peter Port villa annexe was anything to go by, painted glasswork, churchcraft joinery and fine floors might once have primped the interiors, too.

The talismanic owl atop the gable brought no luck to the Naftels. Maude, her father's ultimate lifeline, died at the age of 33 in 1890. Paul Naftel immediately sold the house and moved to Twickenham where he died the following year. Hugh Glazebrook, a portrait painter, bought 76 Elm Park Road and lived there somewhat longer. No.s 74 and 78, also built in about 1884, were similarly first occupied by landscape painters, Henry Pilleau and Pownoll Williams. Pilleau outstayed the Naftels but Williams sold up within two years, abandoning his shopfront studio on the first floor.

Stimulated in part by the local presence of the Chelsea Arts Club, individual artists' houses continued to be built on the old mulberry grove between Old Church Street and The Vale for another 30 years. Chelsea's only other major scene of turn-of-the-century building lay next to the Old Church on Cheyne Walk. Otherwise the district was overrun by studio groups and flats – an indiscriminate phenomenon dating from the late 1870s when the hard-boiled Philistine speculators first saw the gilded, lint-headed Aesthetes coming.

6

HIGH VICTORIAN HAMPSTEAD: FITZJOHN'S AVENUE

IF CHELSEA'S attraction lay in the foggy restlessness and quaint decrepitude of the riverside, Hampstead's lay in its sleepy hollows and bosky high ground. Open-air painters found its breezy commons on the roof of London irresistible. But, until the suburban railways climbed the hill in the 1860s, few such painters could afford to stay from one weekend to the next. In the 1820s Copley Fielding, John Linnell and John Constable, for instance, were each bound to earn a living in Fitzrovia. Yet Linnell returned nightly to his rented farmhouse to discipline his big family, and Constable eventually bought a cottage by the Heath but one too tiny to work in as well.

The first Academician after Constable to buy a house near Hampstead village was the ex-seaman and set designer William Clarkson Stanfield. His successful third career as an easel painter of marines allowed him to relinquish the work that tied him to London's theatreland. From Camden Town he moved farther out to a third-rate Georgian house fronting the High Street on the corner of Prince Arthur Road. Soon after his arrival in 1847 he built a narrowish detached studio in the backyard for the use of himself and his son George Clarkson. It also made a convenient meeting room during the last years of The Sketching Society. But if anyone or anything influenced 'the forcible landscape painter' Mark Anthony to settle nearby in about 1858, it was either his friend Madox Brown[1] or the bother of lugging his traps from Paddington to the Heath every day. Anthony erected a lightweight pavilion (possibly a glasshouse since photography had captivated him at an early date), in the grounds of Whitestone House, then called The Lawn. He retained this prime location overlooking the Vale of Health for nearly half his life.

For some time no other painter managed to improve on Anthony's position although his conditions were really little better than a Barbizon bivouac. Less outdoorsy types, however, were looking more for a halfway house between villeggia-tura and stuffy civilisation. For Paul Falconer Poole ARA, who had something of a reputation as a wife-swapper, a social limbo of this kind was all the more desirable. After circling around Camden Town and Lisson Grove, Poole found a site where he could show a brave face to the world. It was north of Chalk Farm on the corner of

Haverstock Hill and Park (now Parkhill) Road. In 1854 he built Glydder House, a four-square villa that left off the usual stucco coating to expose a scabrous under-clothing of yellow, grey and purple brickwork. At the end of the garden he helped himself to a stable–studio block. Here, when the mood took him, he would paint one of those doom-laden, hologrammatic bible stories; otherwise he would rely on summery picnic scenes. Buyers came forward for both and Poole was elected RA in 1861, not insignificantly the year his mistress became free to marry him.

Alfred Stevens is another man about whose domestic habits there was some prurient speculation. Although he had only been awarded equal fifth prize in the competition for the St Paul's Cathedral Wellington memorial, Stevens was given the commission. This meant that he needed a large workshop over 30′ high in which to assemble the requisite pair of full-sized plaster models. In 1858 a redundant iron church was found for him on the corner of Eton Road and Eton Villas. Work commenced once the church had been converted into both house and studio. In 1862 he was able to rent 9 Eton Villas as well. While Stevens could not have sunk quite as low as Zola's sculptor Mahoudeau (*L'Oeuvre*, 1886), the preparation of just one model reduced him to a truly heart-rending state. Notwithstanding, he salvaged the strength to plan and, in about 1865, to begin building a house of his own on the site of the church. But of the projected four or five storeys[2] of what might have been mistaken for a cinquecento corn exchange by Giulio Romano, only two had been made habitable before he died in 1875. Two further floors together with various ancillaries, perhaps the permanent workshops Stevens had envisaged, were added posthumously in a conventional Italianate manner. A similar stage had been reached with the great monument which, however, was not wholly completed until 1912.

Stevens rented his church from the major local builder, Samuel Cuming. Two or three of the other Eton Villas properties were owned by a rival developer named Richard Batterbury who lived next door to Poole in Bathford Lodge. At least 50 of the plain, brown brick semi-detached houses in Park Road were built by him and his son, Richard Legg Batterbury, between 1850 and 1880.[3] They may not have known that artists had operated in this region several decades earlier, but they did come to realise that watercolourists in particular had taken to their new development. Poole's presence must have helped.[4] But what turned a sprinkling of artistic lessees into a rising flood was the fact that Batterbury Junior had requisitioned the garden ground behind 56–78 Park Road and in 1872 his brother Thomas had designed a string of non-residential studios (1–8 *The Mall*) to go on it. Having been guaranteed options on excellent workspace a mere step beyond the back fence, two illustrators on *The Graphic* payroll, James Linton and Robert Macbeth, had already moved into Batter-bury houses at 60 and 62 Park Road. *The Mall* was so quickly oversubscribed that construction of further working studios related to the existing Batterbury housing stock farther west was proposed. These did not materialise smartly enough, with the result that the Batterburys found themselves putting up one-off units, e.g., for the Green brothers at 88a Park Road (1873), while other individuals, e.g., Ernest Girardot at 51 Upper Park Road (1874), made their own arrangements. Many more painters collected hereabouts simultaneously, either establishing new addresses or replacing residents who had moved on.

73 'Uplands', Paul Poole's house at the top of Arkwright Road, Hampstead, by Theodore Green, 1871. 'The Seven Lumps of Architecture' but architecture nonetheless.

Quick off the mark in this regard was the painter of Frithian vignettes, C E Barnes, who for a brief period after 1871 replaced Paul Poole at Glydder House. Although approaching 64, Poole was enjoying good health and an RA's income topped up by portrait-painting profits. He decided to brandish his senior status by building a grander house in a more commanding position – at the top of Arkwright Road, then a new link between Frognal and upper Fitzjohn's Avenue. The architect T K Green took the plot directly below, building his own house, 'Leyland', there. As Green designed other houses close by, he may have been playing the developer. Perhaps he offered Poole a package deal since he designed 'Uplands' for him, too. It was built, as Pevsner wrote, 'in crude, elephantine Gothic' for £3155 in 1871–2.[5]

Uplands may have looked like The Seven Lumps of Architecture to some, but Ruskin would have been more than proud to stable his pet dragon in it. Indeed, the house would have made a fine snowproof hunting lodge on the edge of Coniston Water. Green employed every motif in the Picturesque canon, from staggered massing to rustic timberwork. Beginning by breaking off a jagged crystal from a conglomerate of brick, stone, slate and glass he chopped and lopped, scored and scalloped, pared and polished the cleavage planes until its inherent order had been fully enhanced, **73**. But on the north-west, Arkwright Road side his effort to evince a natural balance in all but the broad lines was overpowered by the extras in Poole's brief. The portrait sitter's rigmarole was raggedly etched into the elevation: entrance, anteroom, cloakroom and studio, the last marked by a large steel-framed window and a garden bay. As it turned out Poole's truncated room was created in proportion to the short time in which he could make use of it; he died in 1879.

Whereas the style of Uplands belonged more to the 1860s, that of Oak Tree House across the way looked quite advanced for the 1880s. Ideas for Oak Tree House were actually sketched out in 1872, in the early days of the 'Queen Anne' revival. Basil Champneys and Henry Holiday, the team that designed and decorated St Luke's, Kentish Town, were architect and client respectively. Holiday, a stained glass artist, painter and sculptor, and his wife Kate, a clever needleworker, had set their hearts on a Hampstead home. After searching, like Poole, for an elevated spot giving views to

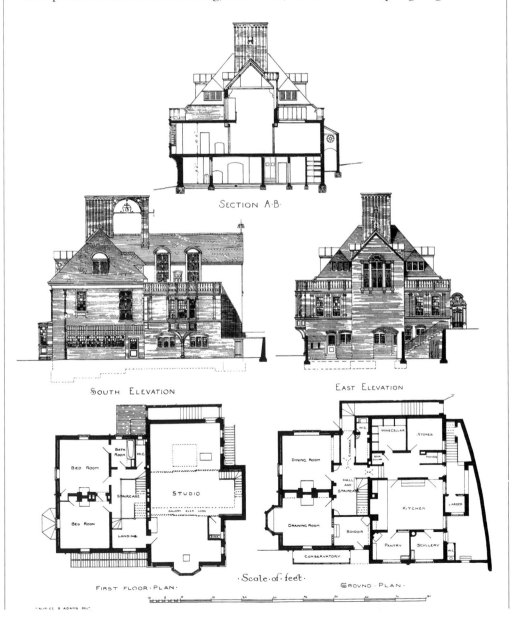

SECTION A·B·

SOUTH ELEVATION   EAST ELEVATION

FIRST FLOOR · PLAN.   ·Scale·of·feet·   GROUND·PLAN.

74 Drawings of Henry Holiday's Oak Tree House, Branch Hill, Hampstead, by Basil Champneys, 1872–4. A fine, early instance of the 'Queen Anne' or London School Board style.

the west over Middlesex, they agreed on a strip of Branch Hill meadow in the lee of a 'particularly beautiful grove of trees . . . with blue hyacinths growing in profusion under them'.[6]

With about £5000 at his disposal, Champneys was asked to design a modern, dry and airy house incorporating studios for Holiday's three main pursuits. He devised a three-storey red brick, red tile composition not remote in its compact, essentially symmetrical form from the late 17th-century Fenton House nearby, **74**. External decoration did not extend much beyond Wrenaissance pilasters and a Tudoresque oriel; the Board school bellcote does not appear to have been built. Champneys nudged the house into the hill, isolating the clammy north side with retaining walls. Additional defences against dampness which he provided included ventilating ducts, cavity walls, and a conservatory or solar energy bank. By placing the studios on the first floor he ended up with ridiculously oversized domestic offices, but these engaged the private rooms so closely that back stairs could be dispensed with. While Kate was given a lady chapel, dim and snug, for her embroidery, Henry obtained an immense, lightsome basilica with one ill-sited fireplace. But it was a modernistic basilica. Hefty partitions suspended from iron joists could be slid across to divide the galleried nave from deep north and south aisles. With its clerestories and mighty Venetian window at the east end, the 30' high nave reproduced the conditions in which the artist's church fittings would ultimately come to be seen. The top-lit north aisle was devoted to painting; the locally lit south aisle, complete with picture slit or 'cartoon slide', to any other modelling, mosaic or enamel work.

Not long after the Holidays moved in on Lady Day 1874, they began to spread their wings. Kate borrowed the south aisle for a music room, going on to commandeer the whole studio for a series of Oak Tree House concerts. Henry, a fervent Gladstone supporter, went further, making the same rostrum available for political meetings. But work came first. Holiday soon realised he needed more light in winter. To this end he erected a whitewashed glasshouse on the southern terrace, **75**. That in turn necessitated the insertion of two more tall dormers over the nave. Then his conscience told him that the stained glass he usually had supplied by Powells of Whitefriars would never match the medieval article. Consequently, in 1890 or '91 he took over the lease of 20 Church Row from the architect Thomas Garner and set up a glassworks of his own in the mews behind. The product was so good that his little firm flourished for about 20 years – until the ageing Holiday felt he had at last beaten William Morris at his own game.

Holiday and his wife knew of the Church Row property because they used to design textile patterns for Garner's Arts and Crafts subsidiary, Watts & Co. Garner had made the upper level of the Church Row coach-house into a drawing office which he shared with his partners George Bodley and George Gilbert Scott Jnr. Bodley already lived at 24 Church Row, so it became doubly handy when Scott moved to No. 26 in 1872. Four years later Scott rebuilt his stabling also, summoning up a quaintly twisted doll-sized studio-house stitched into a tunic of brick-fretted ochre stucco.[7] The Scottish painter Robert Little succeeded to No. 26 in the 1890s; the Will Rothensteins replaced him in 1902.

75 Holiday's studio in 1888, looking into the glasshouse on the southern terrace – spaces made possible by the use of substantial iron beams.

While Scott was getting adjusted in Church Row it was the turn of his neighbour, the *Punch* cartoonist George du Maurier, to move away. His tasteful redecoration of a mongrelly old dwelling opposite Fenton House in 1874 led the *Building News* editor to remark that 'to those whose notions of "furnishing" are as expensive as they are vulgar, it may be instructive'.[8] Many of the gentler readers of *Punch* became wary of taking current fashions too far lest they held themselves up to du Maurier's withering mockery. Others, vulgarians or not, defied criticism by virtue of their complete originality. Such was the case with the Bavarian-born painter Carl Haag. Although his connection with the German court stood him in good stead at the British one, Haag did not really gain any celebrity until he returned from his first trip to Libya with Frederick Goodall in 1858. Sketches he made on this and subsequent journeys to the Near East equipped him with a visual encyclopedia of everyday Arab life. The resulting watercolours, finically accurate and refreshingly radiant, fetched whatever price he cared to ask – his only real English competition being Goodall and J F Lewis.

In *c.* 1871 Haag bought the recently built 7 Lyndhurst Road, renaming it Ida Villa in honour of his wife. There were four storeys already but Haag formed a fifth under a new double-pitched roof to yield a free space about the size of a badminton court. It was reached by a new octagonal staircase tower attached to a back corner of the house. Broad windows with skylights were fixed in the lower slopes of the roof and a lantern was raised along the ridge. Using the bazaarful of Levantine craftwork he had shipped home during his Wanderjahre, Haag concocted a fabulous caravanserai fit for a 'rich, but not oppressively sumptuous Eastern existence'.[9]

No contemporary description of the painter's rooftop studio gives a very clear impression, but it would seem that a striped stone screen ran parallel to one boundary. In between, framed by horseshoe arches and stilted portals, lay a number of divans and furnished recesses, **76**. Daylight entering these was filtered by Cairene lattices; floors and couches were spread with Persian rugs or Palmyran tapestries; walls were lined with gleaming tiles or damascened marble, and the fitted cabinets inlaid with tortoise-shell, mother-o'-pearl, brass and silver. An *Art Journal* writer paid his respects in 1883[10] and went away boggling at the multiplicity of paraphernalia that ranged from assassins' yataghans to Nubian camel saddles, all of it neatly 'strewn about'. He was also a little unnerved by assorted lay figures, dressed for the part, lurking in corners and smoking chibouks. But more remarkable still was the entrance to the so-called Private Apartments. Surmounted by an intricate mashrab-iyya, this tour de force of geometric stonecarving took pride of place among the built-in fittings. Possibly the upper stage concealed a models' room – a secret hareem – or it may have given onto a terrace above the stair tower.

Haag made full use of this and the other studio accessories to cram his paintings with accurate local colour, e.g., *Danger in the Desert* (1871), *Hadji returning to Cairo* (1894). The Lyndhurst Road interior had its precedents and replicas in London, but none could match its absolute authenticity. Haag possessed another studio decorated in primitive Teutonic style in the medieval Roter Turm at Oberwesel, Germany, to which he moved in 1903. Much decorated himself by the Bavarians, French and Turks, he died there in 1915.

76 A divan in Carl Haag's caravanserai at 7 Lyndhurst Road, Hampstead, furnished with a bazaarful of Levantine craftwork.

Lower down the hill, meanwhile, the Batterbury brothers had stepped up their activities. Richard continued building and speculating in ground leases while Thomas joined Mr Huxley to design a sequel to *The Mall* (*Steele's Studios*) on the west side of Haverstock Hill. Then some richer, more established artists came forward. They wanted individually designed, free-standing studio-villas, not just standard family houses with a workshop unit around the corner. It was likely to be James Linton of Park Road who first found out about the Batterbury land in Steele's Road. He bought the plot at No. 35 and commissioned such a residence. Suddenly the grapevine jangled and Batterbury & Huxley had simultaneous orders for comparable houses at No.s 36–39 for the painters C E Johnson, Fred Barnard, Edwin Hayes and G G Kilburne. In fact the houses were built in descending numerical order, George Kilburne's Hawkhurst House going up first towards the end of 1874. Linzell & Son of Tottenham, contractors for *Steele's Studios*, submitted successful tenders for this and the other four houses as well.

It does not take a very sharp eye to see that Batterbury & Huxley have rung five different changes on what is fundamentally the same design. Each house is of four storeys, including a half basement, with a medium-sized studio extending to the rear under its own roof. Considering the depth of the plots in Steele's Road, two storeys would have sufficed, but the basic two-room plan is stacked high to give a grander impression. Hawkhurst House has a crude Gothic character emphasised by multifoil bargeboards reminiscent of Uplands. Briscoe House for the estimable marine painter Edwin Hayes and his son Claude, a passable landscapist, has no character at all, certainly none to warrant its higher price – 'approximately £2000' against 'about £1850'. Warrington House for the popular young Dickens illustrator Fred Barnard reflects the architectural refinement that could be wrung from an extra £300. Stringy chimney stacks reaching well above the ridgeline and the odd pair of tall, slim sashes show Batterbury & Huxley finally catching up with the spirit of the times. Their next move, however, was a rather ill-considered one. Having revealed a capacity to practise Aesthetic tokenism, they then married it to a low-class, draggle-tailed model understood to represent the true Queen Anne style. Morven House, for the land-scape painter Charles Johnson, is the misshapen issue of this alliance. Shamed by this indiscretion, the architects made a pronounced effort to grasp the finer points of the new fashion when they set about Ettrick House for James Linton in mid-1876.

Linton was a high-flyer. Kilburne, the two Hayes and Johnson were all elected members of the New Watercolour Society, but Linton went on to become its long-serving president in 1884 aged only 44; in 1885 he was knighted. From woodblock work he had moved wholly into the more rewarding realm of historical costume pieces and portraits. Sound, mechanical ability enabled him to sink £3000 into the new house in addition to what he had already expended on secondhand fireplaces, doorcases and the like. To supervise the installation of these and to execute other specialist joinery, the architects subcontracted George Eddy, foreman at *The Mall*.

Batterbury & Huxley excelled themselves; they made Ettrick House almost more Queen Anne than Queen Anne, **77**. Yellow brickwork is dressed to the nines in red, with textural contrast provided by rubbed arches and aprons. Unfortunately, though,

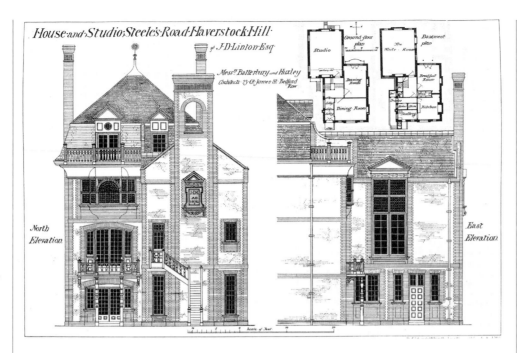

77 Drawings of Sir James Linton's Ettrick House, Steele's Road, Hampstead, by Batterbury & Huxley, 1876–7. A three-dimensional catalogue of 'Queen Anne' trademarks.

the snappy effect of the masonry is spoiled by a mansard roof, for all its adaptability as artless as a newspaper hat. But the flaws in the upper reaches do not detract from the prettiness nearer at hand where the architects' debt to the mastery of Norman Shaw and Mr Eddy is inescapably apparent. The plans work tolerably well, too, differing from Johnson's mainly in their greater formality, efficiency and reference to the garden. Linton similarly made more of his two-storey rearward wing, treating the lower floor as an extension of the studio and reception rooms when entertaining. Ivory white paintwork and a selection of Richard Almond's quietly patterned wallpapers were used to reinforce this relationship. And while the dining room relapsed into dinginess with sludge brown woodwork and a tooled leather frieze, the sunny, vivacious aspect of the house was restored elsewhere by stained glass, tapestries and Italian mosaic pavements.

Without a doubt Ettrick House was once the best of the lot; it spanked and twinked to the tip of its heliotropic finial. It also came closest to being a proper studio-house. But the studio was still a tacked-on affair, oriented no better than the drawing room. Moreover, although these Steele's Road houses appeared good value for money, compared to a totally original design by Webb, for instance, they actually fell far short of it. Nevertheless Batterbury & Huxley became much sought after for the cheaper end of their range, such as it was.

The slalom course of Hampstead Hill Gardens, where another gang of painters lay in wait, happened to be the scene of their next exploits. They led off with a 'Bijou Residence' on the Rosslyn Hill corner for John Ingle Lee in 1875–6. Lee's wickedly irregular site did not stop them easing a loose-jointed Steele's Road Special onto it for just £1680. A *Building News* reviewer agreed that 'The treatment of the roofs and details is pleasingly simple . . . and the general effect is natural, not strained'.[11] It was obviously the design Johnson would have received had not Lee's commission intervened. An Aesthetic School attenuation about the overall mass, the chimneys and window shapes and a happy choice of bricks, in this case greyish Luton purples dressed with Suffolk reds, lift 'Sunnycote' into the cheerful, zany, arty class, **78**. Not much chop as a painter, Lee was sadly unable to live up to the house and it was altered soon afterwards to suit his brother.

The plot below Lee's was no less tricky, but all the illustrator Charles Green required on it for the time being was a hall, a bed-sitter, a studio and a caretaker's room. As for dining arrangements, presumably he would either grill a herring over the fire or join his pen-pals at a tavern in town. To answer his immediate needs, Batterbury & Huxley devised 'Charlecote', a cross between a Queen Anne rout-house and a Renaissance casino. Green was probably delighted to find his budget not only allowed for a decent double-height paintbox but also a gallery that opened onto a roof terrace high enough to give views of the Heath. He transferred here from his temporary Batterbury digs in Park Road in 1877. Four years later he increased the facilities at Charlecote as he turned more to easel painting. Small oils were inter-spersed with crowded watercolour panoramas such as *The Caledonian Market* (1891), but he died relatively young without patently relishing the bruise of the brush any more than the nip of the nib.

One step farther down Hampstead Hill Gardens, yet another B&H budget-beater broke the skyline towards 1879. 'Etherow' was built for Thomas Collier, 'one of the supreme watercolour painters of England'.[12] After spending most of the 1860s in North Wales, Collier shifted his base to Upper Park Road; from there he took after Linton and Green. Etherow was laid out in the usual way but squared up to suggest the sterling solidity of an 18th-century manor house. Nonetheless, by submitting its ruddy, lean features to a slightly gauche asymmetry, a certain genial mien crept in also. Collier's painting room was consistently receptive, letting in peeps of sunlight from the north-east and north-west. It could be equally welcoming in winter since he had taken advice from Linton and Green to have an open fire blazing on one side and a Nuremberg stove chuntering on the other.

At this point the artists' descent on Batterbury & Huxley's office slackened somewhat. Although the High Camp studio-house remained its forte for a few years to come, the opportunity arose for the practice to diversify a little. Not only that, several other minor developers had begun to siphon off potential customers with rentable terraced units and the occasional one-off house. For example, it could easily have been the architect T K Green who offered Frank W W Topham the same sort of deal Poole had entered into earlier.[13]

After their marriage in 1870, Frank Topham and Helen Lemon, daughter of the founding editor of *Punch*, went to ground in St John's Wood. Outgrowing their semi-detached villa and garden studio there, they put Frank's slender gains from his watercolours and historical genre works into 'Ifield', a new studio-house at 16 Prince Arthur Road. The death of Frank's father, Francis Topham Snr, brought an unlooked-for contribution to the building costs early in 1877. Completed by the end of that

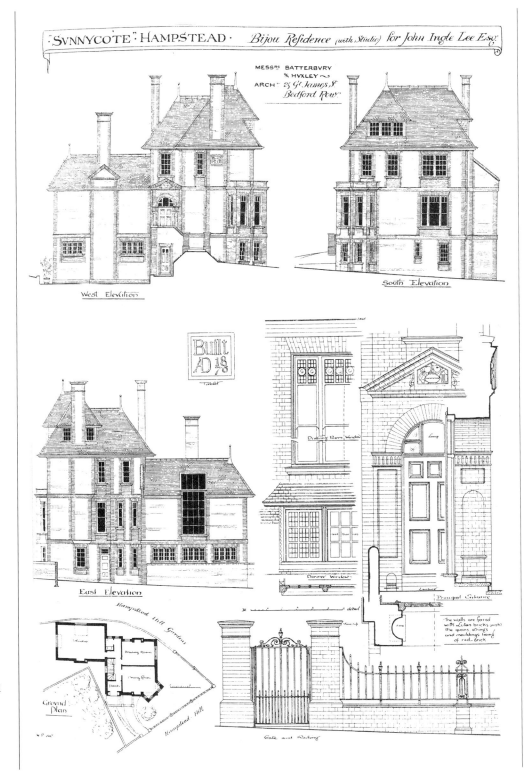

78 John Ingle Lee's 'Sunnycote', Hampstead Hill Gardens, Hampstead, by Batterbury & Huxley, 1876. A high-heeled Aesthetic School house by Hampstead's premier High Camp architects.

year Ifield, like Etherow, clings to a slope dipping to the north-west. It also divides into two distinct parts – a broad service and studio-drawing room block leaning against a narrow bedroom and staircase tower. There are few signs of the architectural times here, the whole rather resembling a residential West Midlands watermill. A catslide of purple tiles sweeps over creamy-grey walls, framing giveaway gallery windows above the service entrance. On the garden side Topham's one extravagance shows itself in the gargantuan Elizabethan north light. This is out of character since, if anything, the style of the house relates to that of Uplands – more 1860s than 1560s, as the pair of bishop's mitre windows by the porch bears witness.

Topham advanced himself signally in his new surroundings (*A Roman Triumph, A Prize in the Lottery*), but his family was steadily approaching its full complement of ten. Provisional measures were taken at the end of 1880 when an extra bedroom was spooned into the studio roof with unabashed expediency. Bursting point was reached in about 1888, however, so the family moved to 'Coneyhurst', near Ewhurst, Surrey, a house only recently built for Miss Mary Ewart by Philip Webb.

Topham's movements almost matched those of Edwin Long, since 1875 an Associate RA. Long celebrated this achievement with a transfer to St John's Wood where he enlarged an already large house. Renaming it 'Longsden', he resided there in some style. However, the overwhelming desire to create his own island in the sun saw him buy a vast beachhead on the Hampstead corniche and consult the daredevils' architect, Norman Shaw. Although he had little hope of upstaging Shaw's golden boys in Melbury Road, he would set the standard for Fitzjohn's Avenue instead – his land stretched from there down Netherhall Gardens to Maresfield Gardens. Shaw tossed off his first sketch plans in November 1876, pencilling in various luxuries he felt certain Long had not meant to be omitted.[14] (Warned that his client might jib at this liberty, Shaw sighed, 'Oh, let him go and paint another nose!') The architect then mulled over the drawings for nearly a year before issuing a revision. A further scheme was agreed with the builders in mid-1878 but even that was changed radically, **79**. Long finally moved into 'Kelston' in March 1880.

Throughout the planning process the original concept of a ground floor studio and living rooms encircling a central 'patio' – what Long believed to be intrinsically Spanish – remained intact. But the studio suite was shunted around and about, ultimately swapping places with the entrance hall. It was then settled that visitors and portrait sitters would enter from the north, Netherhall Gardens side and models from the south, domestic offices side. Sitters were shown into anterooms beside the main entrance before being conducted across a corner of the patio. This 25′-square space, glazed over at high level, paved with coloured tiles and lush with subtropical greenery, must have astonished anyone anticipating the sort of interior suggested by the humdrum 'Queen Anne' exterior, **80**. Crossing the studio threshold the eye was immediately drawn to a gilt-lined apse (allegedly Spanish also, but not unlike Leighton's) at the far end. Much of the light beaming in at calculated angles eddied there, especially that from the elevated north window. A shallow oriel below the north window was soon removed in favour of a smallish glasshouse. Opposite, on the south side. Shaw built in all the adjuncts mapped out on the preliminary plan. Beside the ingle-nook was Long's elaborately screened pipe organ; above these, a nominal gallery; beyond, an easel room and stairs to a handsome billiard room beneath.

'Mr Long . . . now possesses the finest studio in London', announced *The Architect* reporter. 'Studios like this are suggestive of the altered condition of art and artists in England . . .; it seems to be no longer possible for a good picture to be produced unless the painter can regard every stroke of his brush from a long distance.'[15] For his hoarding-size works of biblical subjects, Long required more light and longer distances than most. His rise to RA encouraged him to attempt other huge tableaux and to increase his prices. When his 16′ × 8′ *Babylon Marriage Market* which sold for 1700gns in 1875 fetched a record 6300gns at auction seven years later, he raised them again. In 1883 he opened a Bond Street gallery of his own since the RA could not offer him enough wall space. More hoardings – all lurid, semi-naked slave girls and British Museum furniture – followed, including *Anno Domini*, *Love's Labour Lost* and *Zeuxis at Crotona*, many of them bought by Thomas Holloway, the patent pill tycoon. Long's misplaced popularity as a painter of portraits, e.g., *Princess May* (1887), was similarly sustained by the connections of one wealthy admirer, the Baroness Burdett-Coutts.

A better place to go for portraits, twice visited by the Prince of Wales in the 1880s, lay across Fitzjohn's Avenue at No. 6, otherwise known as 'The Three Gables', the

79 Preliminary ground floor plan of Edwin Long's 'Kelston', 61 Fitzjohn's Avenue, Hampstead, by Norman Shaw, June 1878. The studio suite eventually jutted forward on the east side.

80 View from the Netherhall Gardens side of Edwin Long's 'Kelston' as built by Norman Shaw, 1879–80. Durable Queen Annery without, hothouse Spanish treatments within.

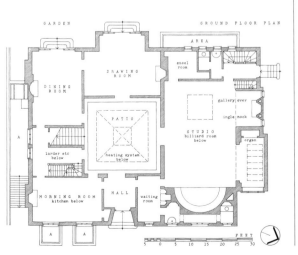

home of Frank Holl. The son of a respected engraver, Holl had already proved himself an outstanding figure painter when Queen Victoria commissioned *No Tidings from the Sea* in 1870; he was then 25. After pursuing comparable themes of misfortune and privation both on canvas and on the woodblock to great acclaim (ARA 1878, RA 1883), he tentatively turned to portraits. In the ten years before his premature death, he completed over 200 of them. 'Probably no portrait painter of any age has executed so much first rate work in so short a time',[16] claimed one; 'six sitters a day killed poor Holl', lamented another.

Built in 1881–2 to designs again by Norman Shaw, The Three Gables represented a reaction to the tired and flat 'Queen Anne' styling of Kelston. In another return to his Old English mode the architect cast a glance at the three-bay front of Marcus Stone's house. Digging deeper into the traditional East Anglian architecture that inspired his earlier New Zealand Chambers in the City, Shaw gathered in and rehashed the essential ingredients: red brickwork, pargeting, ribbed chimneys and Tudor windows, especially his favourite two-tier Ipswich oriels, **81**. On the inside he imparted an Old Englishness by mixing in not only ingle-nooks and panelling but a painting room trumped-up like a medieval hall as well. At the west end of it a convincing 'screens passage' supported a full-width gallery – 'a pretty feature, but of no use whatever'.[17]

As to decoration, Mrs Annie Holl probably had some influence in the living rooms where the emphasis fell on white-painted deal and colour-coordinated soft furnishings rather than stained oak and old leather. The morning and drawing rooms could only be entered from a lofty inner hall set between them. On the near side, this hall, draped from head height in amber plush and patterned with gold stencillings above, was divided from the corridor by a turned wood screen and wicket; on the far side, French doors opened into a cupolar conservatory. While the head of the household tolerated a degree of artistic stuffing here, his studio he kept as bare as a ballroom. Holl was particularly tidy; he was said, in fact, to hold 'a pronounced dislike for that species of litter which, to some persons, has got to be synonymous with art'.[18] Even his frame and properties' store was relegated to the kitchen floor below. Models were obliged to come through this in order to reach a spacious cloakroom behind the screens passage. For the most part, despite a redoubtable north light and its skylight, two flanking windows, an apsidal array and another clerestory range above the gable end, they would have found the studio somewhat funereal. When painting, Holl shrouded nearly all but the central window combination with dark velvet. He would further concentrate this single light source within a hemicycle of floor-to-ceiling curtains. Highlights could be introduced by parting the curtains at appropriate points. Hubert Herkomer, a shrewd portraitist himself, condemned such a practice. He criticised 'a certain sameness in every subject'. 'Holl', he continued, 'never painted an eye in his sitter; it was always in shadow.'[19]

Holl acknowledged that he had been given the hemicycle idea by John Pettie RA. The powerful painter from Haddingtonshire had moved into 2 Fitzjohn's Avenue, on the corner of Belsize Lane, at the end of 1881. 'The Lothians', as it was called, was designed for him in expansive Neo-Baroque style by the Scottish partnership of

81 Plan and view of Frank Holl's 'The Three Gables', 6 Fitzjohn's Avenue, Hampstead, by Norman Shaw, 1881. 'A house good enough for a king.' The curved roof of the conservatory adjoining the inner hall is visible beyond the coach-house.

Wallace & Flockhart. Though the former was Pettie's personal friend, the latter was the executive architect. New to London, William Flockhart seemed to take this opportunity to show his paces. While allowing himself plenty of room to field some preconceived affectations – the lantern, especially – he narrowly avoided summoning up a town hall instead of a town house. Despite insistent vertical accents, a layering of sharp-edged horizontal elements secured the dominance of breadth and gravity. French strains in the plate glass windows, the fluted pilasters and ironwork were

82 William Flockhart's
drawing of 'The Lothians',
John Pettie's house at
2 Fitzjohn's Avenue,
Hampstead, designed in
1880. Flockhart was an able
style-mixer and master of the
expansive gesture.

likewise outpointed by Wrenish mannerisms in the Beer stone dressings and lead-work, **82**.

A close reading of the plans shows The Three Gables possessed more than the one similarity to The Lothians: the same axial corridor leading to a peninsular, ground floor studio; corresponding facilities for models; a downstairs wardrobe; the same off-centre inner hall; and so on. At 50′ × 30′, Pettie's studio was bigger but just as stripped for action. 'Ambition was felt in its space' while 'modesty lurked in its semitones',[20] wrote a fellow painter. In fact a hair-shirted atmosphere prevailed even before it was built. Pettie had bearded Wallace, saying 'Mind you I want a large square room – a workshop, and none of your fal-de-lals and nooks-and-corners and galleries – "nane o' yer whigmaleeries and curlie-wurlies"'.[21] In effect he got two square rooms, the inner with north light, the outer with east, by running a curtain

83 Inner hall of Pettie's 'The Lothians'. It 'fairly sang with canary yellow walls and natural blonde woodwork'.

straight across at the mid-point. What ornament there was tended to the grim and grisly. Pettie grouped it around the fireplaces in each section: claymores, suits of armour, statuettes such as Leighton's *Athlete v Python* and Lawson's *Samson Restrained*, a 'rather stern' bust of the artist, Caledonian rams' skulls, bagpipes, and worse.

Of the living rooms, however, only the traditionally masculine dining room sustained this baleful aspect. The inner hall, for instance, fairly sang with canary yellow walls and natural blonde woodwork, **83**. Light flooded down not, oddly enough, from the lantern but from rearward windows under a toothpaste green ceiling. Opening a sea-green door to the morning room, one would have found a blossomy blue and white wallpaper, a chipper effect contrasted to advantage with an ebonised chimneypiece like a pleached Gothic bower. In 1885 a lady visitor saw that this room had been much lived in. 'Not so the [drawing] room beyond', she shuddered. 'It is a kind of harmony of creams and gold ... There are spindle-legged chairs more effective to the eye than pleasant to the back ... But everything stands in its place, is not strewn about, a danger to itself and the spectator, as is too often the case today.'[22] Selected for special notice was a whitewood fireplace of stylised Oriental fretwork picked out in gold, its overmantel laden with glass and china, a peacock's tail forming the hearth screen.

Greenery-yallery fallalery was not supposed to be part of Pettie's image. Indeed, the Abbotsford stoves in his studio were screened by Highland targes. And it was to the world of Ivanhoe and Cromwell that he really belonged. Bristling, roguish paintings on themes taken from Scott and the Commonwealth propelled him into the RA ranks at a very early age.

Pettie's prowess was enviable and his success so palpable at the city end of Fitzjohn's Avenue that a number of other studio-house builders were soon enticed to the area. John Haynes Williams built the not very beautiful 'Wridhern' at 1 Maresfield Gardens in 1882. In the same year Thomas Davidson took possession of 'Culloden', a Batterbury & Huxley design, at 6 Netherhall Gardens. As usual, Culloden's plan does not deviate much from the B&H norm, and the strenuously staggered outline suggests severe subsidence rather than sensible split-level organisation. A three-stage bow of praiseworthy rubbed brickwork in Renaissance get-up vies with a salient cheese-grater bay verging on the medieval. But a balcony and conservatory are thrown in, while the galleried studio and dining room below it are expensively panelled from top to bottom. Maresfield and Netherhall Gardens also took in sculptors, photographers, even RAs, but the most interesting newcomer hereabouts was the illustrator Miss Catherine Greenaway – after Mrs Merritt only the second woman to build a substantial studio-house in London.

Between 1871 and 1883 some 17 books were issued containing Kate Greenaway's coloured illustrations. *Under the Window* sold over 100 000 copies in Britain and Europe alone; from her last five titles she stood to make £8000 clear profit.[23] Half a dozen more books were in hand and would appear within another two years. Only at this point did Kate feel she could possibly escape from deadly Upper Holloway to salubrious Hampstead. Charily she parted with £2000 for an acre of land in Frognal, and for about the same amount she had her house put on it by Norman Shaw.

At 39 Frognal, Shaw resisted the temptation to concoct a gingerbread cottage for grown-ups. Understandingly, he used his speculative building experience to design a no-nonsense four-bedroom dwelling. Economy is apparent in the simple shapes (unturned balusters, for example) and lightweight construction (tile hanging served to conceal the use of cheap bricks). Other savings resulted from leaving the domestic offices above ground and keeping corridors to a minimum. Shaw's ingenuity played its part, too. Without resorting to back stairs, little sitters were cleverly diverted from the private middle floor, their long climb made less daunting by an early view of the upper landing. A final surprise was to find the painting room turned through 45° to face due north. With the building already ideally placed across the compass in its polite position vis-à-vis the street, here was just the sort of resolution Shaw dared to draw up and pursue, **84**, **85**.

Although most of Kate's limp little people were drawn from the lay figure, local models used to be lured in with promises of afternoon tea. There being no dumb-waiter, old Mrs Greenaway trudged upstairs to serve it in the studio anteroom. This room was also a convenient place to park nannies, and a cosy retreat when it came to fashioning those famous poke bonnets and pinafores. But Kate could actually afford to rest on her laurels by the time the house was ready in 1885. The remainder of her comparatively short life was well provided for. She departed at the top, before the Edwardian greats like Rackham and Dulac had fully made their mark.

Arthur Rackham, incidentally, moved to 16 Chalcot Gardens, Hampstead, in 1907. When first built in 1882 for the indifferent illustrator Towneley Green, this was just an L-shaped cottage, hardly more than studio, parlour and bedroom. There is still both a Cotswoldy and an unusually advanced smooth-skinned look about it. Certainly, of the thinly spread joke-oak treatment within, only a faint hint is given on the outside. Despite his thrift Green fell on hard times. He passed the house to an equally indifferent painter named Adolphus Whalley and went to join his brother Charles in Hampstead Hill Gardens. C F A Voysey enlarged the house for Whalley in 1898. Then, not long after the Rackhams arrived, Maxwell Ayrton knocked the studio into two, cutting up a second window for Mrs Rackham's use below the original one.[24] 15 Chalcot Gardens, dating from 1883, is an artist's house, too, but the studio is separate – a graceless half-timbered kennel at the end of the garden.[25] Once again, but probably for the last time, Batterbury & Huxley own up to the designs. Henry 'Hal' Ludlow, a freelance draughtsman for the magazines, was the client although he appears to have spent little time there.

Meanwhile the self-styled hidalgo of Kelston, Edwin Long RA, was becoming restless. He hankered after another house. Either he wanted a still more imposing residence or he simply could not resist involving himself in the building process. He had recently put a house for letting purposes at the bottom of his garden but there was plenty of room for another. Money was evidently no obstacle; upwards of £6000 came to hand quite readily – liquidity that Henry James could scarcely credit. 'An artist', he wrote, 'whose success in England is, from the foreign point of view, absolutely inexplicable is Mr Edwin Long . . . Mr Long, if I am not mistaken, would be

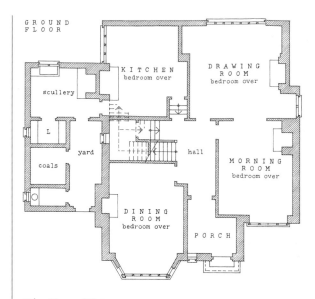

84 Plans of Kate Greenaway's house, 39 Frognal, Hampstead, by Norman Shaw, 1884–5. Shaw lifts a low-budget building out of the ordinary with a diagonal upper stage.

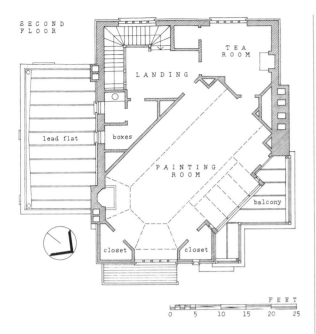

SECOND FLOOR

TEA ROOM

LANDING

lead flat   boxes

PAINTING ROOM

balcony

closet   closet

FEET
0   5   10   15   20   25

regarded in France, in Germany, even in Italy, as dangerously weak.'[26] To mould his new vision Long called in Norman Shaw again. But Shaw, perhaps foreseeing another protracted entanglement, handed much of the control to his chief assistant, William Lethaby.

'Lethaby's Leviathan', built in 1887–8 without too many false starts, was indicative of this architect's subsequent small independent output of grand houses. A variety of subservient elements was clamped onto a monumental longitudinal bulk, a bulk otherwise foreshadowed by Shaw's later Queen's Gate houses. Neither the bullocking brick bays nor the net of weather tiles could restrain it, like a burly rugby prop carrying all assailants before him to the try line, **86**. Sitters and dinner guests faced a heavy slog once the finely-modelled bronze front doors had been opened to them. Acknowledging ancient Carthaginian mosaics set in the porch floor, they then sized up a lengthy gallery lined with pictures, statuary, and the latest in curly electric light brackets, **87**. On the left, a supplementary showroom inspired by Holl's inner hall momentarily modified the view to the garden. To the right opened a dining room almost as vulgar as Millais'. Also on the right, but out of sight, lay the servants' zone, much as it does at the Kennedy house in Chelsea. Sitters reached their objective after a lazy ascent into the unknown. Long's studio, similar in size to his previous one, seemed no better geared to billboard- and portrait-painting although Lethaby improved the service system a good deal.

Long pushed on overconfidently until his sudden death in 1891. Luckily for his widow, however, his reputation was found to rest on earlier work. Along with Millais'

85 Front of Kate Greenaway's 'Camomile Court', Frognal – only the second studio-house built by a woman in London at that date.

86 Western view of Edwin Long's second house at 42 Netherhall Gardens, Hampstead, by Norman Shaw and William Lethaby, 1887–8. A monumental horse pill prescribed to contain Long's megalomania.

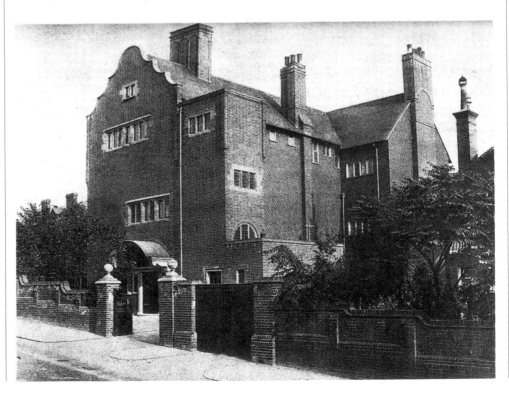

Bubbles, prints of *Diana or Christ?* (1881) issued by Agnew in 1889 actually outsold Hunt's *Light of the World*. Commenting on 19th-century taste, Sickert reckoned 'The nadir of decadent art has perhaps been touched by Long's *Diana or Christ*'.[27] From 1912 to 1921 Sir Edward Elgar lived in the cavernous house. That it was demolished before the war says something unforgiving about 20th-century taste.

Not many London artists built more than one studio-house from scratch, not in the city anyway. The Hon. John Collier was another of them. Had Lady Collier not viewed John's marriage to his deceased wife's sister with so much disfavour he might have remained near her in Chelsea. As it was he decamped to Eton Avenue near Swiss Cottage, resummoning Frederick Waller to design No. 69, North House, in 1889–90. Since much of the west end of Eton Avenue was developed by William Willett, it is quite likely he carried out the building here.

North House does not differ greatly from Collier's More House in Tite Street. Enamel-faced red bricks replace the yellow stocks and buff terracotta the pink stone in another razzle-dazzle display of High Victorian Eclecticism. Clearly complaints were voiced about the old staircase as this one steals the show, bounding up the north front in extrovert arpeggios, **88**. Once again a mid-level studio breaks forward, its extra height jacking up the central bay beyond the eaves line. On the east side the studio opens into a serviceable, sheltered glasshouse. In similar fashion to the arrangements at More House, the floor is fitted with a picture trap and models approached their staircase via the vault beneath.

Having seamlessly rejoined his career, Collier moved away from Godivas and Circes to become a master of the 'problem' picture. Some of the titles of these so-called psychological dramas of upper-class life, in which he had relevant experience, spoke for themselves: *The Prodigal Daughter, Dear Lady Disdain, The Autocrat of the Breakfast Table*, and so on. Collier's rebellious, cynical streak stayed with him till the end; specially made 6'-long brushes enabled him to continue painting from a wheelchair.

During the 1880s and '90s this borderland between Fitzjohn's Avenue and upper St John's Wood soaked up artists as much as any other part of Hampstead. Virtually no one, however, ventured farther west than Kilburn High Road, even though John Rogers Herbert had stolen a march out there as early as 1867. Having rented houses in all the other artistic haunts of London, Herbert chose to build his own house in none of them. He was a real eccentric, 'a profound humorist who joked so seriously that you might almost have taken him for a madman'.[28] George Leslie RA remembered a man whose hair was 'red, long, and very smoothly brushed straight down . . . he had quite a medieval look both in appearance and dress'.[29] His Gothick demeanour he owed to a strong friendship with A W N Pugin and a fervid devotion to Catholicism. When Herbert was ready to build Pugin had been dead some time, so he applied to the architect's slightly cranky son and successor, Edward Welby Pugin. By early 1868 a detached studio had gone up on Herbert's land on the north corner of Quex Road and West End Lane. Within another two years a largish house, 'The Chimes', had been coupled to it. The fact that these buildings did not long survive Herbert's death in 1890 seems consistent with the public outcry over the prominence given to his later paintings at the RA.

87 Plans of Edwin Long's 42 Netherhall Gardens. Most of the rooms look eastwards onto the garden of Kelston.

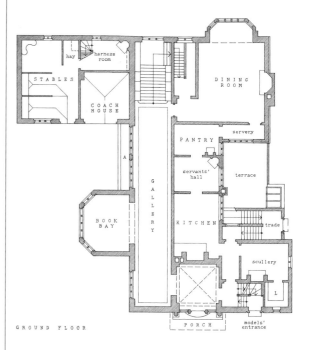

GROUND FLOOR

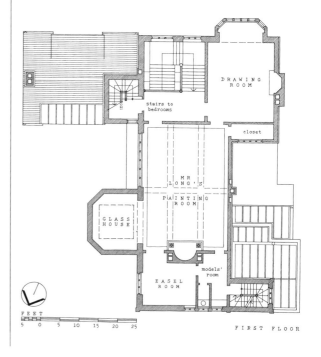

FIRST FLOOR

88 Front of the Hon. John Collier's 69 Eton Avenue, Hampstead, by Frederick Waller, 1890. On the left a glasshouse complements the first floor studio with its glass-roofed bay.

89 John Seymour Lucas's 'New Place', 1 Woodchurch Road, West Hampstead, by Sydney Lee, 1880–1. Mrs Lucas's studio occupies the roof space, her husband's the lower ground floor.

Very gradually other painters discovered Herbert's secret valley; pavilions were raised and garrets converted that have remained discreetly hidden to this day. Compared to these forgotten glades an address in Marylebone did nothing but frustrate an old-fashioned painter like John Seymour Lucas. Thus when he married the children's painter Marie Cornelissen in 1877 Lucas looked to West Hampstead as the place to settle down peaceably. In common with J D Linton, he had collected here a Tudor fireplace, there some Jacobean fittings, and there again a Queen Anne doorcase. These, a brief, and a site at 1 Woodchurch Road he handed to a former painting pupil, Sydney Lee, by then a partner in Lee Brothers & Pain, architects.[30] In spring 1881 the Lucases moved into 'New Place', a strangely hunched Dutch William pensioner, all shoulder-blades, famished features and lean pot belly, **89**.

As to the historical accuracy of Lee's red brick envelope Lucas will have prepared good credentials, perhaps a sketchbookful of East Kent manor-house details. New Place reeks of antiquarian scholarship, especially in the studio which stretches from front to back at lower ground level. (Mrs Lucas had her own east-facing studio under the roof.) Mellow oak panelling encases a genuine old draught lobby and blends into an early English Renaissance gallery front in the best naïve style. Ancient carved oak furniture rubbed shoulders with glowering portraits and numerous legless suits of armour. Lucas drew these props into his paintings, e.g., *After Culloden* (1884), *News of the Armada* (1893). They also came under scrutiny by members of the Kernoozers' Club, a fraternity of arty connoisseurs which regularly met at New Place. Many contemporary military or costumery buffs went away with Lucas's name on their lips, with the result that he preceded most of them to Academy associateship in 1886. For the greater honour, however, he had to wait 12 years on the doormat.

Hundreds of painters never made the first grade in this respect. Quite a few others got a foot in the door but no more. Henry LeJeune, who lived in Goldhurst Terrace, was elevated to ARA in 1863 but rose no higher in 40 years. Yet it was worth persisting, though the tide of fashion worked against older men. George Storey knocked at the seniors' door from 1876 until 1914 before gaining admittance. For 30 years he led his campaign from 39 Broadhurst Gardens, one of a series of new houses with roomy north-lit attics. But 'Dolly' Storey will always be more closely associated with 'dim, divine' St John's Wood – whither the limelight creeps.

7

DECADENT ST JOHN'S WOOD:
GROVE END ROAD

And so that afternoon he took his journey through St John's Wood . . . in the summer sunshine that seemed to be holding a revel over the little gardens; and he looked about him with interest; for this was a district which no Forsyte entered without open disapproval and secret curiosity.[1]

STABBED BY remorse, Old Jolyon Forsyte had set out to reprieve Young Jolyon who lived in shabby rustication at '3 Wistaria Avenue', St John's Wood. Because Young Jolyon was a painter, had twice married beneath himself and produced a son out of wedlock, he had been virtually disinherited by his father and shunned by Forsytes in general. By the same token Holt RA, one of the revolutionary realist painters in George Moore's *A Modern Lover*, lived in seclusion at 'Orchard Villa, Grove Road'. Holt could not bring his wife into society since it was said she sat to half the artists in London. Indeed, the 'faint impropriety' of St John's Wood was familiar to even the least prurient of Victorians. It had long been the haven of kept women and the place where young ladies went to recover from bad colds. These often turned out to be boy colds or girl colds.

In real life the unseemly reputation of the district had its sources in people like the sculptor Musgrave Lewthwaite Watson. Best known for his contribution to the base of Nelson's Column, the quarrelsome Watson spent the later years of his brief life at 13 Upper Gloucester Place. As he lived with 'a young female, the daughter of a publican in Carlisle, but never married her',[2] his acceptance in polite circles was seriously compromised. Of course artists were not solely responsible for loading the meaning of Lower St John's Wood. They were certainly numerous thereabouts, however; since Rossi's day, sculptors had made the zone bounded by the Canal, Edgware and Marylebone Roads particularly their own. A short list of the earlier residents would include the blameless John Graham Lough, the reckless elder E G Papworth, and probably the speediest carver of all time, John Thomas. Other major figures, such as (Sir) Thomas Brock, C B Birch and George Simonds held the fort in these parts in years to come, while Upper St John's Wood gradually took in even more successful academic sculptors than Lower Belgravia.

Nor was there ever a shortage of illustrious painters in the vicinity. C R Leslie RA was not long out of 1 St John's Place, Lisson Grove, before the newly betrothed Samuel Palmer appeared around the corner in Grove Street. The Palmers were still there in 1841 – eking a living from Samuel's teaching fees – when Francis Grant arrived at the Nash-designed Sussex Lodge, Sussex Place, overlooking Regent's Park. In due course, Grant would succeed Sir Charles Eastlake as president of the Academy and be knighted in his turn. From that date forward, the local artistic community hardly required any further vindication of its essential honour and probity. Moreover, Sir Edwin Landseer, the man most people tipped to take Eastlake's job in 1866, had been living close by for all of 40 years. After 18 or so, when his friendship with Victoria and Albert was at its height, Landseer was moved to remodel his over-modest old farmhouse on St John's Wood Road.

Landseer, for all his talents, had little aptitude for business matters. If Prince Albert had decided Thomas Cubitt was good enough to design Osborne then Landseer saw no need to look further afield. Leaving all the arrangements in the capable hands of his friend, the pharmacist Jacob Bell, he went abroad on a long tour. 'Immediately on his departure [the farmhouse] was demolished and in its place uprose a pretentious mansion, retaining of the former humble dwelling only one little sitting room . . . All else was transformed'.[3] Sir Edwin was not wholly sure it was an improvement. In 1850 Bell was detailed to have it tuned up by Henry Ashton, an architect who later had the dubious distinction of designing London's first purpose-built flats. In the end the stuccoed dreadnought contained eight bedrooms, an anteroom for sitters, a 'sketchroom', and two studios, **90**. The upstairs studio was smaller all round by a third than that on the ground floor, which measured 40′ × 24′ × 15′. However, 'Many of the spacious rooms remained unfurnished; others stayed permanently

90 Sir Edwin Landseer's house in St John's Wood Road, St John's Wood, designed by Cubitt & Co. and Henry Ashton, c. 1844–50, from the east.

closed. Only the [main] studio was an unqualified success as it had at one end a space paved and enclosed where animals could be housed when required for models. In this room, half drawing room and half cage, were received some of the greatest people in the land'.[4]

During the bare half of the year that Sir Edwin spent at home, he was looked after by an aunt, his sister Jessica and his resourceful dogsbody, Bishop. None of them could keep him out of mischief though, and his indiscretions amongst the aristocracy were hushed up more successfully than was usual in the Wood. His recourse to the bottle was less well concealed. This followed the first bouts of mental depression that delayed the completion of the Nelson's Column lions and prevented his acceptance of the RA presidency. Sir Edwin died before his time in 1873, the house passing to the landscape and animal painter H W B Davis ARA. Davis was drawn to animal subjects after he had joined Sir Edwin's eldest brother, Tom Landseer, at the nearby 10a–10b Cunningham Place. The amiable engraver moved his business here in about 1850, adding one, if not two, workrooms to accommodate his employees and pupils. Already established in Cunningham Place when Tom came along were three of the late John Constable's children, while 3 St John's Wood Road, two doors east of Sir Edwin, was the home of the three Lucases, John, John Templeton and William.

John Lucas Snr, uncle of John Seymour Lucas, did quite nicely painting portraits of royalty and fashionable society. In 1840 he brought his two young boys to the semi-detached house on the corner of Lisson Grove, remaining there, off and on, for the rest of his life. With a view to both living and working in St John's Wood, he soon built a pair of painting rooms next to the house – after Landseer's, 'the two second studios' in the neighbourhood.[5] His titled lady sitters frequently complained of the fatiguing drive into the suburbs from Mayfair, however, so from time to time he also rented rooms in Newman and Duchess Streets. Having set up in the latter in 1851 and let out his two suburban studios, he suddenly decided he wanted to work in the Wood again. This silly situation led to his taking the lease of a house across St John's Wood Road at 8 Grove End Place[6] and the erection of a third studio there. Within another five years, by which time Lucas had returned to his original address, 7 Grove End Place had also been improved by the addition of a studio. It was here that the RA John Rogers Herbert similarly saw a need to put himself and three sons, all likewise painters, on a more professional footing while retaining contact with his family. The moral viewpoint Herbert displayed in his earnest religious works tended to excuse his stranger behaviour. His habit of speaking in a Frenchified broken English was said to be more than a trifle wearing after a while.

Grove End Place took on fresh significance once the Herberts had departed for Kilburn in 1868. But the life and soul of St John's Wood in 1850s and '60s centred around the streets a little more to the north, especially Grove End Road. Along with its various offshoots, Grove End Road was largely developed in the 1820s. Mr Hall, of Hall Road fame, built some of the grander stuccoed mansions in the area; most of these turned out to be white elephants and ruined him. One exception, however, was 16 Grove End Road which the RA John Jackson of Newman Street adopted as a country house between 1823 and 1831. Other exceptions were the two Hall Place houses taken by Edward Armitage when he was still an Outsider. Although Armitage did very well from gigantic scenes of Eastern barbarism such as Edwin Long prosecuted with equally insulting success, e.g., *Herod's Birthday Feast* (1868), he had the benefit of private means from the start. At his death he left no less than £318 000, the richest estate ever declared by a Victorian painter. Towards the end of the century many more artists could afford the grandeur this wealth represented, but the majority of them set out with houses in the £60–£100 a year bracket – modest houses like the one at 45 Grove End Road that George Hering first occupied in 1853, or the one opposite it at No. 4.

4 Grove End Road had long been a popular address, not least because the garden wall gave the local children an excellent free view of the matches at Lord's on the other side. Armitage, followed by Henry 'Stonebreaker' Wallis, had lived there; in 1865 it was the turn of the historical painter William Yeames. Yeames himself made history not only with *Amy Robsart* (1877) and *When Did You Last See Your Father?* (1878) but also on account of the part he played in the St John's Wood Clique. This latter-day Pre-Raphaelite brotherhood, of which there were likewise seven original members, owes its foundation in 1862 to the man whose sister Yeames married, David Wilkie Wynfield. The other founder members were George Leslie, Stacy Marks, Philip Calderon, John Hodgson and Calderon's brother-in-law George Storey.

Starting with Yeames, each of these painters either enlarged a St John's Wood house, found one already suitably adapted, or ran up a pavilion in the garden. Wynfield squeezed in a shed beside 14 Grove End Road some time after 1867. Leslie doubled the size of 8 Grove End Road in advance of his arrival in 1870. Marks built a garden studio at 15(36) Hamilton Terrace in about 1873; within another decade he had moved to No. 17(40) where he added a painting room, a glasshouse and an aviary. Calderon made no bones of his superior earning power by connecting a sizeable annexe to the former John Jackson house, 16 Grove End Road, in 1876. Hodgson, for his part, owned a house at 5(10) Hill Road which was perfectly ordinary until he invited the Clique to decorate the parlours with jocular episodes from Shakespeare, **91**. Notwithstanding these, Hodgson developed a more profitable stake in Islamic genre as a consequence of a trip to North Africa. In *c.* 1880 he removed his souvenirs – including a Tunisian barber's shopfront – to a much larger house in Circus Road. In the meantime Storey had made a move to the familiar 8 Grove End Place.[7] Storey's star rose rapidly on the strength of heart-tweakers like *Children at Breakfast* (1867) and *Mistress Dorothy* (1873), but he had to back-pedal when it soon levelled out;[8] his defection to West Hampstead in 1885 followed Leslie's escape to Wallingford one year earlier. The Clique survived these losses but finally disintegrated on its 25th anniversary in 1887 with the saddening death of Wynfield.

When Storey slipped into Grove End Place in 1877 he found that his neighbour was John Pettie – since the death of Landseer, the No. 1 painter in the Wood. At the opposite end of the row, at 1 Grove End Place, he saw that Phil Morris had installed himself in an ordered studio and glasshouse designed by T H Watson. Portraiture was Morris's long suit; subject pictures never put him within reach of a wholly custom-

91 Members of the St John's Wood Clique decorating John Hodgson's Hill Road house. From the left: ?Wynfield, Leslie, Hodgson, Yeames and Calderon.

built studio-house as they did a more versatile group of his contemporaries who, like Pettie, were biding their time in 'little league' studios.

Prominent in this group which colonised territory north of the top end of Grove End Road were John O'Connor, Henry Holiday, John MacWhirter and Edwin Long. As early as 1860 the Irishman John O'Connor made an addition to 6 Waverley Place, an end-of-terrace house on land that used to be the Eyre Arms beer garden. Directly north again of Waverley Place lay Finchley Place, a lane serving houses at the Finchley Road end of Marlborough Road (now Place). It was here that the decorative artists Henry and Kate Holiday decided to pitch down in 1868. 'After some searching', Holiday recounted, 'we found an attractive house in St John's Wood: 5 Marlborough Road, which, with our doctor's approval, we took, and moved into before the end of the year.'[9] However, no more than four years passed before the Finchley Place workshop that came with the house was pronounced unhealthy and they made plans to transfer to higher ground in Hampstead. Yet dampness did not deter their successor, Briton Riviere, one of the many *animaliers* choosing to live in the Wood for its handiness to the Regent's Park Zoo. Then it was the turn of MacWhirter to arrive next door at No. 6. Having not so long before tracked his close friends Pettie and Orchardson to London from Edinburgh, MacWhirter was sufficiently encouraged to put down more permanent roots in 1875. Accordingly he erected an austere timber paintbox which also gave onto Finchley Place. Backed by Ruskin, his illustrations and articulate landscapes earned him considerable wealth and respect by the end of the 1870s. As for Edwin Long, he alighted concurrently at 19 Marlborough Hill, forthwith throwing up a villa-sized studio ('Longsden') on the lower part of the garden. But this was to be merely a limbering fling on the showman-dauber's northward road to Fitzjohn's Avenue.

Studio-building throughout St John's Wood ensued with increased vigour after 1875 just as it did in London's other artistic congeries. Developments in this predominantly early 19th-century suburb, however – and it should be fairly clear by now – were more than elsewhere characterised by the cheap-and-cheerful addition to existing housing stock rather than the brand new palace of art on fresh subdivisions. Nevertheless the more professionally presented Calderon, Morris and Long showings of 1875–6 presaged more substantial enterprises altogether. John O'Connor set the ball rolling in 1877. Like David Roberts and Clarkson Stanfield before him, O'Connor resigned his positions at Drury Lane and the Haymarket, opting to become a full-time landscape painter. He and a fellow topographer, James Whittet Smith, pooled the £8000 required to buy and build on adjacent infill sites in Abbey Place – the Abbey Road end of Abercorn Place. For their architect they wanted someone with a reasonably firm-wristed grasp of the 'Queen Anne' style, so they chose Thomas W Cutler.

Cutler used red materials everywhere. Compared to the huddle of pancaked Late Georgian dowagers alongside, the two debutante houses that he designed stand out in a garish flush of rouge, **92**. Carved brick entablatures, tallish chimneystacks and wavy ironwork evoke the period well enough, but the small-paned windows are treated as if they still have thick compo surrounds. O'Connor's sharp-set studio

Tadema made great play of the hinging east side especially. By opening it out, changing the levels and pushing an opera-box gallery across to the conservatory, he teed up several glancing vistas from the body of the house. Most of these were aimed at the priceless onyx screen from the Townshend House Gold Room, which was now placed to stun and diffuse any fierce flashes of westering sun. Others intercepted the immensely tall, double-glazed north window which was designed to beam a painting light to the back of the apse 45 feet away. If not from the outset, at an early stage (when some observers claimed to notice an unprecedented brilliance in Tadema's painting) the apse, possibly the entire ceiling, was coated with aluminium leaf to help it along. Oil, later electric, lamps made good any shortfall on really dull days when even the conservatory was of no use. Certainly, there is hardly a post-1887 Tadema work, e.g., *Silver Favourites* (1903), *The Frigidarium* (1890), that fails either to sublimate these various radiances or convincingly mythologise those penetrating perspectives, **98**, **99**.

In addition to outward signs, one or two other such paintings show that the stylised Pompeian make-up of the studio was carried through the wings towards the garden porch, **100**. Contrary to expectation, the atrium was not open to the sky. It borrowed light from a glass-roofed compluvium (strictly speaking) over the marble basin in the corner. Columns rose up around the basin supporting an upper walkway – which led to the studio and conservatory galleries – and, to soften the midday glare, a muslin velarium. Gilt-capped piers, verde-antico facings and triclinium couches extended the antique theme into the smoking room. But it stopped there; the dining room, in which the shattered cabinets from Townshend House were once again recycled, reintroduced the warm lustre of high quality woodwork. Holly, mahogany, pitch pine, fruit woods, nut woods . . . all these were combined unvarnished in the joinery elsewhere on the ground floor and upstairs. The central hall, however, was painted ivory white. Here the wainscot from Laura's former painting room was re-erected around Tissot's salon fireplace. Over the years the narrow coffers in the panelling were filled with 'calling-card' paintings by appreciative guests. Men like Leighton, Poynter and J W Waterhouse naturally donated appropriate classical subjects.

Many other items inside and outside the house were specially commissioned. A generous host (his 'Twosday' At Homes were legendarily twomultwous), Tadema was also a liberal patron. Alfred Newman was invited to execute the curlicue wrought-iron grilles, crestings, and the singular maulstick-and-palette weathervane.[17] John LaFarge, a contemporary of Tiffany, supplied the stained glass *Peonies* in the atrium; Reynolds-Stephens modelled the copper gallery-front after Tadema's painting, *The Women of Amphissa*. Yet other pieces – busts by Dalou and Amendola, portraits by Collier and Bastien-Lepage – were brought in from Townshend House. But when it came to architecture or furniture, Tadema was very much his own master. Although the house, unlike Leighton's, grew no larger, numerous garden features including the unmistakably Pompeian entrance loggia were added in later years. By 1890 he was often called on by spendthrift Americans to design and decorate grand pianos and living room suites in the manner of his own extraordinary

99 A clockwise move from **98**, showing portions of the silvered apse and the onyx window bay with its Byzantine tracery.

100 17(44) Grove End Road, St John's Wood. Seen from Abbey Road, Tadema's 'Early Christian' studio meets the pagan 'Pompeian' body of the house.

pieces – the schizophrenic Egyptian/Roman divan, for instance. Garden, stage or costume design – all he ever turned his hand to, contributed unfailingly to his wealth and celebrity. A knighthood in 1899, the Order of Merit in 1905, and the RIBA Gold Medal in 1906 crowned a bountiful life devoted to his adopted country. Generous to a fault, however, Sir Lawrence left by far the greater part of his £59 000 estate to the Royal Academy in 1912. Laurence and Anna, who never married and died in obscurity, received barely anything more useful than £100 each.

Sir Lawrence proved to be the last Victorian worthy to keep the Academy flag flapping in Grove End Road even though two or three younger RAs arrived after he did. As it happened, this once much prettier street became an even more de luxe address, statistically at least, than Melbury Road, Kensington. There seemed to be no end to its possibilities. The military painter Ernest Crofts occupied the old Hering house for ten years from 1890. In the same year a fellow battlemonger, A C Gow, moved to No. 15, improving further a villa already extended by Guido Bach. Gow outstayed both Crofts and the landscapist (Sir) Alfred East who dabbled at No. 4 after Yeames had retired. Many other simply able men filled the gaps in between or backed up in the no less sought-after side streets. And the appearance of yet more RAs in the same neighbourhood: H H Armstead in Circus Road, J W Waterhouse in Hall Road, together with the insistent presence of the St John's Wood Art School in Elm Tree Road (founded 1878), demonstrated the range of talent still at hand at the end of the century.

Painters, plainly enough, were very plentiful hereabouts. Even the one senior sculptor mentioned, Armstead, continued to work in distant Pimlico. But in the late 1880s and early 1890s the young, progressive sculptor who rejected High Victorian dignity and moral stiffness in favour of symbolic and sensuous, if not sensual, informality, slipped relatively naturally into the easy-going, all-forgiving Wood. And now, rather than the old-fashioned Canal Zone, they seemed to prefer to work more towards the north-east.[18]

One of the better remembered modern figures was the very deserving Edward Onslow Ford (RA 1895). This most sensitive and skilful modeller established an appreciable yard in 1887 at 62 Acacia Road, on the present St John's Wood Underground station site. His operations were still expanding when he died aged 49 in 1901, having just completed Manchester's mighty *Queen Victoria*. Ford's loss was soon covered by at least three other eminent newcomers: (Sir) George Frampton, (Sir) William Goscombe John, and William Colton. Frampton urgently needed space to model the larger commissions he was beginning to accumulate. Finding what he wanted at 32 Queen's Grove in 1893, he sank his down-payments into modification of the surviving lumpy sheds at the rear. Having married the painter Christabel Cockerell in the same year, he was also obliged to provide for her by extending the house over the side carriageway. Less than ten years later Frampton could charge £1000 for a single stone spandrel carving. 1908, therefore, saw his move to the new, but half-baked, Arts and Crafts-style 90 (now 92–6) Carlton Hill with its inconclusively conjoined studios alongside. Such well-known works as *Peter Pan* and the *Edith Cavell Memorial* were still to come. Frampton's fellow pupil, the Welshman Goscombe John, followed him to *Woronzow Studios*, a speculatively built pair neighbouring Queen's Grove in 1894, and in 1895 Colton, a sculptor of the luscious, fleshly school, set up at the corner of Kingsmill Terrace and Circus Road.

Wholly within the same Finchley Road–Avenue Road realm lived a separate trio of animal painters: Briton Riviere, John Macallan Swan, and John Nettleship. The first two, however, were also creditable sculptors. Riviere took to sculpture more seriously, e.g., *The Last Arrow* (1896), after his rise to RA and his move to 82 Finchley Road in 1880. F W Waller, John Collier's architect, remodelled the existing house on the site, joining on a working area that, like Landseer's, was half painting room and half loose box, **101**. One day Riviere warned a prospective visitor that he was having horses in, 'which add neither to its tidiness nor to its fragrance'.[19] Another caller picked a better time; he found a studio 'full of animal studies, including skeletons of a leopard, a dog, and a cat, with a host of casts of limbs and things'.[20] The back room at 35 Acacia Road, which Nettleship added in about 1884, must have looked similar. Swan, who is noted for his renderings of lions and tigers, cannot have done without a feline skeleton or two either. He drew up at 3 Acacia Road in 1889 and forthwith built the rickety studio adjoining, all broken-backed glazing on the north front, all top-lit animal pens behind.

But it evidently required more than money and sensibility to engender a sculptor's studio-house such as had not been seen since Thornycroft's of 1877. Perhaps (Sir) Alfred Gilbert RA came closest to it by bringing nerve and rage to bear as well. By 1893 Gilbert had passed nearly 20 years of married life at home and abroad without a fitting place he could call his own. That he was gifted enough to go it alone was undoubted; that he could afford to was open to question. He had made a modicum from Winchester's *Queen Victoria* – the much-bedecked monarch shaken wonder-

101 Interior of 82 Finchley Road, Upper St John's Wood, added *c.* 1880 by Frederick Waller for Briton Riviere. The tidier inner section of an animal painter's studio drawn by William Luker.

drugged from Santa's sack; wrested a profit from Manchester's Jeremiah-Time-Bomb *Joule*; lost £4000 on London's fairyland carousel incorporating the aluminium figure of *Eros*; but was once more realistically sponsored for Windsor's spectral *Duke of Clarence* on his panseraphic catafalque. Impatience and impudent self-assurance nullified any other considerations. Thus Gilbert's choice of building site fell on St John's Wood – Sculpturedom – and on Maida Vale, where his parents lived, in particular.[21] Howard Ince, an award-winning young architect who also hailed from Maida Vale, was given his chance to repeat the form he had recently shown in the design of a mansion for a wealthy Swede.

Ince's scheme was finalised by mid-1893. It provided a rectilinear coil of accommodation wherein the principal rooms, except the dining room, looked onto a courtyard, **102**. Distinctively bow-fronted, the dining room shared the grandiose

102 Alfred Gilbert's 16 Maida Vale, St John's Wood, designed in 1893. Howard Ince's thumbnail plan accompanies a view of the courtyard.

Howard Ince inv et delt. March '93

Maida Vale frontage with the models' and assistants' end of Gilbert's workshops. These workshops added up to the largest studio complex ever built in London: the main section alone measured 108′ × 26′ × 28′ – sufficiently big to house two short goods trains side by side. Together with the partly-glazed loco shed doors at the Maida Vale end, the main section sported an equally tall pair between two 14′ side lights facing the courtyard. Whereas most of the moulding and preparatory work was carried out here, Gilbert did his full-size modelling in a personal studio at the north-east end under a truly huge curtain of plate glass. For his sketches and small-scale pieces he could pass beneath a pulpit-like gallery to a more intimate space alongside. A similar great window flanked by deepened reveals gulped at any lumens still at large, **103**. All manner of stores and domestic ancillaries tailed away into a yard beyond.

But the stuff of a sculptor's dreams soon turned into an unremitting incubus. However ambitiously the brief may have been stacked, Ince failed to realise how wildly his cost estimates would be exceeded. Gilbert's impetuosity also contributed to his undoing. For instance, when the people next door appealed against their loss of light, the sculptor bought their house and installed his parents in it. Of course, like

103 Sections and elevations of 16 Maida Vale. Alfred Gilbert's main workshop was 'sufficiently big to house two short goods trains side by side'.

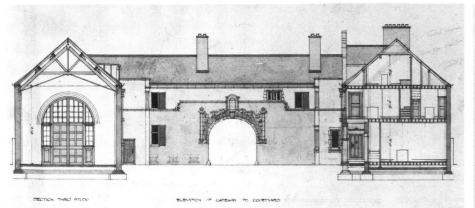
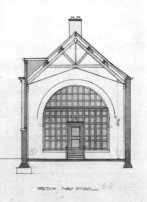
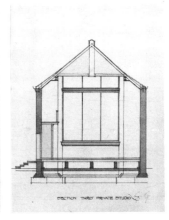
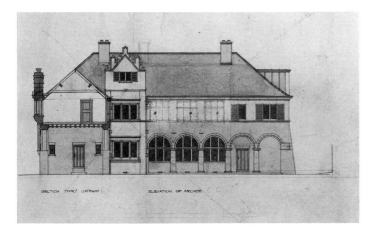
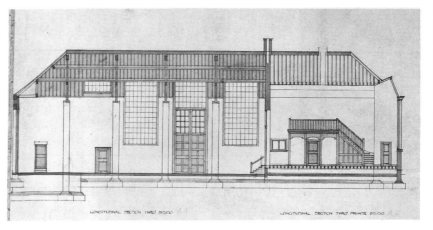

Whistler, he ended up heavily in debt. The house – and there was a touch of the Lethabys about it – could be only thinly decorated. Ince's confused attempts show how invidious the task must have been with a client as creative as this one. Gilbert held out at 16 Maida Vale for six years before submitting to bankruptcy. In 1900 the bailiffs duly claimed the house and he sought exile on the Continent where he was to remain for 26 years. Various sculptors made use of No. 16 while he was away and, after his death in 1934, Sir William Reid Dick occupied it from 1938 to 1961.

It should be made clear that Gilbert was not alone among sculptors stationed to the west of Finchley Road. An eruption of bright sparks occurred in the volatile ground nearby at much the same time. Briefly, then, Roscoe Mullins (Fine Art Society carving, London) took up at the architectural jumble of 24 Greville Road[22] in 1889. In 1891 Harry Bates ARA (*Pandora*; *Lord Roberts*, Glasgow) began the last nine years of his short life at 10 Hall Road, which he enlarged in the typical St John's Wood manner. (Sir) Bertram Mackennal (*Circè*; *Queen Victoria*, Blackburn; RA 1924) established a studio in 1893 at the rear of 87a Clifton Hill, where the terrace was tunnelled through to provide access. And two further pairs of dextrous hands, (Sir) William Reynolds-Stephens (fixtures for St Mary, Great Warley, Essex) and Henry Pegram (*Sibylla Fatidica*; RA 1922) also resorted to St John's Wood in 1895 and 1897, one going to Hodgson's old burrow in Hill Road, the other to workshops at 36 Marlborough Hill.

Having strayed towards Finchley Road again, it is similarly worth noting that Riviere was not alone among painters in the road itself. One of the many converts to Islam, J B Burgess (RA 1888), enlarged No. 60 soon after purchasing it in 1883. The illustrator Arthur Hopkins followed suit at No. 80 after 1884, while in 1892 two more hardy annuals, Yeend 'Dairymaid' King at No. 103 and Dendy 'The Regent Prince' Sadler at No. 44, both went to the architect Frederick Lewis[23] for more of the same: galleried extensions with glasshouses and/or etching rooms attached. In fact Sadler, not Riviere, might have claimed to be the real pioneer of the eastern bloc. First stopping at Finchley Road in 1878, he then transferred to the poet Tom Hood's old house, No. 28. Rooms in this house, which he vacated in 1893, later became those of the St John's Wood Arts Cub – founded early in 1895 by himself and Burgess.

Other characters without whom the Wood would have been the poorer include the minority element of the super-rich and high-born. Neither of the baronets, the English Sir William Eden in Hill Road or the Irish Sir Robert Staples on Marlborough Hill disported other than discreetly, even if somewhat rashly.[24] But Robert Little, a middle-order watercolourist of independent means (his father owned ships), revealed a frivolous streak unusual for a Scotsman. Like Edwin Long at No. 19 some 15 years before, Little built onto 27 Marlborough Hill to quite extravagant effect only to invest in a Hampstead house and studio two years later. Apparently he lived in both at once. At Marlborough Hill he connected a large studio-cum-music room to the semi-detached house by a long, glazed gallery, **104**. His architect could easily have been Flockhart or Stevenson. At 6a Abercorn Place, on the other hand, the architect was probably T H Watson. Designed in Neo-Baroque style on behalf of the wealthy mural painter Sigismund Goetze in 1891, it comprises assorted living rooms subordinate to a studio with outsize north and east side lights under a pyramidal

104 A Bedford Lemere photograph of Robert Little's music-painting room at 27 Marlborough Hill, St John's Wood, taken in 1891. Every luxury from an antimacassar to an electrolier.

roof.[25] Goetze lived here until 1909, when he moved up to Grove House (Nuffield Lodge), Regent's Park. Watson's pupil, Sydney Tatchell, constructed a second studio for him, not unlike the earlier one except far grander – fashioning the existing arc of outbuildings into a highly eventful solid quadrant.

Considering the total number of local artists, only a very few came to appreciate a made-to-measure studio of their own, let alone two of them. Of the better and more conspicuous conversions, Sydney Starr's 38 Abercorn Place should be mentioned. Rebuilt in reasonable imitation of the prevalent George IV style in 1883, it nonetheless leaves no doubt in which direction north lies. A painter of the New English Art Club persuasion (indeed, of what Whistler called the 'Steery Starry Stotty lot'), Starr made his deepest impression in America – his destination in 1889 when he left the house to Charles, the lesser of the Wyllie brothers, marine painters. Otherwise, local artists tended to abet the increasingly slip-shod, shanty-town appearance of the suburb. Melina Place, whence Wyllie hailed, is a case in point. Some of the mingiest studios in the Wood were built here, among them those of *c.* 1886 for Johnny Parker (No. 5, later taken, in his decline, by the cartoonist Phil May[26]) and Henry Macbeth-Raeburn (No. 6, later taken by Harrington Mann of the Glasgow School).

No one could have hoped to halt the visual vandalism these excrescences represent. After all, with only rare salutary exceptions, piecemeal accretion had been the very history of artistic St John's Wood. But, one way or another, it has likewise been the entire history of architecture. St John's Wood continued to degenerate, overrun by institutions, riddled with railways, belittled by high-rise flats. Yet outposts of sanity did exist here and there. Even the crustiest of Academicians, old 'Derby Day' Frith, managed to find an unsullied spot that was forever quiet and sunny in the dead-end at the bottom of Clifton Hill. Nevertheless, to the equally crusty Old Jolyon Forsyte it was still all too seedy and louche for words.

8

MASS-PRODUCED STUDIOS: TERRACES AND FLATS

FOR EVERY custom-built studio in London there would have been another two or three speculatively built ones that could be rented from a landlord. Single units were put up also, but due to the economy of scale these were greatly outnumbered by multiples arranged in terraces and flats. By 1914 some 150 properties of this kind existed, ranging from pairs to groups of as many as 30. Their development runs parallel to that of the individual private house and naturally they are found in the same artistic quarters of the city. If few of them are as extravagant as the one-off houses, others are just as curious or ingeniously planned. A good many are known to be professionally designed but these are not necessarily the more charming examples. Often the charm arises from a conflict between the site and the desirable orientation or the achievement of maximum floor area. Speculators were always trying to capitalise on odd-shaped sites ill-suited to ordinary housing or commerce; backlands and left-over wedges in sought-after areas made particular bargains. Artists could be counted on to take almost any sort of studio space as long as it was cheap.

Discounting rooms of the cut-up window type in the Newman Street region, the earliest instance of deliberate concerted provision for artists is likely to be *Tudor Lodge Studios*, dating from 1843–4. Tudor Lodge, at the Mornington Crescent end of Albert Street, Camden Town, was built in eponymous style for the Paris-trained history and portrait painter, Charles Lucy. Needing space for major canvases, giant cartoons, and several pupils, Lucy therefore attached what was probably an extensive subdivisible shed to the crooked little house. It was certainly big enough for other artists to rent spare divisions. From the outset, then:

> Tudor Lodge was a nest of studios; of these Frank Howard had the largest, Earl Compton the next, and Lucy, with whom Madox Brown worked, the next, John Tenniel being next door to them.[1]

Most of these men were working on their Westminster Hall competition entries at the time. On his move to Barbizon in 1855, Lucy appears to have sold his house but retained ownership of the studios. By 1860 (when Thomas Woolner rented one during the construction of his Welbeck Street shops), two masonry buildings had replaced the original shed. A third one was added to match by 1870. All three directed paired double-hung sashes and skylights squarely to the north across the Tudor Lodge garden.

It is not surprising to find this first development in Camden Town. The overflow from Fitzrovia had been filtering through Somers Town along the Hampstead Road since the early 1800s. A Royal Academician had already spent many years in and near Mornington Crescent before Lucy arrived. So, although they followed hesitantly, Camden Town also claims the next two initiatives, *Stanhope* and *Camden Studios*.

Delancey (formerly Stanhope) Street crosses Albert Street towards its north end. No. 68a was raised over a carriageway to allow access to Stanhope Yard behind. In 1856 Charles Kingston, a City businessman, took possession of 'two back premises' newly built in the yard. Again they were temporarily divided brick structures, outwardly very similar to Lucy's second stage buildings – complete with skylights over broad side lights. By 1866–7 the little terrace had grown by one slightly larger unit. Kingston may have employed his own staff here since, when the painter Albert Ludovici Snr took No. 3 'in the 1860s', he inherited it from 'M. Raymond, a French decorator'.[2] Ludovici's contemporaries included J J Hill and Tom Graham. The sculptors Harry Dixon and Henry Pegram occupied adjacent divisions from the late 1880s onwards.

Camden Studios were erected on a square of land behind the Camden Street Methodist chapel by a cautious neighbouring builder, William Roberts. In three stages between 1865 and 1869 he built a total of nine workshops, all roughly to the same formula. They were set out in two rows, the glazed fronts of one facing the rear

105 *The Avenue*, 76 Fulham Road, South Kensington, from the north. The local developer Charles Freake converted his estate workshops into sculptors' and painters' studios from 1869 onwards.

walls of the other. Henry Bursill, then modelling figures to adorn Holborn Viaduct, was among the sculptors who immediately signed leases for the first three units. Edgar Bundy and Andrea Lucchesi were later tenants of this group which has been replaced in part by a modern substitute.

After 1870 Camden Town ceased to be the centre of speculative enterprise in this regard. Similar developments rapidly materialised in all the parts of London especially favoured by Victorian artists. South Kensington, on a technicality, had already registered a pair of off-the-peg studios in 1859–60. These were the swish three-storey houses for gentleman artists built in Cromwell Place by the local developer, (Sir) Charles Freake. But the time was ripe a decade later for basic, non-residential studios for journeyman artists. Such was the spirit in which the Camden Town groups were conceived, even though there was hardly any stopping poorer individuals sneaking in bed, bath and bain-marie to save renting additional digs elsewhere. Smartly recognising this market, Freake set about realising superior rents from some of his tradesmen's under-used workshops and a mews, which were situated together between Onslow Square and Fulham Road.

Undoubtedly Freake's vision was also sharpened by the recent activities of the sculptors (Sir) Joseph Boehm and Baron Carlo Marochetti.

> A very poor sculptor, Marochetti came over owing to stress of politics in Italy, and obtaining, as a foreigner so often does, patronage out of all proportion to his artistic powers, contrived to earn a living here until 1867.[3]

Almost as soon as he settled, Marochetti established himself on the south side of Onslow Square. In 1849–50 he ran up workspace beside Freake's mews large enough to contain a colossal equestrian *Richard Coeur de Lion* shown by him at the Great Exhibition of the following year. By 1865 his several workshops, incorporating a full-scale foundry, were equivalent in value and extent to five Onslow Square houses added together. At that date Marochetti and his assistant, Sr Baccani, were finally preparing to cast the Nelson's Column lions which had been modelled in the very same shops by Landseer. Another of Sir Edwin's helpers was the sporting painter Charles Lutyens, father of Sir Edwin Landseer Lutyens, who had just moved into 16 Onslow Square.

Marochetti's sudden death late in 1867, and Boehm's plea for premises to improve on those he had recently built too conservatively at 13 Sumner Place, decided Freake to convert the entire collection of buildings behind Onslow Square into rudimentary artists' studios. Three years later an initial three units had been allocated to Boehm, Lutyens, and Marochetti's pupil, the painter Charles Hallé.[4] The total complement of about 20 assorted units was completed soon afterwards. To this day, a forward range of capacious sculptors' shops is separated by a low corridor from a taller, rearward range. North light is contrived to enter at two separately let levels of the latter. Freake must therefore be credited with the first purpose-built, flatted studios to add to his distinctions. The whole block was named *The Avenue*, 76 Fulham Road, after a depleted double line of elms nearby, **105**.

Of all London's studio groups, *The Avenue* might well possess the greatest number of illustrious alumni. Beside Boehm and the other early-comers, there were Elizabeth Thompson (Lady Butler) who painted her startling *Roll Call* here; (Sir) Alfred Gilbert who sculpted the *Shaftesbury Memorial*; Singer Sargent who prefabricated the Boston Library decoration, and so on. But almost comparable lists can be drawn up for the seminal groups elsewhere in the capital. The superlative illustrator A B Houghton, for example, pioneered *St John's Wood Studios* erected at 32a Queen's Terrace in three phases beginning in 1869–70. Early studio-purveyors in Hampstead soon had distinguished names on their books, too. It was the ubiquitous Batterbury family of speculators which set the pace there in 1872 with a discreet, backland development east of Haverstock Hill. Known, by coincidence, as *The Mall*, it consists of eight studios, seven in a row and one detached, planted on gardens reclaimed from Batterbury-built houses in Park (Parkhill) Road, **106**. As the press announced at the time, 'Each studio is 25′ × 20′ . . . and has small waiting rooms, costume room, lobby, and other necessary conveniences' . . . 'The cost of each will be from 325 pounds to 350 pounds'.[5] Attention was drawn to the excellent workmanship and such details as the chimneypots bearing the monograms of the respective occupants. At least three of these men, Robert Macbeth, (Sir) James Linton, and Edward Gregory, made considerable marks in the art world later in life. Since they were so soundly built, the studios have similarly famous associations with 20th-century artists.

Apparently novel, the basic design of both *The Mall* and *The Avenue* studios –

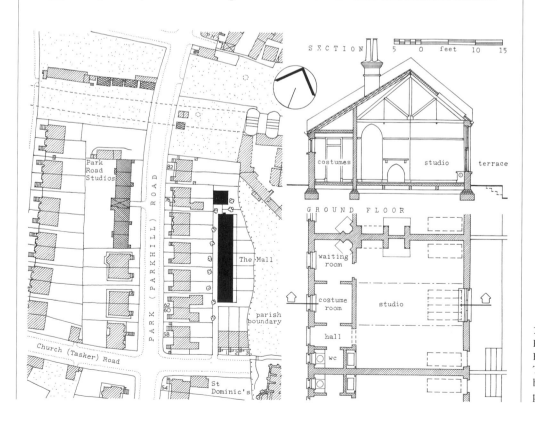

106 *The Mall*, Tasker Road, Hampstead (1872). Eight units designed by Thomas Batterbury and built behind his brother's properties in Park Road.

subsequently wholly typical in London – would in fact seem to derive from the medieval 'hall house'. A certain likeness lies in the double-height space open to the roof, with service rooms opening off it; the storage gallery, or gallery bedroom option, is related just as surely to the traditional upper-level 'solar'. Having achieved such good value for money, Batterbury stuck to these old principles when building the five *Steele's Studios* at 97a Haverstock Hill soon afterwards. Continuing local demand brought new speculators to elaborate on his approach.

In Chelsea the demand proved to be equally strong. The initial development there, *Albert Gate Studios*, actually occurred on the old parish boundary with Belgravia, and its character responds to the connotations of that exclusive district. Between William and Kinnerton Streets stands a tall, bulky building now called Bradbrook House. Before 1872, when Captain Augustus Savile Lumley bought it, it housed a school of anatomy. Lumley was a dashing socialite. While portraiture and caricature could be added to his list of accomplishments, his talent for getting up a charity ball was unapproachable. Indeed, as the *Vanity Fair* editor recognised, '. . . it is not as Lumley the artist in Painting that London best knows Augustus; but rather as the artist in Society, the organiser of amusement, the man of universal acquaintance, and the best of good creatures.'[6] As Lumley's property adjoined 6 William Street he bought that as well, carving out a painting room for himself to begin with. The anatomy school he had converted into a good half-dozen studio-flats. Early tenants of the block, all Lumley's fellow swells, lent it the aspect of a secret playboys' club: (Sir) William Orchardson, the Hon. Archie Stuart-Wortley, the Hon. John Collier, (Sir) Leslie Ward. Both Collier and Wortley camped here while their Tite Street houses were being built. Those former dissection rooms made marvellously convenient, if somewhat macabre, places to inveigle society sitters.

Back in Kensington a number of local investors began to follow Freake's example by building studio-flats, albeit on a smaller scale. Several groups of a few each sprang up beside new railway lines or on otherwise useless, narrow plots. The next showing of any substance and sophistication after *The Avenue* came in 1877–8 with *The Studios, Holland Park Road*, a close of two-storey units planned and built by the major housing contractor William Willett. Sensing the artistic spell which hung over the Melbury Road area, Willett set out to exploit it when an obsolete school site became available next door to Prinsep's house. Behind a formal red brick façade he arranged six amply proportioned, although gardenless, dwellings which benefit from factory-style north-lights over the upper floors. *The Studios* immediately attracted both the couth and suitably spellbound tenant, including (Sir) William Richmond and the Baroness Orczy. In later years many another self-respecting painter, among them John Lorimer and Eleanor Brickdale, worked in an adjacent casbah whose landlords had also muscled in on this Academicians' purlieu. A more picturesque, secluded group of six, however – known at the time of building in 1879 as *Stratford Avenue* – is situated off Stratford Road, near the workhouse. Three of the four units in echelon here are cleverly arranged (although reflected glare may have caused some inconvenience) to enclose private gardens, **107**. Porches with practical double doorways screen the gardens from the main access alley. As at Holland Park Road, provision is

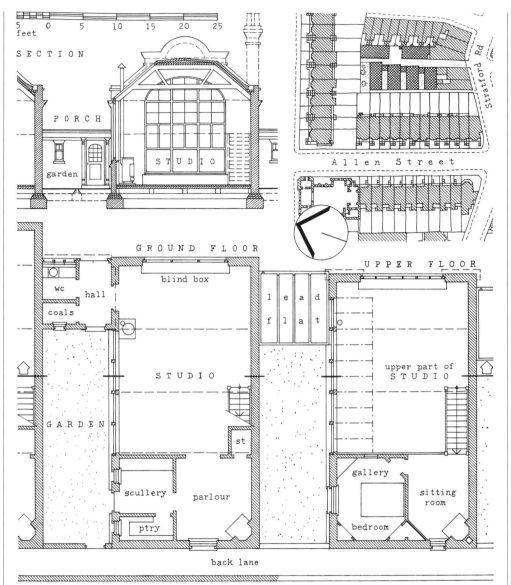

107 *Stratford Avenue*, Stratford Road, Kensington (1879–). Picturesque variety compensates a halfway-successful overall layout.

made for residence around the clock, while the universally familiar studio layout featuring a gallery bedroom becomes particularly apparent. No.s 5 and 6, built slightly later, do not compare so well in plan or decorative character. (Sir) Frank Brangwyn and his travelling companion Arthur Melville worked here during the 1890s. In *c.*1906 Channel P Townsley commandeered the majority[7] of the studios for his London School of Art.

Once invented, the typical studio layout was widely applied to terraces and flats alike. Studio-flats may pass unnoticed where north lies beyond their back gardens, but where tiers of oversized windows distinguish their public face, they tend to be unmistakable. Two such self-evident banks of studio-flats adjoin each other at *75* and *77 Bedford Gardens*, Campden Hill, **108**. Phené Spiers was probably responsible for

108 *77 Bedford Gardens*, Kensington (1882). R Stark Wilkinson's skyscraper contains 10 studios, most of them no more than 19′ × 16′. The adjoining flats, No. 75, are earlier.

the laughably skinny one in 1877. Stark Williamson owns up to No. 77 where the individual units were once no wider. It originally comprised ground floor workshops for the respected clay-modeller Percy Ball – who commissioned the building – surmounted by four storeys of painting rooms and a series of mezzanines at the rear, making ten suites in all. Above the first floor, each front window represents one studio, while on the fourth floor an additional pair of rearward studios was lit by skylights only. The toplit stairwell was generously planned to facilitate the raising and lowering of big canvases. Percy Ball obtained a quick return on his outlay and in 1886, aged 42, went to seek further fortune in Australia. Robert Stark and Harry Bates were two of the sculptors who succeeded to their colleague's tight but ordered appointments.

Even more self-evident in Thurloe Square, South Kensington, are *Thurloe Studios*, built in 1885–7 by the thrifty opportunist William Douglas.[8] They rise five storeys on an acutely tapering site left vacant when the District railway shaved a corner of this early Victorian square some twenty years before, **109**. Few concessions were made either to the prevailing style of the neighbouring terraces or to the comfort of the resident artists. A bunkroom, a scullery and a w.c. come with each of the seven studios, although the spaces clearly become more angular and closet-like towards the thin edge of the wedge. Mezzanines do not seem to have formed part of the original plan. *Thurloe Studios* made excellent pieds-à-terre but would not tempt any best-selling painters. Another flatiron terrace devised for beanpole artists faces the same railway line at Margravine Gardens, Hammersmith.

By the 1890s the Kensington builders had explored several more variations on the same theme. They had already discovered perhaps the most efficient one (for painters, at least) with the living floor-working floor terraces of *The Studios, Holland Park Road*. This solution was soon refined in the shape of the luxurious *Cheniston Gardens Studios* (1883) which rise three storeys per unit. Like the 'hall house' arrangement it was not a revolutionary discovery, however. After all, contract weavers in Spitalfields and, say, Macclesfield, had evolved essentially similar houses in previous centuries. But every new site was subject to different conditions and different forms of building accordingly resulted.

On the site of *43–45 Roland Gardens*, for instance, the precedent existed for skyscraper flats. But the owner of a studio extension directly behind exerted his right to light, with the result that the new block emerged rather lop-sided. A South Kensington architect, J A J Keynes, developed the site to his own designs in 1891–2.[9] At No. *43* a splendid painting room surmounted a maisonette let separately or in tandem, **110**. At No. *45*, entered down the side, the ground floor was let together with the basement. Keynes's scheme appears to partially imitate Col. Edis's *33 Tite Street*, Chelsea; his tenants – Paul Maitland, for example, likewise tended to reveal a Tite Street influence.

In the case of *Roland Gardens*, a very high plot ratio was achieved along with a handsome public image. *Scarsdale Studios* of 1891, again in Stratford Road, reveal a corresponding blend of greed and grace. Two pairs of flats and six working units under their own roofs nestle in a sequestered enclave just 80′ × 80′. The group as a

109

110

111

112

109 *Thurloe Studios*, Thurloe Square, South Kensington (1885–7). Studios were often considered a commercial proposition on otherwise unworkable sites.

110 *43–45 Roland Gardens*, South Kensington, designed by J A J Keynes, 1891–2. A graceful Aesthetic distension narrowly triumphs over an unsettling angularity.

111 Entrance to *Scarsdale Studios*, Stratford Road, Kensington (1891). Modelled tools of trade on the artistic equivalent of a mews arch betray the presence in a mid-Victorian neighbourhood of an otherwise typically secreted studio group.

112 *Pembroke Studios*, Pembroke Gardens, Kensington (1890–1). Studios with chamfered gable ends look north and east onto either public or private gardens.

whole is approached via an archway lodge; in return for his rent the caretaker was expected to monitor comings and goings from the Sunday-suited oriel with its quaintly emblazoned spandrel, **111**. The growing number of liberated maiden ladies who took studios in hideaways such as this in order to pursue useful occupations in the fine arts may have appreciated his presence. *Pembroke Studios*, Pembroke Gardens, put up by the local builder C F Kearley, is another group of 1890–1 which was supervised in the same manner.[10] Two rows of six matching studios border a planted courtyard defended by an ornamental gatehouse, **112**. North lies slightly wide of the long axis of the courtyard so that all but the endmost studios were destined to peer around the corner of the next one in line. But the builder has thoughtfully chamfered both forward corners of each unit and happily solved the problem. The geometric variety introduced by this measure is tempered by uniform wall and window details in attractive 'Queen Anne' colours. Henry Detmold and Henry Ryland were among the first to discover the breadth and simplicity of the interiors.

Most of Kensington's later studio ranges, notably *Edwardes Square*, *Alma* and *Logan Studios*, cropped up not far from Pembroke Square. Probably the last, however, was built in 1911 to a design by the architect Douglas Wells on a sliver of old stable yard in Kensington New Town. Unbelievably, eight separate flats go to make up *St Alban's Studios*, South End. Some of the more hemmed-in ones on the first floor are forced to send up phototropic periscopes within tiny gambrel roofs.

But most have scads of window-wall looking onto a minuscule common patio fairly filled with flowering greenery, **113**. This rookery-nook appealed hugely to young lady artists before they were called away to the munitions factories.

Compared to the modest grandeur of the better Kensington models, St John's Wood and parts north have somewhat less to boast of. Nevertheless, of the schemes to follow the one in Queen's Terrace, *Primrose Hill Studios* or, as it was known early on, Fitzroy Road Studios, bring them certain credit. Here the initiative came from Alfred Healey of Healey & Baker, builders. In 1877 Healey completed ten terraced houses (No.s 31–49, odd) in Fitzroy Road. Behind these he reserved a larger area for 12 terraced studios and a lodge. J W Waterhouse, J D Watson, J C Dollman and Joseph Wolf were able to buy leases in the first row of six in 1878. A second row built by 1881 is separated by the precursor of *Pembroke Studios*' planted courtyard. Units in the second row are jammed in cheek by jowl; they are principally skylit and they have no gardens. The earlier units, with 'double pile' plans, are much roomier; in 1881 the larger end ones, at £65 p.a. rental, cost £20 more than any in the later row, **114**. This extra expense seemed warranted to subsequent tenants like Maurice Greiffenhagen, Reginald Cleaver, and the Arthur Rackhams.

Farther north, Samuel and George Higgins, auctioneers and surveyors of Finchley Road, took after Freake of South Kensington when they converted Clifton Mews into *Clifton Hill Studios* in 1881. Henry Ryland and the co-principal of the St John's Wood Art School, Bernard Ward, immediately rented one each and the enterprise looked like a blue-chip investment. But most of the lower floors were strictly uninhabitable, with the result that rents were kept artificially low to check the rapid turnover of

113 *St Alban's Studios*, South End, Kensington, designed by Douglas Wells, 1911. Eight toy-town flats address their own minuscule civic square.

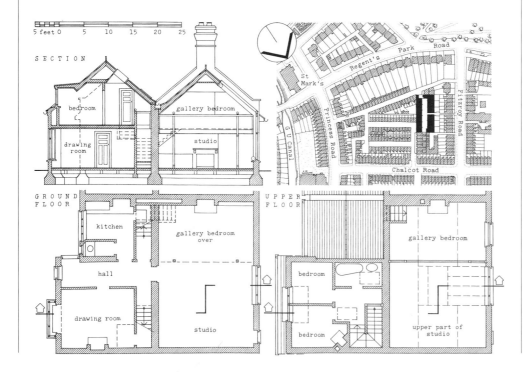

114 *Primrose Hill Studios*, Fitzroy Road, Camden Town (1877–81). Spacious and solidly built terraced units of four different types enclosing a courtyard, formerly planted.

115 *Wychcombe Studios,* England's Lane, Hampstead (1878–80). Two pairs of estate cottages plus the parish workhouse border a forgotten village green.

tenancies thereafter. George Higgins made matters worse in 1892–3 by providing a workshop next door at 87a Clifton Hill for the monumental sculptor, (Sir) Bertram Mackennal. One useful feature of these three two-storey units, however, is the long trap-door in the studio floor above each hallway. The front door fanlight, transom and all, can also be hinged back to admit or despatch really unwieldy canvases.

What appears to be a comparable terrace converted from a mews, *Queen's Road Studios*, 59a Queen's Grove, was actually built from scratch in 1882–3 by John Butler, an ironmonger. Camden Town likewise owed its next offering, *23 Camden Road Studios* (1876), to a plumber and gasfitter. Indeed, people from all walks of life were coming to the aid of the homeless painter. In Hampstead the cause led by the Batterburys was taken up by Thomas Dash Bellamy, a Jermyn Street poulterer. Bellamy joined his brother Charles to finance the building of *Wychcombe Studios*, England's Lane, in 1878–80. The first pair, generously fitted out with 20′-square studios, gallery bedrooms and two or three other rooms, was released in 1879, Robert Macbeth being one of the first takers. A second pair, similar but more restrained, followed by 1880 together with a spectacular three-level construction like a sailmaker's loft, built to order for the marine painter Hamilton Macallum, **115**. 'I should like to be in a conservatory when I paint, so as to get plenty of light all round', he declared.[11] For their forgotten village green setting, units in this group were much sought after by quite accomplished men.

Under hot competition, the Bellamys also built numerous semi-detached houses in the vicinity. Their immediate rivals around England's Lane were Gregory & Bence. Among others, 1–3 Wychcombe Villas and 7–14 Chalcot Gardens display the latter partnership's finer brand of dwelling. With No.s *12* and *13*, products of 1883, they came up with two extremely elegant studio-houses. Aesthetic School attenuation was rarely taken to such heights. A fanciful range of windows with Oriental glazing bar patterns, and balcony railings with sunflower motifs make pleasing contributions to their charm. Gregory & Bence later developed much of nearby Adamson Road, using these highly successful designs again for No.s *14* and *16*, **116**. (Sir) Alfred East claimed No. *16* in 1885; the four storeys cost him only £75 p.a.

Meanwhile *Park Road Studios*, a venture launched by the watercolourists Thomas and William Pyne, had appeared. Planned along the lines of *The Mall* by P F Poole's architect, T K Green, they were offered for rent or purchase in 1880. It was left to the occupant to deploy the back rooms as he or she wished – a 'dressing room' and a bedroom were recommended.[12] Green dwelt on the communal aspect and public frontage of the building to create a variation on the traditional English almshouse, complete with mock belfry. More delightful Aesthetic touches – Japanesy windows, sunflower finials, terracotta plaques – made up for the lack of built-in skylights and sensible doors, **117**. John Nettleship and W H Fisk were early subscribers here, the latter running a painting school in two adjacent units.

A formal public front could mean everything and nothing. A consortium of minor Kilburn developers, including the aptly-named Messrs Pincham and Owers, conveyed just this impression with its *West Hampstead Studios* of 1884 in Sherriff Road. Behind the imposing frontispiece framed by twin bows, the other three units tail away in abject disarray, **118**. No. 5, overlooking the railway cutting, seemed to be the most prized; Bertram Priestman (RA 1923) shared it with Walter West *c.* 1892.

With so much rental accommodation becoming available elsewhere during the 1880s and '90s, Hampstead builders slackened their pace considerably. However, as

116 *14–16 Adamson Road*, Hampstead (1885). Aesthetic School attenuation taken to elegant heights.

117 *Park Road Studios*, Hampstead, designed by Theodore Green in 1879–80. Dinky almshouse charm with an unusual Oriental scrutability. See **106** for location plan.

118 *West Hampstead Studios*, Sherriff Road, West Hampstead (1884). 'Behind the imposing frontispiece . . . the other three units tail away in abject disarray'.

late as 1907 T G Davidson correctly estimated there was life in the market still. His five *Belsize Studios* were conveniently sited in Glenilla Road, Belsize Park, and alluringly presented in Dutch almshouse fashion, the A–B–B–A rhythm of the layout disarmingly accented by a rogue A. Several other configurations could have been devised on this deep plot but, especially with garden and street trees in leaf, one would not wish it any different.

Were it not for the gradual emancipation of women and the continual influx of provincial artists seeking recognition in the capital, far fewer serial studios would have been built later in the piece. Riverain Chelsea and Kensington proper, regions in which developers made comparatively slow starts in the field, nonetheless saw them become the more persistent and stylish providers. Redress for the scarcity of lease-hold premises in Chelsea only began in earnest during the late 1880s. A three-tier, 15-unit block, *Trafalgar Studios* – raised in 1878 in Manresa Road – had at least stopped the gap. The pressure would have eased further had the architect Edward Godwin found a backer for the scheme he drew up in May of the same year. At that time dictating play in Tite Street, Godwin proposed a barrack of no less than 30 studio-flats for an unspecified site.[13] Double-decker studios and interlocking mezzanine living spaces were to have had shared staircases like sets of university college rooms. Different layouts were possible, particularly within the three-level upper flats. All was to be neatly, symmetrically arranged under wide-span flat roofs, **119**.

Having failed to sell this linear block, Godwin began projecting a multi-level one instead. By placing it next to Whistler's White House in Tite Street he did manage to interest a client, but only briefly. Before he could find another, the proposed site was sold to Jackson & Graham, a long-established Oxford Street firm of furnishers. Jackson & Graham seemingly resold part of the site (to Frank Dicey), stole Godwin's concept, and in 1880 called in Col. Edis to build a similar scheme known as *The Studios, 13* (later *33*) *Tite Street*. Edis's diverting street-front decorations do not entirely compensate for the fairly scatty organisation of the building, **120**. Nor should one be convinced by the rationale apparent in the stark, monotone back elevation. Notwithstanding, each rather grand studio measures over 30′ × 20′, with fine south lights answering great gridded north lights which overlook Chelsea Hospital. Annual rents of about £100 did not deter champion portrait painters like Whistler – who returned from Venice to live 'next door to himself' here from 1881 to 1885 – Sargent, Charles Furse, Robert Brough and, much later, Augustus John.

120

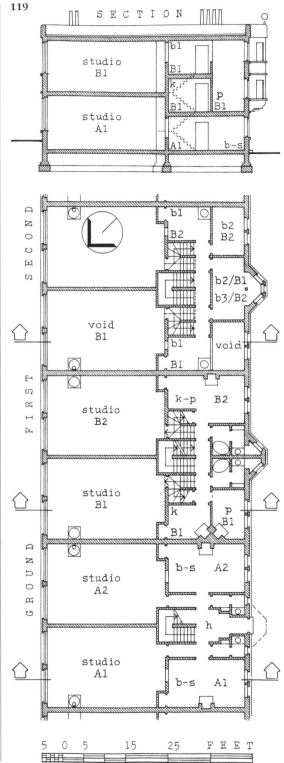

119

119 Range of studios projected by Edward Godwin during his purple period in the late 1870s. Flat-roofed flats interlocking like sets of university college rooms.

120 Studio-flats at *33 Tite Street*, Chelsea, designed by (Col. Sir) Robert Edis, 1880. Trussed like a French tart, they stand between Frank Dicey's No. 31 (left) and Whistler's White House.

Although Godwin was turning away from architecture at this period he had set his heart on building a tower of studio-flats. There is evidence in fact that he had contemplated one as early as 1867.[14] Designed in his Burges-like medieval style, it comprised four double-height floors with mezzanines and a communal kitchen in the basement. The new site he had in mind was the one next door to Frank Miles's passed up by Rosa Corder. Nothing, however, rose upon it even after Godwin himself (so it appears[15]) had wrested ownership from the erstwhile lessee. As the months of delay turned into years, Godwin's personally approached subscribers not surprisingly lost confidence in the exercise. In the end (again, so it appears), he sold his drawings to Denton, Son & North, 'architects',[16] who put up the present building in 1884–5 at a cost of some £7000. *Tower House*, as it is called, also lost face in this process. It shows inside and out how much a typically rhapsodic initial attack from Godwin has been blunted by repeated rebuffs, **121**. Caton Woodville, Robert Macbeth and, once more, Whistler, head the short list of notable painters who lived

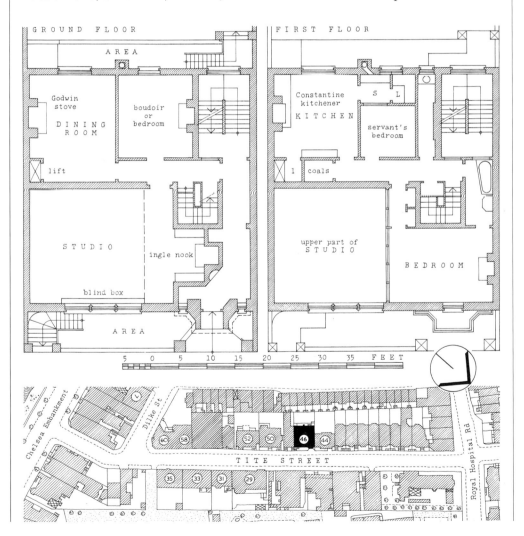

121 Two levels of *Tower House*, 46 Tite Street, Chelsea, by Edward Godwin and others, 1884–5. By inverting the usual family and service zones it was intended to avoid cooking smells and control overhead noises.

here. C J C Pawley assembled a miscellany of Tite Street motifs in his 1894 design of No. *48* alongside.

While the Aesthetes were acting out their private agonies down by the river, quite a number of small studio groups sprang up just off the King's Road. Most of these were doubtlessly prompted by the success of *Trafalgar Studios*. Indeed, the builder responsible there, John Brass, went so far as to convert his own neighbouring villa into another set, *Wentworth Studios* (1885). Later activity remained localised, with

122 Cross-section and plan of *Glebe Studios*, 60–61 Glebe Place, Chelsea (1889–90). The gable end lighting is a masterstroke of which no academic architect would have been capable.

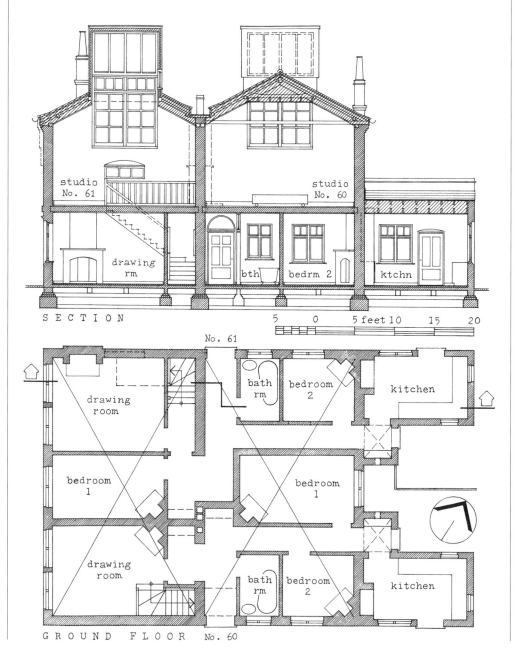

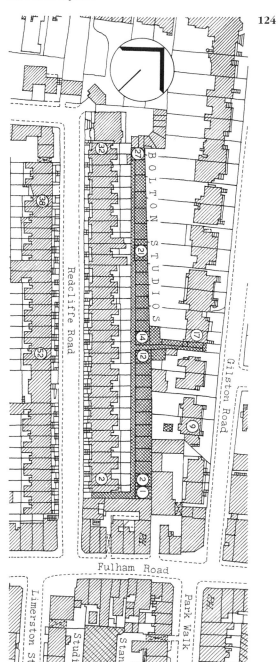

123 *Bolton Studios* taper beyond view between houses in Redcliffe and Gilston Roads, West Brompton.

124 *Bolton Studios*, West Brompton (1883–8). One third of the units are variations on this three-level, space-saving type.

124

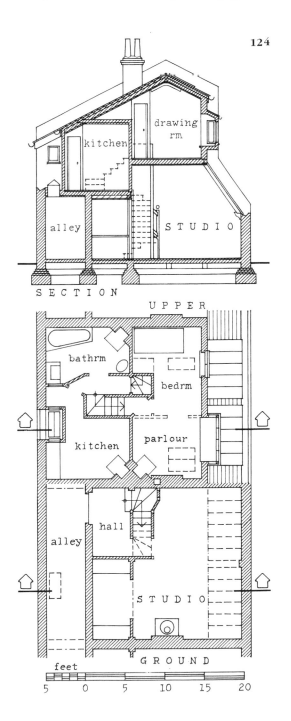

the Manresa Road–Glebe Place axis in particular accounting for more developments per square foot than any other in Chelsea.

The sculptor Conrad Dressler made the first mark in Glebe Place with the glass shacks of *Cedar Studios* (1885–6). Land controlled by the Chelsea Old Church clergy then became available and three more groups materialised in quick succession. *Glebe Studios* (1888–9) at No.s *60–61* gain marginal seniority over the duo at No.s *64–65* and the octet within No.s *52–59*.[17] The local rector himself developed the very agreeable No.s *60–61* and gave his son (who later excelled in the design of chandeliers) one of the first tenancies. There is a Thames-side air about them – north lights like hoist housings, casements, pantiles, and so on – while an impish improvisation has led to the transverse upper storey, **122**. By contrast, the diminutive No.s *64–65* Dance and Smirke with a beguiling urbanity. They are lit mainly through the roof like No.s *52–59*, whose 'picturesqueness is applied', in this case, 'not instinct' as Ian Nairn wrote.[18] These nonetheless intriguing buildings attracted Walter Sickert, (Sir) William Rothenstein and Ernest Shepard among other new-century favourites.

During the 1880s and '90s, more than at any other stage, Chelsea secured its international name as the art centre of London. Multiple studios continued to be built there into the 1910s, notably the *Rossetti* (1894) and *King's House* (1911) groups. But, as those close-grained examples indicate, suitable sites became scarcer and intending builders faced either costly redevelopment programmes or fresh starts on the Chelsea periphery. Astute developers predicted the inner Chelsea property squeeze, directing their efforts early on in West Brompton and Fulham. The sculptor Charles Bacon (of Sloane Street), for instance, fell in with some sharp Scotsmen[19] who levelled slit eyes upon a most unlikely slot of no-man's-land between Gilston and Redcliffe Roads. Between 1883 and 1888 they erected the extraordinary *Bolton Studios* on it – 27 units opening off a 100-yard, dead-straight, dead-end corridor, **123**. The largely single-storeyed No.s 1–20 were built first; extremely constricted plans on several levels were concocted one by one for the remainder which taper to an arm's

123

breadth, **124**. Early denizens included Theodore Roussel, Thomas Kennington and Maurice Greiffenhagen.

Farther west along Fulham Road at No. 454a, another well-circulated commercial sculptor of the day, Louis Fabbrucci, simultaneously set up the six *Fulham Studios*. These occupied not especially desirable warehouse territory backing onto the Walham Green (Fulham Broadway) railway station. James Whistler, perhaps unable to stomach the reappearance of Oscar Wilde on his doorstep, took one of them in 1885. With Sickert and the Greaves brothers wielding the paint-brushes, he transformed it into 'The Pink Palace', **125**.[20] His approaching marriage to Godwin's widow soon led him back to the Tite Street firing-line, however. Many years later in 1913, young Henri Gaudier-Brzeska took another at an annual rent of £26, all in. 'What infinite peace . . . God it's good to have a studio!' he exclaimed.[21] But his consort Sophie, who joined him there in winter of the same year, reacted differently:

> . . . Everything was covered with indescribable filth – the Underground trains which passed just outside the window made a row enough to split my head in two, the draughts on all sides were as if we were on a lighthouse in the open sea . . .[22]

Their trials were just beginning.

Trains also rattled past *St Paul's Studios*, which originally found themselves in the otherwise sleepy Colet Gardens overlooking St Paul's School, Hammersmith. Maj.-Gen. James Gunter of the renowned caterer's family – developers of tracts of West Brompton and West Kensington – financed this splendid terrace dating from 1890, **126**. It was 'specially designed to suit the requirements of bachelor artists, with

125 George Jacomb-Hood's drawing of James Whistler's 'Pink Palace' in 1886 – a unit within *Fulham Studios*, 454a Fulham Road, Fulham (1883–).

126 Frederick Wheeler's original proposal for *St Paul's Studios* (1890–1). Portfolio-toting men and women amble across a quiet Talgarth Road; studio window blinds unfurl from the bottom.

127 *Albert Studios*, Albert Bridge Road, Battersea, designed by W J Chambers in 1898. A philanthropic venture which duly conveys aspects typical of a model village.

128 *Albert Studios*, Battersea. If a double bed were used the kitchen would receive considerably less light.

accommodation for a housekeeper on the lower floor'[23] by Frederick Wheeler at a cost of just £8801. Maiden artists and families were also welcome, as it happened. The frantically Jacobean terracotta work of the exterior is more than matched by the late-Victorian joinery of the interior. But particularly noteworthy are the caparisoned picture slits and the graceful, cheval-glass studio windows with their glazed vaults, some still blackened since the Blitz. Almost certainly the train noises upset lessees like the illustrators Hal Hurst and E T Reed, who came and went quite quickly.

The element of philanthropy in the Gunters' boom-style super-almshouses caught on elsewhere. It was the wish of the director of the Kennerly Reconstruction Co. that *Albert Studios* should not be let to people other than artists.[24] In a cheerful eight-unit row of 1898, these lie a mere river's-width from Chelsea off Albert Bridge Road in Battersea, **127**, **128**. Albert Mansions, in front of the row, were built two years earlier, so it seems that the colourful Juba Kennerley – a sea captain, mining engineer and songwriter as well as a beneficent speculator – recalled his architect, W J Chambers, to mix some model village feeling into the playful Aesthetic tenor of his usual approach. *Albert Studios* are lit from the front and top only, the first two units fitted with wider internal doors for the convenience of sculptors. Omar Ramsden and Alwyn Carr, artists in metal, occupied No. 6 for a period after 1900. Prince Albert would have been pleased to see this venture named after him.

More conspicuous, however, as a memorial embodiment of the world-girdling fine art industry fathered in the reign of Albert and Victoria, is *Lansdowne House*, Lansdowne Road, Notting Hill. William Flockhart designed this golden skybuster in 1900–1 for the South African mining magnate and art lover, (Sir) Edmund Davis.

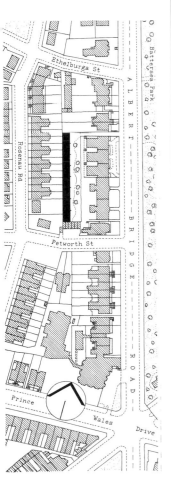

127

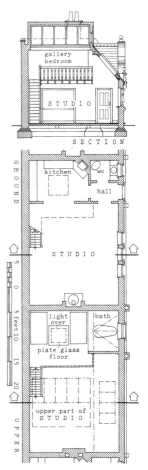

Davis, requiring a London House of more than average size, had already employed Flockhart to unify 11 and 13 Lansdowne Road. For a further outlay, he enjoined Frank Brangwyn and Charles Conder to decorate it. *Lansdowne House*, however, took patronage of the arts to the point of folly. When first built it contained not only two studios and four palatial studio-flats but a common smoking room, a squash court and hydropathic baths, not to mention the passenger lift, the master's motor-house, or his chauffeur's maisonette. All of nine storeys high, it is both powerfully and delicately built, incorporating Scottish turrets and crow-steps of mythical pro-

129 *Lansdowne House*, Lansdowne Road, Notting Hill, by William Flockhart, 1900–1. A 'golden skybuster . . . incorporating Scottish turrets and crow-steps of mythical proportions'.

portions, **129**. Whether or not Davis helped his hand-picked tenants to pay their rent (Ricketts and Shannon, having transferred The Vale Press to this address, shared a flat at about £140 p.a.), he would often entertain them at his somewhat more primitive, but no less prominent, private keep in Kent – Chilham Castle.

Whereas in some quarters mass-produced studios had come a long way since the £13 p.a. units of squalid Stanhope Yard, the provision of raw space almost as cheap still looked a reasonable proposition to developers more than 60 years on. By the end of the Edwardian era, studios could be found from Clapham to Bushey, from Holloway to Bedford Park. Gratifyingly, a large majority survives another 80 years further on. The modern liking for small, self-contained inner suburban properties and one-room living – even if, at £13 per day and more, few artists can now afford them – has tended to make them safe.

9

HOME COUNTY HIDEOUTS

> Lord Egremont hates ceremony . . . he likes people to come and go as it suits them, and say nothing about it . . .[1]

GEORGE WYNDHAM, Lord Egremont of Petworth, knew how to look after diffident artists. Carew, Turner, John Lucas and many others mourned his passing in 1837, for his breed was becoming rarer. Landed aristocrats and county squires who both patronised and played host to parties of townee painters diminished with every new Victorian decade. A few men like William Wells of Redleaf, Penshurst, graciously prolonged the practice till near the mid-century. But after that time, while city-based chiefs of the new industrial and commercial classes virtually took over the role of patron, it was up to the painters to make rural retreats of their own.

Building country houses was a course of action open only to artists of above-average earning power or those on the verge of retirement with life savings in hand. Yet it was also a natural reaction to the temper of the times. Luddites and Chartists had already reacted violently to industrialisation and intense urbanisation. Poets and reformers had been quick to sympathise; artists – more selfishly, more in a bid to preserve their health or retrieve a space for tranquil reflection – began to follow suit. The Picturesque ideal was still a strong force among them when the Plein Air and Pre-Raphaelite proponents recommended that they step out and confront at least some of life's more friendly realities on the spot. Their subsequent quest for authenticity led not only to the hiring of local yokels for models but, in order to put them in context, whole rustic cottages as well. Since it was no longer likely to find these in Hampstead, Chiswick or even Twickenham, the painters reluctantly took to the Iron Civiliser. Rapid expansion of the railway system since 1830 allowed them and their families to travel speedily and cheaply much farther afield. There they could rent one of those cottages for the summer, buy it outright and modernise it, or select land for building anew.

Two pioneers of the London studio-house, John Linnell and Richard Redgrave, also showed themselves to be leaders of the Victorian second house movement. Once he had been elected RA in 1851, Redgrave began holidaying at Abinger, near

Dorking. After a few seasons he bought a farmhouse there. With so many official duties taking his time in London, Abinger landscapes became almost the only paintings he could attempt in later years. Linnell, for his part, thought to revive the country life he had enjoyed before settling in Bayswater. At the age of 57, in 1849, he finally decided he had put aside enough from his portrait practice to be able to buy a personal sketching ground and devote the rest of his days to full-time landscape painting. Although taken by Shoreham, his son-in-law's Kentish 'valley of vision', he plumped for a 20-acre estate, 'Redstone Wood', near Redhill in Surrey. Chastened in these matters, he engaged the architect T H Watson to sort out his ideas for a house to go on it. Nonetheless, 'The original plan of the structure was his own and the execution of the design might have been his too, considering its many defects'.[2] But, with the inclusion of two 40′-long first floor studios – one for himself, the other for his four sons – it served its purpose. Linnell made sure that the windows elsewhere were made 'of the largest size' to command views of his entire domain and at all seasons 'to afford glimpses of the sunset'.[3]

Within five years of moving his family to Redstone in mid-1851, the wily patriarch had bought a further 30 acres adjoining. Within another ten years he had increased his holding to 80 acres and remarried; he was then 74. He ran the household along the lines of an art factory; the boys worked to orders under the name Linnell & Sons. Two or three managed to build independent Watson-designed lodges on the property but they had to pay their father rent for them. Nor could Samuel Palmer be allowed to shirk his contribution. Having extricated himself from London and resettled at Abinger in 1861, the following year he was dragged to a cottage at Mead Vale, Redhill, owned by John Linnell Jnr. No-one escaped until 1882 when, worth

130 One of a series of etchings by the sculptor Richard Cockle Lucas of 'Chilworth Tower', the house and studio-gallery he built for himself near Romsey, Hampshire, in 1854.

some £200 000 and sitting on a real estate goldmine, the old tyrant died, aged 90.

Redstone may have looked peculiar but it was no more odd than '*The Artist's Dream Realised, being a Residence designed and built by R C Lucas, Sculptor, 1854*'.[4] Richard Cockle Lucas (b. 1800), renowned for his portrait medallions, evidently hatched this scheme before he left London in 1849 for the country of his youth. Known as 'Chilworth Tower', his residence went up among rustic-work garden features in a 'dulcet glen' he particularly cherished near Romsey in Hampshire, **130**. At first sight Chilworth Tower appears to be a church with a house attached. But then a resemblance to Fonthill Abbey is not exceedingly remote either. In fact the ostensible nave section with its skylight and crudely glass-tiled bay contained Lucas's gallery-studio. One of his many grubby etchings of the building (subtitled 'How the parasite strangled the patron') pictures masses of plaster busts and uncommissioned heroic groups arranged inside. Outside, the walls were dotted with mottoes and posers such as 'Live to learn', 'Science demonstrates not an atom of matter is ever lost. Can, or will, intellect perish?' Apparently such philosophy was born of Lucas's deliberations in the sky-parlour, or observatory, on top of the tower. This tower at least, unlike the one at Fonthill, did not perish until about 1950.

Exploration of the counties south of London gathered momentum during the 1850s. Interest swung to the east when a number of former Redleaf regulars agreed that Cranbrook in Kent should become the rendezvous for their summer furlough. From 1854 onwards, F D Hardy, his teacher Thomas Webster RA, and John Horsley invested in old houses in and near the village. Supplemented later by three or four other households, the settlement came to be labelled the Cranbrook Colony. Loosely united in its aim to paint characterful contemporary scenes, particularly proverbial domestic situations, it did manage to represent the age quite truthfully. Horsley, once he was certain to clear the RA hurdle, asked Norman Shaw (who was just starting out in practice) to improve his house at Willesley. In 1868 Shaw came back to add a studio which, even in the backwoods, the prudish Horsley insisted should have a separate models' entrance. Shaw also made Webster's Cranbrook house more comfortable for his declining years.

Meanwhile another pioneer London studio builder, J C Hook ARA, had been sizing up Redgrave's patch and the prolific watercolourist Charles Davidson had established himself near Linnell. Hook was then on the point of turning from history pieces to rustic genre and coastal subjects. Support for his notion was sufficient[5] to convince him he ought to renounce London life completely. His first move was to Abinger but this did not suit so he tried Hambledon. After a period there which saw his rise to RA he invited his brother, Adam Hook, an architect, to build him a new cottage on a site near Witley. But 'Pinewood', completed in 1860, did not satisfy him either. Hook then acquired a number of acres at Churt, close to Farnham, and made yet another start, this time to his own designs. It turned out to be 'just such a house as an old English Franklin, had he been a man of culture, might have built of yore'.[6] 'Studios above and on the ground level were laid out with prescience, the latter opening on a large conservatory.'[7] Content at last with 'Silverbeck', as he called it, Hook remained from 1866 until his death aged 88 in 1907.

Both Hook's sons, Bryan and Allan, also painters, followed him to Churt and fixed up self-contained lodgings down the lane. They all shared the main house, however, and another studio on a heathery ridge some way distant: a genuine sky-parlour, specially equipped for the study of clouds. But painting became almost a sideline as they all set about developing the Silverbeck property into a biodynamic smallholding. Although the Linnells had kept hens and bees in Bayswater, the Hooks might well have been England's first artist drop-outs. They grew their own vegetables, planted an orchard, and harvested their own corn which they ground in a small private watermill. They bred and slaughtered their own sheep and chickens. And, it was said, they hardly ever seemed to have a bad year. Hook Senior lent a strong hand in all this, even at the age of 70 or more. A grand old fellow, he held that 'a house was not worth going into unless it had a baby and barrel of beer on tap in it'.[8]

'Hooksville' outstripped 'Linnellsville' but really it was no more a single-minded artistic community than the Cranbrook Colony. Perhaps The Ancients, of whom Samuel Palmer was a member, was the last of these. At one point William Morris interested his principal decorating and furnishing designers in a kind of mini-phalanstery to be joined to his Red House at Upton in Kent, but the idea was abandoned. Morris returned to London in 1865, just six years after building that famous house – not least a place to protect his bride from upper-class snobbery.[9] Roddy Spencer-Stanhope did not last any longer at 'Fairmile', a house near Cobham, Surrey, which Morris's architect was next to provide. The trouble in this case was Stanhope's asthma; it finally forced him out of Britain altogether. Burne-Jones remembered a lovely house with a garret studio, yet 'Just a bit over-severe . . . a bit gloomy perhaps'.[10]

While Burne-Jones was not called upon to help decorate Fairmile as well, he was soon in demand by Birket Foster at his new house. Foster had been saving against the day when he could lay aside engravings for books in favour of the arcadian watercolour drawings by which he was becoming so much better known. The death of his wife in 1859 hastened a connected decision to build in Surrey. Hearing that Hook was leaving his Hambledon cottage he decided to buy and modify that while continuing to look for his dream-house site. In this he again trailed Hook to Witley, choosing a spot on top of Wormley Hill. By 1863 Foster and the architect Decimus Burton had combined to build 'The Hill', a picturesque pastiche of medieval elements more in the Shropshire vernacular than the Surrey, **131**. Foster remarried in 1864 and sustained a great celebrity for the rest of the century. He was quickly able to increase the house to princely proportions and thereby to entertain on a grand scale. Burne-Jones was commissioned to supply designs for stained glass, mantel tiles, a frieze and a screen; Stacy Marks was let loose in the summer-house; Foster's brother-in-law John Dawson Watson began frescos in the second and larger, hall-style studio. Charles Keene and Fred Walker were frequently invited to represent the life and soul of the parties.

Foster's house signalled the advent of the more grandiose manor of the nouvelle richesse. It also indicated the vitality of the contemporary art workers' grapevine. In no time, (Sir) Henry Cole of South Kensington had built almost next door, Edmund

131 'The Hill', Witley, Surrey, as it appeared in 1898. Birket Foster stands before the house he began building with some help from Decimus Burton in 1863.

Evans the colour printer (another Foster relative) had done likewise, and Helen Allingham was on the way. Through a similar series of social and professional connections, the marine painter E W Cooke (RA 1863) came to raise 'Glen Andred' just beyond Groombridge on the Kent–East Sussex border. Cooke had recently consulted Decimus Burton in London; he knew Horsley from the Redleaf days and the Academy; and Horsley recommended Norman Shaw. His site he obtained via separate channels. Having pulled together schemes drawn up by Burton and Cooke himself, it took Shaw from just April to August 1866 to get the contractor started. He used Glen Andred to advance further aspects of his 'Old English' idiom, fairly well succeeding to relate it to its county stylistically. In Cooke's time it had dozens of rooms, among them a large greenhouse, a library and a study, the latter with northern and western outlooks, but no formal studio.

Not to have a proper studio in such a house was puzzling to Frederick Goodall, Cooke's fellow RA and another familiar of Redleaf vintage. Goodall had been imagining his own withdrawal to the country for many years before he saw Glen Andred, a magnificent pile close by called Leys Wood, and Horsley's new Cranbrook studio, all designed by Norman Shaw. Only then did he know he had found an architect worthy of the Goodall site. In 1856, although no more than 34, Goodall had profited to such an extent from his provincial genre pieces that he could afford a comfortable existence in Camden Square and the title to 100 acres of the Harrow Weald. His switch to Egyptian genre, following a tour of the Bible Lands in 1858–9, then had Gambart offering £6000 for his sketches alone. By 1870, when he was legally able to build, a 30-acre portion of his Harrow land had been wisely planted and Shaw was left to work his magic on it without fear of overspending.

132 Frederick Goodall's 'Grim's Dyke', Harrow Weald, Middlesex, from the west. Norman Shaw's design of 1870 gives the impression of a manor-house established and added onto for centuries.

Were it not for Goodall's insistence on a painting room oriented strictly north–south, the house would have assumed a predictable rectilinear outline parallel to Grim's Dyke, an ancient earthwork crossing the grounds. Yet the offset studio–kitchen wing perhaps looked less calculated than the other historical accidents of the rambling composition. Moreover, it suggested the overlapping vistas up and down the corridor and ensured the bay for sunset studies in the studio would be ideally placed. Jackson & Shaw (Prinsep's builders) excelled themselves for a sum in the region of a very reasonable £7000 and Goodall sampled all the 'Old English' luxuries of Leys Wood at a reduced scale, **132**, **133**. But it was not long before Goodall complained of time wasted travelling, of the scarcity of experienced models and the poor standard of local schools for his children. In 1880, therefore, he sold up and moved back to London. He bought 62 Avenue Road, Hampstead (once Gambart's), redecorated it with Egyptian salvage and indulged his expensive tastes until he faced insolvency in 1902, two years before his death. In 1890 'Grim's Dyke' passed to W S Gilbert of comic opera fame who made further additions – including the fruity alabaster studio fireplace – to those already carried out by an interim owner.

This 'Artistic House for an Artist by an Artist' set a standard only the watchfully

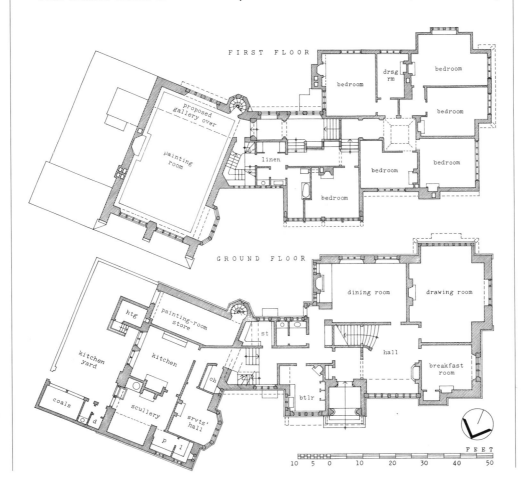

133 Preliminary plans of Grim's Dyke, Harrow Weald. While the bulk of the house was best placed parallel to the Dyke, the studio had to face due north.

extravagant could emulate. Thomas Woolner and Sir Arthur Clay, the latter a rich amateur painter, supply two cases in point. Both men seemed to catch the 'Old English' bug but failed to catch Norman Shaw. They went to Frederick Cockerell instead. In 1872 Woolner had him remodel 'Cranesden', a mostly Elizabethan farmhouse at the centre of an 80-acre estate just south of Mayfield in East Sussex. The insertion of a period house front from Shrewsbury had the effect of inviting comparisons with Birket Foster's muddled mansion. Although his involvement there was not full-time like Goodall's, Woolner also pulled out after ten years, 'tired of the bothers of farm and land'.[11] But the profits of the sale soon revived him. Four years later, in 1886, he bought 132 acres within view of Tennyson's Blackdown property near Horsham and tinkered with another farmhouse. Of course he sold up again shortly before he died, wealthier than ever, in 1892. For Sir Arthur Clay, Cockerell started from scratch and built a Tudoresque stone homestead incorporating a sizeable studio at Shere, Surrey, in 1874.[12] G F Watts RA would go to Cockerell for his new London house simultaneously, but at an earlier stage the tender-hearted painter was intent on leaving London altogether.

Since the Holland Park house in which he had been living with Val Prinsep's

134 Plan and sections of 'The Briary', Freshwater, Isle of Wight, designed by Philip Webb in 1872–4. George Watts's seaside rest-home for himself and the Thoby Prinseps.

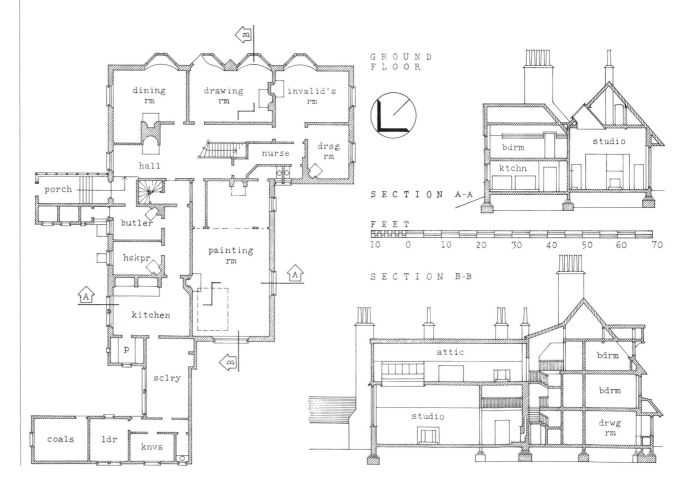

parents was scheduled for demolition early in 1874, both parties had to find an alternative. Watts's debt to the Prinseps, and Tennyson's account of the restorative climate of the Isle of Wight, inclined him to build a joint resort close to the poet's former home at Freshwater. The depleted health and prosperity of his erstwhile hosts and the fact Mrs Prinsep's sister, Mrs Cameron, also lived by the bay made up his mind. Clearly impressed by Val Prinsep's house, Watts handed the task in good time to Philip Webb. Although the contract did not run smoothly,[13] a typically idiosyncratic but lovable seaside rest-home – 'The Briary' – resulted, **134**. Notwithstanding, it also provided a practical base for Watts, having one voluminous painting room under the main roof and another equally large studio suite, presumably for sculpture, a few yards off. Lady Ritchie wrote of these 'sacred temples' where visitors were made to 'put their shoes off, so to speak',[14] in her novella, *From an Island* (1877). But the Divine Watts tended only to winter there, especially after Mr Prinsep died in 1878. By that time, Watts had already built again in London. Portraiture being his prime source of income, he could never escape the necessity of keeping studios in the capital.

Another Victorian polymath, (Sir) Hubert Herkomer (surely the model, together with Felix Moscheles, for the diabolical Svengali in *Trilby*), likewise financed a major building programme on the strength of a portrait practice for which he retained a studio in Cadogan Square. Since 1873, the date of his first marriage and first big sale at the Academy, Herkomer had been living modestly with his parents just outside Bushey in Hertfordshire. Ten years later the family's fortunes and the local landscape had changed considerably. Both his wife and mother had died; a large timber-framed studio-drawing room had been built to link the semi-detached cottage to its mate; behind, even larger, fully equipped joinery and printing shops had also been erected, along with a smithy, a drawing office, two teaching studios and a glasshouse – the nucleus of the Herkomer Art School, in fact. Herkomer himself had recently returned from America, his first visit. During his stay he had produced a 400-guinea portrait once every five days, although it required a team of Swedish masseurs to keep him up to the mark. By maintaining this hectic pace for the rest of his life, he would earn in excess of £250 000 from portraiture alone.

Widowed twice over by the end of 1885, Herkomer made a second trip to America. While in Boston he persuaded H H Richardson, the foremost East Coast architect, to accept a portrait of himself in exchange for a set of elevations and construction details. These were to fit plans already prepared by Herkomer[15] with a view to building a palatial new studio-house on another field he had bought at Bushey. Receiving the drawings early in 1886 he saw Richardson had suggested a house of 'the greatest dignity . . . using 13th-century Gothic with a Romanesque feeling'. 'It will be an addition to England', he wrote in his diary, 'unique as it is noble.'[16] This second American trip also allowed Herkomer personally to entreat his Cleveland-based uncles – Anton, a weaver, and Hans, a woodcarver – to help execute the furniture and fittings in the Bushey workshops. For he intended to buy nothing for the new house, 'but everything must be made in that place, from the carving to the entire metal- and stonework'.[17] Yet no expense would be spared either.

Uncle Hans and family agreed to go over to continue the carving and cabinetmaking long since begun by Hubert's father, but Uncle Anton would send curtains and covers from Cleveland. Hundreds of tons of rough, grey tuffstein were imported from Bavaria and construction got under way later in 1886. Though Herkomer declared himself satisfied with it, 'Lululaund' (so-named after his second wife) was still unfinished in 1894 when the clan moved in. In the meantime Hubert converted a chapel on his property into a 150-seat theatre. From 1887 he wrote, scored, designed, produced, directed and took the leading roles in a series of 'pictorial music plays' enacted there. These performances were temporarily memorable for their innovative stagecraft, if little else. His third marriage took place to Lulu's sister,[18] and he fathered two more children. In 1889 *The Chapel of the Charterhouse* became the second of his subject pictures to be bought (for £2200) from the Chantrey fund, hastening his rise to RA the following year. Between a craze for making decorative enamels and the invention of 'Herkomergravure', he held the Slade professorship at Oxford, taught at his school – by then a rampant institution[19] – while etching, mezzotinting, watercolouring, touring and portrait painting at his usual feverish pitch.

135 'Lululaund', Sir Hubert Herkomer's studio-castle at Bushey, Hertfordshire, designed by the Herkomer Gemeinschaft and H H Richardson, 1885–94. The upper stages of the tower were never completed.

136 Plans and sections of Lululaund dated June 1888. These drawings were followed until 1892; the plans and roof structure were subsequently rationalised somewhat.

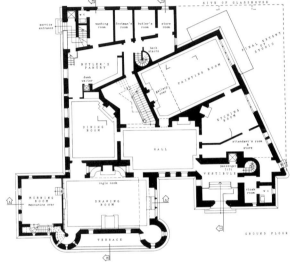

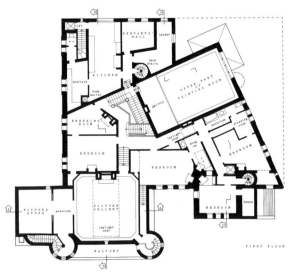

There could be no doubting that Lululaund cost its builder close to £75 000, **135**. Richardson's massive masonry specification must have inflated the tender but Herkomer's intransigence over his cranky, amateurish planning will have put a bubbly figure on it in the first place. As at Grim's Dyke and 17 Grove End Road, the ideal or polite orientation of the house as a whole lay at odds with that of the painter's studio. Yet, unlike Shaw and Alma Tadema, Herkomer could not control or take advantage of the clash of axes, saddling himself with grossly irregular rooms and lobbies, **136**.

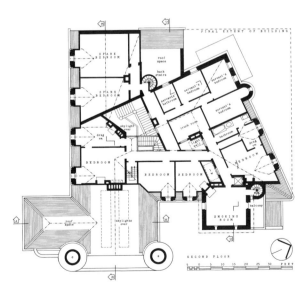

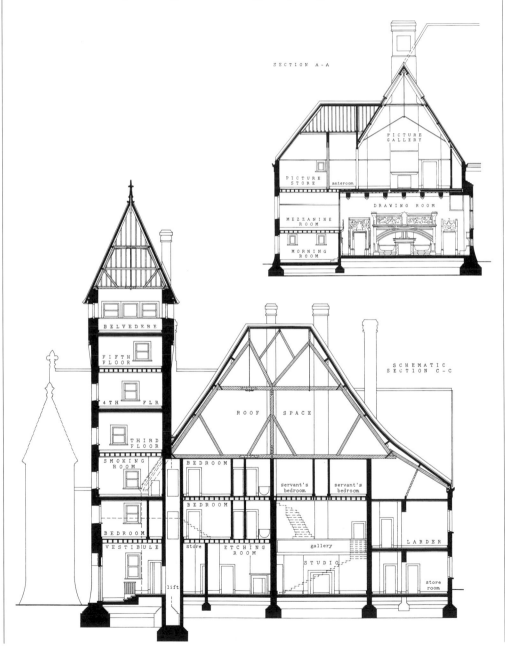

Nevertheless these deformities were to a great extent camouflaged by Uncle Hans's spiky Gothick decor – itself enveloped day and night in a sedative gloom only spasmodically relieved by home-generated electric light. Defending the prickly woodwork, Herkomer argued that he had instinctively recreated the chiaroscuro of his native Tannenwald with all its intertwining twigs and lichens, **137**.

An American reporter predicted that the house would not contain 'a single inch of dull, meaningless, stupid detail, of laborious ugliness, or cheap sham'.[20] Well, there was indeed little that could be called cheap sham. Thousands of man-hours went into the cathedral-quality carving, the glittering chased and repoussé cabinet fronts, the baronial ironmongery, the brilliant brocades and upholstery fabrics. Most of the walls were partly lined with incised oak panelling. In the stair hall, priceless, stately sequoia was used in planks 30′ × 3′, while elsewhere it was shaped into stupendous sinewy beams. Above the dining room dado, the walls were laminated with crimped and lacquered aluminium foil, a surface eventually overlaid by a pastelly low relief figuring a chorus line of dreamy Rhinemaidens in a Jugendstil vortex of diaphanous drapery. Both the drawing room and studio received similar metallic finishes, but tempered by a black scrim, the one said to be brassy, the other silvery, **138**.[21] Further modelled decoration, in this instance, extravagantly gilt, appeared upstairs in the master and main spare bedrooms. Pure copper leaf on the ceiling of the former added a twinkling iridescence to a sparkling golden shimmer.

From the polychrome patterns on the gable end to the pewterwork nymph blocking her ears which surrounded the front door bell, from the guardian angel in blue enamel gracing the hall to the silver cutlery and dinner service, everything bore the handwrought hallmark of Herkomer's originality. If ever Britain possessed a

137 The drawing and dining rooms at Lululaund: a marriage of Strawberry Hill Gothick and Bavarian Art Nouveau arranged by Celtic fairies.

Wagnerian Gesamptkunstwerk, the Schloss Neutuffstein qualified without question. Although Sir Hubert von Herkomer, as he had become by 1907, lavished royal ransoms on the motoring, gardening and film-making interests[22] that preoccupied him after the art school had been wound up, he still had £41 319 in reserve at his death in 1914. Thus he could have afforded to complete the mighty watchtower after all. Unfortunately, hindsight reveals that it would have disappeared with the rest within another 40 years anyway. *Im Hause Liegt das Glück*, inscribed on the door-knocker, turned out to be a hollow promise.

Herkomer's style of life was all but unique in the home counties in his day. Yet while the archetypal second-home builder, like today's stockbroker, would turn almost naturally to the Guildford–Maidstone belt, the 1880s also saw many out of the ordinary departures. A few of the really wealthy gentlemen, Landseer and Millais for instance, whom one would expect to own splendid country seats, owned nothing of the sort. Such engaging fellows, they were forever invited to someone else's house – anywhere between Balmoral and the Château Marochetti at Passy. Others were inveterate travellers, always on the move. Leighton would set off to Morocco or

138 Sir Hubert Herkomer, *A Zither Evening with My Students* (1901). Herkomer entertains in his extended Lululaund studio to which a small glasshouse has been joined.

Moldavia at a moment's notice. Before he built Lululaund, Herkomer arranged annual sketching tours in Wales, taking his studio with him. This consisted of a demountable hut with a revolving floor.[23] Millais owned a similar contraption which he used to send ahead of him by rail. Several marine painters went one better with their self-propelled studios: Henry Scott Tuke cleared the hold of his brig *Julie* to make a space fully 60′ long; Napier Hemy's sloop, the *Van de Velde*, contained a mahogany saloon with excellent light all round; and George Vicat Cole fitted out a steam launch for tootling up the Thames Valley.

Water of all sorts, of course, afforded an unfailing source of subject matter and recreational potential for those of either the most retiring or robust dispositions. The Royal Tapesty Works art director H Henry followed Willam Morris up the Thames to Old Windsor, where Maurice Adams installed him in a particularly frilly 'Queen Anne' studio-house.[24] W L Wyllie, on the other hand, established a veritable crow's-nest overlooking the Medway at Rochester, while the outdoorsy Stanhope Forbes contingent commandeered every under-used sail loft from Fowey to Newlyn along the Cornish Riviera.

But, notwithstanding the number of alternative boltholes, the acknowledged weekenders' playground remained that aforementioned Guildford–Maidstone horse-latitude. Two RAs, Holl and Watts, certainly went a long way to reaffirm its significance. Holl began by renting a Tudor manor house close to Gomshall in the early 1880s. Very soon afterwards he brought in his London architect to build 'Burrows Cross' nearby. This was an informal, typically Shavian, two-storey country house sprouting in all directions at once. In the meantime, Boehm, who already had a compact, gingerbread house near Dorking ('Bent's Brook' by Col. Edis),[25] replaced Holl at the old Gomshall place. Boehm continued to follow Holl's example in reverse order, engaging Edis again in London. The inextinguishable Watts, however, could not revert to any of his previous architects for yet another venture he conceived in 1889. Three years before, aged 71, he had remarried. But this act failed to relieve him of his pestiferous neighbour Mrs Barrington, so the Wattses decided to isolate themselves at Compton, near Guildford – buying sufficient surrounding land to discourage Mrs B's pursuit. Intended to be a mere Wendy house despite the mega-studio in the brief, 'Limnerslease' ended up with no less than 43 rooms. Perhaps that explains why George & Peto, the architects who built it in 1890–1 in an academic local vernacular, reputedly omitted the staircase connecting the two upper floors.

After his stay at Kelmscott with the Morrises, Rossetti, too, suffered a kind of persecution, in his case largely illusory. In reclusive mood he took himself off to one of several J P Seddon-designed beach-houses at Birchington, near Westgate-on-Sea in Kent. The inconsolable old reptile eventually succumbed to his excesses here in 1882, whereupon Alfred Gilbert[26] made use of the same forlorn, quiescent lair. Indeed the popularity of these bungalows, as they were called, caused many more to be built in the vicinity by other architects. Others again, among them the Seddon trainee Charles Voysey and his contemporary Robert Briggs, were able to prop up their private practices with bungalow commissions elsewhere, not solely seaside locations. In fact Briggs, 'a slick draughtsman, but in the flesh too frightful',[27] could be unctuously flexible in his interpretation of the article. In 1891 he wrote:

Suffice it to say that what we mean by a bungalow is an artistic little dwelling, cheaply but soundly built with a proper regard to sanitation, and popped down in some pretty little spot with just enough accommodation for our particular needs. It is not necessary that an English bungalow, like its Eastern original, should be a one-storeyed building.[28]

An example which Briggs directed specifically at an artist embodied, if it did not actually overfulfil, all these qualities for a sum estimated at £900. Interestingly the blunt smoking room-belvedere also lay at the thorax of an emergent 'butterfly' plan, **139**.

Voysey likewise attracted a number of artist clients by flying kites in pro-Arts and Crafts publications. Not such a fashionably tricksy architect as Briggs – though assuredly a more versatile designer – he could nevertheless match him for cost-saving ability. Thus his more workaday 1895 scheme commanding a view of Studland Bay, Dorset, for the dramatist Alfred Sutro and his wife, the painter Esther Isaacs,

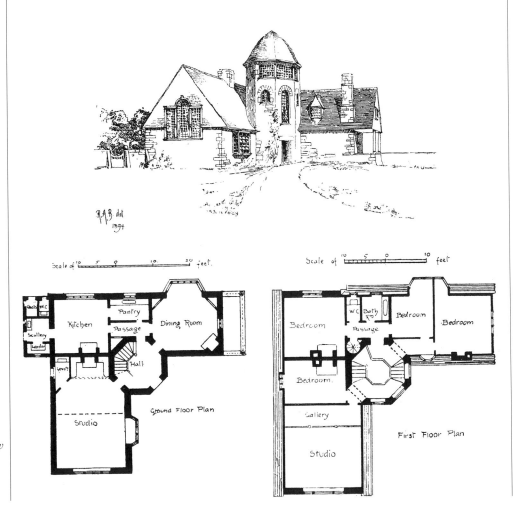

139 *An Artist's Bungalow with Studio*, a project by Robert Briggs, 1894. Briggs had the knack of designing by committee single-handed.

came in at £1194, excluding overmantel reliefs by Frampton, **140**. In spite of the shortcomings of the bedroom floor, Mr Sutro retained great faith in Voysey as later furniture designs, projects[29] and improvements in his hand would make clear.

Sutro's 'Hill Close' could no more be called a bungalow in today's terms than the Briggs effort, but it was as much an 'artistic little dwelling' as the 'House for an Artist in Surrey' devised by M H Baillie Scott and Seton Morris. Like Voysey, Scott sets out to construct simply, deferring mildly to traditional forms and materials. Then he disjoints and stratifies the major plan elements: quarrying into corners, breaking out bays, attaching lean-tos, until his idea of picturesque articulation is complete inside and out, **141**. But, in Voysey's view, Scott overdoes the interiors: 'By the popular sin of lavish multiplication of pattern, colour, texture and form the effect of breadth is destroyed, and there is no repose.'[30] Without a doubt the 'mad, worrying movement, vulgar glitter and display'[31] inadvertently conceals some of the more ingenious quaintnesses such as the shuttered studio-gallery halfway up the attic staircase.

Fortunately Baillie Scott had few opportunities to exercise his decorative flair on a

140 Drawings of Alfred Sutro's 'Hill Close' near Swanage, Dorset, by Charles Voysey, 1895. The north elevation, especially, anticipated a style popular 30 years later.

141 *House for an Artist in Surrey*, a project by M H Baillie Scott, 1895. Dining room and plans. 'Mad, worrying movement' inside; outside, 'more gables than a lazy man would care to count on a sunny day'.

N-E ELEVATION

N-W ELEVATION

GROUND FLOOR

UPPER FLOOR

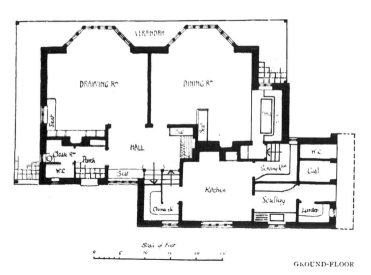

GROUND-FLOOR

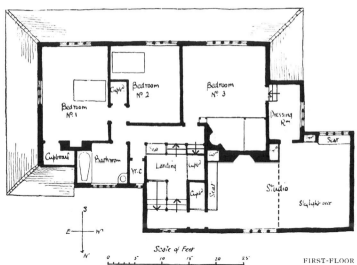

FIRST-FLOOR

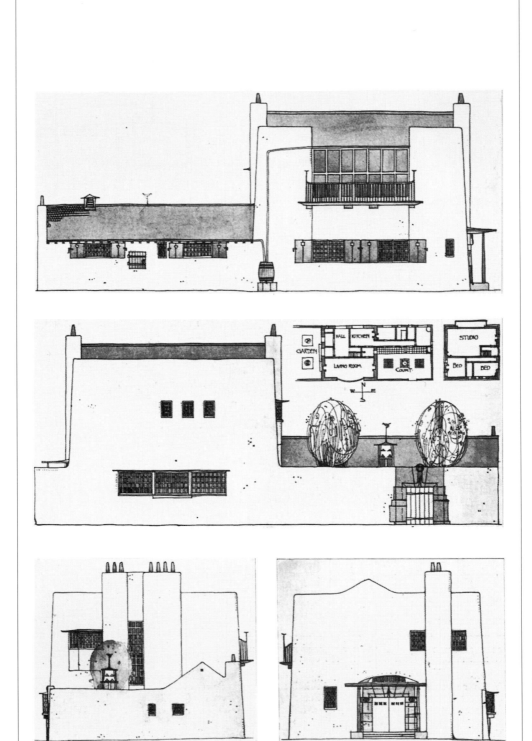

142 Charles Rennie Mackintosh's projected *Country House for an Artist*, 1900. Elevation and plans. Partly Scottish, wholly matchless.

large scale. His functionally intensive, highly interactive planning, however, called up imitations and refinements right around the country – from Sundial Cottage at Northwood for Walter West by Arnold Mitchell to Munstead Wood at Godalming for Gertrude Jekyll by (Sir) Edwin Lutyens.[32] When he eventually did get to design a real Artist's House (for Mrs Branson at Letchworth, Hertfordshire, in 1906), his once effortless injection of harmonious variety had become more a matter of self-conscious distortion.

This nationwide, Free Style free-for-all merged imperceptibly with the Bungalow Binge which continued to divert the eccentric fringe and from which few architects of the new century were immune. But the way ahead, if only the British realised it at the time, lay with men of the vision of Charles Rennie Mackintosh. Yet works like Mackintosh's exquisite country studio-house project of 1900, **142**, merely passed into oblivion like a spooky iceberg on a tide of indifference.

10
NOT A COMMON HARTIST'S STUDIO: PHOTOGRAPHIC ESTABLISHMENTS

IN 1860 *Punch* issued a du Maurier cartoon showing three cigarette-puffing artists trooping into a photographer's rooms. Confronting the leader, a mincing operator in cravat and cape announces that smoking is forbidden.

'Oh', gasps Dick Tinto, 'A thousand pardons! I was not aware that —'
Here he is interrupted with dignified severity:
'Please to remember, Gentlemen, that this is not a Common Hartist's Studio!'

The common artists are taken aback by this class distinction. Really they should not have been surprised. By that date photographers had been putting on airs for nearly 20 years. Photography, unlike the newer vogue for cigarette smoking, had briskly become popular at all levels of society. Portrait painters, especially miniaturists, felt understandably threatened by it, however. But at least there was some truth in Alfred Chalon's observation that, though cheaper, photography did not flatter, and that inexpert tinting with dyes could not match skilful brushwork in oils or watercolour.

Richard Beard, as any enthusiast will tell you, opened London's first daguerreotype portrait establishment in 1841. Designed by Beard himself, it was situated atop the Royal Polytechnic Institution on the west side of Upper Regent Street. George Cruikshank's drawing presents no common studio but a small rotunda, **143**. Cornice-mounted cameras are aimed at a throne which backs onto a darkroom bitten out of the circular plan. A contemporary initiate recorded how she sat '. . . under a glass dome casting a snapdragon blue light, making all [the attendants and customers] look like spectres . . .'.[1] Beard's first real competitor, Antoine Claudet, also started business in 1841. His studio above the Adelaide Gallery, off Adelaide Street, Strand, had more the appearance of a large greenhouse.[2] Once the two rivals began to realise considerable profits, there was a rush to obtain daguerreotype licences for English use. Following Claudet's example, totally glazed attics began to appear in quick succession along London's major shopping streets. (At a high level the light was unimpeded and the working day potentially longer.) The number of portrait studios rose to 66 by 1855; in 1861 it exceeded 200, of which 35 were in Regent

143 George Cruikshank, *A Photographic Phenomenon*, *c.* 1841. Richard Beard's kiosk at the Royal Polytechnic Institution.

Street.[3] Most of these latter by no means complemented the skyline of the regal Regency terraces. However, Count Ostrog's 'Walery' studio – a classical sky-parlour designed by T H Watson to crown the central pavilion of Soane's No.s 156–172 – did nothing if not reproduce the novelty value of Beard's original rooftop kiosk.

Abolition of the patent rights covering Daguerre's and newer, improved processes in the early 1850s, accelerated the spread of photographic businesses to the suburbs. Roof-level glasshouses were favoured for high street locations but ground-floor studios in select neighbourhoods definitely had their advantages. Not every customer was willing or able to climb ten flights of stairs and, besides, photographers required a fair-sized bleachfield for printing purposes. Provision also had to be made for the equestrian portrait. André Disderi, who ran studios in Brook Street, Mayfair, catered for the mounted sitter in the grounds of Hereford Lodge off Old Brompton Road, South Kensington.[4] It was Disderi & Co., along with another French outfit directed by Camille Silvy, which popularised *carte-de-visite* photography in London from 1859 onwards. In 1859–60 Silvy reconstructed premises bought from Caldesi & Montecchi at 38 Porchester Terrace, Bayswater – none other than John Linnell's former address.

144 An inexpertly taken photograph by Camille Silvy of the rear of his *carte-de-visite* premises at 36–38 Porchester Terrace, Bayswater, 1862.

By 1864 his operations had been carried over into Linnell's studio annexe and he was employing up to 40 assistants, **144**. Superior artistry and acumen brought Silvy such a significant share of the hugely voluminous and lucrative *carte-de-visite* market that he retired comfortably, aged only 33, in 1868. No wonder cartoonists thought these fellows a bit uppity.

Despite the reverses of fortune suffered by some of their fellow pioneers, portrait photographers like Silvy soon obtained reputations for great wealth and showmanship. This was especially true of the French, both in Paris and in London. More so than the portrait painters', the service they offered belonged to the commercial realm; for the most part they projected their image through city centre studios. Were they to take it, however, the opportunity existed to make their own houses the vehicle of self-advertisement inside and outside working hours. Some idea of domestic facilities suitable for practitioners in the English capital was given in 1859 by the French architect Hector Horeau. His scheme's full title, *Résidence d'un Photographe à Nothing Last word près London N.E.*, reveals its element of Utopian fantasy, **145**. Intemperate elevations 'in a rather naïve and démodé troubadour style'[5] belie the prevalent classical signature of the plans. But, oddities aside, the

145 *Résidence d'un Photographe à Nothing Last word, près London N.E.*, designed by Hector Horeau, 1859. A suburban mansion with a Parisian-style top floor studio.

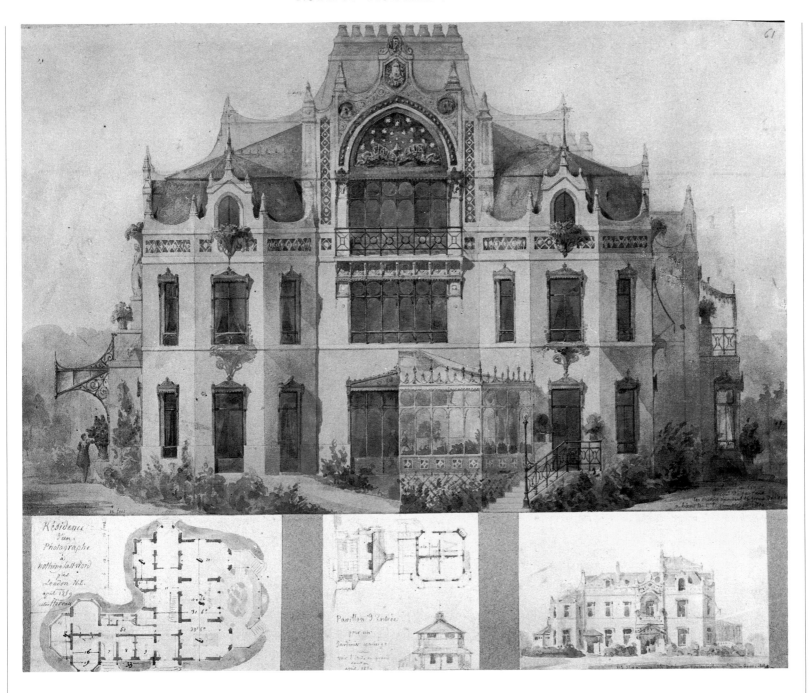

proposal was nevertheless a circumstantially plausible one. Determined to please, Horeau shows on the side view that the northern gable (decorated with a majolica design spelling out FIAT LUX – Let there be Light) could be replaced by a conventional rooftop glasshouse.

A realistic picture of live-in arrangements lower down the celebrity scale is supplied by F D Hardy's painting of 1862, *The Young Photographers*, **146**. Here the studio, equipped with typical props, is attached to an ordinary house in a country town. While his wife is distracted from her tinting and framing responsibilities, the adult photographer shows sample plates to a wide-eyed local couple. Perhaps the photographer is an ex-miniaturist. If so, his new commodity is evidently slow to win acceptance: the struggle to support numerous children is telling on the upkeep of the parlour.

Off-broadway professionals in suburban London do not seem to have indulged themselves to a much greater degree than Hardy's progressive provincial. Thomas Fall, from 1874 onwards a self-employed photographer who specialised in portraits of children and animals, was able to build his own house and studio at 40 Netherhall Gardens, Hampstead, by 1881. A flimsy subsidiary structure with a basement darkroom, the studio was demolished only ten or so years later when Fall moved elsewhere. Predictably enough, people like him gravitated to all the other artistic quarters of London as well. Charles Praetorius, for example, placed a decorative glass marquee on the forecourt of 12–14 Clareville Grove, Brompton, in 1892; *c.* 1898 Frederick Hollyer, another man chiefly engaged in reproducing works of art, erected a garden studio behind 9 Pembroke Square, Kensington; G C Beresford, renowned for portraits of the cultural élite, launched his practice from a ready-made studio-house at 20 Yeoman's Row, near Knightsbridge, in 1902.

146 Frederick Hardy, *The Young Photographers* (1862). Conventional studio props are visible in the lean-to glasshouse at the rear.

If the scores of similar domestic studios around London were outwardly less than spectacular – or too elegantly fragile to have survived – some of the workshops built by amateurs were not always prepossessing either. Julia Margaret Cameron, the famous shutterbug who went lion-hunting on the Isle of Wight in the 1860s, made no special effort to glorify hers:

> I turned my coal-house into my dark-room, and a glazed fowl-house became my glass house. . . . The society of hens and chickens was soon changed into that of poets, painters, and lovely maidens. . . . I longed to arrest all the beauty that came before me.[6]

This longing Mrs Cameron shared with D W Wynfield, to whom she owed 'all she ever knew' concerning wet-plate technique. Wynfield's half painting, half picture-taking studio in St John's Wood was essentially similar to the one built for the use of Mrs Henry St John Mildmay alongside the Mildmay country house near Sevenoaks in Kent.[7] Until the roll film camera arrived in 1888, photography was not a hobby to be trifled with, but neither was it reserved for rich Aesthetes. Accordingly, in about 1883, a photographer and 'architectural woodworker' named James Parkinson felt it his duty to show ordinary mortals how to construct a studio of their own, **147**. His aim, as he set out in *Amateur Work*:

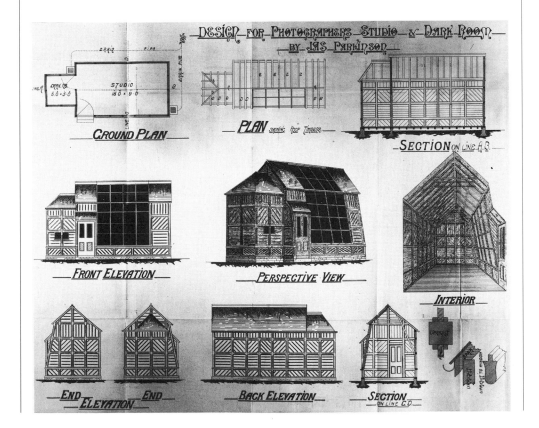

147 James Parkinson's designs for a do-it-yourself studio and darkroom, *c.* 1883. A garden pavilion not unlike a London cabmen's shelter.

. . . is not as many recommend, to knock up any kind of a shed, and think it will do, but to give carefully-prepared plans and specifications for a studio that will be an ornament to the garden and a credit to its builder, as well as useful.[8]

This done, he went on to describe the merits of various accessories, assuring that a judicious selection from the following priced list would serve the average hobbyist quite adequately:

Backgrounds, etc.	£	s	d
Empire Patent Backcloth, 8′ × 6′	1	5	0
Fancy Painted Interior, 8′ × 7′	2	2	6
Fancy Painted Landscape, 8′ × 7′	2	2	6
Art Curtain, 10′ long		15	6
Real Skin Rug (photogenic colour), 6′ × 3′		15	0
Imitation Grass Mat, 6′ × 4′		12	6
Fancy Velvet Cushion & Drapery	1	1	0
Basket Artificial Flowers (arr. for photo)		5	0
Imitation Tree Trunk (carton pierre)	1	15	0
Furniture			
The Argyll Chair, 5 changes	3	10	0
The Sultana Chair, 3 changes	6	10	0
The Aesthetic Poser, 6 changes	10	10	0
Small Fancy Table	2	10	0
Garden Balustrade	5	10	0
Appliances			
Emmerson Head & Body Rest	2	10	0
Portable Head-screen	1	10	0
Concave Side Reflector	1	0	0

Items similar to these are visible in Poyet's engraving of a grander French establishment of the same period, **148**.

Opportunities to produce commercially profitable images due to the development of better quality materials, more convenient processes, and endless new applications, brought more and more photographers into the field. In England as a whole the total number stood at 2534 in 1861. Between 1871 and 1881 this rose 41 per cent; in the next ten years it jumped a further 59 per cent, to nearly 11 000.[9] Competition to attract personal customers became increasingly fierce in London. Despite the connotations of a company name like 'Carl Vandyck, Photographic Artist', 'Argent Archer, High Art Photographer Royal' definitely had a superior ring. Passenger lifts, such as those William Barraud and Martin Jacolette advertised, gained favour with portrait subjects averse to the usual tedious ascent. J E Mayall's electric light installation, 'the most powerful in London', provided versatility and longer opening hours. Reduced-scale furniture enhanced the stature of smaller patrons. All these gimmicks helped to make one studio more fashionable than the other.

149

148 A professional photographer's glasshouse of the 1880s fully equipped with backdrops, studio furniture and technical devices.

149 Entrance front and plan of Elliott & Fry's South Kensington establishment at 108–110 Old Brompton Road – the result of William Flockhart's reconstruction in 1885–6.

148

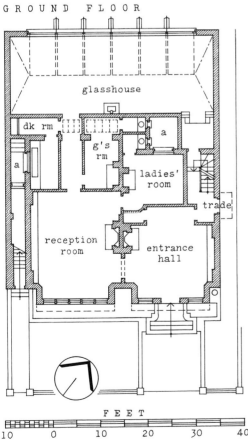

149

G R O U N D   F L O O R

glasshouse

dk rm

g's rm

a

a

ladies' room

trade

reception room

entrance hall

F E E T

10   0   10   20   30   40

In this connection Messrs Elliott & Fry of Baker Street, where photographers came two a penny, tried a different approach in 1885–6. They appointed William Flockhart to convert two semi-detached houses around the corner from Queen's Gate, South Kensington, into a new establishment embracing as much of 'the homely character and quiet of the private house'[10] as possible, **149**. Flockhart disposed of £3000 remodelling the fronts in the latest red brick, Harrington Gardens style, while tying together the interiors with passably consistent Jacobethan motifs. Mr Fry untied them again with a mixture of 18th-century and Aesthetic School furniture; pictures by Rossetti, Sandys and Herkomer hung on the walls. W A S Benson designed the light fittings, and Alfred Newman, the art-metalworker concurrently contracted by Alma Tadema, executed the railings and nameplates. A supplementary ladies' dressing room was situated on the first floor and, above that, 'a very complete set of apartments for the resident operator'. The operator's glasshouse, fitted with white and dark blue blinds from end to end, closely resembled the contemporary French model mentioned earlier. It continued in use by photographers until 1919.

By increasing the 'facility of access', Elliott & Fry intended their South Kensington branch to appeal to 'Ladies in Court Dress or other elaborate costume'. This gambit failed to lower the premium on premises nearer Mayfair, Knightsbridge and Buckingham Palace, however. Maull & Fox therefore found themselves well placed at 187 Piccadilly. Unwilling to move when their landlords, Hatchards, decided to redevelop in 1908, their glasshouse was rebuilt over the bookshop more or less as it was before, **150**[11]. M. Lafayette also capitalised on the position he obtained at 179 New Bond Street. His London headquarters stood out by virtue of a polychrome faience pediment incorporating a rising sun and the royal coat of arms. A small gallery of

150 Former Maull & Fox premises on the top floor of 187 Piccadilly, Westminster, as rebuilt on the site in 1908.

151 An Edwardian photograph of H Walter Barnett's 'Electric Light Studio'. At night the rooftop glasshouse glowed like a beacon above Knightsbridge, Belgravia.

photographs adjoining the waiting room, proto-Art Nouveau decor, and electric lighting further distinguished Edmund Wimperis's remodelling of 1896. But Lafayette's trump card was undoubtedly his patent system for ridding the glasshouse of fog – 'one of the most deadly enemies of the camera'.[12] Just the same, any number of competitive innovations could not have put H Walter Barnett out of business. Barnett made his supremely prominent building into a three-dimensional advertising hoarding. Open on the occasion of their majesties' evening levées, it glowed like a beacon on the Knightsbridge side of Hyde Park Corner, **151**.

Roll up! Roll up! But, please to remember, no smoking.

11
FICTION AND FACTION
IN STUDIOLAND

JUST AS nearly every major Victorian architect was called on to design a studio, there were few major Victorian writers who did not exploit the image of an artist in his typical setting. Two of the better-known 19th-century English novels in which this image features largely, *The Picture of Dorian Gray* (1891) by Oscar Wilde and *Trilby* (1895) by George du Maurier, each open with descriptions of that object of intense public curiosity. Wilde introduces Basil Hallward's painting room:

> The studio was filled with the rich odour of roses, and when the light summer wind stirred amidst the trees of the garden, there came through the open door the heavy scent of the lilac, of the more delicate perfume of the pink-flowering thorn.
>
> From the corner of the divan of Persian saddlebags on which he was lying, smoking, as was his custom, innumerable cigarettes, Lord Henry Wotton could just catch the gleam of the honey-sweet and honey-coloured blossoms of a laburnum . . .; and now and then the fantastic shadows of birds in flight flitted across the long tussore-silk curtains that were stretched in front of the huge window, producing a kind of momentary Japanese effect.

Du Maurier presents a scene in Paris well before the influence of the Aesthetic Movement had been felt. He begins[1]:

> The big studio window was open at the top, and let in a pleasant breeze from the north-west. The big piano lay, freshly-tuned, alongside; opposite was a panoply of foils, masks, and boxing gloves. The walls were of the usual dull red, relieved by plaster casts of arms and legs. There were also studies in oil from the nude: copies of Titian, Rembrandt, Velasquez . . . . Along the walls, at a great height, ran a broad shelf on which there were other casts – a little flayed man threatening high heaven, a lion and a boar by Barye, an anatomical figure of a horse. Near the stove hung a gridiron, a frying-pan, a toasting fork . . . . On the floor lay two cheetah skins and a large Persian praying rug.

. . . And an immense divan spread itself in width and length and delightful thickness just beneath the big north window – a divan so immense that three well-fed, well-contented Englishmen could all lie lazily smoking their pipes on it at once without being in each other's way, and very often did!

Little had changed over the years in a way. But du Maurier's half gymnasium, half museum lumber room rather than Wilde's sensory saloon created the more lasting popular impression. Beyond that, the public would have been no more surprised to read of a detached peer smoking (opium-spiked) cigarettes within such a place than of three ordinary, friendly gentlemen-artists smoking plain tobacco. In fact no artist was ever thought to be entirely ordinary, friendly or gentlemanly. Novelists tended to cast him either as a one-stroke prodigy with exemplary manners and taste (Gaston Phoebus in Disraeli's *Lothair*), or as a loaded symbol of the suffering creator sunk in Bohemian dereliction (Claude Lantier in Zola's *L'Oeuvre*). The latter role matched the popular conception of the studio and usually prevailed. Yet, of course, like everyone else he actually fell somewhere in between and much was made of the company he kept, both reputable and disreputable, but always colourful, **152**.

Du Maurier had plenty of personal experience to draw on when he set the scene in the Place St Anatole des Arts. For example, along with Fred Walker and Val Prinsep, models for the characters 'Little Billee' Bagot and Talbot 'Taffy' Wynne in *Trilby*, he was an honorary member of the St John's Wood Clique. These artists, including David 'Winkie' Wynfield, George 'Dolly' Storey, John 'The Dodger' Hodgson and Philip 'The Fiend' Calderon, used to get up more uproarious charades, fancy dress balls and tableaux vivants than most. Sometimes, their wives in tow, they would join Eyre

152 George du Maurier, *All as it used to be*, an illustration from *Trilby*. Svengali keeps his hypnotic eye on Trilby and Little Billee at a Sunday afternoon party in the Quartier Latin.

"ALL AS IT USED TO BE"

Crowe and the *Punch* columnist Frank Burnand to spend a weekend at Hever Castle. On other occasions they would leave the makings of a barbecue at the Spotted Dog in Neasden, ramble all day, return to their grilled cutlets and play croquet on the tavern pitch; 'Ever on Thee', the Clique's bibulous motto, was engraved on little gridiron badges. They would also rigorously 'grill' each other at the end of sketching evenings conducted in rotation in their own studios. On one occasion Fred Walker sent in his contribution from Torquay – a mirage peopled by his madcap friends, **153**.[2]

A less cohesive group was that which gathered at different stages around the charismatic Gabriel Rossetti. Painters, poets, cranks, critics, models and minders all came to recline in the arch-Pre-Raphaelite's 'lordly pleasure marquee', set up in a gardenful of exotic animals at 16 Cheyne Walk, **154**. Many of the pets in the legendary menagerie were named after Royal Academicians. There was a great variety but Rossetti regretted not having an elephant; he would have trained it to wash the windows. And it would have made little difference to the garden, which was '. . . large, and so neglected and untrimmed as to be a veritable wilderness'.[3]

Painters' gardens were habitually in this condition. Even Basil Hallward's rarefied surroundings saw '. . . bees shouldering their way through the long unmown grass . . .'.[4] According to George Eliot, it was a phenomenon which dated back to the days

153 Fred Walker, *A Vision of 'the Clique'* (1864); left to right: Hodgson, Storey borne by Leslie, Wynfield (with family tree), Yeames (with wedding ring), Marks, Calderon and Walker.

of Piero di Cosimo in Florence. In her novel *Romola* (1862–3), she takes the reader to Piero's studio where the open door:

> . . . showed a garden, or rather thicket, in which fig trees and vines grew in tangled trailing wildness among nettles and hemlocks. . . . It seemed as if that dank luxuriance had begun to penetrate even within the walls of the wide and lofty room . . .[5]

Wildlife had begun to penetrate it too, since several pigeons and a white rabbit felt quite at home there, while 'three corpulent toads were crawling in an intimate and friendly way near the doorstone'.[6] Here was a situation which Edward Lear envied a good deal. Writing to his Pre-Raphaelite 'Uncle' Woolner about the studio-villa he was building at San Remo in 1870, he added his thoughts on the new garden:

> I shall have 28 olive trees & a small bed of onions: & a stone terrace, with a gray Parrot & two hedgehogs to walk up & down on it by day & by night.[7]

Ten years later poor Lear was forced to build a second villa which, in order not to confuse his cat, the redoubtable Foss, was laid out on an identical plan to the first. The household at Grim's Dyke, once it had passed to W S Gilbert, likewise revolved

154 (Sir) Max Beerbohm, *Dante Gabriel Rossetti, in his back garden*; left to right: Whistler, Swinburne, Watts-Dunton (admonishing), Rossetti, Meredith, Burne-Jones, a Cornforth-like model, Morris, Ruskin (foreground), Hunt, Hall Caine.

around the pets. Servants had to suffer laying places at table for them and so on. Grim's Dyke had been a safari park since the day Goodall introduced Jacob sheep and Egyptian goats to feature in his Arabian genre pieces. Like Madox Brown's Clapham Common lambs, they 'used to behave very ill',[8] nibbling to the quick the palm saplings Goodall had grown from date stones.

In a manner of speaking, Rossetti did get his elephant in the end. A cockney model of mammoth proportions, she was called Fanny Cornforth. To his consternation she was considerably less tractable than his late wife who, at the height of their Pre-Raphaelite fervour, lay three-quarters drowned in a bath posing for Millais' *Ophelia*. Models were frequently asked to take up undignified and exhausting poses yet, because the going rate was reasonable (Cope was offering an off-duty guardsman 12 shillings a day in 1843[9]), there was no lack of them, **155**. Whole families of handsome Italians were said to live in West Kensington surviving on an ability to represent *contadini* and ancient Romans. Some were given extra responsibilities and even got ahead of their station, like du Maurier's handy individual:

> I sit for the 'eads of all 'is 'oly men. I order 'is frames, stretch 'is canvases, wash 'is brushes, set 'is palette and mix 'is colours. All 'e's got to do is just to *shove* 'em on.[10]

With others, as Madox Brown found when retouching his *Christ Washing Peter's Feet* in 1856, it was a matter of pot luck. The Messiah he was recommended turned out to be (in Brown's own words) 'a brute of a model, a hugh accadimician with a beard and muscles all over like all accadimy models, too stiff to take any pose except the Apollo Belvidere'.[11] The right model – Storey's 'Dorothy' and Herkomer's Chelsea Pensioner, for instance – could make an artist's name for him. And a model's finest hour had come if, on Academy election night, he or she could win the traditional steeplechase to take good news to the new member.

Academy membership eventually required a turn of duty on one or another of the many internal committees. Students had to be visited; the Benevolent Fund had to be administered; Old Master Winter Exhibitions, Banquets, Ballots and so on all had to be organised. Stints on the committees responsible for sifting the works sent in for the annual summer show and their arrangement in the galleries were probably more arduous than most. Ten RAs served on the Selection Committee, **156**. They spent several days assessing thousands upon thousands of pictures, their own prejudices and preferences soon becoming apparent. While Leighton would baulk at absolutely any view of Whitby and W B Richmond damned anything Impressionistic, Herkomer once threatened to resign until a Sargent portrait was accepted. The selection made, it would pass to the grimly named Hanging Committee comprising five painters, one sculptor, one architect and one engraver. The hangers' work involved jigsaw-puzzling on a grand scale, with countless trips in search of likely looking pieces. For this task old George Richmond took to a wheelchair. Young George Leslie then dared to ride around on a tricycle – quite slowly after the time he came to grief over a box of screws.

155 T Walter Wilson, *The Last Call*, representing Charles Bell Birch at work on *The Wounded Trumpeter* (1879). Some figure models really had to earn their pay.

156 Reginald Cleaver, *The RA Selection Committee* (1892). A gang of ten sifts the thousands of pictures submitted for inclusion in the Academy's annual exhibition.

MR·J·C·HORSLEY.   MR·H·S·MARKS.   MR·W·BROCK   SIR·J·MILLAIS   MR·J·C·HOOK.   MR·W·O·ORCHARDSON
MR·ALMA·TADEMA   SIR·F·LEIGHTON.   MR·HAMO·THORNYCROFT   MR·J·PETTIE
MR·EATON (SEC).

Whether or not an artist belonged to the Academy or one of the alternative exhibition societies, there was always a kerfuffle before Sending-In Day. It paid to complete your exhibits well in advance since the public insisted on an inspection in your own studio first. As nothing could prevent this fashionable invasion,[12] Outsiders generally opened their doors on the fifth Sunday preceding the RA submission and RAs on the fourth. Stacy Marks felt that only 'humbug, hollowness and hypocrisy' came of these 'Picture' or 'Show Sundays'. People showed themselves to be rude and ignorant; they thieved and gave the staff colds. Furthermore, they often mistook the appointed day and very rarely bought anything. Residents of studio groups, however, were known to enter into the spirit: clubbing together to hire decorative models or a costumed blackamoor to conduct visitors around the various booths. Acceptance of pictures culminated in Varnishing Day, an opportunity for invited exhibitors to repair chipped frames or to alter effects compromised by the gallery lighting. In fact, three such days were allotted to Academicians, but only one for everyone else; in other words, in the lead-up to the RA show, varnishing could readily become an all-in parlour Wall Game, **157**. On those days you might have caught Turner shamelessly daubing neighbouring works with opaque toner while the pure pigment he had piled onto his own landscape made it shine like the view from an open window. After Varnishing Day came Charwomen's Day, which was followed in turn by the Press and Private View Days.

This intense opening to the London cultural season was inevitably the occasion of numerous receptions and arty parties. The latter, however, might take place with less ceremony at any time of the year. At 'Perspective', the Richmond mansion of the munificent patron Mr Halket Grosvenor in G B Shaw's *Immaturity* (1879), the 'artistic congress' on Easter Sunday always drew a large crowd. Nonetheless, 'People who disapproved of felt hats, tweed and velveteen clothes, long hair, music on Sundays, pictures of the nude figure, literary women, and avowals of agnosticism, either dissembled or stayed away . . .'.[13] Consequently an 'idealised Bohemianism' prevailed, although discussions could become overheated, as Shaw amusingly relates. Just the same, parties were usually all-male, evening affairs, dedicated to smoke, spirits and slander – or, when Stacy Marks, the famed painter of birds, played host, 'Pipes, Poultry and Potations'. Easily the most popular were those given by Arthur Lewis, the convivial Conduit Street mercer and amateur painter. Good Arthur moved from Jermyn Street to the ducal Moray Lodge on Campden Hill in the early 1860s, attaching to it a big saloon especially for these Saturday entertainments. Sentimental glees sung by a 25-voice choir – formerly the Jermyn Band and latterly The Moray Minstrels – selected tobaccos and choice oysters ('The amount we consumed on one occasion was 278 dozen, as I happen to know', wrote Felix Moscheles[14]) were 'the order of the evening', **158**. Sadly for the men, Kate Terry outlawed these tobacchanals after her marriage to Arthur in 1867. Miss Terry was not the only one to disapprove of the artist's love of the weed as Frith discovered at about the same time. Resting from his labours before Sir Edward Cust, one sitter among very many to appear in a vast group portrait, the painter asked if he would mind him lighting a cigar. 'Not in the least,' replied Sir Edward, 'if you don't mind my being sick, which I certainly shall be the moment you begin.'[15]

Arthur Lewis needed no other claim to fame, but in 1863 he founded the Hanover Square Arts Club, having earlier been prime mover of the Junior Etching Club. This minor version of the exclusive Kensington-based organisation was launched in William Gale's studio at Langham Chambers, themselves the headquarters of The Artists' Society and The Langham Sketching Club. The last-named club operated on Friday nights from October to May. It was an offshoot of the former Society 'for general study from the life' first incorporated in 1830 and re-established with its own studios, library, gallery and chambers in 1854 at 1–3 All Souls' Place, Marylebone. Clubs such as these which enabled elected subscribers to come together for recreational drawing sessions rather than disciplined academic exercises naturally had many antecedents. Among the more venerable was the one recrystallised in 1808 by Francis Stevens, J J and A E Chalon: The Sketching Society. Formed 'for the purpose of combining social intercourse with the cultivation of their art', its members met weekly during the winter until 1851, by which time the elder Chalon had attended

157 George du Maurier, *Varnishing Day at the Royal Academy.* Men and women clamber over one another to add final touches to their exhibits.

158 T Walter Wilson, '*The Knight of the Hill's' Studio Smoke.* A tobacchanal held at Arthur Lewis's Moray Lodge, Campden Hill, where artists are the life of the party.

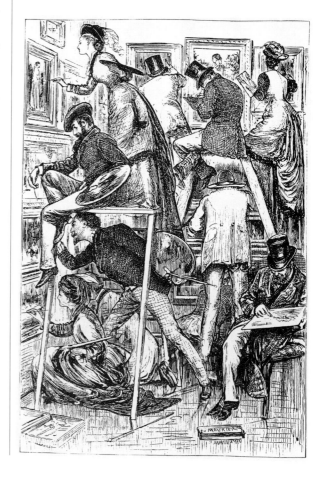

reduced that to sign language, the teacher and his methods cultivated many a future champion. Having become a living legend, Leigh could not prevent Thackeray poking fun at him, alias Gandish, in *The Newcomes* (1853–5). Accompanied by the smarmy Smee RA, Col. Newcome inspected the school with a view to enrolling his 16-year-old son, Clive. On their way through the students' room, the statue gallery and the 'hatrium', Gandish showed off a personally signed specimen of High Art – a 'haltar-piece', in fact – for which he never could get his price. 'I should think it *is* high art', whispered old Smee; 'fourteen feet high, at least!'[18]

Col. Newcome's tour closely resembled a real one which Mr Frith Snr undertook in 1835 on behalf of his 16-year-old, William, at an older, rival school founded by Henry Sass (alias Barker[19]) in Bloomsbury Street. Sentenced to two years here as a boarder, young Frith became all too familiar with 'a long corridor off which were the little rooms that Sass called the "Studii", for the separate use of the advanced students', and, at its end, 'a large circular hall . . . built on a reduced scale in the proportions of the Pantheon in Rome'.[20] Top lighting, also in the manner of the Pantheon, made this the perfect statue gallery. Above the studii lay 'an upper school, much smaller than the lower gallery, but built precisely on the same plan'.[21] Boarders enjoyed the privilege of meeting hallowed figures such as Wilkie, Constable and Martin ('certainly one of the most beautiful human beings I ever beheld', Frith recalled) at family dinners and conversazioni. Wilkie was once pleased enough to

162 The Henry Sass–Francis Cary Art School on the corner of Bloomsbury and Streatham Streets, Bloomsbury.

flatter Sass, telling him he could teach a stone to draw. 'And so it is,' he rejoined, 'but I can't teach that C— anything.'[22] We only have Frith's word that he did not actually say 'F—'.

Sass was forced to retire through mental illness, having taught for some 22 years. F S Cary took over the school in 1842. As the mini-Pantheons were probably cheaply made up in lath and plaster it is likely Cary rebuilt the premises as they stand today, **162**. Other less reputable classes likewise prepared students for entry to the Academy where the full course entailed between seven and ten years' study.[23] No painting was attempted before two years were up; access to the living model followed later still. Women, moreover, were not admitted to the RA Schools before 1860 and then only by default. Not until 1893 could they study from the partially draped male nude there. For these reasons, beginners wishing to advance more rapidly either went to the Continent where teaching was more liberal and efficient, or to a London school run on Continental lines. With the government education system absorbing most of the better teachers, atelier-style classes tended to be maverick institutions. The St John's Wood Art School began to rival Heatherley's (formerly Leigh's) in 1878;[24] Herkomer took his first pupils at the Bushey labour camp, later to become a veritable archipelago, in 1883. Several smaller outfits like Louise Jopling's in Clareville Grove and Logan Place, and the Cope and Nicol studios in Pelham Street, prospered over the same period. Remarkably enough, Heatherley's, at over 125 years old, is still kicking. And another, the Byam Shaw school – a mere stripling of 80 or so – founded by two graduates of 'The Wood', still keeps it up to the mark.

Schools, it goes without saying, were the nurseries of friendships and ideological factions: the RA gave rise to the Pre-Raphaelite Brotherhood and its medievalist revival; Leigh's brought together the St John's Wood Clique on the side of historical romance. Whatever their particular gospel, such groups were traditionally united in their efforts to obtain decent exhibition space, proper recognition and a fair price for their work. Certainly no small portion of an unaccredited, unaffiliated artist's daily round was spent chasing these essential requisites. As Edward Lear observed:

> The walking-exploring-noveltyperceiving & beautyappreciating part of the Landscape painter's life is undoubtedly to be envied:– but then the contrast of the moneytryingtoget, fuss-trouble & bustle is wholly odious & every year more so.[25]

Thus it happened that the Pre-Raphaelite faithful attempted to promote their art by setting up the Hogarth Club. The Clique replied by infiltrating the Dudley Gallery committee. Despite the closure of the friendly British Institution, increasing numbers of private galleries like the Dudley espoused most causes satisfactorily until the mid-1880s. But then even the Grosvenor revealed its true colours when asked to represent the Glasgow Boys, the Newlyners, the Bomb-Throwers – flat brush painters fresh from Parisian ateliers, or the London Impressionists. Following meetings first in Luke Fildes's house and later in *Wentworth Studios*, Chelsea,[26] these revolutionaries launched joint redress through the New English Art Club and its virtual Salon des

Refusés at the Marlborough Gallery from 1885 onwards. Close either side of this date the long unrequited female and applied art lobbies attained their objects too – one with the Society of Lady Artists at Suffolk Street, the other with the Arts and Crafts Exhibition Society at the progressive New Gallery in Regent Street. In those days a ginger group, that is any assembly with a vested interest in red hair, seemed to have an even chance of success.

The NEAC had no formal headquarters since its leading lights were also largely those of the Chelsea Arts Club. This licentious playgroup was founded in 1890 in rooms at 181 King's Road taken over from a political league by the slippery Scotsman, Jimmy Christie. Larger premises, sustained on the proceeds of a series of infamous summer balls, were later obtained in Old Church Street. As much as in any other decade, St John's Wood also lent asylum to the renegade element in the 1880s. But there the moves to establish a cooperative bar and cheap table d'hôte for local artists came mostly from the Continentophile old guard. Dendy Sadler and J B Burgess RA are acknowledged to have originated the St John's Wood Arts Club in 1895. But it was not until 1900 that Sadler's former rooms at 28 Finchley Road – entirely similar to those in Chelsea – were opened for use as a permanent home. Alfred Gilbert presided at the inaugural jollifications, **163**.

It is a measure of the energy of Victorian worthies that they could combine work and play so freely. Often their professional facility was such, however, that only the latter required any special practice. One of the more tireless organisers, Walter Crane, readily turned a dab hand at tennis. But he positively recoiled from the bloodlust of a Millais or a Stuart-Wortley. Millais was known to sit sketching in Wharncliffe Chase with a shotgun across his knees. If a duck should stray before his field of view he would blast it from the sky and carry on drawing with total equanimity. Jacomb-Hood managed to go riding every second day; he was often joined by Solomon Solomon who enjoyed a weekly outing with the Surrey Staghounds. Aware that Sir Francis Grant also rode to hounds, Disraeli obviously thought this was Leighton's style, too. In his novel *Lothair* (1870), the Leighton figure, Mr Phoebus, sails off on his steam yacht to a private Aegean island. There he pursues a life 'partly feudal, partly oriental, partly Venetian, and partly idiosyncratic'. In between keeping a grand studio, running an academy and reviving the gymnasia he conducts wolf hunts:

> . . . and that was a remarkable scene. The ladies, looking like Diana or her nymphs, were mounted on cream-coloured Anatolian chargers with golden bells; while Mr Phoebus himself, in green velvet and seven-league boots, sounded a wondrous twisted horn rife with . . . musical and learned venerie.[27]

During his time at Orme Square Leighton can at least be said to have done a spot of pistol shooting – the targets set up at one end of the studio. Clearly it gave him the edge over his colleagues because, soon after May 1860 when they all enlisted in the 38th Middlesex Artists' Rifles Volunteer Corps, he emerged the natural choice for commanding officer. There had been fear of a French invasion since early the previous year, and it occurred to Edward Sterling, Henry Phillips and Cave Thomas,

163 Sydney Hall, *The St John's Wood Arts Club* (?1895). Hacker traces Tadema's silhouette onto the clubroom wall while (left to right) Sadler, ?Burgess, Ford, Voysey, Collier, Hopkins and a waiter look on.

164 Godfrey Merry, *An Encampment of (20th Middlesex) Rifle Volunteers* at their summer camp on the church plateau, Aldershot, 1884.

among others, that London's artists, musicians and actors should form not just a detachment, but a crack defence regiment.[28] A similar proposal – to train a corps d'élite from the ranks of the RA and its students – was put forward in 1803 by Martin Archer Shee, but not implemented. Nor could Leighton, in the event, always depend on his fellow Academicians. Asked by him to accept a higher rank, Leslie (he of the St John's Wood Clique) had to confess that punctuality was not his strong point. True, he wore a watch chain, but it ended in a latchkey and a corkscrew. Nevertheless the Artists' RVC was impressive for its force of numbers and its superior marksmanship. This it practised anywhere between the Hythe Academy and the range in Marlborough Place, St John's Wood, **164**. After 1888, having become the 20th Middlesex, it attended drills in a new hall in Bloomsbury designed by (Sir) Robert Edis, Leighton's successor as colonel-commanding. Edis eventually led a contingent of Artists into the Boer War.

For the most part, the painters took soldiering no more seriously than the theatricals they produced in their studios. There was even a side-swipe at the volunteer movement in *The Colonel*, a little burlesque devised by Frank Burnand which Whistler, Wilde and Miles performed once or twice early in 1881. Burnand could have taken his theme from *Patience*, although he and Arthur Sullivan had been in cahoots since 1866, when they adapted *Cox and Box* for the Moray Lodge company.[29] While du Maurier played Box, several other *Punch* men also lined up, including Mark Lemon and John Tenniel. These latter two, along with George Cruikshank, Frank Topham Snr and Frank Holl Snr, belonged to another troupe known as The Histrionics. Profits from their repertory of comic sketches usually went to the Artists' Benevolent Fund. Mark Lemon brought experience from an earlier period still, having been a member of Dickens' Guild of Literature and Art. A favourite venue of that belaboured engine was Egg's Bayswater studio. Leech, Mulready, Webster and Frith were among the thespians who regularly appeared there.

Of course the show went on in the country, too. Webster, Horsley and Hardy, all sons of musicians, got together around the studio piano at Cranbrook; Birket Foster hosted less sober sessions at Witley, especially near Christmastime. Charles Keene suggested that Foster's singalongs would gain in spontaneity if the studio windows were decorated with a selection of words and music. (This notion was taken a stage further by Thomas Rooke who painted folk dance steps on his parlour floor in Bedford Park.) Then there were the cricket matches . . . Edwin Abbey, a foreigner, earned no respect in Fairford until an artists' eleven he brought up from London defeated the local club by ten wickets. One wonders whether this victorious team ever met the one fielded by the boys down at St Ives. Did these extraordinarily resourceful artists take the lead and make home movies as well? Of course they did, and in colour, too. Many painted their own magic lantern slides, after Gainsborough's early example; it only took imagination to animate the scenes and splice the frames.

12

RIVERRUN AND ENVIRONS:
A RALLYING ROUND

FOR MANY decades just a small Middlesex village on the road to Fulham, Little Chelsea by 1865 lay in the midst of the burgeoning London suburb of West Brompton. Late in the previous century Mary Moser RA had dallied in Seymour Walk; now there were signs that an artistic element had come to stay. Maull & Polyblank, the photographers, had taken up at 252 Fulham Road and Morton Edwards, secretary of the Society of Sculptors, had put a deposit on 16 Hollywood Road. This latter, a wee building in naïve Romanesque opening from the rear of 27 Cathcart Road, was the work of Corbett & McClymont, builders of the Redcliffe Road terraces and much else in the vicinity.[1] Containing two equal-sized ground level shops and one other chamber, it proved to be a sound speculation. Edward Hughes, nephew of the Pre-Raphaelite Arthur Hughes, who had leased another Corbett & McClymont house in Finborough Road in the meantime, held the tenancy from 1891 onwards.

Corbett & McClymont and their backers took care not to compromise the tone of their estate by encouraging the settlement of artists too openly. The fact that a life class in Limerston Street had attracted 300 students within four years of its establishment in 1872[2] showed the area might easily be overrun. But it was not until 1883 that the builders joined in the wholesale and wholly covert provision of artists' accommodation by making a start on *Bolton Studios* between Redcliffe and Gilston Roads. Later in the 1880s individual settlers began forcing the pace south of Fulham Road on the estates largely developed by the more amenable Gunter family. Fred Brown, NEAC founder and soon to become Slade Professor, headed a gang of ex-*Bolton Studios* men who gathered in Netherton Grove. In due course, garden-studio fever hit the surrounding streets, Gunter Grove in particular. Following the lead of the sculptor Alfred Drury, nearly every second property along its west side sported a one-man factory unit by the end of the century.

Nonetheless, it took all this time and longer for a proper studio-house to appear. In 1903–4, 3a Seymour Walk went up to designs by C H B Quennell for the art-metalworkers Omar Ramsden and Alwyn Carr. These talented craftsmen,[3] who worked in the Art Nouveau style, promptly advertised their business by erecting splendid wrought iron gates incorporating their colophon, a pair of dragons, and a figurine of St Dunstan, patron saint of goldsmiths. The house, however, is a job-lot of bumps, bays and bulges. Various workshops, studies and living rooms are subservient to a pine-panelled upper studio where the Neo-Tudor motif gives rise to heraldic stained glass, kingpost trusses, and a gallery. Ramsden & Carr, both Roman Catholics, prospered on the strength of church and city corporation commissions until 1919, when Carr set up independently in Melbury Road.

Contemporary with St Dunstan's is the original fabric of 8–9 South Bolton Gardens. The present building is a vile remodelling of twin studio-houses designed in a thoroughly stripped mullion-and-transom manner by Walter Cave. Sir William Orpen occupied the eastern one, No. 8, almost from the beginning, **165**. Another hugely successful portrait painter of Irish stock, Sir James Shannon, used No. 9 during the 1910s in addition to his Holland Park studio. It is some wonder that Orpen who in his

165 Sir William Orpen, *Summer* (*c.* 1910). Billy-O shows himself, a model, and Cupid before the original studio window at 8 South Bolton Gardens, West Brompton.

prime could ask up to £3000 for a single ¾-length, should be satisfied with the basic amenities here for so long. Twenty-odd years passed before he bought No. 9 as well and in 1929 allowed Forbes & Tate to nullify Cave's modular simplicity and substitute a creole gumbo of Spanish Mission and Colonial Adam ingredients.[4] Billy-O then had room to spread his eclectic furnishings and a mechanical toy collection the rival of Alma Tadema's for the two years that a chronic addiction to the bottle would leave him.

'Go west along the Cromwell Road until your cab horse drops dead, and then ask.' 'The Grange', North End Road, since 1867 the home of Edward Burne-Jones and family, was so remote that these were the best directions to reach it you could get. Over a century had elapsed since the early English novelist Samuel Richardson lived in the same house, yet it remained just as much out of the way. After redecorating it in The Firm's taste and repairing the ceiling that Morris's over-enthusiastic dancing brought down at the house-warming, Burne-Jones dreamed away the years in a Cockaigne he rarely liked to leave.

By 1882, however, the great demand for and increasing size of his canvases caused him to build a garden studio. W A S Benson, the brother of a stunner he had solicited four years earlier, designed a 'long, white, roughcast' and skylit shed against the Lisgar Terrace boundary, **166**. Sunday visitors were fobbed off with this relatively spruce lumber room, while the bashful druid continued working in the self-confessed 'Augean' house studio. Books and folios, stacked in teetering but highly

166 Interior of Sir Edward Burne-Jones's skylit garden studio at 'The Grange', North End Road, West Kensington, designed by W A S Benson in about 1882.

specific piles on the floor there, were the bane of 'Little Rookie', his faithful assistant Thomas Rooke. Grandchildren were forbidden entry; all they knew was that 'Sinister people called "models" lived there who had trays taken up to them at lunch and tea time'.[5] Sustained demand persuaded Burne-Jones to have Benson improve the house studio lighting as well, **167**, for '. . . it is strange to remember that the Brotherhood of Artists who so loved Beauty did not love light, but lived in a tinted gloom through which clear spots of colour shone jewel-like'.[6] Benson was also relied on to make up Arthurian props for the painter's pictures and, in about 1889, to expand the family's holiday cottage on the green at Rottingdean. One grandchild later broke a discreet silence over the shortcomings of Benson's new work and the excruciating discomfort of the Pre-Raphaelite furniture in general.[7] Like Watts, Burne-Jones could not really cope with the real Victorian world. But though he shrank from public exposure, his art and his industrious gentility were much admired by eminent public figures, Gladstone especially. Thus no sooner had he resigned his Associateship of the RA than he was offered a baronetcy – an honour, unlike Watts and despite considerable misgivings, he was finally not too modest to accept. He was, after all, an outstanding designer.

It was not until Burne-Jones started to reorganise his operations at The Grange that any other artists of consequence saw fit to settle in West Kensington. But once the Irish sculptor Albert Bruce Joy built his workshops on a cheap railway embankment off Beaumont Avenue in 1882–3, a handful of Aesthetic adventurers rushed to stake claims on the land farther west. John Dixon Batten, fairy tale illustrator, tempera painter, chromoxylographer and Burne-Jones disciple, had barely turned 26 when he moved into 5 Margravine Gardens. His bespoke red brick studio-cottage of 1886 looked directly towards the Sir Coutts Lindsay folly which had risen the year before in Colet Gardens. Several hyperbolically arty houses sprang up at the same time in Challoner Street, one of them, No. 3, occupied from the outset by Maria Spartali and her husband. *Margravine* and *St Paul's Studios*, the former a speculation by Sir Coutts's builders, capitalised on some of the remaining railway edges.

A further, nicely calculated instance of this approach, half speculation and half self-interest, fills a gap between the old West London line and Avonmore Road. It consists of a five-storeyed double studio-house commissioned in 1888 from James MacLaren by the established sculptor Richard Hope Pinker. Ten years earlier MacLaren had projected a seven-bedroom painter's house for an open site near Parson's Green.[8] Although it looked plausible enough, he had actually thrown against an overgrown round tower quite unrelated pieces of 'Queen Annery' already patented by Stevenson and Champneys. On another job in Scotland he was guilty of directly copying a Norman Shaw composition. But interim employment with Godwin and the work of the new craft guilds kindled an original spark in him at Avonmore Road. A concentration of organic stone carving on the right-hand side there denoted Pinker's residence; on the left, above the sculpture workshops, are the meaner windows of the tenant painter's studio suite, **168**. The fortified parapet and the Indian-style spiked helmet crowning the tenant's staircase are features MacLaren had just tried out on a school building in Stirling. This arrangement of workshops flowing through

167 Sir Edward Burne-Jones's house studio – incorporating improvements by Benson – at the rear of 'The Grange', West Kensington, in 1954.

168 Richard Hope Pinker's 22 Avonmore Road, West Kensington, by James MacLaren, 1888. A pace-setting, yet assured proposition, ordered and compact.

to Addison Bridge Place will have made life easier for Pinker when he came to handle monolithic works like the 32-ton Empress ordered by the government of British Guyana.

In those days, if you caught the train at Addison Bridge, as likely as not it would swing around the Kensington and Richmond spur and land you at Turnham Green.

Little Rookie had the option of doing this at the end of a working day at The Grange. After 1878 he would walk on a bit farther to 7 Queen Anne Gardens, Bedford Park – a new house built for him by W Wilson, to whom the general layout of that progressive estate is likewise attributed. Wilson appears to have limited himself to a smallish finite envelope and tried to impose an early 18th-century symmetry on it. In fact the outward regularity of the upper storey is fairly deceptive while the unbalanced lower one belies a 20th-century modernity. Rooke's studio in the north-east corner required extra clearance, so it was set down a few steps and the floor above jacked up. But as the 11′ ceiling height still proved insufficient on occasions, a trapped opening in the floor was contrived into which oversized canvases could be lowered.[9] Although the change of level affected all the other rooms the overall result was unusually pleasing.

Founded in 1875 by a brother of one of the Grosvenor Gallery directors, Bedford Park and its resident Aesthetes came in for a good deal of facetious criticism, some of it even-handed, nonetheless; for instance, G K Chesterton noted in *The Man Who Was Thursday* (1908) that 'Saffron Park':

... was described with some justice as an artistic colony, though it never in any definable way produced any art. But although its pretensions to be an intellectual-centre were a little vague, its pretensions to be a pleasant place to live were quite indisputable.[10]

And so they were.

The illustrator and marine painter Joseph Nash Jnr may not have had his late

169 Joseph Nash's woodcut of the studio Maurice Adams designed for him at 36 The Avenue, Bedford Park, in 1879. Practical solutions derived from traditional architectural shapes.

170 Plans, side and front elevations of the Forster house, 14 South Parade, Bedford Park, by Charles Voysey, 1891. 'A stand against the surrounding Aesthetic folksiness.'

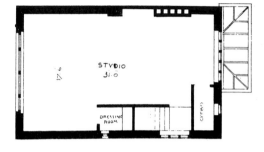

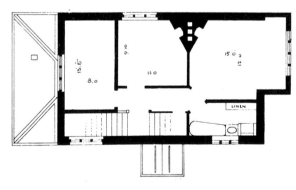

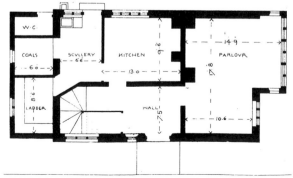

father's gifts, but his particular patch of Bedford Park was well enough chosen. In 1878 Nash returned from a teaching post in Guernsey to spend his inheritance on a studio-house designed by Maurice Adams at 36 The Avenue. Connected to the bulk of the accommodation by a corner hallway, the handsome, spacious studio is distinguished by a plain plaster ceiling of crossing vaults, **169**. In addition to a fancy oriel or 'combination window' facing due north, there are French doors giving onto a decent stretch of garden on the east. Two years later Adams, a devoted Vernacular-Queen Anne Revivalist, elaborated his line in tile hanging, pargeting and composite windowcases for Nash's fellow artist on *The Graphic* staff, John Dollman The larger half of a semi-detached pair, Dollman's 14 Newton Grove was said to depend entirely 'on the commonsense convenience of its interior arrangements, and the picturesque proportions of its elevations for all the effect that has been aimed at'.[11] From the first floor studio two doors opened onto balconies; a third one served a small glasshouse from which an exterior models' stairway led down to part of an old Acton orchard. Adams also designed for Dollman some 'Queen Anne' studio furniture comprising bookcases, a costume wardrobe, an engraver's desk and a models' throne, all fussed over most preciously. Indeed, there is every indication that:

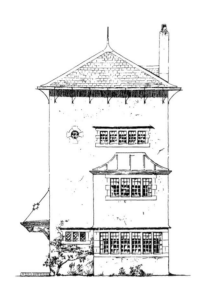

> With red and blue and sagest green
> were walls and dado dyed,
> Friezes of Morris there were seen
> and oaken wainscot wide.[12]

Not yet 30 when the house was built, Dollman went on to paint in oil (*Emigrants, The Death of Oates*) and watercolour. He became well known for his animal subjects and comic strips, too. With Norman Shaw as consultant, Adams went on to build the Chiswick School of Art in Bath Road.

By 1890 Bedford Park was nearing its total of nearly 500 red brick, red tiled houses and Charles Voysey had had a hand in none of them. The Wilson Forsters from Stoke-on-Trent had requested sketches for a site at 14 South Parade but they had since gone quiet. When in 1891 they re-appeared with more money Voysey quickly added a storey to his previous design. Nonetheless, he kept the total cost down to just £494.10.0. In this connection it was reported that:

> . . . so much has the architect studied to avoid elaboration that he has found it necessary to prepare 18 sheets of contract drawings so that the contractor may not put in *the usual thing* – 'ovolo mouldings, stop-chamfers, fillets', and (what without irreverence might be termed) 'damnation' generally![13]

Voysey expressed his disgruntlement in the non-suburban form, abrasive materials and contrary colour scheme of the tichy studio-house, **170**. Virtually the only decoration consisted of brackets and corbels in the shape of baleful grotesques. But, while making a stand against the surrounding Aesthetic folksiness, the tall building was also very much a product of Voysey's current obsession with tower houses. In effect this private whim denied the Forsters a thoroughly functional fulfilment of their brief; far from a remedy, the two-storey wing added in 1894 merely represented the architect climbing down a little. The occupants go quiet again until about 1910 when Mr Forster, a versatile but mediocre artist, turns up in Bushey in charge of an arts and crafts school.

Two of the better Bedford Park artists, Blair Leighton and Cecil Aldin, contented themselves with studios extended behind their houses in Priory Avenue. A smattering of pavilions, a range of units in Gainsborough Road, and the roomy attics purposely provided in many of the houses designed by Norman Shaw catered for the considerable number of lesser lights.

Voysey attempted to foist a tower on another client wishing to build near Brook Green,[14] but he had more immediate success with a distinctly bungaloid solution at 17 St Dunstan's Road, Hammersmith. This house for the decorative painter Bill Britten was much the more workshop-like of his two published proposals; the living quarters were pushed to one end to give maximum studio space, **171**. Drawings dated 1891 show that, in addition to a three-way choice of side lights, a good thousand square feet of glass was to be fixed over both north and south roof slopes. Despite obvious budget restrictions, Bainbridge Reynolds was appointed to execute a Mackmurdo-esque iron palisade. Britten also allowed Voysey to treat him to a birdbath supported by fretwork satyrs, as well as a pair of figurative porch brackets similar to the Forsters'.

17 St Dunstan's Road is not a square peg in a round hole to the extent 14 South Parade is, but all the trademarks of Voysey's waspish style – a style almost fully mature at only its third or fourth outing – are apparent again here, not least these mordant idiosyncrasies. Though clearly open-minded, Britten belonged to an older school. Typical products of his bungalow were the mosaic designs for St Paul's Cathedral which he prepared in conjunction with the painter-sculptor (Sir) William Blake Richmond RA.

Richmond was to Hammersmith what Burne-Jones was to West Kensington.[15] In 1870 he bought Beavor Lodge, Beavor Lane, from a horse trainer. This was then so isolated that he could keep pigs, heifers, a donkey, a goat, and sundry other farm animals. He forthwith adapted the coach-house for use as a modelling shop, while a large detached room the horse trainer had built 'for his girls to dance in' he converted into a lordly galleried painting saloon. A technician in the Leighton mould, Richmond made a competent, if reluctant, portrait painter. Believing himself secure in his garden studio, he was deeply embarrassed on one occasion when Princess Louise arrived early for her sitting to catch him touching up a coloured, nude foundation sketch. Not long afterwards the same royal personage, who had called unexpectedly, was announced at the studio door by his servant. 'Tell her to go to the devil!' he roared; but Princess Louise had followed unbidden and in she walked.

Partly to protect his privacy and partly to keep more big works on the go, Richmond rented extra studios in Holland Park and Chelsea. But he retained Beavor Lodge for nearly 50 years, during which time – from Morris's Kelmscott Press to Christopher Whall's stained glass studio, from Cobden-Sanderson's Doves Bindery to

171 Drawings of 17 St Dunstan's Road, Hammersmith, for W E F Britten, by Charles Voysey, 1891. A bungaloid studio-house similar in organisation to many speculative terraced examples.

FRONT ELEVATION
NORTH

WEST ELEVATION

the Stablers' pottery – that part of Hammersmith took its special place in the history of English applied art.

Heading back into the hurly-burly of old Kensington, right to the very top of Campden Hill, you could winkle out another of the late Victorian art publishers. Andrew White Tuer, co-director of the Leadenhall Press and a jolly artist in his own right (e.g., *Luxurious Bathing* – 12 etchings, 1879) spent £5750 rebuilding 18 Campden Hill Square.[16] This rebuilding of 1887–8 included an arresting four-storey block at the back incorporating coach-house, stables, and self-contained studio suite, now numbered 26 Aubrey Walk. Tuer's idea of raising north lights to recapture the view over the square-side houses below caught on rapidly. At least six adjoining premises were similarly adapted within as many years. Stable buildings in Hillsleigh Road behind houses on the east side of Campden Hill Square also became targets for conversion. Here the trend was initiated by Matthew White Ridley who launched his art school at No. 2 in the early 1880s. Both the book decorators Heywood Sumner and Walter Crane made use of the Ridley studio over the next decade, while Rex Vicat Cole installed himself at No. 9 in 1895.

Before descending the hill, it is worth casting a glance at Percy Macquoid's Yellow House of 1892 at 8 Palace Court, Bayswater Road. Macquoid, an illustrator, genre painter and connoisseur, rather surprisingly obtained his design from George & Peto, a firm not a little prone to garbling its historical quotations. In this case, however, the architects managed a colloquial Belgian Renaissance utterance with mustardy terracotta facing in reply to the blazing red Flockhart job on the corner. Although now part of a private hotel, Macquoid's undemonstrative between-floors workroom is still discernible at the rear.

1892, particularly, saw renewed activity down in the establishment heartland of Melbury and Holland Park Roads. Both Thornycroft and Prinsep were expanding their houses, 25-year-old Graham Robertson began a new one, and (Sir) James Shannon remodelled another. Robertson, aspiring portraitist and litterateur, snared one of the last plots in Melbury Road, within yards of his teacher Albert Moore's recently abandoned 1 Holland Lane. The painter-architect Robert Oliver concocted a Stuart-fronted, Elizabethan-backed design to be built in two uneasy stages – rather like Prinsep's house.[17] Unfortunately the first stage, a most unpredictable half of the full picture, was to remain just that, even after Robertson had sold his interest and moved to Witley. In the meantime the society squire and his tenant, Arthur Melville, made do with not much more than a grand stairhall, a studio overlooking Holland Park, and a billiard room. Shannon's view to the north, on the other hand, was curtailed by Colin Hunter's Lugar Lodge. Otherwise he was quite famously lodged next to Leighton in the old Holland Estate farmhouse which had been rejigged and gentrified for him by relatives of Slade Professor Fred Brown.

Although Leighton's death seemed to put a brake on studio building hereabouts, it continued notwithstanding, and there was no reduction in the turnover of personnel. Phil May, for instance, turned up at 7 Holland Park Road in 1892, quickly joining his Australian friend (Sir) John Longstaff across the way in Rowsley House, itself lately vacated by Ernest and Henrietta Normand. Somehow less accountable was Holman

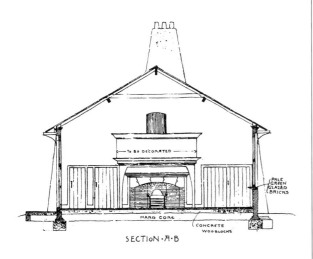

SECTION · A · B

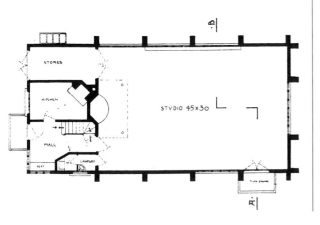

Hunt's choice to spend his last seven years at 18 Melbury Road and its benighted hutch alongside. Quite the antithesis of this situation is to be found nearby at 49 Addison Road, where the classical charade-painter Herbert Schmalz had a radiant church hall added on by (Sir) John Simpson. In the following year, 1895, Simpson devised a similar studio for (Sir) Arthur, son of the late Charles West Cope RA, whose memorial he had also just designed.

Arthur Cope belongs halfway back up the hill; he succeeded George Vicat Cole RA at the somewhat eldritch Little Campden House. When Byam Shaw first visited Cole's son Rex there it was already the scene of two artists' premature deaths. He rang the bell at the garden gate 'and it opened with a jerk. Walking in he found no one there or behind it (it was worked by an underground wire) and, seeing a rather large garden between himself and the house, he bolted'.[18] Rex decided against keeping on the 200-year-old relic; instead he shifted to Campden Hill Square only, as previously noted, to fall in with Walter Crane. Crane, for his part, was still bearing the cost of moving up to 13 Holland Street and it was not until 1898 that he could build a studio of his own. In fact he built two little ones, perhaps to the designs of Lionel Crane, in the alley opposite – just a few doors from the pavilion left behind by his short-lived contemporary, Randolph Caldecott.

Especially within Old Kensington, pavilion and studio-house sites of any size that were not largely the result of demolitions naturally became more scarce as time went by. Therefore four buyers still in the market as late as 1910 counted themselves lucky to find suitable vacant plots in St Mary Abbot's Place, a cul-de-sac off Kensington High Street just beyond Edwardes Square, already the location of the compact, five-unit *Warwick Studios* dating from 1883. William Colton ARA, a sculptor deservedly respected for the realism of his voluptuous female nudes; Frank Calderon, principal of the Baker Street School of Animal Painting which he aimed to decentralise; Fred Appleton, an artist preceded by a fairly slender reputation; and (Sir) William Llewellyn, lately the popular choice to paint Queen Mary's state portrait while not yet one of the Academy's chosen, all adopted designs in a passe-partout Village High Street style by the architects Gale, Gotch & Leighton. Whereas Colton, at No.s 3–5, satisfied himself with a modest dwelling and detached workshops, Calderon, at No. 9, commissioned a dominant three-storey house together with comprehensive new facilities for his painting school. These included a barn-sized skylit atelier separated by a courtyard from a general assembly room, a horse stall, kennels and coops, and specific entrances for both large animals and students. Teaching was resumed here upon completion of the buildings in 1912, but ceased completely during the Great War, leaving Calderon with excess accommodation. In 1912 and 1913 Appleton, at No. 11, and Llewellyn, at No. 15, moved into multi-gabled houses similarly secluded at the head of pleasant gardens reaching down to the northern boundary of *Pembroke Studios*. Llewellyn's richer, more orthodox studio-house withstood the increased social exposure resulting from his knighthood and ironical subsequent elevation to RA, but after Lady Llewellyn's death in 1926, it seemed only an address in The Dukeries on Campden Hill would befit the impending office of Academy president.

Over the earlier end-of-century period, developments in South Kensington tended to be no more discrete than this concerted settlement in St Mary Abbot's Place. Yeoman's Row is a case in point. In 1896, after complicated manoeuvres involving an obscure Arts and Crafts guild, vacant land on the west side of Yeoman's Row plopped into the hands of W H Collbran, an architect first sighted much earlier in Eldon Road, Kensington. Collbran then sublet three plots to three maiden artists, Ida Lovering, Emily Campbell-McCallum and Sarah Vaughan. They, in a venture probably unique in London's building history, jointly obtained studio-house designs from another architect, William Barber.[19] More than that, all three buildings were double, if not triple, houses, **172**. From the outset in 1898 each house is listed with up to four tenants – mostly women, although the illustrators Dudley Hardy and Ad Birkenruth were also taken in. Despite Barber's apparent determination to avoid the economies of standardisation, the houses originally looked all of a piece. But, excited by a very full brief, he fooled himself that visual balance achieved through asymmetry was not a matter calling for careful calculation. Notwithstanding, Miss Lovering, who specialised in chalk portraits of children, was at first given a creditable, relatively lean design at No. 24.

172 Revised designs for the double and triple studio-houses for three maiden ladies at 24–28 Yeoman's Row, South Kensington, by William Barber, 1898.

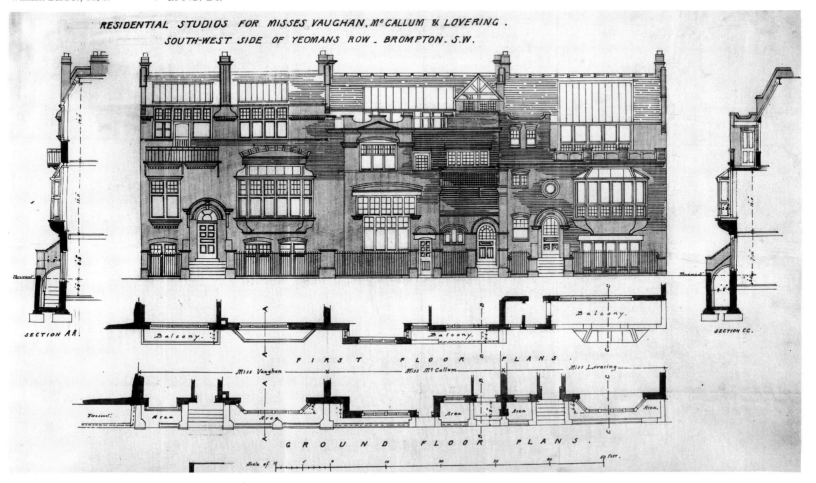

RESIDENTIAL STUDIOS FOR MISSES VAUGHAN, McCALLUM & LOVERING.
SOUTH-WEST SIDE OF YEOMANS ROW. BROMPTON. S.W.

Most other bright spots in South Kensington, like those northwards of No. 24 in Yeoman's Row, come under a separate heading. To uncover more artistic free-masonry, more women and rarer entertainment generally requires, therefore, a visit to Chelsea. This was the scene of cooperation between the Century Guild leader, Arthur Mackmurdo, and the Australian-born Mortimer Menpes, 'painter, etcher, raconteur and rifle shot'. Menpes had penetrated the Whistler studio in the early 1880s, learning the Master's secrets and (allegedly) borrowing his ideas to create the celebrated 'Home of Taste' on Fulham Road. A decade later he had engaged Mack-murdo to demolish a corner dwelling behind Sloane Square at 25 Cadogan Gardens and replace it with a five-storey studio-house – worth £4000 even without second fixings on the ground and lofty first floors.[20] After consulting Mackmurdo, Menpes took the measurements of these empty rooms to Japan. There, basing his scheme on high-class traditional fittings, he supervised the prefabrication of all the joinery. Together with a fabulous collection of loose furniture, porcelain, bronzes, lacquer-ware and fabrics, he had it shipped back to London for installation.

On the ground floor the main and servants' entrance lobbies converged from west and north onto a top-lit inner hall, **173**, visited at intervals by the staircase; a square dining room occupied the north-west corner. Above the dining room on the first floor lay the studio with its token galleries and three northern bay windows lined internally with translucent shoji, **174**. The remaining space on the same level was largely taken up by an equal-sized common room complete with two tokonoma. To each room Menpes allotted a floral theme (camellia, chrysanthemum, peony, and so on) which was particularly noticeable in the Osaka fretwork of the modular doors and ceilings. Slatted timber friezes, or ramma, set on a gold ground like the fretwork, were aimed to correct the vertical and un-Japanese emphasis of Mackmurdo's basic structure. Dynamic rectilinearity, unpatterned walls, plain carpets, furniture disposed like rocks in the gravel of a Zen temple garden, wall-mounted electric lamps, dark lustres and golden highlights – a formula so enlightened it made Whistler apoplectic-ally jealous.

It seems Menpes spent only 1897 to 1899 acting the Sloane Square daimio before rejoining his travels. Within six years these gave rise to innumerable exhibitions and more than a dozen illustrated books, many with texts by his daughter, Dorothy Menpes. For a period giving his closest attention to etching, the artist passed through Tite Street on his way to Pangbourne, where much of his middle life was devoted to commercial colour printing at the Menpes Press. A real love of cherry blossom never left him, however, such that a retirement venture resulted in the Menpes Fruit Farm Ltd.

Whereas Mackmurdo had little or no experience building houses for artists,[21] C R Ashbee was twice able to test his ideas on his family while experimenting with real projects for others. Ashbee's first essay, 37 Cheyne Walk of 1893–4, accommodated his mother, his sisters and himself. No. 37 incorporated rooms for music, needle-work and painting along with a drawing office. To some extent, the internal decor-ation exhibited the abilities of the Guild and School of Handicraft which the architect-designer had founded five years earlier in the East End. Ashbee's subse-

173 Inner hall, 25 Cadogan Gardens, Chelsea. Fittings and finishes prefabricated in Japan were applied to the house Mortimer Menpes designed in consultation with Arthur Mackmurdo from 1892 onwards.

174 East end of the studio, 25 Cadogan Gardens. 'Furniture, disposed like rocks in the gravel of a Zen temple garden.'

quent architectural works in London were almost exclusively sited along Cheyne Walk, a fact that can be shown to be due to personal leasehold interests. Thus, although he was a proven socialist worker, it tempers Goodhart-Rendel's view that 'If you had taken him up, you really were in with the revolutionaries'.[22]

Protracted negotiations with clients who were unsure of themselves, and numerous false starts, preceded the second essay, 72–4 Cheyne Walk of 1896–8. In the end the Glasgow Boy Edward Walton and his wife agreed to share the double plot at No.s 72–3 with the Midlands sculptor, John Wenlock Rollins. Ashbee launched No. 74, a typically unconventional artist's house with a strategically dominant studio as a speculation. That he and Janet Forbes, his bride of 1898, were then able to occupy and gain title to it, may be attributed to the Forbes' refreshment of the Ashbee finances. Rollins's No. 72 mainly comprised a ground floor carriageway leading to a 32′ × 22′ skylit shed at the rear. His sitting room (lower stage of large oriel), bedroom and bathroom suite bridged the full length of the carriageway. Walton's spacious No. 73 took up the rest of the five-storey building, sandwiching a double-

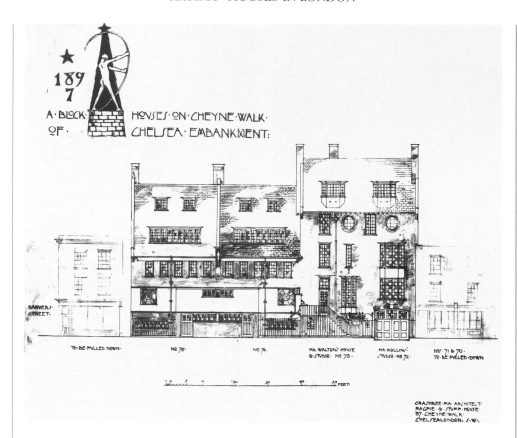

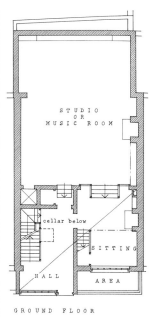

175 No.s 72–75 Cheyne Walk were conceived by Charles Ashbee as a single entity. Common factors in the design at this stage give it the strength to support selected variants.

height studio between the upper ground floor and the attic bedrooms. While the placement of the street-front windows bore an undeniably rational relationship to the rooms behind, their shape and number were chosen more to effect an asymmetrical unity-in-diversity. In this regard Ashbee's judicious assimilation of schemes such as Shaw's 6 Ellerdale Road and Swan House, Godwin's White House and MacLaren's 22 Avonmore Road ensured the indisputably happy outcome.

No. 74 formed part of the same yellow brick, green tile composition, although its separate contribution to the total picture of studied randomness was made in a lower portion of red brick and white roughcast. Again, a special window shape signalled the position of the studio gallery. In this instance the studio was assigned to the ground and first floors and the kitchen promoted to the second, right alongside the dining room, **176**, **177**. On the whole the plan was a good one, shortening floor by floor to avoid excessively deep upper rooms. If nothing else did, the ground floor studio suited frail old Whistler when he and his wife's family rented the house for the 15 months prior to his death in July 1903. Venomous to the last, Whistler objected to the woodwork stained Baillie Scott green, the dining room frieze depicting the Diamond Jubilee pageant in crimson and gold, and the stained glass spoiling the river view – all evidence, he felt, of 'the disastrous effect of art on the middle classes'. Had he lived a little longer he would surely have met (Sir) Jacob Epstein who replaced Rollins at No. 72 in 1908. Gaudier-Brzeska, for one, found him there later on, 'doing

176 Plans of 74 Cheyne Walk, Chelsea, built as a speculation by Charles Ashbee in 1897. 56 years have elapsed since Richard Redgrave first explored this arrangement (**25**).

FIRST FLOOR

THIRD FLOOR

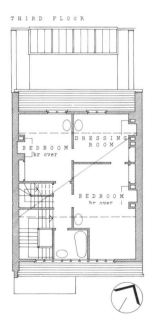

177 Early photographs of the ground floor music room–studio at 74 Cheyne Walk. Joinery and decoration supplied by Ashbee's Guild of Handicraft made for a total work of art.

most extraordinary statues, absolute copies of Polynesian work with Brancusi-like noses'.[23] There is at least some truth in Goodhart-Rendel's uncharitable observation.

While No.s 72–4 were being built, several more designs for local sites diverted the Ashbee office. One, for the Jubilee frieze painter Max Balfour, involved restoring and adding a studio to No.s 118–9 Cheyne Walk (Turner's last refuge). Another, a studio-house project for Walton's friend (Sir) James Guthrie, would have been a blend of No.s 73 and 74 distinguished by two superbly owlish gallery windows. A further project, variously providing for four and seven half-serious tenants, among them Edwin Abbey, Singer Sargent, Augustus John and the sculptor John Tweed, was mostly the work of young Charles Holden. A block of studio-flats named *Danvers Tower*, it was to be built on the present site of Crosby Hall. The only other job to get off the ground entailed two rebuildings next door to the office. No. 38 Cheyne Walk was commissioned by the still life painter, Miss Clara Christian; No. 39 – a conventional family house and a much more realistic proposition because of it – was put forward as a freehold speculation, **178**.

Anything but conventional, Miss Christian's house contained three studios and the entrance to a fourth in the back garden. The three house studios came in three different sizes and possessed three different modes of lighting. Foreknowledge of Ashbee's sign language would lead one to suppose a gallery lurked behind the cobwebbed oculus in the jagged gable. Yet there were few internal luxuries; plain-ness, even old-fashioned thrift, pervaded the rooms whose lines partially echoed those formerly on the site. In the same spirit Ashbee quoted the Georgian character of the earlier houses externally, reassembling terrace alignments, rephrasing window rhythms, and redistributing common materials. Guild-crafted iron railings like those at No.s 72–3 further betokened the attempt to provide an outline continuity. For a few years before her sudden death in 1906, Miss Christian was joined at No. 38 by (Dame) Ethel Walker. Clara and Ethel had already shared studios in Pembroke Gardens and Tite Street.

Ashbee was far from done with Cheyne Walk; he was still hopeful of commissions in 1914. But of the numberless schemes he prepared – from a hall of residence for London University to a collection of 17 studio units based on the Trinity Ground almshouses – only two were built. Mrs William Hunt, an art collector, occasioned the mismatch of No. 74 at No. 75 in 1901–2 and Mrs Adeline Trier, a flower painter, mothered the vulgar bulk of No. 71 in 1912–13. The latter, which sported a painting room under the roof, showed Ashbee's aesthetic finesse heavily compromised by the glib mechanisms of the Neo-Georgian vogue.

Some of the pleasanter early George V houses in Chelsea, neither too coarse nor too dainty, lie in a region north of the Kings Road – between Manresa Road and Park Walk. The Vale, especially, provides a fair selection. Well into the Edwardian years, however, The Vale was a shady, time-forgotten lane bordered by five or six cottages. Attention was drawn to it afresh when Whistler took cottage No. 2 in addition to his Pink Palace at Walham Green. Charles Ricketts and Charles Shannon, publishers of *The Dial* and founders of The Vale Press, followed him to the same address in 1888. No. 1 was acquired simultaneously by the newly wed de Morgans, William and Evelyn.

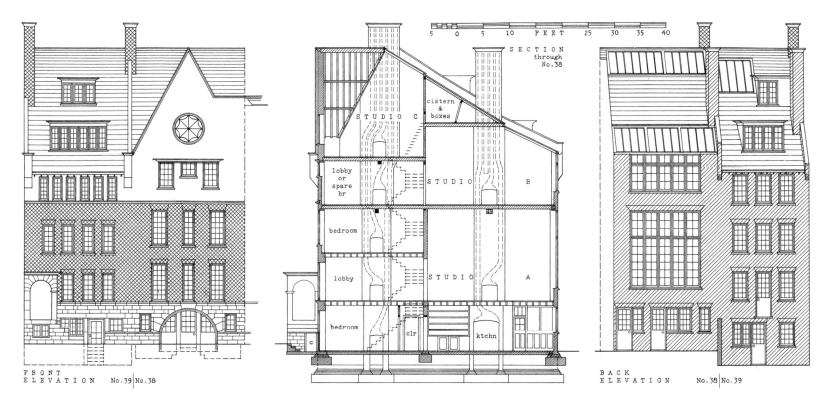

178 Elevations of No.s 38–39 Cheyne Walk, Chelsea, and a section through Clara Christian's No. 38 showing its three studios – designs of 1898 by Charles Ashbee.

For the duration of their trips abroad the de Morgans let the cottage, together with the painting and craft room which they had attached, to Walter Sickert and his Chelsea Life School. Only the sculptor Stirling Lee, who was forced to leave his shops in Manresa Road and convert a YMCA hall on the King's Road corner instead, stayed any longer than the de Morgans. In about 1909 he moved to Vale Studio A, the lower floors of a new house some distance along. The upper floors, Vale Studio B, were independently occupied by Henry 'Terrible' Tonks, the surgeon turned Slade School tutor.

This first sign of redevelopment saw the de Morgans off. They transferred to the top end of Old Church Street, not very cleverly knocking two terraced houses (one of them of ill repute) into a single entity with a top storey studio for Evelyn. Only with the 1890s did any major change begin to come over Old Church Street. In 1891 Captain Adrian Jones, the army vet turned sculptor, arrived at No. 147 and proceeded to mock up the colossal Hyde Park Corner *Quadriga* in the backyard. Three years later Felix Moscheles was building on the Elm Park Road corner, and within another seven the management of the Chelsea Arts Club had merged two old villas at No.s 143–5. All went ominously quiet for a while and then Augustus John bobbed up at Robert Hannah's No. 153. Although he stayed there only briefly, John soon decided he would build a house of his own in the area. Accordingly in 1912 or '13 he bought a smallish plot between Old Church Street and The Vale in Mallord Street. His architect, a Dutchman named van't Hoff was, so the story goes, the first man to volunteer his services when John made an impetuous appeal in the local alehouse.[24] Ready for occupation in July 1914, the house showed itself to be almost as much Neo-Plastic as Neo-Regency in conception. Indeed, John felt the rectangles had been overdone. Yet, as a cure for his restlessness it worked tolerably well.

Various less significant studio-houses sprang up close by at the same time, three of them on corner sites. One, 113 Old Church Street, is an uninspired double-decker in which the children's portrait painter John DaCosta had the principal interest. But by far the most noteworthy is No. 117, a truly imperious design from the hand of William de Morgan's former associate, Halsey Ricardo. Since the house was a wedding present for his daughter Anna and her husband, the architectural subject painter Charles Maresco Pearce, Ricardo pleased himself what he did with it. True to form, he played Lutyens's 'High Game' with it just as he had with the Debenham commission in Addison Road. Above and below the giant Georgian order caging the bedroom floors, the reception and painting room floors express themselves at will. Piano nobile windows appear at ground level; traditional, square attic windows discountenance the gablets; a runaway pilaster grafts itself to the off-centre chimney stack, and much more, **179**. Both the genuine Queen Anne sashes and the flush-pointed red and blue brickwork are used to field further baroque roguery on the garden front. Unanswerable Renaissance elements are introduced along with an exercise in Moresque (or Maresco) arcading, all enlivened by hierarchical wrong-footings and surface patterns as jazzy as Argyll socks.

While Maresco Pearce was thoroughly spoiled, he clearly found the garret studio a trifle gloomy. Tactfully he refrained from raising the right hand gablet to match the central one until after his father-in-law had died.[25]

Altogether too few artists' houses of the loving craftsmanship typical of this era survive in London. At least one other, not quite in the same class but certainly worthy of notice, rewards a final journey to a region otherwise moribund in studio-building terms – Hampstead. 'The Atelier', George Swinstead's house in Kidderpore Avenue, diplomatically separates the L-shaped lodge Voysey built for his father and St Luke's, an Anglican church designed by Ricardo's master, Basil Champneys. Swinstead, a proven plein air painter, commissioned it in 1901 from Arthur Keen, a one-time Norman Shaw assistant who was said to embody 'everything connected with detail, tidiness, law and order'.[26] Nevertheless, and contrary to Shaw's injunction, 'Keep it quiet', Keen crammed the street front with stylised vernacular features very nearly to the point of anarchy, **180**. Rounded forms, folded and feathered planes, and sea-weedy squiggles worked into the thick whitewash hint shyly at the French allegiance of the design, an allegiance later declared in the name. But behind the façade the organic knobbliness is abruptly disengaged. A capacious galleried glasshouse, its gable end a network of lozenged panes, nestles against the returning wing. French doors open into a backyard once Swinstead's pride and the subject of his account, *My Old-World Garden and How I Made It in a London Suburb* (1910). Poor transcription in the past has led credulous readers to believe this rare volume was in fact two separate titles.

Ah, those were the days. There has been no period since to match the Edwardian

179 117 Old Church Street, Chelsea, built for his daughter and Charles Maresco Pearce, his son-in-law, by Halsey Ricardo in 1914–15. Further baroque roguery enriches the garden front.

for the craftsmanship and character of its domestic architecture. Craftsmanship began to die out when men like Mr Green, Halsey Ricardo's foreman of works at Chelsea, went to Flanders in 1915 never to return. Character was erased by post-war demoralisation, austerity, and the adoption of inappropriate foreign and machine-age fashions. Very few could afford to uphold sentimental Arts and Crafts principles any longer, let alone the cost of building – suddenly inflated two to three hundred per cent – using materials handwrought by artisans whose loyalty and masonic expertise, or 'guildworthiness', was already succumbing to the levelling catch-cries of mass enfranchisement policy. Yet active neglect, commercial greed and a failure both

180 George Swinstead's 14 Kidderpore Avenue, Hampstead, by Arthur Keen, 1901. As near as English architecture came to *Olbrichstil* or *le style Guimard*.

HOUSE AT HAMPSTEAD
ARTHUR KEEN · ARCH?

to acknowledge and admire these artists' houses for the cultural monuments they are, have done more damage than any war. Thirty years elapsed after Lord Leighton's death before his house was begrudgingly rescued for posterity. Lululaund was ruined by 1940, tramps and vandals having been allowed to mutilate and loot it. Whistler's White House was demolished in 1965 without any appeal to the Anglo-American fund that could have reconstructed it as an Aesthetic Movement masterpiece. Sir Lawrence Alma Tadema's palace survives by some miracle, but it is barely recognisable – gutted, subdivided and purposely unmaintained. It is high time to cherish actively the few treasures that remain. May the steps taken recently to preserve Thomas Woolner's workshops and Linley Sambourne's house develop into determined strides elsewhere also.

NOTES AND REFERENCES

The following abbreviations are used in the References to all chapters and in the Gazetteer:

A	*The Architect*
AJ	*The Art Journal*
BA	*The British Architect* (Manchester)
BN	*The Building News*
Br	*The Builder*
DNB	*Dictionary of National Biography*
MA	*The Magazine of Art*
SoL	*The Survey of London*, F Sheppard, ed., GLC

All works cited were published in London unless otherwise stated.

CHAPTER 1

1   The 36 original members of the RA elected in 1768 were:

John Baker	John Gwynn	Paul Sandby
George Barret	Francis Hayman	Thomas Sandby
Francesco Bartolozzi	William Hoare	Dominic Serres
Agostino Carlini	Nathaniel Hone	Peter Toms
Charles Catton	Angelica Kauffmann	William Tyler
Mason Chamberlin	Jeremiah Meyer	Samuel Wale
William Chambers	George Moser	Benjamin West
Giovanni Cipriani	Mary Moser	Richard Wilson
Francis Cotes	Francis Newton	Joseph Wilton
George Dance	Edward Penny	Richard Yeo
Nathaniel Dance	Joshua Reynolds	Johan Zoffany
Thomas Gainsborough	John Richards	Francesco Zuccarelli

   – S C Hutchison, *History of the RA 1768–1968*, Chapman & Hall, 1968.
2   Extrapolated from A Graves, *Dictionary of Contributors to the RA 1769–1904*, (1905) Kingsmead Reprints, 1970.
3   Sir J Summerson, *Georgian London*, Pleiades Books, 1945, p. 43.
4   Another way of soliciting buyers was to advertise in the press. Antonio Canaletto, working in London at the mid-century, is known to have placed newspaper notices inviting the public to view recent paintings at his lodgings in Beak Street, Golden Square. *SoL 31*, ii, 1963, pp. 174–5.
5   John Harris, *Sir William Chambers*, Zwemmer, 1970, pp. 164ff.
6   Although over a third of the first RAs was not English-born.
7   *European Magazine*, June 1801, p. 442, *ex SoL 34*, 1966, pp. 502ff.
8   James Northcote, *Life of Sir JR*, i, 1819, pp. 46, 47.
9   F W Fairholt, *Homes, Works and Shrines of English Artists*, Virtue, 1873, p. 36, quoting Allan Cunningham.
10 *SoL 34*, p. 509.
11 Leicester Fields was a veritable hotbed of artists during the mid- and later 18th-century. At least one other painter, the part-time architect James 'Athenian' Stuart, is reported to have tacked on a gallery (No. 35, 1769–88). *SoL 34*, p. 505.
12 If, as it could be proposed, Wilson's actual lodgings were No.s 10–11 (formerly Sir Peter Lely's, *c.* 1651–80), or No. 12 (formerly Sir James Thornhill's, 1722–34), the inevitable alterations attendant upon each of these painters' considerable practices may have survived to be at his disposal. See *SoL 36*, 1970, pp. 88ff.

CHAPTER 1 *continued*

13   *SoL 36*, pp. 10ff.
14   L Cust, *History of the Society of Dilettanti*, Sir Sidney Colvin ed., 1898, 1914.
15   For a full account of Schomberg House and its rich variety of tenants, see *SoL 29*, i, 1960, pp. 371ff.
16   Accounts differ as to whether Carlini was born in Geneva or Genoa.
17   As such they conformed to the metropolitan Building Acts of 1707 and 1709 which ensured they would be less poky and more soundly built.
18   Extract describing 50 Rathbone Pl., W1 from an undated (early 1801) letter sent by John Constable. *JC's Correspondence*, ii, R B Beckett ed., Suffolk Records Society, Ipswich, 1965, p. 33.
19   Among consultants to the landlords was Charles Bridgeman, the garden designer, who took 8 Henrietta St (11 Henrietta Pl.) in 1725 but lived in Broadwick St, Soho; James Gibbs also built houses at 5, 9, 10 and 11 Henrietta St. He lived at No. 5, overlooking his church, from 1730 until his death. Others whose careers were fostered by the Harleys included the sculptor Rysbrack: in Vere St 1725–70, and Wootton the sporting painter: at No. 23 in the square itself, *c.* 1730–65. P Willis, *Charles Bridgeman*, Zwemmer, 1977, pp. 30–31.
20   *Sale Catalogue* of 24 Cavendish Sq., February 1771, V & A Library, London.
21   *Ibid.*
22   Sir J Summerson, *op. cit.*, p. 146.
23   Most of the details concerning Chambers's developments in Berners St are recounted in John Harris's monograph (*op.cit.*), pp. 11, 12, 72ff.

CHAPTER 2

1   Auction particulars, 25.5.1829.
2   A Cox-Johnson, *JB, RA 1740–1799*, St Marylebone Society, 1961, pp. 17ff.
3   Mrs A E Bray, *Life of TS, RA*, John Murray, 1851, pp. 29–30.
4   Sir Joshua saw this painting as an allegorical attack on himself and the shine he had taken to Miss Kauffmann. See M Butlin, 'An 18th-century Art Scandal', *Connoisseur*, 5, 1970.
5   *SoL 29*, i, 1960, p. 376.
6   *Ibid.*, pp. 375–6.
7   Sir J Burke, *English Art 1714–1800*, OUP, Oxford, 1976, p. 256.
8   Drawings survive in a private collection of a house Barret proposed to build in this locality.
9   Thomas Sandby was the designer of Virginia Water, Windsor, for example.
10   Girtin may have lodged with Smith while improving some of the publisher's Morland Gallery plates with J M W Turner.
11   W Combe, *History of the Principal Rivers of GB*, ii, J & J Boydell, 1796, p. 3.
12   J Harris, *Sir WC: Knight of the Polar Star*, Zwemmer, 1970, p. 242.
13   See A Livermore, 'Sandycombe Lodge', *Country Life*, 6.7.1951.
14   T H Ward and W Roberts, *Romney: A Biographical and Critical Essay*, i, Agnew, 1904, p. 68.
15   R Ellis, 'Romney's Two Hampstead Houses', *Camden History Review 5*, Camden History Society, 1977, *passim*.
16   *Ibid.* Probably James Wyatt's pupil S (Samuel?) Bunce. Since Bunce is said to have been living in Rome in 1790, Flaxman may have met and commended him to Romney. H M Colvin, *Biographical Dictionary of British Architects 1660–1840*, John Murray, 1954.
17   E Bell, 'GR's Studio at Hampstead', *M'sex and Herts Notes & Queries*, i, Hardy & Page, 1895, pp. 66–8, quoting Hayley.
18   The original state of the building has been obscured by Sir Clough Williams-Ellis's alterations of 1929 onwards.
19   Romney would have had to paint at least 12 ¾-lengths at his 1776 price merely to pay the £210 p.a. ground rent charged to Cotes in the previous decade. (Gainsborough would have had to paint maybe five, Sir Joshua perhaps four or fewer.) Romney's income in 1786, however, was £3504. T H Ward and W Roberts, *op. cit., passim*; G Rudé, *Hanoverian London 1714–1808*, UCLA Press, Los Angeles, 1971, p. 69.
     It is surprising, really, that neither Gainsborough nor West bought the lease of 24 Cavendish Sq. after Cotes died.
20   D Goldring, *A Regency Portrait Painter, The Life of Sir TL, PRA*, MacDonald, 1951, pp. 244–5.
21   Stroehling attempted to charge two teenagers £500 each for portraits which they understood were to cost only £50. Farington reckoned '£100 would be large payment'. K Cave, ed., *Farington Diary*, ix, Yale, 1982 (28.6.1810, p. 3677). An Irish portraitist, T C Thompson, used the Egyptian studio from 1818 to 1830.
22   In the introduction to his *Household Furniture and Interior Decoration* of 1807, Thomas Hope had warned that 'Modern imitations . . . [of real Egyptian monuments] . . . composed of lath and of plaster, of callico and of paper, offer no one attribute of solidity or grandeur to compensate for their want of elegance and grace, and can only excite ridicule and contempt'. Stroehling's design, on the contrary, has a pleasing integrity.
23   Arguably the same job, though Soane died in 1837. C J Richardson, *The Englishman's House*, J C Hotten, 1871, pp. 339–40.
24   'My room was so small,' Haydon noted, 'the air so confined, the effluvium of paint so overpowering' and the casts he had taken of the Elgin Marbles so hemmed him in that '. . . people advised me to move if I wished to save my life.' *Autobiography of BRH*, OUP, Oxford, 1927, p. 347.
25   *Ibid.*, p. 348.

CHAPTER 2 *continued*

26 *Ibid.*, p. 350.
27 'Constable thought it a very fit house for an artist, but grumbled that Leslie had moved "sadly out of the way – but it is quite the country." ' J L Fraser, *JC 1776–1837*, Hutchinson, 1976, p. 158. C W Cope, P F Poole and J S Westmacott were subsequent lessees; Cope complained of dampness and church mice in 1839–40. C H Cope, *Reminiscences of C W C. RA*, R Bentley & Son, 1891, p. 120.
28 *SoL 40*, ii, 1980, pp. 295, 317.
29 R Gunnis, *Dictionary of British Sculptors 1660–1851*, Abbey Library, 1961.
30 Auction particulars, 25.5.1829.
31 Formerly the RA William Hamilton's. *SoL 33*, i, 1966, p. 139.
32 John Tallis's remarkably faithful *London Street Views* of 1838–40 show several houses similarly affected in Charlotte St, including the former No. 88, then lately occupied by (Sir) William Boxall. Cut-up windows still exist at (today's numbering) 53, 57 and 63 Charlotte St, / Grafton Way, and 50 Greek St. See, also, the old photograph of 17 Red Lion Sq. in G H Crow, *William Morris: Designer*, The Studio, 1934, pp. 28, 37.
33 Some time after settling here in 1781 Farington tacked on an 'Anteroom' and a 'Great Painting Room' at the rear. K Cave, *op. cit.* (9, 11.4.1810, p. 3631).
34 See E H Shepard, *Drawn from Memory*, Penguin, 1975, p. 125.
35 W P Frith RA reckoned Reynolds's room was built 'about 1815', but Whitman says otherwise. Frith's friend Augustus Egg lived at Ivy Cottage *c.* 1847 to 1854. A Whitman, *S W R, Engraver*, G Bell & Sons, 1903.
36 Conveyance document 5.10.1849. Mansell Collection.
37 The phrase is Raymond Lister's. Linnell may have added an extra storey or two at various stages. A T Story, *Life of JL*, i, R Bentley & Son, 1892, pp. 248–9.
38 A T Story, *ibid.*, ii, p. 33. For example, the painter James Barry's house in Castle St W1 had 17 windows; his bill for 1804 was £7.15.0. (Receipts at Marylebone Library.)
39 *SoL 38*, 1975, p. 34.
40 Cope appears to have lived at No. 28 from 1841 but the studio did not take the shape shown until 18.3.1847. C H Cope, *op. cit.*, pp. 167–8.

CHAPTER 3

1 K R Towndrow, *Alfred Stevens*, Constable, 1939, *passim*.
2 Richard Westmacott RA, Professor of Sculpture at the RA, retired to 1 Kensington Gate *c.* 1857, however.
3 Bridell built the studio behind No. 8 just before his early death in 1863.
4 A H Palmer's *Life* (1892) is quoted in R Lister, *SP – A Biography*, Faber, 1974, p. 192.
5 *The Art Union*, 1847, p. 230; C H Cope, *Reminiscences of C W Cope, RA*, R Bentley & Son, 1891, p. 135.
6 Tor Villa stood – facing south at the corner of Campden Hill Rd – on the gardens of the present Tor Gdns.
7 F G Stephens 'JCH RA', *The Art Annual*, 1881. (Hook was probably obliged under the conditions of the ground lease to build a pair of houses. See A J Hook, *Life of JCH RA*, 1929, p. 84.) The 'campanile' may have been better called an Italian 'torre' or 'tor'.
8 Horsley may have come because a studio was being joined to his permanent home, (now) 128 Kensington Church St. This was a mere 22′ square, first floor infilling. A tier of sashes – a cut-up window projecting into the sky, in fact – chamfered the N-E corner so that the painter could profit from extra depth along the diagonal axis (J C Horsley, *Recollections of a RA*, A Helps ed., John Murray, 1903, p. 350). George Smith and (Sir) W F Douglas succeeded Horsley at 2 Tor Villa; another Scot, Thomas Faed RA, lived in nearby Sussex Villa 1865–76. See also D Goldring, *South Lodge*, Constable, 1943, and Ballantyne's painting of Phillip's painting room.
9 A J Hook, *op.cit.*, p. 84.
10 Frith once admitted that it was a toss-up whether he would become a painter or an auctioneer. Whistler, arch-enemy of the subject painter, rejoined, 'He must have tossed up!' On the subject of *Derby Day*, the commissioner, Jacob Bell, had specified a size between five and six feet in length; Frith managed to increase this commensurate with his vision. His house was, indeed, superior to other Pembridge Villas at the time. The junior of the two tumblers who came to 'sit' for their part in *Derby Day* returned from the lavatory, exclaiming, 'Oh, father! such a beautiful place! all mahoginy, and a chany [china] basin to wash in!' – W P Frith, *My Autobiography and Reminiscences*, i, Richard Bentley & Son, 2nd edn, 1887, p. 251.
11 Thackeray in *Our Street* portrayed him as the risible George Rumbold ARA as early as 1848.
12 M S Watts, *GFW: The Annals of an Artist's Life*, i, Macmillan, 1912, p. 140.
13 *AJ*, 1855, pp. 152–3, 249–50. Edward Salomons ARIBA may have been the consultant architect.
14 M S Watts, *op. cit.*, p. 290. Cased in brickwork, The Tin Pot survived until the 1960s. The catalogues of several companies, e.g. Harbrow's, still listed iron studios after 1900. The extant prefabricated sculpture studios of the RCA on Queen's Gate SW7 were erected very early this century.
15 R Engen, *Victorian Engravings*, Academy Editions, 1975.
16 P Ferriday, 'The Victorian Art Market', *Country Life*, 9.6, 16.6.1966, *passim*.
17 E Aslin, 'The Rise and Progress of the Art Union of London', *Apollo*, No. 1, 1967, p. 14; R Engen, *op.cit.*
18 Early lessees of Freake's in Onslow Square included the sculptor Baron Marochetti and the South Kensington Museum director (Sir) Henry Cole.

CHAPTER 3 *continued*

19   William Tasker or even Thomas Cundy III may have been the designer – *SoL 38*, 1975, *passim*.
20   A drawing of the front façade is given in *Br* 12.2.1859, p. 115.
21   *SoL 38*, 1975, p. 289. Sir Coutts was distantly related to both Lord Eastnor and Admiral Bethune, the intervening leaseholder at No.4.
22   J G Millais, *Life and Letters of Sir JEM*, i, Methuen, 1902, p. 363. Millais may have been told of the availability of No. 6 but brushed aside by Sir Coutts. If so, his misfortune was compounded when Freake decided later in 1861 to add one more house to the west side terrace. Freake dared to build it on the garden of his own house (facing Cromwell Rd), thereby shutting out Millais' light and air. Lord Thynne took the new house.
23   A Woolner, *TW, Sculptor and Poet*, Chapman & Hall, 1917, p. 205.
24   At the astonishing rate of three corbels per day they burst forth into 'violets, roses, thistles, ivies, geraniums and other things lovelier than their names.' *Ibid.*, p. 213.
25   Buckingham Palace Road. The painter Arthur Hughes shared this 'nasty wood house full of clay and water tubs' for a period around 1855. See B Read, *Victorian Sculpture*, Yale, 1982, pp. 47, 50.
26   Swinton's account books – SNPG.
27   *BN*, 10, 17.2.1860.
28   Another saving on the original contract, the gallery appears not to have been built until 1865.
29   Listed in Swinton's will.
30   *BN*, 29.10.1880.
31   A couple of rows of Dutch pantiles were used to cope the eaves level cornice – a planted fossil recalling former London building practice.
32   In Paris, it was under the roof at 21 rue Pigalle (9), no distance from the Jollivet house.
33   *BN*, 9.11.1866, p. 747.
34   E W Godwin, in *BN*, 30.11.1866, pp. 799–800.
35   Fireplaces beneath windows are not particularly unusual. There is one in the upper hall of Romney's house. Aitchison installed another here – in the library of stage 2. Leighton bought and commissioned many works of art for the house, from embroidery by Gertrude Jekyll to *Icarus* by Alfred Gilbert.
36   E Haweis, *Beautiful Houses*, Sampson Low *et al.*, 1882, pp. 8, 9.
37   The heavy masonry surround which Aitchison first proposed is unlikely to have been built. It had a close resemblance to a Parisian design in *BN*, 12.12.1862, p. 454.
38   Aitchison introduced would-be Islamic patterns into two small windows either side of the recobbled eastern bay. Dating from early 1870, they give a foretaste of the phantasmagoria pieced together later in the decade. (RIBA drawings collection)
39   L V Fildes, *Luke Fildes RA, A Victorian Painter*, Michael Joseph, 1968, p. 65.
40   Leighton had always intended to give Crane and Burne-Jones a free hand to cover the inside of the Arab Hall dome with mosaics.

CHAPTER 4

1   A similar masonry pattern was used on Spencer-Stanhope's 'Fairmile' of 1860 and again here when Webb added a superb two-pronged Vanbrughian gable to the north elevation in 1873.
2   W Crane, *An Artist's Reminiscences*, Methuen, 1907, p. 166. Crane was able to move into Beaumont Lodge, Shepherd's Bush, just vacated by Edward Poynter. The stables there had been converted into a roomy studio by Webb in 1870.
3   The Etching Club held together until 1885 with Cope, Redgrave and Horsley staying the distance. Heseltine's contact with this circle is interesting in view of the clientèle Horsley generated for Shaw following their first job together.
4   In 1882 Stone had Mervyn Macartney raise the central oriel to the ceiling line in order to eliminate the shadow cast by the external cornice. Fildes (see text, below) had this done in 1881.
5   Another of the ladder-framed windows balanced the dining room design as built, but only to worsen the external effect.
6   L V Fildes, *LF RA: A Victorian Painter*, Michael Joseph, 1968, p. 43. Fildes's grandmother provided most of the money to build the house (p. 36).
7   *Ibid.*, p. 133.
8   He was probably helped by his old sparring partner, W E Nesfield.
9   W G Robertson, *Time Was*, Hamish Hamilton, 1931, p. 58.
10   *BN*, 7.3.1879, p. 261.
11   W G Robertson, *op.cit.*, p. 59.
12   W Blunt, *England's Michelangelo*, Hamish Hamilton, 1975, p. 122.
13   *Boadicea* remained in the plaster *c.* 1871–97, well after Thomas's death. Completion of this and *Commerce* may have forestalled an earlier move from 21 Wilton Place SW1. B Read, *Victorian Sculpture*, Yale, 1982, p. 59.
14   Hamo had in fact kept a flat at Wynnstay Gardens, off Allen Street, Kensington, since 1884 (*Post Office Directory*). He relinquished it once 2a Melbury Road had been built. (The façade of No. 2a was not original. Belcher had designed one the same for a building at Mark Ash, near Abinger, in 1888.)

CHAPTER 4 *continued*

15 The gluey foundations that caused Fildes extra expense may account for this strategy.
16 M D Conway, *Travels in South Kensington*, Trübner & Co., 1882, p. 196.
17 See Gazetteer.
18 *SoL 37*, 1973, p. 57. (Sir) Will Rothenstein occupied the house between 1920–5.
19 *Ibid.*, p. 70.
20 Later 110 Palace Gardens Terrace – see M D Conway, *op.cit.*, pp. 178ff.
21 These quotations are from E Haweis, *Beautiful Houses*, Sampson Low *et al.*, 1882, pp. 45–52 – one of the best records anywhere of an Aesthetic Movement interior.
22 A notable survivor is 32 Campden Grove; see *SoL 37*, 1973, p. 54 and Gazetteer.
23 F G Dumas, ed., *Modern Artists*, i, Chapman & Hall, 1882, *passim*. Boehm carved the seal fountain.
24 In 1886 Millais gave his third daughter Alice in marriage to Charles Stuart-Wortley, MP and future Baron Stuart of Wortley. S-W's brother Archie made use of the Palace Gate studio after 1896.
25 *BN* reporters who saw T H Watson's design at the RIBA rooms wrote: '. . . why he should have taken the trouble to make a drawing of it, or, having done so, should have exhibited it, we are at a loss to conceive'. *BN*, 26.6.1868, p. 427. Watson's work is in fact sufficiently sensitive to be indistinguishable from the original portion of the house. Evidently he demolished Alfred Corbould's flimsy studio annexe, replacing it with the gabled masonry wing bordering Eldon Road. Adjoining the stairhall, which this wing incorporates, he built Edward Corbould's north-lit studio and a lumber room of equivalent size beneath. These comprehensively put paid to Alfred's big stable and the rest of the back garden.
26 Kensington Planning Application Case 317, Kensington Library. The names Maj.-Gen. James Pattle Beadle and James Prinsep Barnes Beadle indicate a relationship to Val Prinsep's mother's family – one well known in the Indian service. Young James's connections in the London art world will no doubt have been partly the result of old Val's doing.
27 Natorp lent him antique furniture to draw, for instance. They may have already met in America.
28 C M Mount, *John Singer Sargent*, Cresset Press, 1957, p. 122. On the other hand it has been said that Natorp may have ghosted Sargent's little-known bronzes.

CHAPTER 5

1 In February Mrs Langtry had put down a deposit on a studio-flat in a block Godwin was planning to develop (ultimately *Tower House*, Tite St). The private house was estimated to cost £2642 and the scheme advanced some way before abandonment. Godwin *Sketchbook*, E.255, V & A Museum.
2 See E V Lucas, *E A Abbey, RA*, i, Methuen, 1921, pp. 74, 75.
3 T Pocock, *Chelsea Reach*, Hodder & Stoughton, 1970, p. 75. M D Conway writes, also, of a gloomy staircase brightened up by lemon yellow walls above a golden dado dotted with butterflies in *Travels in South Kensington*, Trübner & Co., 1882, pp. 183–4.
4 W M Rossetti, *Some Reminiscences of WMR*, i, Brown, Langham & Co., 1906, *passim*. Swinburne left in 1866, WMR in 1874. Frederick Sandys, probably with his gypsy girlfriend Keomi, stayed some six months in 1866. DGR and WMR were not the first Pre-Raphaelite Brothers to live in Chelsea. Hunt was at Prospect Place (*c*. 60 Cheyne Walk), 1850–4; Collinson at 11 Queen's (Royal Hospital) Rd, 1855–60.
5 *Ibid.*, p. 273.
6 O Doughty, J R Wahl, eds, *Letters of DGR*, ii, Clarendon Press, Oxford, 1965, pp. 511–13.
7 V Surtees, ed., *Diaries of GPB* (1941), Real World, Norwich, 1980, pp. 49–51, 101. The house was actually called North House (in relation to Cheyne Row) at first.
8 This famous green paint, a perfect foil for blue and white porcelain, survives in the basement china closet. *Tatler*, June 1982 gives some photographs.
9 Walton, who also stayed with his architect at this time, was waiting to move into 73 Cheyne Walk. Apparently he took advantage of Boyce's disordered affairs to steal a fireplace for installation at the new house. *Ashbee Collection*, Chelsea Public Library.
10 *BN*, 27.6.1879, p. 720.
11 E V Lucas, *op.cit.*, p. 79.
12 *BA*, 1879, p. 106.
13 M Girouard, *Sweetness and Light*, Clarendon Press, Oxford, p. 180.
14 A mildly conciliatory drawing had been submitted in January (see Girouard, *ut supra*, p. 180). This showed the higher parapet containing a Japanesy mosaic panel.
15 *Ibid.*, p. 181.
16 S Weintraub, *Whistler: A Biography*, Collins, 1974, p. 225.
17 E V Lucas, *op.cit.*, pp. 80–1.
18 F Bickley, *The Pre-Raphaelite Comedy*, Constable, 1932, p. 58. Cremorne was the pleasure garden at the lower end of Cheyne Walk.

CHAPTER 5 *continued*

19 Possibly Pellegrini's contribution; the plans reflect the two plots. There was then enough space to let out a couple of ground floor rooms. Godwin drawings and *Sketchbooks*, E.244, 245, V & A Museum.
20 *BA*, 1879, p. 106.
21 E Harris, 'CP: Man and "Ape"', *Apollo*, No. 1, 1976. Ape left Archie £221.15.8.
22 E Haweis, *The Art of Decoration*, Chatto & Windus, 1881, pp. 51–2.
23 *BN*, 7.3.1879, p. 261.
24 *Ibid.* The rear elevation, however, really *did* end up downright ugly.
25 Miles's helter-skelter staircase, for instance, was made up in natural sycamore with brass-capped posts whereas Whistler's featured inlaid ivory bands.
26 See H M Hyde, 'OW and his Architect', *Architectural Review*, March, 1951.
27 G P Jacomb-Hood, *With Brush and Pencil*, John Murray, 1925, pp. 113ff. His architect was Alexander N Paterson, brother of one of the Glasgow Boys.
28 For an example of Howell's winning ways, see *BA*, 13.12.1878, pp. 231–3. Regrettably the trial described here was scheduled to be heard at the same time as *Whistler v Ruskin*. Otherwise the painter, with Howell as witness, would undoubtedly have won his costs. Whistler agreed with him: 'You would have won the case and we should all have been in Newgate'.
29 W G Robertson, *Time Was*, Hamish Hamilton, 1931, p. 191.
30 Sargent first took the studio and rooms above Whistler's in winter 1885 – C M Mount, *JSS*, Cresset Press, 1957, p. 92.
31 L V Fildes, *Luke Fildes, RA: A Victorian Painter*, Michael Joseph, 1968, p. 67.
32 C M Mount, *op.cit.*, p. 243.
33 Of the Gloucester firm, F S Waller & Son, and brother of the painter S E Waller. FSW would appear to have designed No. 50, FWW No. 52.
34 R Hart-Davis, ed., *Letters of OW*, R Hart-Davis, 1962, pp. 464, 499.
35 L Jopling, *Twenty Years of My Life*, Bodley Head, 1925, pp. 134ff., 145–155.
36 *BN*, 28.4.1865, p. 298. Drawings at V & A Museum. Naftel fortunes plotted by courtesy of Mr Stephen Furniss.

CHAPTER 6

1   Brown lodged in the High Street for 21 months from mid-1852 while he worked on *Work*.
2   S Beattie, *RIBA catalogue of Stevens drawings*, 1975, pp. 48ff.
3   Richard Batterbury Snr of Bathford, Somerset, had retired by 1871; Richard Jnr, aged 26 at the same date, was already in charge of 24 men and 5 boys. (Hampstead census return)
4   His second wife's younger son, Thomas Danby, and her son-in-law, John Mogford, settled at 11 and 17 Park Rd in the late 1860s. See Gazetteer under 36 Upper Park Road, also.
5   *Br*, 8.4.1871.
6   H Holiday, *Reminiscences of My Life*, Heinemann, 1914, pp. 237ff.
7   This little building foreshadowed the handsome house designs of 1877 for Salisbury Street, Hull.
8   *BN*, 22.12.1876, p. 621.
9   M Phipps-Jackson, 'Cairo in London', *AJ*, 1883, p. 74.
10 *Ibid.*, pp. 72–5.
11 *BN*, 27.10.1876, 23.2.1877.
12 M Hardie, *Watercolour Painting in Britain*, iii, 1967; *BN*, 12.1.1883, p. 40.
13 The existence of a clique comprising F W W Topham, Poole, Thomas Danby, Francis Holl Snr, W W Deane and others adds some credence to this claim. Another long shot is Saxon Snell.
14 See three preliminary plans plus the near-final sketch elevations in the RA collection, Burlington House.
15 *A*, 15.11.1879, p. 286.
16 *DNB*.
17 H Zimmern, *MA*, 1885, p. 150.
18 *Ibid.*
19 H Herkomer, *My School and My Gospel*, Constable, 1907, p. 17.
20 E Pinnington quoted by M Hardie, *John Pettie*, A & C Black, 1908, p. 117.
21 M Hardie, *ut supra*, p. 116.
22 H Zimmern, *MA*, 1885, p. 93.
23 *DNB*.
24 D Hudson, *Arthur Rackham*, Heinemann, 1960, p. 70.
25 Neither should 1 Wychcombe Villas – same side, nearest Haverstock Hill – be overlooked. It is also of 1882–3.

CHAPTER 6 *continued*

26 H James, *Atlantic Monthly*, August 1882.
27 W R Sickert, *Fortnightly Review*, December 1928.
28 G A Storey, *Sketches from Memory*, Chatto & Windus, 1899, p. 330.
29 G D Leslie, *Inner Life of the RA*, John Murray, 1914, p. 150.
30 *BN*, 7.9.1888, p. 302.

CHAPTER 7

1   J Galsworthy, *The Forsyte Saga*, i, Heinemann, 1922, p. 67.
2   R Gunnis, *Dictionary of British Sculptors 1660–1851*, Abbey Library, 1951.
3   A M W Stirling, *Victorian Sidelights*, Ernest Benn, 1954, p. 89.
4   *Ibid.*, p. 90.
5   A Lucas, *JL, Portrait Painter 1808–74*, Methuen, 1910, p. 30.
6   1–8 Grove End Place was a ragged line of Italianate houses between Grove End Road and Hamilton Mews, renumbered *c.* 1870 as 33–19 (odd) St John's Wood Road. Lucas was able to reclaim his original house in 1856 mainly due to the suicide of his tenant, the painter Matthew Wood.
7   (Sir) W Q Orchardson, followed by Heywood Hardy, had preceded Storey to 8 Grove End Pl./19 St John's Wood Rd. Pettie landed next door just before Orchardson slipped away again.
8   *Fun's Academy Skits* of 1882 found a target in Storey's *Coracles on the Dee – Llantysilio*. The comment ran, '*Coracles on the Dee – Verysillyo*. You will see that the coracles are most coracley drawn'.
9   H Holiday, *Reminiscences of My Life*, Heinemann, 1914, p. 159.
10 *Br*, 10.10.1885, p. 496.
11 A M W Stirling, *op.cit.*, pp. 142ff. The London Sketch Club had its headquarters hereabouts later in the piece.
12 *Ibid.*, p. 168.
13 *Ibid.*, p. 186.
14 Quoted by V Swanson, *Sir LA-T*, Ash & Grant, 1977, p. 31.
15 H Zimmern, *50 Years of Art: 1849–99*, The Art Journal, p. 261.
16 See *A*, 31.5, 7.6.1889 for further illustrations.
17 *Br*, 18.9.1886, p. 412.
18 George Simonds – brewer, banker, sculptor, master of the Art Workers' Guild – at 'Priory Studios', Lodge Road, from 1887, was a significant exception.
19 C L Hind, 'Painters' Studios', *AJ*, 1890, p. 138.
20 *Ibid.*
21 16 Maida Vale. By coincidence the old house here once belonged to Robert Jackson, John Thomas's chief assistant in the 1840s and 1850s.
22 Berlin-born Otto Weber, animal painter, established this studio *c.* 1874. Goscombe John replaced Mullins early in the new century.
23 *BN*, 5.5.1893, pp. 601, 619; 25.11.1892, p. 735. Except for Sadler's, these extensions actually belonged to houses in lower Hampstead.
24 Eden advanced Reynolds-Stephens to the Hodgson house, since renumbered. It was he who, in 1894–7, crossed swords with Whistler in the *Baronet v Butterfly* duel. Young Staples no sooner built than he moved away.
25 Possibly this studio (also known as 2a Nugent Tce), since considerably altered, was initially superimposed on the one Edward Gregory ARA used 1879–89.
26 May's name is a reminder of the large assembly of great black and white artists in the Wood then and earlier, e.g., Sir John Tenniel, A B Houghton, J D

CHAPTER 8

1   F M Hueffer, *Ford Madox Brown*, Longmans, Green, 1896, p. 38. Perhaps Charles Compton is meant.
2   A Ludovici Jnr, *An Artist's Life in London and Paris*, Fisher Unwin, 1926, p. 10.
3   Rev. W J Loftie, *Kensington, Picturesque and Historical*, Leadenhall Press, 1888, p. 217.
4   Rate Books; D Stroud, *The South Kensington Estate of Henry Smith's Charity*, H S Charity Trustees, 1975, pp. 30, 33.
5   *A*, 17.8.1872.
6   *Vanity Fair*, 3.1.1874, 'Men of the Day No. 76'.
7   No. 6 may not have been part of the school, but there are skylights over the bedrooms suggesting their use as individual painting rooms.
8   *SoL 41*, 1983, pp. 70, 81.
9   *Ibid.*, pp. 153–4.

CHAPTER 8 *continued*

10   Unfortunately, as at *Scarsdale Studios* and here, these lodges were themselves converted into studios of sorts along the way.
11   *BN*, 7.3.1879, p. 261.
12   *Ibid.*, 3.9.1880, p. 270.
13   In his talk at the AA in March 1879 Godwin talked of stables 'at the back of Gower Street' which recommended themselves as sites for studios. *BA*, March 1879, p. 106.
14   RIBA Drawings Collection.
15   See M Girouard's version in *Sweetness and Light*, Clarendon Press Oxford, 1977, pp. 183ff. and *Country Life*, 23.11.1972, pp. 1370–4. Thomas Henry Watson may have been Mrs Bagot's architect.
16   *BA*, 22.5.1885, p. 252.
17   The atelier of M. Hubert Vos is said to have opened in two studios early in 1889. *A*, 25.1.1889.
18   *Nairn's London*, Penguin, 1966, p. 134.
19   *SoL 41*, pp. 175–6; Kensington Public Library Records.
20   When Walter Dowdeswell visited for the *AJ* in 1887 it was painted 'white tinged with yellow'. A Sickert etching of the studio is in the BM collection.
21   H S Ede, *Savage Messiah*, Gordon Fraser, 1971, p. 135.
22   *Ibid.*, p. 137.
23   *BN*, 13.3.1891, p. 364.
24   *Ex inf.* Mrs G M Hyams.

CHAPTER 9

1   A Lucas, *John Lucas, Portrait Painter*, Methuen, 1910, p. 13.
2   A T Story, *Life of JL*, ii, R Bentley & Son, 1892, p. 32.
3   *Ibid.*, p. 33.
4   BM Prints & Drawings collection; *DNB*.
5   '. . . for colour, indescribable charm, [Hook] is pre-eminent even to hugging him in one's arms. A perfect poem is each of his little pictures', Ford Madox Brown writes of the 1856 RA exhibition. V Surtees, ed., *Diary of FMB*, Yale, 1981, p. 174.
6   F G Dumas, ed., *Modern Artists*, ii, Chapman & Hall, 1884, p. 220.
7   F G Stephens, 'JCH His Life and Work', *Art Annual*, 1887, p. 16.
8   G D Leslie, *Inner Life of the RA*, John Murray, 1914, pp. 104–7.
9   An extension to accommodate the Burne-Joneses was tendered for in 1864 (*Br*, 27.8.1864). E W Godwin's Harpenden, Herts, house, built in 1869 for himself and Ellen Watts was a similar result of Victorian social pressure.
10   M Lago, ed., *B-J Talking*, John Murray, 1982, p. 77.
11   Amy Woolner, *TW, Sculptor and Poet*, Chapman & Hall, 1917, pp. 290–2, 327–8.
12   *BN*, 6.11.1874, illustrated.
13   Work began in mid-1872. For the procedure, see RIBA catalogue of Webb drawings.
14   A Ritchie, *From an Island*, Smith, Elder, 1895, p. 268.
15   *American Architect and Building News* of 9.7.1887 reported that '. . . the Brookline architect took the plans, already laid out by the painter's talented *wife*, and worked them into available shape' [my italics].
16   J S Mills, *Life and Letters of Sir HH*, Hutchinson, 1923, p. 165.
17   *Ibid.*, p. 131.
18   Holman Hunt, John Collier and the architect Lionel Crane also married a deceased wife's sister.
19   Over 100 pupils were resident at Bushey by 1889; by 1900 some 62 studios at or near Bushey were built or occupied by graduates.
20   *American Architect, op.cit.*
21   *MA*, 1901, p. 402. Another source describes the walls as 'greenish-gold' – A L Baldry, *HvH*, George Bell, 1901, p. 111.
22   See W C Brookes, 'Has Herts the oldest film studio in England?', *Herts Countryside*, August 1973.
23   J S Mills, *op.cit.*, pp. 100–125; Madox Brown was possibly coveting something similar in 1857. See V Surtees, *op.cit.*, p. 195.
24   £3688 worth; *BN*, 5.5.1882, p. 540.
25   *BN*, 5.8.1881. Another work of interest nearby was John Belcher's unassignable 'Mark Ash' studio of *c.* 1888 at Abinger. Belcher also designed studios at Brenchley, Kent, either for the wildlife illustrator Harrison Weir or the Alfred Sassoons. *BN* 11.2.1881, *A*, 8.4.1887.
26   Gilbert then trailed Boehm to the old Gomshall manor house. Orchardson also had a house at Westgate-on-Sea at this period, while Solomon Solomon allegedly glazed the mouth of a cave in the coastal cliff-face to make himself a seascaping eyrie at the same resort.

CHAPTER 9 *continued*

27 Sir N Pevsner quotes Goodhart-Rendel in A Service, ed., *Edwardian Architecture . . .*, Architectural Press, 1975, p. 480.
28 A précis of his *Bungalows and Country Residences* (1891) appeared in *The Studio*, No. 3, 1894, pp. 20ff.
29 Especially a studio-house on an adjoining site 'for the use of W J Margetson' born out of a preliminary dual studio scheme, also of 1897. See RIBA catalogue of Voysey drawings.
30 *The Studio*, No. 9, 1897, pp. 28–35.
31 *The Studio*, No. 21, p. 246.
32 *Br*, 5.5.1894, p. 550; Godalming: a fairly direct result of Lutyens's father taking a house on Thursley Common from 1876 onwards.

CHAPTER 10

1 C Colvin, ed., *Maria Edgeworth: Letters . . .*, OUP, Oxford, 1971. Letter of 23.5.1841. The blue light observed may have been due to sodium compounds in the lantern glass.
2 Site of the first London Salon des Refusés in 1847, i.e., before the Pre-Raphaelite furore. Banks & Charles Barry Jnr remodelled Claudet's studio here in 1855.
3 Asa Briggs in *From Today Painting is Dead*, Arts Council, 1972, p. 14.
4 Disderi & Co. operated here between *c.* 1860 and 1869, in which year Walter Bentley Woodbury (patentee of the Woodburytype photographic process in 1865) established his Photo-relief Printing Company on the same site. Woodbury's works survived until 1876 when the land was set aside for redevelopment. (Contemporary advertisements.)
5 F Loyer, 'La Grande Kermesse d'HH', *Monuments Historiques de la France*, April, 1979, pp. 8–16. For a HH scheme that was built in London, see *Br*, 26.2.1859, pp. 145, 155.
6 Quoted from *Annals of a Glass House* by B Hill, *JMC and Her Sisters*, Peter Owen, 1973.
7 C W Cope began his *Cdr Cameron's Reception at Shoreham* here in 1877. C H Cope, *Reminiscences of CWC, RA*, Richard Bentley & Son, 1891, p. 333.
8 F C Young, ed., *Amateur Work, Part 12*, Ward, Lock & Co., *c.* 1883, pp. 34–6, 212–216.
9 W J Reader, *Victorian England*, Batsford, 1974, p. 125.
10 *BN*, 14.5.1886, p. 777.
11 See *SoL 29*, i, 1960, p. 262.
12 *Builder's Journal*, 10.3.1897, pp. 66–7.

CHAPTER 11

1 Abridged but not misrepresented.
2 H S Marks, *Pen and Pencil Sketches*, Chatto & Windus, 1894. Marks explains the Walker drawing in vol. i, p. 90.
3 T Watts-Dunton, *Aylwin* (1898), 22nd edn, Grant Richards, p. 232.
4 O Wilde, *The Picture of Dorian Gray*, Magnum edn, p. 10.
5 G Eliot, *Romola*, i, Blackwood and Sons edn, pp. 283–4.
6 *Ibid.*
7 Quoted in Amy Woolner, *Thomas Woolner RA, Sculptor and Poet*, Chapman and Hall, 1917, p. 284.
8 V Surtees, ed., *The Diary of F M Brown*, Yale, 1981, p. 76.
9 C H Cope, *Reminiscences of CWC, RA*, Richard Bentley and Son, 1891, p. 147.
10 M H Spielmann, *MA Annual*, 1887, p. 136.
11 V Surtees, *op.cit.*, p. 184.
12 Luke Fildes received nearly 700 visitors on 18.4.1883 to see his *Village Wedding*. In later years the figure would often exceed 1000 – L V Fildes, *LF RA, A Victorian Painter*, Michael Joseph, 1968.
13 G B Shaw, *Immaturity*, Constable, 1921, pp. 104–5.
14 F Moscheles, *In Bohemia with du Maurier*, Fisher Unwin, 1896, p. 132. Moscheles points out that Arthur Lewis is 'the great sculptor', Sir Louis Cornelys of Mechelen Lodge, Campden Hill, in *Trilby*.
15 W P Frith, *My Autobiography and Reminiscences*, i, Richard Bentley & Son, 2nd edn, 1887, p. 355.
16 J Hamilton, *The Sketching Society 1799–1851*, V & A Museum, 1971, pp. 17, 10.
17 Previously Leigh, with Charles Lucy and John Foley, had taught at the Dickinsons' Maddox St school, itself a successor to one run by C E Butler Williams.
18 W M Thackeray, *The Newcomes*, Macmillan, 1901, p. 185.

CHAPTER 11 *continued*

19 In fact Gandish has more Sass in him than Leigh, but Gandish's school is the one 'in a certain lofty street in [north] Soho'. Sass died in 1844, so Barker strictly represents F S Cary.
20 J C Horsley, *Recollections of a RA*, Mrs Helps, ed., John Murray, 1903, pp. 23–4.
21 W P Frith, *My Autobiography and Reminiscences*, i, Richard Bentley & Son, 1888, p. 38.
22 *Ibid*, p. 40.
23 Hence Millais began at Sass's aged 9, Horsley and Rossetti aged 13.
24 An advertisement in *The Year's Art* of 1890 announced that 201 of the 304 RA probationers between 1880–90 had been taught at St John's Wood. Ex-Wood pupils also took 80 per cent of the RA prizes between 1886–8.
25 Letter to Emily Tennyson, 10.5.1865, quoted in Lady Strachey, ed., *Later Letters of EL*, Fisher Unwin, 1911.
26 See L V Fildes, *op.cit.*, p. 145, and G P Jacomb-Hood, *With Brush and Pencil*, John Murray, 1925, pp. 77ff.
27 B Disraeli, *Lothair*, OUP, 1975, p. 296.
28 W Richards, *His Majesty's Territorial Army*, iii, Virtue, 1911, pp. 81–2. The idea was mooted at Phillips' studio, 8 St George St, Hanover Sq.; John Ballantyne painted the subject.
29 A musical travesty of *Box and Cox*, first performed at The Adelphi on 11.5.1867.

CHAPTER 12

1 *SoL 41*, 1983, pp. 175, 218. *Cf.* 41 Cathcart Rd/7 Oakfield St.
2 Victor Barthe's practice class. See T Pocock, *Chelsea Reach*, Hodder & Stoughton, 1970.
3 P Cannon-Brookes, 'OR – Artist Goldsmith', *Connoisseur*, April 1974.
4 C Hussey, 'Sir WO's Studio', *Country Life*, 20.9.1930.
5 A Thirkell, *Three Houses* (1931), OUP, Oxford, 1950, p. 19.
6 W G Robertson, *Time Was*, Hamish Hamilton, 1931, p. 73.
7 A Thirkell, *ibid*, pp. 80, 104.
8 *BA*, 18.1.1878, p. 30.
9 The trap was carefully placed at right angles to a high side light. E A Abbey used this expedient at Fairford. Even though his studio there measured 75' x 42' x 17', he had to dig a trench to accommodate his Royal Exchange panels. E V Lucas, *EAA, RA*, ii, Methuen, 1921, p. 345.
10 J M Dent & Sons edn, 1958, p. 5.
11 *BN*, 13.8.1880, p. 182.
12 Anon., 'The Ballad of Bedford Park', *St James's Gazette*, 17.12.1881.
13 *BA*, 18.9.1891, p. 209; *The Studio*, No. 11, 1897.
14 In Aynhoe Rd for Miss Forster. See Gazetteer.
15 George Hemming Mason ARA who reached Theresa Tce (King St) in 1864 was probably the pioneer Victorian in these parts. Frederick Stacpoole (ARA), the engraver, arrived soon afterwards.
16 *Br*, 1.10.1887.
17 *SoL 37*, 1973, pp. 149–50.
18 R V Cole, *The Art and Life of Byam Shaw*, Seeley, Service & Co., 1932, p. 28.
19 *SoL 41*, 1983, pp. 125ff.
20 Menpes's choice of architect may have partly resulted from interest taken in Mackmurdo's 12 Hans Rd on the same Cadogan Estate. *Br*, 28.5.1892, 14.10.1893.
21 The 'House for an Artist' project which appeared in *The Hobby Horse* and *BA*, 4.1.1889 is hard to take seriously. Equally infantile designs (1904–5) of unbuilt houses for Selwyn Image exist also where a Voysey influence is apparent (Morris Gallery, Walthamstow).
22 Sir N Pevsner, 'G-R's Roll Call' in A Service, ed., *Edwardian Architecture . . .*, Architectural Press, 1975, p. 479. Ashbee's biographer substantiates the architect's property dealings here. But, while many unrealised schemes were commercially speculative, the sheer numbers of them for immediately local sites tend to flesh out an ulterior romantic vision of a pre-Embankment Chelsea villagescape. – A Crawford, *CRA: Architect, Designer and Romantic Socialist*, Yale, 1985, *passim*.
23 H S Ede, *Savage Messiah*, Gordon Fraser, 1971, p. 147.
24 M Holroyd, *Augustus John*, ii, Heinemann, 1975, pp. 120–30.
25 Presumably. Drawings in RIBA collection; illustrations in *Architectural Review*, 1919, p. 105.
26 *Br*, 13.1.1939, p. 116.

13
GAZETTEER

PART ONE:
MULTIPLE STUDIOS

19th-century groups of two or more units, plus the earlier 20th-century examples, are listed below in the alphabetical order of London's postal districts.
In addition to those set out on page 223, the following abbreviations have been used as an aid to document these buildings:
(6) number of units in the group;
† known to be demolished; **a** architect or designer;
b builder; **p** proprietor; **o** occupiers of some importance, given chronologically;
RA membership is indicated if it was applicable during the period of occupancy.
All artists are painters unless otherwise stated.

N7

Brecknock Studios (9) *c.* 1896 †
114a–116 (former) Brecknock Rd
p *?Samuel Sharp*
o *A Rackham*, illr; *S Nicholson Babb*, sc
Terrace of 6 small units plus 3 larger ones one year younger. Out of the way; cheap and basic.

NW1

Camden Studios (9) 1865–9 †
28a (former) Camden St
b, p *William Roberts*, bldr
o *H Bursill*, sc; *J H S Mann*; *Haynes King*; *E Bale*; *R T Waite*; *E Bundy*; *A Lucchesi*, sc; *J D Penrose*
Pioneering utilitarian group adjoining the builder's yard. Popular with Society of British Artists members.

21 Camden Road *c.* 1890 †
o *G A Lawson*, sc; *E Geflowski*, sc; *C J Allen*, sc
Single canal-side workshop discovered by Lawson

in 1879. Extended and converted into several factory-like units.

23 Camden Road Studios (5) 1876 †
a *H T Bonner* of Lewisham (*BN* 9.6.1876)
p *William Edwin Heath*, engineer & gasfitter
o *N E Tayler*; *A H Marsh*; *J H Hooper*
A roof-lit terrace 'of an Italian Gothic character . . . in white Suffolk bricks, with Bath stone dressings'; the internal walls were painted 'in cool tints with dados'.
See *Hogarth Stus W1*.

Primrose Hill Studios (12) 1877–81
Fitzroy Rd
p, b *Alfred Healey & Baker*, bldrs, dvlprs
o *J D Watson*, illr, ptr; *J W Waterhouse RA*; *J Wolf*, animal ptr; *J C Dollman*, illr, ptr; (*Sir*) *H Thompson*, surgeon; *P M Feeney*; *C Whymper*, ptr, illr; *C E Fripp*; *L Calkin*; *M Maris*; *T J Lloyd*; *C Schloesser*; *W Logsdail*; *J D Penrose*; (*Sir*) *E Waterlow*; *R Cleaver*, illr; *M Greiffenhagen*, illr, ptr; *A Rackham*, illr; (*Sir*) *H Wood*, musician; *P Caulfield*
Extravagantly appointed units with a choice of sizes but, like *Pembroke Stus W8*, the front row only has gardens. Communal reserve now invaded by cars: a layout not unlike the piano factories which

operated contemporaneously in this locality. Referred to in Joseph Hatton's *By Order of the Czar* (1890).

Stanhope Studios (3) 1856–67
68a Delancey St
p *Charles Kingston, John Kingston & Co.*, mrchnts
o *A Ludovici Snr*; *J J Hill*; *T Graham*; *F R Stock*; *H Dixon*, sc; *H Pegram*, sc; *C J Fox*
Typical carriageway entrance; stable yard appearance; side- and skylit, terraced brick sheds originally let at 5/- a week each. After *Tudor Lodge Stus NW1* these form the imperfect model for all later such groups.
Still recognisable in the late 1980s.

Tudor Lodge Studios (3) 1844–60–70
Albert St
p *Charles Lucy*, ptr
o *C Lucy*; *F M Brown*; *?Charles Compton*; *F Howard*; *?(Sir) J Tenniel*, illr; *J Ritchie*; *J Brett*; *T Woolner*, sc; *E C Barnes*; *C W Nicholls*; *C A Smith*; *Maresco Pearce*
Supposedly temporary buildings at first. Extant tall and galleried units are lined up rhythmically with ideal orientations, although the skylights are too flat. Essentially the earliest suburban multiple studios – the initiative, significantly, of an artist of the Pre-Raphaelite persuasion.

NW3

14, 16 Adamson Road (2) 1884–5
p *Gregory & Bence*, dvlprs
o *(Sir) A East*; *L Raven-Hill*, illr, cartoonist; *R Bevan*
Sublimated garret studio-houses of the same design as 12, 13 Chalcot Gdns NW3, but in reversed format.

Belsize Studios (5) 1907
Glenilla Rd
p *T G Davidson*
o *G S Knowles*; *C M Q Orchardson*; *C A P Walker*; *T M Hemy*; *N Hemy RA*
Pleasing Dutch Colonial design wherein the detached studio pavilion browses the forecourt jungle like a pregnant albino rhinoceros. Generous rear gardens.

12, 13 Chalcot Gardens (2) 1883
p *Gregory & Bence*, dvlprs
o 12: *G F Wetherbee*; *N P Davies*; *Jessie Macgregor*
o 13: *G Montbard*; *S P Hall*, illr
Remarkably elegant, tall Aesthetic School houses by talented anonymous designer. Compare *14, 16 Adamson Rd NW3.*

13a Heath Street (3) *c.* 1893
p *Charles Bean King*
o *J Nesfield Forsyth*, sc
Redevelopment by owner of early Heath St numbers said to contain 3 studio-flats. Two floors of 28 Church Row next door, also owned by King, apparently converted after 1895 as well.

22 King Henry's Road (3–4) 1869
o *E Barclay*; *William Davis*; *F W W Topham*; *A H Marsh*; *H Woods*; *(Sir) S L Fildes*; *E J Humphery*; *L J Pott*; *H Scott Tuke*
3 or 4 flats with big N windows. Transitional between Fitzrovian painting rooms and the new studio units of nearby Camden Town. See Luke Fildes literature.

151a, b King Henry's Road (2) *c.* 1906
o *L T Watts*; *E Vincent*; *Pickering Walker*
Leonard Walker builds the detached street-front studio in 1901 on a former bicycle circuit marked out for a road. Surplus area is appropriated for cheaply built pair with basic facilities.

The Mall (8) 1872
Tasker Rd
a *Thomas Batterbury* (*A* 17.8.1872)
b *Richard Legg Batterbury*
p *Batterbury family*
o *R W Macbeth*; *E F Brewtnall*; *A S Coke*; *E J Gregory*; *(Sir) J D Linton*; *W B Morris*; *R T Waite*; *C W, W J Morgan*, ptr, sc; *(Sir) G Clausen*; *E Bale*; *W M Fisher*; *J Scott (RI)*; *N Tayler*; *Constance Phillott*; *R Sheppard*, sc
E W Godwin, archt and sometime art critic of *The Architect*, visited 'some Outsiders' at *The Mall* in 1876, noting that they seemed 'just now to be more than usually proud of the horny hand of industry. Its portrait and all the minutiae of its surroundings are "took" with a force and realism rarely accorded, unless specially paid for, to the soft hand of beauty or the nervous hand of thought'.
(*A*, Vol. 15, 1876, p. 156).

Park Road Studios (7) 1880 †
Parkhill (formerly Park) Rd, N end
a *Thomas Knolles Green* (*BN* 3.9.1880)
p *Thomas & W B Pyne*, ptrs
o *G F Wetherbee*; *F H Potter*, ptr, archt; *W H Fisk* (school); *R Morley*; *W Duncan*; *H T Schafer*; *J T Nettleship*, animal ptr; *F Bodkin*; *J S Hill*; *H Macbeth-Raeburn*, engrvr; *N Macbeth*; *L Baumer*, cartoonist; *F Roe*; *B Bradley*, illr
Local architect perhaps took note of St Pancras Almshouses nearby when giving these studios a jaunty institutional air. A piece of Aesthetiana regrettably lost.

Steele's Studios (4 + 1) 1874
97a Haverstock Hill
a *Batterbury & Huxley* (*BN* 8.5.1874)
b *Linzell & Son* of Tottenham, £2314
p *H R Robertson*; *M & D W Stretch*
o *H R Robertson*, ptr, etchr; *M Stretch*, illr; *A McLean*; *W E Marshall*; *G A Lawson*, sc; *A J Whalley*; *J S Hill*
Batterbury's next job after *The Mall NW3* – similar designs and again a row of units with one detached. Eight units were planned for this site (*A* 17.8.1872) but briefs and ownership bids had apparently not been settled even in 1875. No. 1a is added by 1879.

Vale of Health Studios *c.* 1890
o *W R Stevens*; *T Taylor*; *H Hollingdale*
Precursors of the Henry Lamb–Stanley Spencer–William Coldstream legend.

Warwick Studios *c.* 1887
South End Green/Fleet Rd
p *Mr Quennell*
o *Alma Broadbridge*; *Lucy H Bell*
Sheds.

Well Mount Studios (2) 20th-C.
Well Rd
o *M Gertler*, etchr (1932–3)

Such is the value of traffic islands in NW3. Vorticism and the factory aesthetic.

Wychcombe Studios (4 + 1) 1879–80
England's Lane
p *Charles F & Thomas Dash Bellamy*, dvlprs
o *E Barclay*; *R W Macbeth*; *J T H Macallum*; *A H Burr*; *T Green*, illr; *J Y Carrington*; *J W North*; *S P Hall*, illr; *D Farquharson*; *S E Waller*; *A L Burroughs*; *C M Q Orchardson*; *J Aumonier*; *Edyth Starkie*; *A Rackham*, illr
Two speculative pairs and a commissioned one-off double studio (for Macallum), all professionally designed with above-average amenities. An artistic backwater by investors active in Chalcot Gdns and Steele's Rd. Popular with Scots.

NW6

St James Mansions (2 +) *c.* 1890
West End Lane
Articulated block of flats topped by original, purpose-made garrets within the individual mansard roofs. Typical of the rooftop studios added to taller houses in this locality.

West Hampstead Studios (5) 1885
Sherriff Rd
p *Richard Pincham*, dvlpr
o *J W West*; *R Holyoake*; *H Sykes*; *B Priestman*; *Alfred Withers*
A château-esque front, to be sure, but the rest amusingly niggardly. Rooftop devices crane for light except on end unit (later divided) which is well served. Squeezed behind shops next to railway.

NW8

Clifton Hill Studios (6) 1881
95a Clifton Hill
p *S & G Higgins*, auctnrs, srvyrs
o *B E Ward*; *H Ryland*; *S Goetze*; *F Brooks*; *F Bowcher*, sc, mdllr; *Savile Lumley*; *G L Stampa*, cartoonist; *Alyn Williams*, min. ptr; *(Sir) W Reid Dick*, sc
Reconstruction of the W end of Clifton Mews. Storerooms opposite are also upgraded *c.* 1892 when remainder of mews is converted into sculptor's workshop (No. 87a).

23–25 Marlborough Place (2) *c.* 1876 †
o *L J Pott*; *H A Olivier*
Stable-loft studios of shaky lineage backing onto

NW8 concluded

Langford Close. Possibly built by Alfred Scorer; since ruined.

Marlborough Studios (3) 1899
12a Finchley Rd
p *Samuel & George Higgins*, est. agnts, srvyrs
o *R E Higgins; T Robertson*
No.s 10 & 12 Finchley Rd were successively the offices of the Higginses – promoters of *Clifton Hill Stus NW8* and possibly *St John's Wood Stus NW8* – from about 1869 onwards. A pair of galleried paintboxes with a third bungalow bunged in front.

Queen's Road Studios (3 + 3) 1882–
59 Queen's Grove
a *?Albert E Pridmore*
p *John Butler*, ironmonger
o *Theodore Cook; H Lyndon; C P Knight; A Altson*, illr; *E Crofts; W Paget*, illr; *H A Olivier*
Butler followed the 3 mews conversions (perhaps seeing what the Higginses had done) with a formless collection of sheds, including his own workshops and forge, behind the terrace facing Queen's Grove.

St John's Wood Studios (7) 1870–74–91 †
Queen's Tce (W)
a *F J Chambers* (phase 2)
b *A & W Garnar* (*Br* 8.8.1891)
o *J W G Pringle; A B Houghton*, illr; *Peploe Brown; R Monti*, sc; *V Bromley*, ptr, illr; *A H Tourrier*, ptr, illr; *W S Coleman*, dsgnr, illr; *W C May*, sc; *S J Solomon; Y King; E de Martino; W L Wyllie; A Maclean; A Dixon; W R Colton*, sc; *A H Buckland; Isabel Pyke-Nott*
Three very large units are built in the first phase; 4 units half their size and some shops follow. Possibly by the dvlprs of *Marlborough Stus NW8*. A hodge-podge, but handy to the local and to the St John's Wood Arts Club.

3, 5 Wellington Place (2) 1911
o *Bee Belton*, photo
Part of development fronting Wellington Rd.

Woronzow Studios (2) 1890
9a, b Woronzow Rd
a *Albert E Pridmore*
b *Taylor & Son*, £754 (*Br* 10.5.1890)
p *John Butler*, ironmonger
o *C O Skilbeck; C K & Gertrude Warren; (Sir) W G John*, sc
Semi-detached pair of small, standard units on the rear garden of 33 Queen's Grove, backing onto

George Frampton's sculpture studio. By proprietor, and possibly archt, of *Queen's Rd Stus NW8*.

SE3

Art Club Studios c. 1883
46 Bennett Park, Blackheath
p *Bennett Park Art Club & Studio Building Co. Ltd*
o *G Pope; Terrick Williams; A A Hunt*
Arose in response to the Lee & Lewisham Government School of Art, established opposite in 1880.

SE11

Kennington Studios c. 1897
Princes (Cleaver) Square
a *Ralph Nicholson*
b *Marsland & Co.*, £915 (*Br* 11.6.1881)
o *I Fripp*, ptr, stnd gls dsgnr; *T Tyrrell*
A subsequent adaptation of the buildings of Kennington Park Road (or South London Technical) Art School, established in 1879. See S Beattie, *The New Sculpture* (1983).

SW1

Albert Gate Studios (7) 1872–
6 William St/Kinnerton Place
p *Capt. Augustus Savile Lumley (ret.) & John Savile Lumley*
o *A S Lumley; (Sir) W Q Orchardson ARA; James Webb; H Cameron; (Sir) L Ward*, caricaturist; *W Linnell; Hon. J Collier; J Varley Jnr; Hon. A Stuart-Wortley; R C Belt*, sc; *Mrs E M Ward; Herman Herkomer; J Charlton*, illr, ptr
Somewhat like Benjamin West's establishment of 100 years earlier in Newman St W1, an orderly domestic front conceals anomalous elements behind: a seminal S-W London group in a converted block more lately called Bradbrook House. Clonal studios were also set up in the tiny forecourt ostlers' houses.

Bloomfield Studios (3) c. 1878
13, 13a Bloomfield Place, Pimlico
p *J & W H Newson*, bldrs
o *T Phyffers & R Fallon*, wdcrvrs, scs;

Maud Earl, animal ptr; *W E F Britten; (Sir) L Ward ('Spy')*
Stables between Pimlico Rd and Bloomfield Pl. converted into a few largish workshops. The Catholic Phyffers survived, in straits, to serve Bentley after the Pugins. Reconverted; still nominally Newson's.

Chester Studios (2) 1887
17 Gerald Rd
p *Mrs E M (Henrietta) Ward*
o *Mrs E M Ward; Noel Coward*, dramatist, pu
Pair of discreet flats, one for letting, behind Chester Houses. Extra income for the widow of an RA. Married at 16, she outlived him by 45 years.

2 Spenser Street 1872–3 †
o *F Sandys*, illr, ptr; *(Sir) W Q Orchardson ARA; R W Allan; A Moore; T H McLachlan; (Sir) A East ARA; (Sir) J Lavery; C B Phillip*
Sandys was set up here from the beginning by his patron, Cyril Flower, later Lord Battersea, to deny him an excuse for failing to fulfil his commissions. A distinguished company of Scottish ptrs suggests there was more to these early flats than the building demolished c. 1980. Albert Moore died at this address.

West Eaton Place (4) 20th-C
Grosvenor Studios
Conversions which barely qualify. Forced to the edge of Belgravia like the Kinnerton Pl. examples.

SW3

80–82/63–59 (former) **Cadogan Square** (3)
c. 1882 †
p *Charles Bacon*, sc
o *C E Perugini; G Pope; P Ball*, sc
Matching units on the S-E fringe of the incomplete square; demolished by 1888. Possibly related to 121 Sloane Street SW3, (see Gazetteer Part Two).

Carlyle Studios (4) 1881–2 †
rear 296 King's Rd
p *T H Lee*, srvyr
o *G P Jacomb-Hood*, illr; *T Roussel; H Pennington*, illr; *S J Solomon; A Drury*, sc; *J W B Knight; (Sir) W G John*, sc; *E Crowe; F Sandys*, illr, ptr; *G Chowne*
Sizeable spaces suitable for all trades; formerly stables.

SW3 continued

Cedar Studios (4) 1885
45–46 Glebe Place
p *Conrad Dressler*, sc
o *A Hartley; (Sir) S H W Llewellyn;*
A Baccani, sc; *F Pegram*, illr; *A G Walker*, ptr, sc;
C Praetorius, photo; *J W Rollins*, sc; *R Gray*
Flimsy hot-houses (or 'glass shacks' – R Gray) and
brick sheds extending the enterprising Dressler's
Cedar House Studio around its garden.

Chelsea Manor Studios (11 +) 1915
Flood St
p *W J Garlick*
o *Margaret McD Mackintosh*, dsgnr;
M & D Donaldson
A roof-lit pair in a formal block on the street guards
the entrance to a warren of saw-toothery behind.
Cf. *Stanley Stus SW10.*

1, 11, 11a Cheyne Gardens (1886–7)
o *H C Christie*, sc; *W Wiehe Collins*, illr;
L Raven-Hill, illr
Gracile red brick studios terminating contemporary
terrace. No. 1 is integral with house No. 1; self-
contained duo at the N end is largely rebuilt.

Garden Studios (5) 1884; 1890 †
1 Manresa Rd
p *G Chapman; Edward Holland*, archt, dvlpr
o *T Riley; A Hitchens; Amédée Joubert*, dcrtr;
C Praetorius, photo; *Clare Atwood* (school)
Initially one pair behind 278 King's Rd; another
unremarkable pair plus glasshouse is added in 1890
behind No. 276 by local architect.

26, 27 Glebe Place (2) *c.* 1892
o *D Knowles; W Linnell; G Henry* ARA;
Derwent Wood, sc
Double-decker pantechnicon altered over the years;
originally, in all likelihood, the doing of the
figurative sculptor, Gio Fontana, of 25 & 25a
Glebe Pl.

52–59 Glebe Place (8) 1888–9
a *W H Collbran* or *Elton Hawkins*
p *Robert King*, dvlpr
o *H Vos* (school); *W Sickert; H C Clifford;*
(Sir) W Rothenstein; J DaCosta (school);
R Anning Bell, dsgnr; *E H Shepard*, illr; *A Mann;*
W J Neatby, ceramic dsgnr; *G Coates; Helen McKie*
Also known as Glebe Studios. At the front: back-
and side-lit galleried studios, large and lofty. At the
rear: roof-lit square studios with ancillary rooms on
two sides, low-built and relatively confined. Bulky,
punchy, ultra-Dutch facades. Fine photos featuring
exotic additions appear in *World of Interiors*, April
1985.

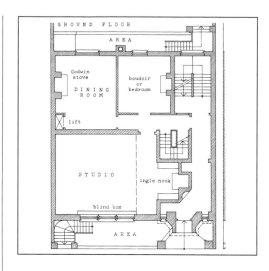

Glebe Studios (2) 1888–9
60, 61 Glebe Place
b (*George Mercer*, crpntr)
p *Revd Gerald Blunt: Anglican Church*
Commissioners
o *Arthur Cadogan Blunt*, dabbler;
F H Townsend, illr
Studio-house nirvana. Admirable resolution of
gable-end lighting despite staircase position in No.
61. Axes of storeys adventurously overlaid.

64, 65 Glebe Place (2) 1890
o *F Pegram*, illr; *R Gray; Maud Porter;*
C M Sheldon, illr; *O Eckhardt*, illr
Skilfully rendered anonymous architectural exercise
on site of former non-conformist chapel. Rearward
unit gains more light and privacy.

Great Cheyne Studios 1890 †
14a Cheyne Row
p *W L Barker*
o *A Pocock*, mason; *G Schaub*, electro-depositor;
T Hughes; H Hughes-Stanton; F W Sargant, sc;
J Tweed, sc; *H Knight*
Local landlord adds extensive studio to stables. Up
to 6 assorted artist-craftspeople here in late 1890s,
early 1900s.

Hans Studios (2) 1893
43a Glebe Place
o *Mary Sargant Florence; Margaret McD &*
C R Mackintosh, dsgnr & archt, ptr
Hugger-mugger pair with periscopes. Earlier partly
workspace rented by Italian masons and Conrad
Dressler of No. 46. Reputedly a safe house for
Suffragettes.

Joubert Studios (5) 1890 †
Jubilee Place/King's Rd corner
p *Amédée Joubert & Sons*, dcrtrs etc
o *Philippe L, Félix, J Amédée Joubert*, crvrs, scs;
(Sir) A Streeton; O Wheatley, sc; *(Sir) W Nicholson;*
W J Donne
Initially Jubilee Studios – No.s 2–4 tiny units, No. 1
only twice as big – built in conjunction with Joubert
Mansions by proprietors of 'The Pheasantry',
152 King's Rd.

King's House Studios (4) 1911
396 King's Rd
p *George White*, printer
o *H Gandy*
White gains ownership of his own printery, yard and
stationery shop (ceased trading 1979), then builds
handsome King's House flats and, finally, 4 studios
in crook of King's Rd kink. Neatly contrived row
with roof terraces.

Merton Villa (2) *c.* 1880 †
280a King's Rd
p *Mrs J B Philip*
o *T S Lee*, sc; *(Sir) J J Shannon; C Buhrer*, sc;
L Holst
After J Birnie Philip's death here in 1875, his
sculptural commissions are completed by Sgr
Fucigna. Philip's daughter Constance and son-in-law
C G Lawson stay until 1882. As the villa is
subdivided, Lee establishes a foundry and painters
invade.

5 Mulberry Walk (2) 1914
o *Miss Elliott; Baron A Rosenkrantz*, stnd gls dsgnr;
C Shepperson, illr
Pretty Neo-Georgian domesticity, prevalent in this
precinct, is interrupted by the hard realities of this
purposeful, end-of-the-era building.

Oakley Studios (1 + 6) 1880– †
Upper Cheyne Row
p *A Mossop*
o *Angelo Castioni*, sc; *C Dressler*, sc;
A Hutchinson, sc; *A W Bowcher*, sc; *E Lanteri*, sc;
P E Stretton, animal ptr; *Biglioski Bros*, scs; *H Speed*
Castioni present from *c.* 1878 at Oakley Cottage
(originally 4th along from Oakley St, S side).
Ghostly Cottage Studio survives but units 1–6 – a
shed divided into garage-sized cells – do not.

141a Old Church Street (2)
No. 141 taken by Thomas Nelson Maclean, sc, in
1875. *C.* 1888 he joins a workshop to the N (owner
Mr Turk). After his death in 1895 another storey is
added; remodelled later still.
Cf. 13a Pembridge Place W11.

SW3 continued

Onslow Studios 1892–1900 †
183 King's Rd
p *W H Martin*, operator
o *C E Holloway*; *C Buhrer*, sc; *H G Fell*;
T F Catchpole; *A S Haynes*; *V Rolt*; *H Speed*
C. 1884 Martin, of The Soudan Syndicate etc.,
appears to build a new house beside Onslow
Cottage, the basis of Onslow College of Art &
Science (est. 1882). Once the Chelsea Arts Club
gathers steam at No. 181, Martin gradually builds up
to 12 sawtooth-lit units behind No. 183, depressing
their rateable value, perhaps, by keeping them in
the college's name.

Radnor Studios (2–5) c. 1878 †
3 Radnor Walk
o *H R Bloomer*; *R A M Stevenson*; *W F Mitchell*;
(Sir) J J Shannon; *A Hartley*; *(Sir) F Short*, engrvr;
(Sir) W Reynolds-Stephens, ptr, sc; *E Holland*, archt;
H Enfield; *C Rea*
'A hole of a place . . . with two desperate studios in
the backyard. . . . I remember that I wanted to lean
my head against the wall and cry.' – E V Lucas, *E A
Abbey RA* (1921). Dickensian refuge for transients,
not all of them hopeless; some facing hard times.

Rossetti Gardens Mansions, St Loo Mansions
1888–90
Flood St, St Loo Ave
a *Frederick Hemings*
b *?H Johnson* of Wood Green
p *Henry C Pennell*
o *J L Barnard*; *W E F Britten*; *L Raven-Hill*, illr;
G D Giles; *Ellen G Cohen*, ptr, sc
Airy attics adapted from the start to suit artists: a
late instance of the garret studio. Hemings also built
nearby and began the vast Albert Court behind the
Albert Hall in SW7.

Rossetti Studios (7) 1894
Flood St
a, p, b *Edward Holland*, archt, dvlpr
o *Ada Holland* (*Mrs Sachs*); *W Maud*, illr; *R Brough*;
H Thaddeus; *A John & (Sir) W Orpen* (Chelsea
School of Art, 1903–6); *G W Lambert*
Apparently built by 1890 but not occupied till 1896
despite the '1894' date tablet. Rossetti House flats
also by Holland who, with Ada, is up for
embezzlement in 1901. Like *The Avenue SW7*, three
2-storey units with rear entrances and picture slits
overlook 4 cloistral singles with corridor access via
caretaker's lodge. Clever, remarkably modern
medium-density housing. Originally £1 per week
each.

St Leonard's Studios (2) 1887
Smith St
a *Walter J Ebbetts*
b *H Baylis*, £615 (*Br* 23.4.1887)
p *Cocks & Elsworthy*, est. agnts
o *(Sir) W Reynolds-Stephens*, ptr, sc;
J W Godward; *W von Glehn*; *M Lawrence*, sc
Owners buy last two houses in St Leonard's Tce and
extend studios over half their gardens. One of the
dinkier pairs in London; split-level; practical double
doors.

Smollett Studios (2) c. 1905
19–21 Cheyne Row
p *Mrs Ellen Barker*
o *Mary Sargant Florence*
Undemonstrative workshop plus glasshouse
beneath painter's studio.

The Studios, 13 (33) Tite Street (3) 1880
a *(Sir) R W Edis*
p *Jackson & Graham*, furnishers
o *J McN Whistler*; *B E Cammell*; *Mrs A Murch*;
M R Corbet; *J S Sargent RA*; *(Dame) Ethel Walker*;
Clara Christian; *F Barnard*; *C Furse*; *C Perugini*;
E B Smith; *R Brough*; *F C Cowper ARA*;
G Philpot; *A John RA*
Study, bedroom, scullery and bathroom come with
each grand studio. Lower one has 18′ × 12′ north
light; others 12′ × 12′ – all with 2′ square panes.
Fine spaces and (once) fine fittings. Elements of
Edis's Woolner job of 1860 reappear here 20 years
on.

Tower House (4) 1884–5
28 (46) Tite Street
a *Edward W Godwin*
b *Macey & Sons*, £6923 (*Br* 2.8.1884)
p *Bailey, Denton, Son & North*, dvlprs
o *G D Giles*; *R C Woodville*; *J McN Whistler*;
R W Macbeth RA; *G Philpot*; *R Christie*
BA 22.5.1885 points out the advantage of having the
kitchen and servant's room above the dining room
and 'best bedrooms'. It alludes also to the goods lift
from the basement (as at *The Studios* opposite and,
later, *Thurloe Stus SW7*) where there is extra storage.
Cheap stone trim outside; oak work by M Allô of
Ghent inside. Top floor views unbeatable.

30 (48) Tite Street (3+) 1894
a *Charles J C Pawley*
o *Maud Porter*; *Ellen Sparks*, leatherwkr;
W F Mayor; *E Skinner*
Narrow flats displaying an amalgam of Tite St styles
by prominent mansion block designer (Victoria St,
Drayton Gdns, Melbury Rd) on a half plot vacant
since the 1870s.

Trafalgar Studios (15) 1878–9 †
Manresa Rd
b, p *John H Brass* of Manresa Rd
o *J E Christie*; *J H Thomas*, sc; *W Holman Hunt*;
G P Jacomb-Hood, illr; *B Bradley*, illr;
E Onslow Ford, sc; *J M Jopling*; *H LaThangue*;
W Trood, *J Emms*, animal ptrs; *F W Lawson*;
E Dade; *P W Steer*; *A Toft*, sc; *Mary E Kindon*;
Edith & Nelson Dawson, ptrs, mtlwkrs;
A Grimshaw; *C P Sainton*;
(Sir) F Brangwyn; *G D Giles*;
(Sir) L Ward, caricaturist, *W M Hale*; *C Condor*;
M L Fairfax, illr; *C M Pearce*
5 basic units on each of 3 floors in industrial-style
mill on E-shaped plan; lower ground floor with
projecting glasshouses and gardens. Porter's lodge
also. See G P Jacomb-Hood, *With Brush and Pencil*
(1925) for life & times of occupants.

Turner Studios (6) 1897
66–71 Glebe Place
p *?Cornwallis West*
p *F Lynn Jenkins*, sc; *G Moira*; *H M Marshall*;
T Sheard (school); *Sir W B Richmond RA*
Bland almshouse-like 2-storeyed terrace, but upper
levels overlook lightsome glazed spaces; now
mostly carved up. Casements became a Glebe Place
vernacular.

Wentworth Studios (8+) 1886 †
Manresa Rd
b, p *John H Brass* of Manresa Rd
o *W Holman Hunt*; *J Havard Thomas*, sc;
G P Jacomb-Hood, illr, (school with
W Thomas Smith); *F M Skipworth*;
(Sir) F Short, engrvr; *(Sir) S H W Llewellyn*;

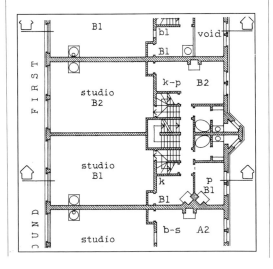

SW3 concluded

Edith & Nelson Dawson, ptrs, mtlwkrs; *E Dade*;
A Hartley; *(Sir) F Brangwyn*, ptr, dsgnr;
C J Watson; *F Pomeroy*, sc; *A S Hartrick*;
Carton Moore Park, illr; *H Poole*, sc;
W J Neatby, ceramic dsgnr; *E Sullivan*, illr
Brass meets with success at *Trafalgar Stus SW3* next
door. He then converts his own villa, extends
behind, and adds a further 5 units – triplets and
twins – parallel to each other across a courtyard.
Former tenants keep allegiance. NEAC and the Arts
Club Ball nurtured here. See G P Jacomb-Hood,
ut supra, and J Bignell, *Chelsea Seen* (1981).

4 Yeoman's Row (4) 1900-2
a, **p** *W H Collbran*, archt, dvlpr
b *W Mitchell & Son* of Dulwich
o *Hayes*; *Birkbeck*
The Yeoman's Row story is best followed in *SoL 41*.
Attractive compact building with typical 1900-style
pylons (spoilt) and grids, incorporating 4 studio-
flats and a shop.

6, 8, 10 Yeoman's Row *c.* 1923
No.s 6, 8 and 10 were originally built *c.* 1892 as the
first stage of stables and rooms for the Egerton
Place mansion flats. Another, No. 12, added *c.* 1896,
completed half the scheme. No.s 6, 8 and 10, at
least, converted into appealing studios in the 1920s.

14, 16, 18 Yeoman's Row (9) 1898-9
b *Charles E Bassington* of Camberwell
p *W H Collbran & ditto*
o *A Ludovici Jnr*, ptr, illr; *Anne J Challice*;
Lady Egerton; *Douglas Wells*, archt, ptr;
R J E Moony
Originally known as 1–3 Egerton Place Stus. (For
'Egerton Stus', see Brompton Rd SW3 in Gazetteer
Part Two). High-density, no-frills paintboxes; £30
p.a. basement, £60 p.a. upper floors in 1905. No. 18
(top) converted in 1935 by Dr Wells Coates into a
Dymaxion studio-house – *Archl Review*, vol. 82,
1937.

SW4

Eagle House *c.* 1897
cnr Clapham Common S Side & Narbonne Ave
Two strikingly skylit studios behind suave turn-of-
century house said to have been a surgeon's, but a
painter has left a tell-tale mark on it, too.

SW6

Chelsea Studios *c.* 1920–
410–416 Fulham Rd
J W Godward, ptr, builds studio at No. 410 in 1894.
Mario Manenti (1885–1954) establishes sculpture
foundry behind own house at No. 416 *c.* 1920; adds
3 studios with rooms behind No. 414 in 1925–6;
buys No.s 410 & 412, adding 6 more residential
studios to rear of No. 412 by 1930. Subsequent
addition of further 10 units behind No. 416
completes 'Italian Village'.

404a–d Fulham Road (4) 1899
p *W Mainwaring Palin*, ptr
o *W M Palin*; *W Wiehe Collins*, illr; *W L Hankey*, illr
Four units builts between former No. 404, owned
by Palin, and Stamford Bridge Athletic Ground.
Three remain, crammed against cliff-face of football
stadium wall.

Fulham Studios (5) 1890– †
452b Fulham Rd
o *W Smith & R G Wheaton*, archl scs
String of basic workshops between Fulham Rd and
railway line. Popular with Latin masons.

Fulham Studios (6) 1884 †
454a Fulham Road
p *?Aristide Louis Fabbrucci*, sc
o *A L Fabbrucci*, sc; *Alice Chaplin*, sc;
J McN Whistler; *W Sickert*; *A Drury*, sc; *C B Birch*, sc;
H J Stock; *R Sheppard*, sc; *P R & H Montford*, scs;
A Broadbent, sc; *H Gaudier-Brzeska*, sc
Similar to *452b Fulham Rd*, attracting superior
talents. Whistler's h.q. during his notorious RBA
days when the fawning assistance of Sickert and
Mortimer Menpes ('The Kangaroo') sharpened his
gentle art to a needle point. Gaudier-Brzeska was
jealous of the 'furnace to do plaster moulds' in the
largest unit: No. 6 – once Fabbrucci's.

The Glasshouse (5) 1906
11, 12 Lettice St
b *?W N Froy* of Hammersmith
p *Mary Lowndes & Alfred J Drury*, stnd gls
dsgnrs
o *ditto*; *Leo Malempré*; *Henry Holiday*, ptr, dsgnr
Pinched, railway-cheapened redevelopment site.
Two adjoining houses included in the scheme.
Almost a railway signal box with swingeing
windows, but not beautiful. Important Arts & Crafts
Movement stained-glass workshops and showrooms
still active.

Pomona House (6) *c.* 1897
111 New King's Rd
a *?F A Powell*; *?C R Guy Hall*
p *Charles J Praetorius*, photo
o *A Dixon*; *Charles E Dixon*, photo;
C Praetorius, photo; *E A Thiede*
After an unsettled career in Chelsea and South
Kensington Praetorius invests the profits from his
Art Reproduction Co. Formerly a symmetrical
building with similarities to *Edwardes Square
Stus W8* and *Alma Stus W8*, but still eye-catching.

St Oswald's Studios (5) 1902
80a Sedlescombe Rd
a *Walter Cave*
b *Wenden & Co.* of East Ham
o *H Davie*; *W Smith & R G Wheaton*, archl scs;
A Campbell & F Christmas, stnd gls dsgnrs;
F C Tilney; *J A Stevenson*, sc
Part of the surrounding estate for which Cave
supplied standard house designs. Reputedly flanked
an archery ground; hence the stout fence and linear
form. Flexible narrow spaces and storage galleries
bordering the length of the studios which can be
divided easily. Economy plus.

Stamford Bridge Studios (4+) *c.* 1886 †
16 Wandon Rd
p *Marwood Gooding*
o *G Merry*; *E W Roberts*; *G F Carline*; *Ida Lovering*;
S Nicholson Babb, sc; *O Sheppard*, sc;
O Ramsden & A Carr, slvrsmths; *H Ospovat*, illr;
L S Merrifield, sc
Shanty-town; no more, no less. 6/- a week in 1890.

SW7

Alexandra House 1884-6
Bremner Rd
a *C Purdon Clarke*
b *Lucas Bros*; (Doulton ceramics)
p *Royal College of Music & Royal Academy*
Garret studios, once with a view over Kensington
Gardens, for female art students in a hall of
residence.

The Avenue (20+) 1870–
Sydney Close, 76 Fulham Rd
b, **p** *(Sir) Charles Freake*, dvlpr
o *Sir J E Boehm RA*, sc; *C Lutyens*; *C E Hallé*;
C Hunter; *F Dicey*; *Sir C B Lawes*, sc;
Sir F S Haden, etchr; *R C Belt*, sc; *R Glassby*, sc;
A Bruce Joy, sc; *E Thompson (Lady Butler)*;

SW7 concluded

J Wolf, animal ptr; *J Willis Good*, sc; *W Linnell*; *Anna Lea Merritt*; *(Sir) A Gilbert RA*, sc; *Sir E Poynter RA*; *C & J Stuart*; *E O Ford ARA*, sc; *M R Corbet*; *A Toft*, sc; *G E Wade*, sc; *J Tweed*, sc; *H Harvey*, sc; *J S Sargent RA*; *P W Steer*
A culturally sensitive entrepreneur, Freake cleverly completed the conversion of Strong's Place mews, already substantially undertaken on behalf of Baron Marochetti, to launch the speculation in cheapish artists' accommodation in S-W London. Boehm's leading hand in the tutorship of Princess Louise was lent, it is said, in the absence of chaperon and assistants here. Poynter, ensconced on his mezzanine, would startle importunate callers when they knocked at his downstairs door by whispering into a speaking tube with a concealed outlet. A hive of industry especially congenial to sculptors. See *SoL 41*, pp. 102–3 and G B Shaw, *Love Among the Artists* (1888), Constable, 1924, pp. 288–9.

Clareville Studios (7) 1889 †
27 Clareville Grove
o *Louise Jopling*; *D Hardy*, illr; *E T Reed*, illr; *W G King*; *F Sandys*, illr, ptr; *R Jack*; *J W Swynnerton*, sc; *Annie Swynnerton*; *H Quilter*, jnlst
Row of plain units on W corner with Clareville St. Jopling conducted a painting school at No.s 1 & 2 *c*. 1889–92. See her *20 Years of My Life* (1925). Outline plan at Kensington Public Library.

Clareville Grove 1889–
Following the eponymous group at No. 27, other studios appeared by degrees at 1a, 5a (by 1891) and 3a, 3b, 5b (all by *c*. 1903). 1a started life as a kindergarten. Blitz-rattled assortment sheltering lesser lights.

4, 5 Cromwell Place 1859
a *?William Tasker*
b, **p** *(Sir) Charles Freake*, dvlpr
o *3rd Earl Somers*; *Sir Coutts & Lady Lindsay*; *R Cholmondeley*, ptr, sc; *C Couzens*, min, ptr; *Hon. A Stuart-Wortley*; *Sir J D Linton* (school *c*. 1892); *Sir J Lavery RA*
Earliest pair of off-the-hook gentlemen's studio-houses in S-W London, strategically placed next to Albertopolis. Only No. 5 survives as such, but without its star-spangled ceiling – a scheme repeated for Lindsay at his Grosvenor Gallery. Occasionally let to friends.

151a Gloucester Road (4) 1884–
p *?F Holdstock*; *Sarah Paskell*;

J H Bridgewater;
o *H P MacCarthy*, sc; *G G Manton*; *A J Elsley*; *Alice Grant*
Samuel Paskell's picture restoration workshops appear to have been converted after his death. Badly shaken in the Blitz, little evidence remains.

Oratory Studios (2) 1894 †
16 Fulham Rd
b, **p** *King & Co.*, bldrs
o *S F Monier Williams*, archt; *E Stourton*, sc; *C G Anderson*
Also a coach depot, coal merchants' yard, estate agent's shop and a house.

43–45 Roland Gardens (4) 1891–2
a, **p** *J A J Keynes*
b *Clarke & Co.* of South Kensington
o *Sarah Vaughan*; *P F Maitland*; *Prof. G Sauter*
Elegant and luminous in a blaze of red brickwork, now a little dulled. See *SoL 41*, pp. 153–4. Keynes was providing Martin Jacolette's photographic studios at 42 Harrington Rd SW7 at the same date. Refer, also, to 45 Evelyn Gdns SW7 (Gazetteer Part Two).

49 Roland Gardens (5) 1892–3
a, **p** *J A J Keynes*
b *Sherries & Co.* of Chelsea
o *G Petrie*; *F M Lutyens*; *J S W Hodges*; *Mrs Barnard*; *Mary Carlisle*
A rookery of average aspect containing 3 flats and 5 studio-flats with N-lights cascading down the rear façade. Clearly Keynes also designed No. 47 – the local studio-mania has infected it, too.

Sussex Mansions (2) 1896–8
Sussex Place (Old Brompton Rd)
a *W H Collbran*
b *Rider & Sons*; *Carmichael* (*Br* 25.4. & 25.7.1896)
o *Josephine White*
Collbran was a crypto-studiophile. Cf. the contemporary *4 Yeoman's Row SW3* which has similar rectilinear features. Basements and tiny rear yards. Also cf. the later rear of Thurloe Court, 117 Fulham Rd SW7.

Thurloe Studios (7) 1885–7
5 Thurloe Square
a *?C W Stephenson*, srvyr
b, **p** *William Douglas*, bldr, dvlpr
o *H R Bloomer*; *L C Powles*; *A J Ryle*; *C G Anderson*; *A F Hughes*
An extreme example of the developer's conviction that artists would rent a cheap studio, no matter what size or shape. But only slender talents ever visited this wickedly opportunistic sliver of Aesthetic attenuation both vertical and horizontal.

SW10

Bolton Studios (27 +) 1883–8
Redcliffe Rd/Gilston Rd
a *?F N Kemp*
b *?A McClymont*
p *C Bacon*, sc; *Misses Bacon*; *W R Andrew*
o *C Bacon*, sc; *St G Hare*; *M Greiffenhagen*, ptr, illr; *T Roussel*; *T B Kennington*; *R Harris*; *H Ryland*; *J W Godward*; *A or L Grimshaw*; *G D Giles*
No.s 2–20 are single-storeyed and similar, No.s 21 27, mostly £90 p.a. by 1900, are on several levels and each slightly differs from its neighbour. All are equally claustrophobic. Rumour has it that there was a central kitchen and room service – and that not all the Edwardian lady residents earned a living by the brush alone. A unique but doomed building.

8, 9 South Bolton Gardens (2) 1903; 1929
a *Walter Cave*; *Forbes & Tate*
b *F G Minter*
p Sub-lease from *Gunter Estate*
o *(C Desclayes*, stnd gls dsgnr); *(Sir) W Nicholson*; *Sir W Orpen RA*; *Sir Hugh Lane*; *A P Garrett*; *Sir J J Shannon RA*
Formerly numbered 5, 6 Osborne House Studios; now, remodelled, the only survivors of a project including 4 other houses (*Br* 6.2.1904, 9.10.1931; *Country Life* 20.9.1930). Judging by the painter's taste in decoration Osbert Sitwell did not call Orpen the 'supreme Irish carpenter and flashlight photographer' without reason.

17a, 19a Edith Grove 1902
o *C Praetorius*, photo; *(Mrs W de Morgan)*
Undistinguished detached pair in hotbed of similar developments. By 1915 No. 25 Edith Grove has 7 residents, 5 of them maiden lady artists.

Gunter Hall Studios (4) 1921–4
Gunter Grove
p *?Percival Landon*
o *C D Ward*
Formerly stable ground beside the W Brompton Congregational Chapel (later a public hall, etc.). Not unlike *St Oswald's Stus SW6* in shape, they were possibly originally entered from *Milton House SW10* (*q.v.*).

Harley Studios (2) 1894
16, 17 Cresswell Place
p *?C E Melchers*
o *J Tweed*, sc; *W B Fagan*, sc; *D A Thomas*, sc
Bolton Mews redevelopment. Ordered facade, matching windows; common hallway, economical plan. All much spoiled.

SW10 concluded

Milton House (2–3) 1922
2 Fernshaw Rd
p *F E Williams*
o *H Poole*, sc, dsgnr
Several flats and sculpture studios converted from a former girls' reformatory. Somehow linked to *Gunter Hall Stus SW10*.

Raeburn Studios (3) 1910
11 Edith Grove
o *H E Compton*; *A Bentley*; *M Osborne*
Part of the piecemeal development between Edith and Netherton Groves. Childe & Doubell, stnd gls ptrs, at No. 7 *c.* 1895 onwards. A little backland village.

Redcliffe Road 1903–
p (*A*) *G S Foster*; (*B*) *E R Johnson*
o *N Hardy*; *Miss Campbell-McCallum*; *B Evans*; (*E Bawden*; *E Ravilious*)
From 1903 (*A*) converted No.s 34, 37, 38 and (*B*) No. 52 into studio-flats by remodelling façades and roofs of 1860s terraced houses. Some 10 houses were altered by 1920s. No.s 33, 34, 43 known as *Cathcart Stus*; No.s 52, 53 as *Holbein Stus*; No. 37 as *Tenniel* or *Leighton Stus*. Usually 3 units in each; some now reconstructed. A response to the success of nearby *Bolton* and *Stanley Stus SW10*.

5 Seymour Walk (2) 1893–7
o *Jane Griffin*; *G H Chadburn*; *Edith Maryon*, sc
The late Regency Holly Lodge is overrun by lady

artists after 1885. A small studio is added, then another similar. On the face of it these are taken over and combined into one larger (extant) workshop *c.* 1910 by Ramsden & Carr of St Dunstan's Studio next door (3a Seymour Walk).

Stanley Studios (9 +) 1896
Stanley Mansions, Park Walk
p *Alice G McKay*
o *May L Lucas*; *Fanny Stable*; *Sarah Vaughan*
As with *Rossetti Stus SW3* where provision for supervision is likewise included, the flats were built first (1890–2). A corral of close-grained, skylit units popular amongst, and perhaps devoted to, lady artists.

SW11

Albert Studios (8) 1898
Albert Mansions, Albert Bridge Rd
a *?W J Chambers* (*Br* 25.6.1898)
b *C Fifield* of Woking, £1500
p *Juba Kennerley & J Halley*, archt
o *A G Morrow*; *Ramsden & Carr*, slvrsmths; *N H Hardy*, illr
Exquisite row incorporating Picturesque devices, looking onto mansions' garden while only a short step from Battersea Park. Halley and Chambers put up Albert Palace Mansions nearby; Kennerley and, presumably, Chambers put up Cranbourne Court: up the road, nearer the river.

Anhalt Studios (2) *c.* 1907
Anhalt Rd
o *P R Montford*, sc; *R G Wheaton*, sc
Diminutive pair with front doors at the 'back' leading to useful double-height spaces.

W1

8 Fitzroy Street *c.* 1878– †
o *Weedon Grossmith*; *W Cave Thomas*; *C E Holloway*; *F S Richardson*; *J McN Whistler*; *W Sickert*; *A John*; (*D Grant*; *Vanessa Bell*)
A 'vast rambling rookery of a place' – M Lilly, *Sickert* . . . (1971). See also Q Bell & A Garnett, *V Bell's Family Album* (1981) – it contained twin studios: '. . .They were huge and reached by an iron passage which reverberated like stage thunder as people walked along it'. One of a few old Fitzrovian houses which were more than just flats with cut-up windows, e.g., 10 Fitzroy St W1 and *Hogarth Stus W1*. Known later as Whistler Stus.

Hogarth Studios 1876–80
64 Charlotte St
p *William Edwin Heath*, engineer & gasfitter
o *W Logsdail*; *W Goodall*; *Gibbs & Howard*, stnd gls ptrs; H R Bloomer; *T R Miles*; *J Aumonier*; *C E Holloway*; *C O Skilbeck*; *C N Worsley*; *Baroness E Orczy*; *O Fleuss*, stnd gls ptr
Victorianisation of 100 year-old terraced house. Indeterminate alterations not likely to be by same designer as that of Heath's *23 Camden Road Stus NW1*.

Langham Chambers (5 +) 1854–70 †
All Souls' Place
p *G Stainer & others*
o *Wyon dynasty*, mdlsts, scs, ptrs; *J Soden*; *Lowes Dickinson*; *J Luard*; (*Sir*) *J E Millais ARA*; *W C Dobson*; *M F Halliday*; *W Gale*; *A J Stark*; *H W B Davis*; *L Duncan*; *M Stone*; *C Schloesser*; *F D Millett*; *Sir D Murray RA*; *V Davis*; *H Field*, archt; *R Bunny*
Premises enlarged and adapted for The Artists' Society (est. 1830) and the Langham Sketching Club (est. 1838). Studios and chambers for use of Society members on a residential hotel basis. Dating from the 1850s, these are thus almost the earliest of studio groups. Bombed 1940.
See *Country Life* 13.11.1980.

Langham Studios (3) *c.* 1855–1910
5 All Souls' Place
a *?Horace Field & Ptnr*
p *Jonathon Soden*, ptr, *& successors*
o Include some *Langham Chambers* lodgers
As it does on other adjoining sites, the Artists' Society, whose h.q. lay opposite, more or less commandeers rooms on this property which wraps around the dead end of All Souls' Pl. A mixed redevelopment *c.* 1910 of a conversion *c.* 1880 embraces formal studio-flats on a repeated plan. Sweetly scaled, with historical motifs.

W2

Fulthorpe Studios (4 + 4) *c.* 1898– †
3, 5 Warwick Ave
o *?G C Hards*; *Win Austen*; *S Kent*; *A Ludovici Jnr*, illr; *A & S Kendrick*; (*L Freud*; *F Topolski*)
Assorted units, 8 in all by the 1920s, within and without decrepit old houses. On the site of Rembrandt Gardens.

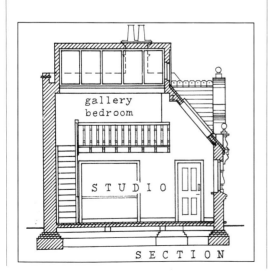

gallery
bedroom

STUDIO

SECTION

W2 concluded

Hurlingham House Studios (2) *c.* 1909
3–5 Blomfield Crescent (Westbourne Tce Rd)
p *?Frome & Son*, landlords
o *James L Henry*; *L Edith C Maryon*, sc
These 2 detached units were built on garden
ground when adjoining terraced houses dating from
the 1850s were converted into flats. Straightforward,
well-lit spaces with minimal extras; delightfully
embowered in summer.

Queensborough Studios (3) *c.* 1890
Queensborough Tce Mews
p *Frederick J Foxley*
o *J A Cull*; *C Sims*
Three preposterous flats buttressed by a stair tower
built over the Circle Line.

W4

Gainsborough Studios (4 +) *c.* 1894
10 Gainsborough Rd, Bedford Park
o *M M Giles (Mrs B Jenkin)*, sc; *E W Cook*;
D Carr, ptr, archt; *Hely Smith*; *F Jackson*
Two parallel pairs in double and single storey
versions built on less desirable land adjacent to the
railway. A late response to the artistic appeal of
Bedford Park.

Woodstock Studios (5) *c.* 1910
Corner of Woodstock & Bedford Rds
o *P A Staynes*
Probably ad hoc adaptations of Powell's estate
workshops and builder's yard. Frederick William
Peel was 'architect to the estate' at the time. Altered.

W6

The Grove Studios (2 + 1) *c.* 1891–5
17 Adie Rd
o *A M Pearson*; *M W Webb*; *P J Thornhill*;
O Fleuss, stnd gls ptr
Ultra-basic pair nonetheless designed with some
care, and a foreign later addition.

Margravine Studios (4) 1890
2–8 Margravine Gdns
b, p *(Gibbs &) Flew*, bldrs
o *N H Hardy*; *C M Padday*; *W F Mayor*; *F Brooks*;

A P Garrett; *E O Hoppé*, photo
Ubiquitous local speculating builders (known to
their creditors as 'Glue & Fibs') making the most
acute part of their 2–12 Margravine Gdns
railwayside wedge into low-class artists' dwellings.
Cosmetic 'Queen Annery' including apposite
terracotta 'margravine'; train-spotters' stair-tower at
apex of site.

Orchard Studios (3) *c.* 1887
15a, b, c Brook Green
Semi-detached red brick couple with cart before
the-horse plans. A later bungalow unit adds to the
visual discomfort. Contemporaries of *Brook Green
Stus W6* across the Green.

W8

Alma Studios (3) 1898–1903
Stratford Rd
a, p *Charles R Guy Hall*, archt
b *John Barker & Co., Bldg Dept*
o *J W Schofield*; *H Morley*; *P Wyndham Lewis*
Originally conceived as 'Wynnstay Stus'; reworked
and redesigned 1902–3 (LCC Planning Applctn
Cases 719, 834, 874). 3 flats with south-side
balconies and a range of tiny rooms beyond
yawning N-lights, the roof window framed by crow-
stepped parapets. Cf. *Edwardes Square Stus W8*.

6 Bedford Gardens (2) *c.* 1871
b, p *Jeremiah Little*, bldr
o *E S Kennedy*; *James Archer*; *W L & C W Wyllie*;
G C & W C Horsley; *O Scholderer*; *L Bogle*.

12 Bedford Gardens (2) *c.* 1871–
b, p *Jeremiah Little*, bldr
o *F D Hardy*; *H Speed*; *G Motra*;
F Lynn Jenkins, sc
Like preceding example, crude rebuilding by local
developer on ground laid waste and cheapened by
new Underground line. Early Kensington flats.

55a (75) Bedford Gardens (3) *c.* 1877
a *?R Phené Spiers*
o *A Stokes*; *J B Yeats*, illr, ptr; *H J Ford*, illr;
A D McCormick
Relatively early double-height studio-flats with
pretentious superficial treatment; deemed just wide
enough for thinnifer artists.

57 (77) Bedford Gardens (10) 1883
a *R Stark Wilkinson*
b *Perry & Co.* of Bow

p *Percy Ball*, sc
o *P Ball*, sc; *R Stark*, sc; *A Tomson*;
(Sir) S H W Llewellyn; *P Craft*; *P M Lindner*;
H Bates, sc; *Baron A Rosenkrantz*, stnd gls dsgnr;
G I Bulleid
Ball probably met Wilkinson through Doultons.
Good use of a 'typewriter' section to provide
skylights atop side lights as Ashbee did later.
Finding themselves confined from the outset,
residents annexed adjoining units on the same floor
whenever they could. A curiosity.

20, 20a Campden Hill Gardens *c.* 1895
o *Mary Breakell*; *L T Watts*
Pair of flats substituted for proposed end-of-terrace
house. Completely altered (*SoL 37* p. 96;
Br 1.4.1871).

28, 28a Campden Hill Gardens *c.* 1872
p *?Jeremiah Little*, bldr
o *J J Napier*; *A Wasse*; *Lisa Stillman*;
A Birkenruth, illr; *H Grant*
Ungainly flats squeezed in behind No. 30.

Campden Hill Studios (2) *c.* 1879 †
Campden Hill Rd, S of Phillimore Walk, W side
a, p *W A S Benson*, archt
o *W A S Benson*, archt, mtlwkr; *E J Sartoris*;
A Lemon; *(Sir) E Burne-Jones ARA*;
Edward Clifford; *R & H Stiles*, photo;
Argent Archer, photo
Unassuming semi-detached units with glazed
gablets – photos at Kensington Public Library.
Benson's sometime client, Burne-Jones, worked on
the vast *Arthur in Avalon* here *c.* 1884 onwards.

Cheniston Gardens Studios (3) 1882
b, p *Taylor & Cumming* of Kensington, bldrs,
dvlprs
o *M J Moberly*; *P F Maitland*; *A Jones*, sc; *L Calkin*;
H Hampton, sc
Sheer luxury for the time. Service zone below;
dining room/parlour and bedroom at ground level;
galleried studio above. Opportunistic use of dead
corner in the Gardens – largely by the same
builders. Cf. *St Paul's Stus W14*.

Edwardes Square Studios (6) 1892–3
a *Charles R Guy Hall*
b *Leslie & Co.* (*Br* 22.10.1892, 10.12.1892), £2537
p *John Crowle*, dvlpr
o *W Wontner*; *H J Ford*, illr; *F S Beaumont*;
H Macbeth-Raeburn, ptr, engrvr; *J Y Hunter*;
A Stokes; *F Cadogan Cowper ARA*; *P Annigone*
Crowle and Hall were also responsible for the
former stables and granaries adjacent. Pleasantly
sited spacious flats on a symmetrical plan. Florid
heraldic frontispiece by illiterate carver.

W8 continued

18 Kensington Court Place 1883–4
a *?W G Flint*; *?H Powys Adams* (*SoL 42*,
H Hobhouse, ed., GLC 1986 p.51)
p *Barker & Roscoe*, est. agnts, srvyrs, dvlprs
o *A Mackworth*; *H Glazebrook*;
W G Collingwood; *A Lemon*; *C Shepperson*, illr;
F Appleyard; *G Lenfesty*
Mixed 'Queen Anne-ish' development including 2
or 3 modern garret studios by speculators who own
up to other tall blocks of flats in this immediate
vicinity and the South Kensington Station buildings.

Kensington Studios (7) 1888
(Tarn Mews)/Kelso Place
b *?Charles Liney*
p *?Charles Liney*; *Cecil Crofton* (Kens. Vestry Mins
1888–9)
o *C Sillem*, animal ptr; *Isabel G White*;
Millicent E Gray, illr
Like *Camden Stus W1*, this graceless group built over
the railway line in down-market territory may be
attributed to the builder whose yard adjoined. Both
the plans (some units are impossibly polygonal)
and the lighting suggest buildings previously in
different use.

Kensington Gardens Studios (5–7) *c.* 1904
27a–29a Notting Hill Gate S
a *?R Phené Spiers*
o *E Mills*; *P Wyndham Lewis* (*c.* 1937–57)
Variety of sizeable working and residential units in
region of present Rabbit Row. Over-building of this
class of studio and noisy location led to lack of
interest. Interior photos in Lewis literature.

Logan Studios (2) 1905
1–2 Logan Place
a *?Gilbert Jenkins*
p *?Hugh Muir*
No. 1 originally matched the more-glass-than-wall
No. 2. Largish, attractive late-comers which appear
to have links with the later No.s 3–8 Logan Pl. next
door as well as the earlier 22 Cromwell Rd West SW5
studio behind. Reconstructed for recent theatrical
use.

2a, b Pembroke Road (3–4) *c.* 1900
o *Sydney Newcombe*, archt;
Bertha Newcombe
Infill in highly susceptible part of Kensington. Self-
effacing, defensive façade possibly by Newcombe
who designed studios in Pembroke Square.

Pembroke Studios (12) 1890
Pembroke Gdns
a *?Rolfe & Matthews*
b *Charles F Kearley* of Kensington, bldr, dvlpr
o *H E Detmold*, ptr, illr; *A Mann*; *H J Draper*;
H Ryland; *O von Glehn*; *A Sassoon*, ptr, sc;
Clara Christian; *(Dame) Ethel Walker*; *J Y Hunter*;
D Hockney
Erected on a residual pocket of market garden by a
merchant builder who put up several local blocks
of mansion flats. Certainly one of the more
considered and ostensibly desirable groups in
London, but half the units came without private
outdoor space and none had residential amenities
worth speaking of. High rents will also have
contributed to a lack of popularity early on.

Pembroke Walk Studios (6) *c.* 1902
Pembroke Walk
o *T H Liddell*; *Effie Stillman*, sc;
E Gordon Craig, illr, dsgnr
Half the back gardens of 38–42 Pembroke Sq.
belonged to No. 40. Three mutually respectful units
built on this tranquil site immediately became
associated with 2 more – initially used as
gymnasiums – behind No.s 43–44. A 6th unit,
possibly the earlier building behind 8 Pembroke Rd
(occupied by the illr Alfred Chantrey Corbould), or
maybe a converted portion of the builder Thomas
Heath's workshops, completed the original
grouping.

St Alban's Studios (8) 1911
South End
a *R Douglas Wells*, archt, ptr
p *Charles Saunders*, est. agnt, srvyr; *R D Wells*
o *R D Wells*, archt; *Lillian Hall*, min. ptr;
Miss Murray, photo
An unlikely, half-timbered and Tudoresque, 2-
storeyed toytown on a half-doughnut plan – scaled
so diminutively that neighbourliness is essential. See
SoL 42, H Hobhouse, ed., GLC, 1986, p. 148. Built
on the site of Clarendon Mews (by Frederick
Saunders, bldr).

Scarsdale Studios (10) 1890–1
Stratford Rd
b *Goddard & Sons* of Farnham
o *G Cowell*, ptr, sc; *J S Fox*; *F S Beaumont*;
Edith Sprague
Expropriation of parts of the adjoining Stratford Rd
terrace (1863) provided the site. Carriageway
topped by a much-altered caretaker's perch. Some
flats with mezzanines, but mostly factory units with
north-light roofs and a press of ancillaries at the
gallery end. Typical Victorian ingenuity in the
functional tradition.

Stratford Avenue (6) 1879–82
Stratford Rd
b *G C Butt* of Bayswater
p *Francis W Dollman*, solicitor
o *P T Williams*; *(Sir) A S Cope*; *C P Downing*;
C T Garland; *R C Woodville*; *W Prehn*, sc;
G H Barrable; *J W Nicol*; *J R Weguelin*;
(Sir) F Brangwyn, ptr, dsgnr; *A Melville*;
Dorothy Woolner; *W J Donne*;
London School of Art
First 5 units built within 2 years; No. 6 later; porter's
rooms later still. Superior plans but with limited
application to this site. A blend of sophistication
and picturesqueness results from the designer's
artful intent. Butt had just built 11–13 Stratford Rd,
while Dollman had financed the building of 1–27
Scarsdale Villas (*SoL 42*, H Hobhouse, ed., GLC,
1986, pp. 232, 235).

38a (32a) Victoria Road (2) *c.* 1880
S-W cnr St Alban's Grove
p *T O Barlow RA*, engrvr
Puzzling, but it seems this pair of well-matched
studio-flats was added to the much older Victoria
Rd house (Auburn Lodge). Horace Field made
alterations for C E Perugini, ptr, on his succession
to Auburn Lodge in 1891. Probably privately let.

Warwick Studios (5) 1883–4
St Mary Abbot's Place/Kensington High St
b *T Pink & Co.* of Vincent Square
o *H C Harper*; *(Sir) P Burne-Jones*; *H G Stormont*;

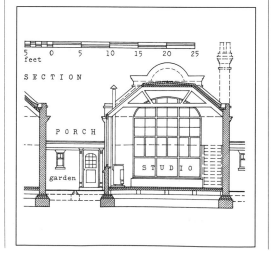

W8 concluded

W G Robertson; P A Hay; Miss C I Verner; F Baden-Powell, ptr, sc; J G Borglum, sc; A Fisher, dsgnr, slvrsmth (school); F F Foottet, etchr; T H Liddell

Largely top-lit single-storey units in a four-square block behind 1–3 Warwick Gdns, with a frontage to Kensington High St. Such a valuable position led to redevelopment: conversion into 2-storey flats called Warwick Close in the 1920s. While a teacher at the Central School of Art, Alex Fisher held private classes (1896 onwards) here, convenient to his own studio down the lane. Robertson describes a visit by Ellen Terry in his *Time Was* (1931). (My thanks to Mr Roderick Ham.)

W11

Lansdowne House (6) 1901
Crnr Lansdowne & Ladbroke Rds
a *William Flockhart*
p *(Sir) Edmund Davis*, mining mogul
o *C Rea; Constance Halford*, ptr, sc (*Mrs Rea* 1907); *C Ricketts*, ptr, illr; *C Shannon*, ptr, illr; *G W Lambert; G Philpot; F Cayley Robinson*, ptr, illr; *J Pryde*, ptr, illr; *V Forbes*
Belle Epoque opulence par excellence – a monument to British cultural imperialism. Only 1 of the 6 luxurious double-height studio-flats remains as such, but it is still outwardly a grand stock brick edifice. See Ricketts & Shannon literature for interior photos.

42 Linden Gardens (?3) *c.* 1880
p *Edouard Rischgitz*, grangeriser
o *Rischgitz family; Ada Bell; Anne Marks*, illr; *L Thackeray*, illr; *G W Bayes*, sc
c. 1878 Thomas Creswick's house (built by Thomas Allason, archt, *c.* 1827) and studio (*c.* 1840) pass from Mrs Creswick to The Linden Club. Rischgitz develops extra studios, 'Cambridge Lodge', as adjacent tube line downgrades the property. Popular with lady flower ptrs.

14a, b Pembridge Crescent, (2) 1882
a *H A Rawlins*
p *B E Ward & G G Manton*, ptrs
o *H S Mendelssohn*, photo (both units)
Pair of 28′ × 19′ units on a back garden site. Varied slightly from the original proposal (Kens. Bldg Applctn Case 312); now greatly altered. Ward was head of the St John's Wood Art School, Manton a portraitist.

13a Pembridge Place (3) 1878
o *Dorsfield Hardy; F D Hardy; E B Leighton; James Archer*
Three flats like a glass-fronted 4-drawer filing cabinet on an infill site. Similar to *55a/75 Bedford Gdns W8*.

22a, b Pembridge Villas (2) *c.* 1901 †
Chepstow Villas crnr
b, p *Brodrick Bros*, bldrs
Converted stable buildings which were in existence 30 years earlier.

W14

Addison Studios (6) *c.* 1887 †
(21–31) Blythe Rd
o *A F & W J Muckley*, illrs; *C Sims; A P F Ritchie*, illr; *J Hassall*, illr
Four matching units plus one larger and another larger again, all with extra rooms, of undetermined form.

12 Beaumont Avenue (1 + 3) 1883–95
p *Albert Bruce Joy*, sc
o *A B Joy*, sc; *G W Joy; Mme Cassavetti*, sc; *S G Mawson*, sc; *C A Bird; H Becker*
The Irish portrait sculptor builds the studio-house here but leaves it in 1899 after attaching fair-sized units. Possibly a foundry incorporated early on.

Brook Green Studios *c.* 1885
2 Dunsany Rd
p *Frederick & Francis Hawkes*
o *Arthur Hill; Alyn Williams*, min. ptr; *J W Forster*
A private art school with transient staff and students in a compact block. Converted into flats. Hill learned to forge Alma Tademas.

1 Challoner Street 1887
a *?Francis L Pither* (*Br* 11.6.1887)
b *?Stephenson* of Bishopsgate
Fourth of four arty red brick houses (e.g., sash horns resemble the stylised clouds in Japanese prints) has built-in access to polyvalent rear building. Shady history involves kindergarten, dancing school, studios, gambling den, etc. *Ex inf.* Xian Morgan. House No. 3 occupied by Mrs Maria Spartali Stillman from 1886. No. 2 with studio from *c.* 1890.

11 (51–57) Holland Park Road (4) *c.* 1886 †
o *A Wasse; S Paget*, ptr, illr; *R Peacock; P Buckman*, illr; *G Spencer Watson; J H F Bacon; Eleanor F Brickdale*, illr

Purpose-built N-S line of units on S side of Holland Park Rd, opposite Prinsep's house. G L Taylor's E F Brickdale exhibition catalogue (1972–3) gives photo of her here.

17 (39) Holland Park Road (2) *c.* 1880–1901 †
o *J W Wilson; J H Lorimer; Prof. G B Amendola*, sc; *E Hopkins*, illr; *L L Brooke*, illr, ptr; *P A Hay; Gifford Lenfesty; H P Clifford*
Giff & Cliff ran a painting school within, shortly before a storey was added to this early St Mary Abbot's Terrace mews conversion, making 2 studio-flats

32a, 32b Holland Park Road (2) 1900
a *Albert E Cockerell*
p *?Henry S Coxeter*
o *R Peacock* (32a); *P A Hay* (32b)
Parisian-style ateliers on the site of St George's Riding School: separate 5- and 3-storey studio houses not unlike concurrent designs on Cheyne Walk SW3 by C R Ashbee. Stepped roof terraces compensate for a high plot ratio.

St Paul's Studios (8) 1890–1
135–149 Talgarth Rd
a *Frederick Wheeler* (*Br* 1.3.1890)
b *G Jervis Smith* of Streatham, £8801
p *Maj.-Gen. James Gunter*
o *H Macbeth-Raeburn*, ptr, engrvr; *P M Feeney; H Sidney; W H Margetson; S Lewin; Gertrude Hammond; A D May; O Scholderer; H Hurst*, illr; *L Speed*, illr; *E T Reed*, illr; *W Logsdail*
BN 13.3.1891 illustrates the original proposal ranged along Colet Gardens where the pavilionised composition overlooked St Paul's School. Metal window frames and iron railings replaced timber designs such that these matched the mechanical precision of the terracotta façade. Chimneypieces, staircases and the mouldings generally were also custom-designed and exuberant – amazing at a mere £1100 per 3-storey unit.

9 St Paul's Studios (5 +) 1885–6
Colet House, 151 Talgarth Rd
a *Fairfax B Wade*
b *Gibbs & Flew* of West Kensington
p *Sir Coutts Lindsay*
o *A D May; F Lutiger*, mtlwkr; *Sir E & (Sir) P Burne-Jones*
Little-known work by Wade; possibly envisaged as an artists' club. On the top floor (perhaps divisible into 2 or 3) is the largest studio in London at 75′ × 35′. Two galleried studios plus generous living rooms and ancillaries, all symmetrically disposed, lie on the 2 lower floors. Separate access to basement

W14 concluded

and top floor via flanking turrets. Mid-floor columns spoiled lower studios; rents were perhaps too high anyway. In vain Sir Coutts anticipated many tenants like Sir Edward with huge works like the unfinishable *Arthur in Avalon*. With his marriage and the Grosvenor Gallery slipping from his control, to build this was sheer folly. Sale of the Scottish estates followed. (My thanks to Miss Helen Wright of The Study Centre.)

The Studios (6) 1878
20–30 Holland Park Rd
b, **p** *William Willett Snr*, bldr, dvlpr (Kens. Planning Applctn 29.7.1878)
o *H Helmick*; *H Schmalz*; *W M Fisher*; *H Cook*;
W R Symonds; *A N Burke*;
(Sir) W B Richmond ARA, ptr, sc;
Alice Swan; *A C Gow ARA*; *C F Murray*;
Baroness E Orczy; *H Speed*; *A McCallum*; *S W Lee*
Early studios de luxe by a progressive developer who consolidated the principle of roof-lit workrooms on upper floors to maximise site coverage. Some meddling at the turn of the century is evident.

BUSHEY, Hertfordshire

Meadow Studios (19) *c.* 1887 †
High Rd, Bushey, near Clay Hill
o *H S Bridgewater*, engrvr; *M Flower*;
A T Haddon; *A U Soord*; *Amy Sawyer*;
Win Freeman; *G Harcourt*; *J W Whiteley*;
R Wheelwright; *P M Teasdale*
A large group of free-standing and semi-detached, timber- and steel-framed, iron-clad bungalows each accommodating 2 or more artists in tiny bunkrooms either side of cramped studios. Built in response to the requirement for Herkomer School students to be Bushey residents. Herkomer said he himself financed a block for male students.

13

GAZETTER

PART TWO:

INDIVIDUAL STUDIOS

A list follows of studios built for individual and, usually, personal occupation between 1864 and 1914. One or two noteworthy items either side of these terminal dates are also included. Such a list cannot be made entirely comprehensive; there were, and still are, others of this period unaccounted for – some of them significant, too. A number of informal or undemonstrative sculptors' shops have been unavoidably overlooked while country houses and photographers' premises have been omitted altogether.

In the case of studios other than studio-houses the dates given alongside them refer to the additions or alterations.

The code of abbreviations is the same as that used in the Multiple Studios section, plus a further five.

† known to be demolished; **a** architect or designer; **b** builder; **p** proprietor;

o major occupiers, given chronologically.

RA membership is indicated if it was applicable during the period of occupancy.

All artists are painters unless otherwise stated;

C conversion; **E** extension; **G** garden pavilion; **H** studio-house; **M** miscellaneous.

EC1

83 City Road
E 1865 †
a *John W Dennison*
b *Anley* (*Br* 21.1.1865), £536
p *George Tutill*
A landscape ptr who also made regalia, the local speciality, built this unusually easterly studio at an early stage. William F Callaway, a portraitist, lived next door.

N7

294 Camden Road
E 1874–81 †
a *C E Evans*
b *R Perkins* (*Br* 21.5.1881)
p *William Small*, illr

NW1

2 Hanover Terrace
E 1892
a *Delissa Joseph* (*Br* 20.2.1892), £248
p *Mr & Mrs Arthur Lewis Raphael*

Osnaburgh Street
Numerous 'nasty wood houses full of clay and water-tubs', as John Ruskin called them, were in use here from the early 1800s to the early 1900s. Peter Rouw, William Behnes, John Foley and (Sir) Thomas Brock were among the sculptors; William P Frith, William Gale the painters. All rebuilt.

47 Regent's Park Road
G 1893
a *H Helsdan*
b *Cauley* (*BN* 20.5.1893), £345

27 St Augustine's Road
G 1867– (†)
a *Frank Huddlestone Potter*

b *Aylett* (*Br* 11.5.1867), £125
p *William Oliver Williams*;
Joshua H S Mann (–1880–)
No. 16 renumbered. Muddled council records suggest this modest scheme was abandoned.

Stanhope Street
  39 M –1845 †
        o *Thomas & Mary Thornycroft*, scs
 101 M –1850 †
        o *Thomas Woolner*, sc; *Jonathon E Soden*
 171 M –1875 †
        o *Hamilton Macallum*; *Albert Moore*;
        Tom Lamont; *William C May*, sc
A shabby area – a remnant of the Quickset Row era – neither Somers Town nor Camden Town, popular with sculptors.

NW3

Adelaide Road
  5 G *c*. 1890 †
      o *Robert Kemm*; *Edgar Bundy*

NW3 continued

66 G *c.* 1890 †
   o *William Stott* of Oldham; *Wright Barker*
118 G *c.* 1884 †
   o *John Sturgess*, animal ptr
120 G *c.* 1887 †
   p *James Ricks*
   o *George W Smetham-Jones*

62 Avenue Road

E (1880) †
p *Frederick Goodall RA*
Goodall came by the house via Ernst Gambart,
Joseph Gillot and Col. Mapleson. He converted the
gallery/ballroom suite which Gambart had added in
the 1860s into a large studio-saloon. This he
'orientalised' with Islamic architectural salvage.

Chalcot Gardens

15 G 1883–5
   a *Batterbury & Huxley*
   b *J W Dixon* of Highgate (*Br* 31.3.1883), £2500
   p *Hal Ludlow*, illr
   o *A C E Hill*; *Alfred Weatherstone*, stnd gls ptr;
   Hugh Riviere
'Raithby' plus the sizeable pavilion. House not
occupied until 1885 when it was let.
16 H 1882–3
   p *Towneley Green*, illr; *Adolphus J Whalley*;
   Arthur Rackham, illr; *Edyth Rackham*
See D Hudson, *Arthur Rackham* (1960) pp. 70–1.
Not stylistically a Batterbury & Huxley design;
altered by C F A Voysey and others.

Christchurch Hill

G *c.* 1890 †
p *Harvey E Orrinsmith*
'Sunnybank' plus a small outhouse.

Church Row

12 C 1901
   o *Miss Beard*
20 M *c.* 1875
   p *G T Pilbeam*
   o *Thomas Garner*, archt; *George Bodley*, archt;
   Henry Holiday, dsgnr; *William Glasby*, gls wkr
Studio over coach-house (rebuilt by Holiday after
1890 to accommodate his glass works), formerly
the architects' drawing office.
26 M 1876
   a *George Gilbert Scott Jnr*
   p *Rev. R R Watts*
   o *G G Scott Jnr*, archt; *Robert Little*;
   Mary Lovell
Pretty mews studio-house,
now 25 Perrin's Walk.

27 C *c.* 1888 †
   p *Miss M Gillies*
   o *James Webb*; *?Sir Charles Holroyd*, ptr, etchr

East Heath Road

E *c.* 1875 †
p *Walter Field*
A landscapist of private means, Field added to the
already vast mansion, 'The Pryors', which was
situated on the edge of the Heath itself.

1 England's Lane

H 1882
p *Thomas Dash Bellamy*, dvlpr
o *Francis S Walker*, illr, ptr; *David Farquharson*;
James S Crompton; *John C Halfpenny*
One of the three Wychcombe Villas built for the
Bellamy brothers, its style and scale perhaps
influenced by the adjacent Gregory & Bence
houses. See *Wychcombe Stus NW3*.

69 Eton Avenue

H 1890
a *Frederick W Waller*
b *?William Willett Jnr*
p *Hon. John Collier*
o *Reginald Barratt*, illr, ptr

Eton Villas

M –1858–65– †
a *Alfred Stevens*
p *James Cuming*, dvlpr
o *Alfred Stevens*, ptr, sc, dsgnr;
James Aumonier, sc (1903)
Prefabricated iron church converted into makeshift
residential sculpture shop next to 9 Eton Villas
which Stevens rented from 1862 onwards. All parts
except the equestrian figure of the Wellington
Memorial group were modelled here. *C.* 1865
Stevens began building his own masonry house and
studios on the church site. The house was
completed posthumously.

Fellows Road

74 E *c.* 1878 †
   p *John & James Syer*, ptrs; *Edward
   Hacker*
   o *Arthur Hacker*
98 E 1885–
   p *Frederick E Bodkin*, ptr
   o *Tom Graham*
Bodkin also owned No. 96, first occupied by
Gordon Browne, illr. No.s 82 and 84 were built by
the Bayes family while No. 86 was taken by Thomas
C Gotch, James S Hill, Francis B Berry and others.
100 E *c.* 1886
   p *Henry Garland*, ptr
   o *Luis R Falero*

Pre-conceived addition in the same style as the
house, quickly let to a Paris-based painter.
102 E *c.* 1885
   p *Alfred S Coke.* ptr; *A L Salmond*
   o *Ernest E Briggs*; *Rudolf Blind*;
   Thomas G Appleton

Finchley Road

103 E 1893 †
   a *Frederick J Lewis* (*BN* 5.5.1893)
   b *Myring & Co.* of Abbey Road
   o *H Yeend King*; *Haynes King*
A 10'-square glasshouse on the south side served to
supplement the overhead lighting of the 28' × 25'
main space. A models' room situated under
another, smaller studio was accessible via the
eastern (house end) gallery.
325–7 E 1878
   a *William Smith*
   b *Patman & Fotheringham*
   (*A* 2.3.1878), £1830
   p *James Forsyth*, sc, crvr;
   James Nesfield Forsyth, sc;
   John Dudley Forsyth, stnd gls ptr
New house (Ednam House), showrooms, studio
and workshops for reputable wood and stone
carvers next to the Finchley Rd L&NWR station.
These buildings survive, much altered.

Fitzjohn's Avenue

2 H 1881–2 †
   a *Wallace & Flockhart*
   b *S Dowsing & Son* of Notting Hill
   p *John Pettie RA*
'The Lothians'. *BN* 4.11.1881; *MA* 1885
3 C *c.* 1910
   p *Philip de Laszlo*
A house larger in extent than Long's 'Kelston';
capable of holding 200 guests at a buffet lunch.
Altered.
6 H 1881–2 †
   a *R Norman Shaw RA*
   b *William Tongue*
   p *Frank Holl RA*
'The Three Gables'. *BN* 8.9.1882; *MA* 1885
61 H 1876–81
   a *R Norman Shaw RA*
   b *Braid & Co.*
   p *Edwin Long RA*
'Kelston'. *BN* 10.2.1881
75 H 1871–2
   a *Theodore Knolles Green*
   b *Wicks, Bangs & Co.* (*Br* 8.4.1871), £3155
   p *Paul Falconer Poole RA*
'Uplands'. A prime example of Victorian 'outrage'
according to the *Architectural Review* of
c. 1965.

NW3 continued

39 Frognal
H 1884–5
a *R Norman Shaw RA*
b *Rider & Co.*
p *Kate Greenaway*, illr
The artist's mother and brother were also accommodated in the house, now added to, which cost approximately £1500, while £2000 was paid for the acre of land, long since subdivided. See Spielmann & Layard, *Kate Greenaway* (1905).

Hampstead Hill Gardens
1 **H** 1876
    a *Batterbury & Huxley*
    b *J O King* of Primrose Hill (*Br* 14.8.1875), £1680
    p *John Ingle Lee*
'Sunnycote'. Added to for H B Lee by Holliday & Greenwood. (Architects: Batterbury & Huxley, *Br* 18.8.1883.)
3 **H** 1877
    a *Batterbury & Huxley* (*BN* 26.7.1878)
    b *Manley & Rogers* of Primrose Hill
    p *Charles Green*, illr, ptr
    o *Towneley Green*, illr
'Charlecote'. Initially a working studio with caretaker's rooms. Additions designed by same architects (*Br* 21.5.1881) but built by James Holliday Jnr of Brixton.
9 **H** 1878–9
    a *Batterbury & Huxley*
    b *Manley & Rogers* of Primrose Hill (*BN* 12.11.1883)
    p *Thomas Collier*
'Etherow'. Arthur G Bell and Alfred D Fripp, ptrs, also gave addresses in this street during the 1880s.

Hampstead Heath
G *c.* 1858 †
o *Mark Anthony*; *Charles F Cleverly*
An early pavilion sited in the grounds of 'The Lawn'.

2 Harley Road
E *c.* 1885
o *Charles E Marshall*; *Henry Pegram ARA*, sc

Haverstock Hill
38 **G** *c.* 1890 †
    p *Col. Davis*
    o *?Leicester Burroughs*; *John H Killick*; *Robert Abbott*
Numbered 38 Rosslyn Hill, on the S corner with Pilgrim's Lane.

51a
    E *c.* 1890 †
    p *C W Ryalls*
    o *Horatio Hollingdale*
112
    G 1854 †
    p *Paul Falconer Poole RA*
    o *Edward C Barnes*
Glydder House. Poole lived here until 1873, Barnes until 1875. George Barham added a glazed link to the rearward outbuildings in 1885. See Parkhill Road NW3.
126
    G *c.* 1892 †
    p *J E Anderson*
    o *Mansell, Hunt, Cally & Co. Ltd*
192
    G *c.* 1892 †
    o *Boobyer*; *Alice Mulley*

4 Keats Grove
E *c.* 1894
p *W P Bodkin*
o *John James Frazer*

14 Kidderpore Avenue
H 1901–2
a *Arthur Keen*
p *George Hillyard Swinstead*
One of the finer Arts & Crafts studio-houses, although the scullery and servery have been ripped out, a balcony added above the bay and hardly a leadlight remains. Swinstead was evidently a painter, like Hamilton Macallum, fond of sunny effects; both men were probably obliged to wear hats in the studio. Partly illustrated in Swinstead's *My Old World Garden . . .* (1910).

151a King Henry's Road
M 1901
p *Leonard Walker*, ptr, stnd gls dsgnr
Leonard, nephew of Fred Walker and sometime teacher at the St John's Wood Art School, planted this simple, smithy-like shop on a 'cycle ground'.

7 Lambolle Road
G *c.* 1893 †
p *J Galloway*
o *Nathan C Bechmann*

14 Lancaster Grove
E *c.* 1892
p *H Cheesewright*
o *Daniel J Noyes*; *?Dora Noyes*

7 Lyndhurst Road
C 1871 †
p *Carl Haag*
Ida Villa – said to have been taken after his marriage in 1866 to Ida Büttner. Aladdin's Cave under a raised roof. Gutted.

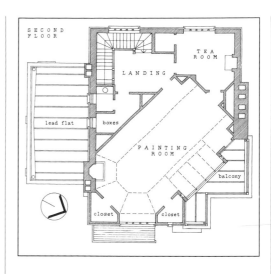

7 Maitland Park Villas
E *c.* 1885 †
p *Robert Thorne Waite*
One of the original residents of *The Mall NW3* who clung to the locality. *AJ* 6.1892 reported his studio was 'big enough for a military painter'.

1 Maresfield Gardens
H 1882
p *J Haynes Williams*
o *(Sir) Ernest Waterlow*
'Wridhern'. Possibly built according to a sketch by Batterbury & Huxley – Williams also had an early interest in *The Mall NW3*. Vital detail has been stripped as a result of subsequent maintenance.

Netherhall Gardens
6 **H** 1882
    a *Batterbury & Huxley*
    b *Holliday & Greenwood*
    p *A S Thomas Davidson*
'Culloden', later Frazer House. Illustrated in *BN* 4.8.1882; interior photos in the GLC collection. Altered.
9 **G** *c.* 1884 †
    p *Samuel Fry*, sc; *Caroline Fry*, ptr
'Sompting'. Two, probably three, of the Victorian also-rans.
40 **E** 1881 †
    p *Thomas Fall*, photo
'Wensley'. The Yorkshire-born photographer added a private studio (he owned commercial premises elsewhere) to a house bought more or less 'off the hook'. Whereas the house survives, the studio was replaced by the present fine billiard saloon and conservatory – possibly Flockhart's work – for, it

GAZETTEER, PART TWO

W8 continued

transpire by the architect'. John Oldcastle, writing of the mansion in the *Magazine of Art* (1881, pp. 290–5), admitted. 'It has not been built in order that it might abide as a monument of taste, but chiefly that it might stand as the beautiful house of a household'. By 1878 that household embraced the Millais' 8 children, up to 6 servants including governess and tutor, perhaps a studio assistant, perhaps a house guest – maybe 18 in all. For a decade following 1881, family holidays were regularly taken at a rented house in Effie's country at Little Dunkeld, Perthshire.

37 **H** 1870
- **a** *Frederick Pepys Cockerell*
- **p** *Reginald Cholmondeley*, sc
- **o** *Frank Baden-Powell*

The Red House; later Langton House. Sir Edward Sutherland occupied it for most of the remainder of the 19th-century. Cockerell's curving unification of vertical light and sloping light in his studio window design eliminated the horizontal bar of shadow almost universally met with. In about 1876 such *un châssis courbe* was developed in scale at 57 boulevard Arago, Paris 13ème (†, *Revue Générale d'Architecture* 1878), for the painter Lehoux, but the idea gained little or no further favour either in London or on the Continent.

Palace Green

1 **H** 1867–9
- **a** *Philip Webb*
- **b** *Messrs Ashby*
- **p** *George Howard, 9th Earl of Carlisle*

'That they [the authorities disinclined to approve the design] are unable to discover what actual style or period of architecture I have used I take to be a sincere compliment', wrote Webb. 'Every separate detail was his own', wrote George Jack. – A Service, ed., *Edwardian Architecture and its Origins*, (1975), p. 17. *SoL 37* reproduces plans and good early photos.

x **G** 1878 †
- **a** *Edward W Godwin*
- **b** *Longmire & Burge*
- **p** *HRH Princess Louise*, sc
- **o** *Sir Alfred Gilbert RA*, sc (–1934)

A 2-roomed workshop with anteroom and ancillaries built against existing walls in proper Queen Anne style at the S-W corner of the Kensington Palace grounds. *BA* 3.12.1880; drawings at the V & A. Enlarged somewhat by the time it was assigned to Sir Alfred.

80 Peel Street

H *c.* 1878
- **p** *Matthew Ridley Corbet*

- **o** *Edwin Abbey*, illr, ptr;
Matthew White Ridley; *(Sir) Frank Dicksee RA*;
Sir William Russell Flint RA

In *Drawn from Memory* (1957), E H Shepard illustrates the disruption he caused as a boy at a Dicksee social gathering during the 1890s. See also plates 10 and 31 in A Palmer, *More Than Shadows* (1943) for studio interiors in Flint's time.

Pembroke Cottages North

G *c.* 1898
- **o** *(Sir) William Rothenstein*; *(Augustus John)*;
Clemence & Laurence Housman, illrs

Pembroke Road

3 **G** 1891 †
- **a** *R Phené Spiers*
- **o** *Louise Jopling-Rowe*

Transferring her art school from Clareville Grove SW7, Louise had new premises set against the Logan Place boundary here. LCC Planning Applctn Case 529, 7.8.1891 *et seq.* An interior sketch at the V & A shows Spiers's modification of the main house; photo in *Windsor Magazine* 6/11.1906.

7 **G** 1892 †
- **o** *Everard Hopkins*, illr

(48) **E** *c.* 1875 †
- **o** *Frederick Havill*; *Oswald Sickert*;
Mason Jackson; *Arcangelo Bere*

Originally 'The Willows'. After a period as a gymnasium, the building was split into two studios: 12a & 12b Pembroke Gardens.

Pembroke Square

6 **G** 1914
- **a** *(Sir) Guy Dawber*
- **p** *Miss E F Robinson*

Like Mrs Jopling-Rowe's at Pembroke Road, Miss Robinson's architect ran foul of the local regulations governing boundary set-backs. Dawber's drawings were approved only upon their fourth presentation. LCC Planning Applctn Case 1386. No. 5, also, may lay claim to a pavilion even later than 1914.

8 **G** 1890–8
- **p** *Frederick Hollyer Snr & Jnr*, photos

The Hollyers had owned No. 9 for some years previously. Sir Edward Burne-Jones employed these photographers to copy his paintings and drawings.

16 **G** 1912–13
- **a** *Sydney Newcombe*
- **p** *R J Barrett*

17 **G** 1903–13
- **a** *Sydney Newcombe*
- **p** *R J Barrett*

---

18 **G** 1903–13
- **a** *Sydney Newcombe*
- **p** *R J Barrett*

This garden structure together with those at No.s 16 and 17 – all virtually unrecognisable now – are covered by LCC Planning Applctn Cases 847 & 1301. Newcombe, too, had called the planners' bluff.

(43) **M** *c.* 1902
- **o** *Edward Bradbury*, fencing master

Two studios at the rear of No.s 43 and 44 are initially used for Bradbury's School of Physical Culture. They are soon numbered 3 & 4 *Pembroke Walk Stus W8*.

Phillimore Gardens

1a **G** ?1866 †
- **o** *(Sir) William Q Orchardson ARA*;
Oswald von Glehn;
Robert Sauber (school)

Presumably built for Orchardson at what is an early date for the region. See also 22 Cromwell Road West SW5.

35 **C** *c.* 1882
- **p** *Samuel Pepys Cockerell*

Although practical from the painter's point of view (obtaining for him or her unobstructed light while leaving the garden unencumbered), a roof conversion done on the cheap rarely enhanced an established neighbourhood.

Phillimore Walk

(13) **M** *c.* 1895 †

A short-lived mews conversion.

(69) **M** *c.* 1895
- **p** *?Lear & Drew*

St Alban's Grove

(1) **C** 1845–58 †
- **o** *James Legrew*, sc; *Alfred Elmore RA*

(1a) **G, M** 1852–61 †
- **p** *Richard Ansdell RA*, ptr, animal ptr
- **o** *Andrew C Gow ARA*;
Christabel Cockerell; *Sarah Vaughan*

Lytham House. While still living in Victoria Road, Ansdell built a fair-sized studio-cum-observation booth in the paddock adjoining Legrew's house. In 1860–1 he added a 3-storey Low Renaissance mini-palazzo of five bays in grey brick. This agglomeration was let in the interval between Ansdell's death and the establishment there of the Kensington High School for Girls. Mostly rebuilt since.

St Mary Abbot's Place

3–

5 **G** 1910–11

W8 concluded

a *Gale, Gotch & Leighton*
b *J Marsland & Sons* of Walworth
p *William R Colton RA*, sc

Colton initially excelled at small-scale enamelling (an interest he shared with Alexander Fisher of *Warwick Stus W8* opposite), but by 1911, having executed the Royal Artillery War Memorial in St James's Park for instance, he was in the big league. A defector from the sculptors' haven in St John's Wood, Colton rose to RA a year before his early death. Detached workshops here are reached via a carriageway and double doors opening from the street.

4   **C** 20th-c.
A converted outbuilding behind 9 Warwick Gardens W14.

9   **E** 1911–12
  a *Gale, Gotch & Leighton*
  b *Kilby & Gayford*
  p *W Frank Calderon*, ptr, animal ptr (school)
Frank and his future wife were formerly near neighbours in St John's Wood. Colton (see No.s 3–5 above) knew them since he had modelled a bust of Mrs Calderon's father, the veteran sculptor H H Armstead RA, in 1903–4. Relocating the School of Animal Painting ('Live Animals Six Days A Week') here from Baker Street W1 did not pay off, but the new facilities could be and were let conveniently due to built-in separate access. The Calderons later retired to Seaton Bay, Devon.

11   **E** 1912
  a *?Gale, Gotch & Leighton*
  b *C F Kearley* of Kensington
  p *Frederick E Appleton*
A thoroughly hidden-away house by the builder of *Pembroke Stus W8* in similar style to the (supposed) architects' other offerings in this backwater. History does not speak any more publicly of the resident.

12   See 17 Warwick Gardens W14.

15   **H** 1913
  a *Gale, Gotch & Leighton*
  b *Parker & Sons* of Peckham
  p *Sir S H William Llewellyn RA*
A steady stream of portrait commissions enabled Llewellyn to leave an unprepossessing Aubrey Walk walk-up studio and build this more accommodating, very English 3-storey house which opens on the south side to a garden. Retaining his architect Arthur Leighton, Sir William erected Little Blundell House on Campden Hill after leaving here in 1926.

1 Scarsdale Villas
G *c.* 1894
o *Leonard L Brooke*; *Walter T Barkworth*; *David McGill*, sc

38 Sheffield Terrace
H 1876–7
a *Alfred Waterhouse RA*
b *W H Lascelles* of Finsbury
p *Edward Conyngham Sterling*; *Helen Sterling*
o *(Sir) William Rothenstein* (1920–5)
Despite – or, perhaps, due to – his heavy current workload, Waterhouse mustered a cavalier approach to the soldier-painter's encumbered brief. Evidently Sterling was determined the nation's most august architect should put his stamp on the design: a self-assertive if somewhat improper building on a fine, clear-cut plan. Halsey Ricardo may well have borne in mind this model as he turned his knowing hand to 117 Old Church Street SW3. (My thanks to Cdr & Mrs Drage.)

1–2 Tor Gardens
H 1851–2 †
a *James Clarke Hook, Adam C Hook*
p *J C Hook ARA*
1 Tor Villa and 2 Tor Villa were semi-detached houses. The Hooks occupied No. 1 with its relatively novel open-plan first floor. William Holman Hunt, Robert Martineau and Michael Halliday, Pre-Raphaelite adventurers all, rented it 1856–66. Alfred Hunt succeeded them; Edward Lear, Hunt's mock nephew, stayed in 1858. John C Horsley ARA, George Smith (d.1901) and (Sir) William F Douglas rented No. 2.

15, 16 (17, 17a) Vicarage Gate
M *c.* 1890
o *Arthur Wasse*; *Henry Wilson*, archt, sc; *William G Hunt*, archt

Victoria Road
2 (25)   **E** 1896
  a *H G Ibberson*
  p *Herbert Hampton*, sc
  o *Frank Baxter*, sc
More a zooscape for a mountain goat than a contextual addition, but artists will be artists. LCC Planning Applctns 679, 689.

7 (39)   **E** 1846– †
  p *Richard Ansdell ARA*
  o *Henry N O'Neil ARA*; *John Charlton*; *Arthur Marsh*; *Harold Burke*
Argent Archer photograph in Kensington Public Library (St Alban's Grove, S-E corner of Victoria Road intersection). Rebuilt 1981.

8 (41)   **G** 1862–3 †
  p *(Richard Ansdell)*; *Frederick & Eliza Bridell*, ptrs
  o *Charles Martin*; *George Vicat Cole ARA*; *Samuel Sidley*
Rebuilt.

28 (81)   **E** ?*c.* 1910
  o *(Basil Thomson)*
Southernmost house on the E side. Occupied 1857–73 by John Wright Oakes, ptr; separate entrance built 1919.

29 (52)   **E, E** 1850–68
  a *(Thomas H Watson, BN 26.6.1868)*
  b *Daniel Edwards* of Hampstead
  p *Alfred H Corbould*, ptr, animal ptr; *Edward H Corbould*, ptr, illr
  o *Richard Caton Woodville*, illr, ptr
Eldon Lodge. Struggling, perhaps, to pay off Edwards, Alfred Corbould finally took the lease of his house, studio and stable early in 1855. Conceivably the studio was exclusively for human portraiture while the similarly N-facing, and otherwise oversized, stable was specially adapted for studying horses and dogs. The character of Edward Corbould's reconstruction of Eldon Lodge's back half may be understood from a reading of *SoL* 42, (1986), p. 142. Edward's motto on the building, *Qui invidet minor est*, is dated 1868. (My thanks to Messrs John Greenacombe & Andrew Saint.)

38a (32a)   **C, E** 1845–55–79–
  o *James Uwins*; *Thomas Uwins RA*; *Thomas O Barlow RA*, engrvr; *Charles Perugini*
Auburn Lodge. Thomas Uwins's job as Surveyor of the Queen's Pictures brought him to his relative's house here for its convenience to Kensington Palace. Like the royal drawing master Edward Corbould (see No. 29 (52) above), Uwins floated in and out of Kensington New Town before settling permanently. Rooms and windows enlarged by Uwins and Barlow. Barlow family added studio-flats behind in St Alban's Grove; Perugini added balcony and back porch in 1891 to designs by Horace Field. These became bays in 1922.

44 (20)   **G** 1843–67– †
  o *John Bell*, sc; *Martin Heade*; *Henry C Whaite*
Formerly 1 Marlborough Terrace. At the rear was the colonial workshop built by Bell who soon moved next door to 15 Douro Place. Hence also known as 16 Douro Place.

46 (16)   **E** *c.* 1880
  o *(Thomas F Marshall*; *William E Marshall)*; *William Lomas*; *Harry Woods RA*
Formerly 'Walton Villa', Madeley Villas. Lomas, who probably added the back room, replaced the Marshall family which had been resident here since 1851. Midlands painters, of whom the Marshalls were typical, formed a certain coterie in and around Victoria Road during its early years. Other 19th-c. garden studios may pass unrecorded in this once sought-after locality.